Trials and Tribulations of International Prosecution

Trials and Tribulations of International Prosecution

Edited by Henry F. Carey and
Stacey M. Mitchell

LEXINGTON BOOKS
Lanham • Boulder • New York • Toronto • Plymouth, UK

Published by Lexington Books
A wholly owned subsidiary of The Rowman & Littlefield Publishing Group, Inc.
4501 Forbes Boulevard, Suite 200, Lanham, Maryland 20706
www.rowman.com

10 Thornbury Road, Plymouth PL6 7PP, United Kingdom

British Library Cataloguing in Publication Information Available

Library of Congress Cataloging-in-Publication Data

Trials and tribulations of international prosecution / Henry F. Carey and Stacey M. Mitchell.

p. cm.

Includes index.

ISBN 978-0-7391-6940-7 (cloth : alk. paper) — ISBN 978-0-7391-6941-4 (electronic)

1. International criminal courts. 2. Prosecution (International law)—Case studies. 3. International criminal courts—Case studies. I. Carey, Henry F., 1953– II. Mitchell, Stacey M.

KZ7230.T75 2013

345'.05042—dc23 2012046384

™ The paper used in this publication meets the minimum requirements of American National Standard for Information Sciences—Permanence of Paper for Printed Library Materials, ANSI/NISO Z39.48-1992.

Printed in the United States of America

Contents

Introduction

Current Issues Confronting International Criminal Prosecutions

Stacey M. Mitchell and Henry F. Carey

The twentieth century has been dubbed the "age of politically sanctioned mass murder."[1] The mass murders by the Khmer Rouge, Hitler, and Saddam Hussein's regimes among others are what Drumbl refers to as "extraordinary crimes."[2] They differ from ordinary crimes in that crimes against humanity, many war crimes, and genocide are committed by collectives against collectives. Moreover, murders, rapes, acts of torture have group component traits, as well as individual participation that does not fit into legal paradigms of individual criminal deviance.[3] Because these crimes violate universal *jus cogens* norms, they are seen as violating the conscience of humanity, even if they do not necessarily violate the consciences and norms of the societies in which they occur. Whether or not perpetrators really believe they have done nothing wrong because they were merely targeting "enemies," such prosecutions inevitably are difficult because they are commonly perceived as politically motivated and biased.

Because there have been few domestic prosecutions of *jus cogens* crimes, international prosecution has been established for these "core crimes."[4] This is thought to serve justice, as well as to deter and punish criminals. International prosecutions are alternatives or supplements to truth or other fact-finding commissions, which involve broader investigations of crimes without necessarily holding individuals responsible for violations of international criminal law.

A lasting legacy of the Nuremberg and Tokyo tribunals, the concept of individual responsibility is commonly considered to be one of the merits of the international criminal model because it avoids the creation of collective guilt. This makes such prosecutions politically controversial and difficult to induce true accountability, which would deter future crimes, as well as alter national narratives of innocence. Consequently individual responsibility may or may not induce a "cathartic or healing effect [that] may contribute to peace."[5]

International courts, including the International Criminal Court (ICC), hybrid tribunals, and the *ad hoc* tribunals with superior jurisdiction—the International Criminal Tribunal for the former Yugoslavia (ICTY), the International Criminal Tribunal for Rwanda (ICTR)—have been lauded as effective tools with which to fight impunity. They focus largely on prosecuting the "big fish": military and political leaders who are the "architects" of egregious crimes. By incapacitating extremists, the ICTY, ICTR, and other courts have arguably established important legal precedents and institutions that have changed international criminal norms, defused intolerance, and created conditions for peace.[6]

International tribunals are not solely concerned with the utilitarian goal of deterrence although it has been cited as one of the foremost rationales for punishing human rights offenders.[7] Other goals include retribution, reconciliation, and strengthening the rule of law. These goals are inter-dependent,[8] meaning they all improve or deteriorate together, depending on how the courts behave, how the international community, domestic leaders, and civil societies perceive trials, and how they respond to those perceptions.

A key indicator of successful prosecution is whether domestic prosecutions are induced as a result of international trials, as well as broader formal or informal domestic investigations and greater national debates about historical crimes. Without some degree of accountability induced from international prosecution, future governments in the immediate country can be expected to perpetrate such crimes again whenever they so feel the need. A trend of increasing use of domestic criminal courts to try mass murderers may be the result of the establishment of international prosecution in the mid-1990s, as well as an indication that states prefer dispensing justice rather than leaving it to the ICC.[9] However, the adequacy of national criminal courts depends on factors including political will and stability, as well as credible institutional development which most post-conflict countries lack in varying degrees.

A hypothesis test of whether the international criminal courts induce more domestic prosecution would be whether the international criminal trials of perpetrators of extraordinary crimes increase greater awareness of and reliance on international law as a tool in not only domestic trials, but also in domestic politics and discourse. If international law conditions the norms used to resolve disputes by threatening legal punishment of these international crimes,[10] they may also "blunt the hatred of the victims and their desire for revenge."[11] Thus prosecutions are closely linked with peacemaking and peace building; hence the role of the United Nations Security Council (UNSC) in the justice process.[12]

As Schabas explains, prosecutions by international and/or domestic courts today are contrasted with the Nuremberg and Tokyo tribunals, which were products of the unconditional surrenders of Germany and Japan.[13] However, both of these courts, by most accounts, *did* change national narratives of innocence (in Germany more than Japan), inducing political systems and attitudes which had no role for denial of past crimes or justification for future ones. Many of the cases with which international criminal courts *now* contend, however, concern crimes perpetrated in ongoing conflicts or where peace agreements result from negotiations born of war weariness rather than victory. Thus, there is no shame of defeat which might induce the broader purposes achieved by the two post-World War II tribunals.

The chapters in this volume examine the multitude of factors that contribute to the successes or failures of prosecutions of violators of international humanitarian and criminal law. The contributions to this volume add to a current trend in scholarship about the international criminal justice model, which Fichtelberg characterizes as a shift from explaining why and how tribunals are established to whether or not they actually fulfill their mandates.[14]

Fichtelberg characterizes the dominant scholarship as a legalistic approach, reflecting a "fundamental faith in the value of legal norms and procedures."[15] Within this group, however, are skeptics and advocates. Skeptics focus their criticisms largely on the perceived negative impact international mechanisms of justice have on the core principles of sovereignty and non-intervention, as well as diplomatic relations between states. They contend that threats of trials undermine diplomatic solutions to war when the indicted criminals are real or potential interlocutors. Advocates, on the other hand, emphasize the value international tribunals have for the rule of law. Interestingly, neither group fully addresses the successes of international courts.

An alternative approach to legalism discussed by Fichtelberg is constructivism, which evaluates the extent to which international criminal prosecutions affect international and domestic criminal norm formation and implementation, and any consequent normative shifts on perceptions of impunity, as well as international and domestic courts themselves.[16] A hypothesis test of constructivist approaches would include changes in public opinion which would support or oppose prosecutions of major violators of international criminal law. Some of the contributions in this volume tackle this issue by addressing international and domestic criminal norm change and its influence on domestic and international criminal prosecutions.

Although they acknowledge and examine serious weaknesses in the international criminal justice regime all of the contributors to this volume agree that international and hybrid tribunals have made substantial contributions to the development of international criminal and procedural law.

Clearly, norm change at the level of international criminal law is the clearest contribution accruing from international prosecution. In the *Akayesu*[17] case, for example, the ICTR clarified aspects of the definition of genocide under international law, the type of intent required for the commission of genocide, and for the first time, established rape as a genocide-related offense.[18] Moreover the *Kambanda* case marked the first conviction of a former head of government for the crime of genocide.[19]

The ICTY reinforced the norm that no longer privileges sovereign or head of state immunity, by indicting and trying a number of high profile offenders. In *Krstić*,[20] the Court elaborated further on the *mens rea* element of the crime of genocide, and in *Tadić* the ICTY contributed to the formulation of the doctrine of joint criminal enterprise (JCE), and articulated the principle that international humanitarian law applies to intra-state as well as inter-state conflicts.[21] These precedents set by the ICTY and ICTR have been and continue to be influential on international and hybrid courts, as well as national courts.[22]

Moreover the ICC and the Special Court for Sierra Leone (SCSL) are responsible for the indictment, trial and/or conviction of a number of military and militia leaders for the enlistment and use of children for combat, including Thomas Lubanga Dyilo and former President of Liberia Charles Taylor, respectively. The ICC has also made substantial contributions to the development of international procedural law, laying out in its statute rules governing the manner in which investigations are to be conducted and evidence admitted, rules governing the administration of the Court, and the protection of witnesses and basic trial proceedings.[23]

Despite these significant accomplishments, ICC arrest warrants following the indictments of Joseph Kony of the Lord's Resistance Army and President Omar Hassan Ahmad al Bashir of Northern Sudan demonstrate that courts remain embedded in international and domestic politics. This challenges the legal authority and political credibility of the ICC as an institution of justice.[24] Moreover political and other groups are *still* excluded from the protections of the *United Nations Genocide Convention* (UNGC).[25] And it was only in June 2010 that the crime of aggression was formerly defined and officially added to the jurisdiction of the ICC. Of course the weakness of the definition of aggression, in addition to a seven year moratorium on its implementation, will likely enable many countries to avoid accountability for past (and present) misdeeds.[26]

Moreover the various difficulties associated with complementary jurisdiction means the ICC might be sidetracked into dealing with admissibility and jurisdictional challenges from states who claim that they have investigated and cleared potential defendants, rather than actively fulfilling its mandate. Relying on referrals from the UNSC as a method to avoid jurisdictional problems adds the burden of obtaining support from the United States, China, and Russia, three countries that have not yet ratified the Rome Statute.

Advocates for the ICC nevertheless contend that complementary jurisdiction places the onus of prosecution on domestic jurisdictions where it should be. In this light, the ICC is theoretically effective as a court of last resort. Yet others contend that this hope is seriously misplaced.[27] After all, indictments have only occurred for Africans. The behavior of states clearly demonstrates a lack of commitment and enthusiasm for the prosecution of perpetrators of international crimes."[28]

This problem is further aggravated by the fact that the ICC, like the ICTY and ICTR, "needs artificial limbs to walk and work. And these artificial limbs are state authorities."[29] The ICC depends heavily on inter-state cooperation to arrest and extradite war criminals, as well as a legal case that the country with territorial or citizenship jurisdiction is not credible. More generally the powers granted the ICC and the various ways in which member states can opt out of compliance demonstrate that the international criminal justice regime has hardly achieved "post-Westphalian" status,[30] or for that matter the "communitarian cosmopolitan" status wherein the international community stands solidly united in the pursuit of justice for violations of *jus cogens* norms.[31] In practice, the strength of the ICC and many hybrid courts is a function of the political will and correlation of forces in international politics.

As Michael Thurston discusses in his chapter, with regard to the ICTY and ICTR, political will is demonstrated through the use of prosecutorial discretion by these courts. Whether or not uncooperative states will be coerced into compliance with the courts or not is a function of how they are perceived by the international community: as aggressor (e.g. Serbia) or victim (e.g. Rwanda). This of course raises problems of selective prosecution.

Moreover if states refuse to cooperate with the ICC, there is little the Court can do. Instead the ICC "(through the Assembly of States Parties) can only fall back on the usual international law mechanisms for inducing compliance with international obligations. It lacks any special authority, or power, or means of putting into effect its orders, or generally discharging its mission, on the territory of a recalcitrant state party."[32] As long as the great powers are divided over specific indicted war criminals, ICC member and non-member states will normally be unable to cooperate. Renegade states can then disregard ICC international arrest warrants in the name or "guise of state sovereignty."[33] If this continues, ICC will "have little more than normative impact."[34] Such sovereignty constraints impose similar obstacles on other issues of intervention, such as the emerging Responsibility to Protect (R2P) doctrine authorizing coercion to provide humanitarian relief and, where necessary, remove murderous governments.[35] R2P and the ICC are both are intended to respond to and prevent *jus cogens* violations. They also face similar hazards as Benjamin Schiff addresses in his chapter which compares the establishment and purposes of the ICC with the formulation of the R2P norm.

Political will, specifically the relationship between the will of domestic and international actors and the process of post-conflict justice, also impacts domestic prosecutions, as well as the work of the hybrid courts. Beth Dougherty's essay about the arrest of Charles Taylor addresses the degree to which Taylor's pursuit was shaped by the conflict between the US Congress and the presidency, two branches of government with opposing ideas about Taylor's fate. Johanna

Herman's contribution assesses the efforts of the Cambodian state to limit the process of justice for the victims of the Khmer Rouge. Stacey Mitchell's chapter on *gacaca* tribunals examines the efforts of the Government of Rwanda to curtail the justice process and subsequently the "truth" about inter-group violence in Rwanda. Joanna Quinn's contribution assesses the effectiveness of local conflict resolution mechanisms being used in the north against President Museveni's own efforts to achieve peace in Uganda. Lastly Jo-Marie Burt explores the impact of domestic and international actors and institutions on the creation of an accountability environment in relation to the prosecution of former president Alberto Fujimori and others in Peru. She suggests that continued domestic support for trials will likely be a function of the extant political environment in Peru. All told these chapters demonstrate that political will can be an asset to, or in the alternative, an inhibitor of prosecution.

Many contributors to this volume also evaluate the practical limitations encountered by the international criminal justice model as a whole. For one thing, case law is a subsidiary means of determining international law, since legal precedents are not automatically binding on other international courts.[36] This derives from the civil law tradition of most of the world's countries. Consequently different international and domestic courts will continue to have different views on various aspects of the law,[37] which can lead to forum shopping. Added to this is the fact that judges in the ICTY and ICTR have relied on the *Vienna Convention on the Law of Treaties,* Article 31,[38] which permits looking at legislative history if the ordinary meaning of the text is unclear, to interpret a court's statute. The result is a problem of consistency.

These differing interpretations create challenges for substantive criminal law.[39] James Larry Taulbee's essay examines the obstacles international tribunals encounter in developing the legal concepts of crimes against humanity and war crimes. Similar to Kelly-Kate Pease's chapter in this volume about the case against Charles Taylor in the SCSL, Taulbee examines the ICTY's formulation and use of the JCE doctrine to demonstrate the problems that a lack of uniformity creates for the legitimacy of the international criminal model as a fair and impartial vehicle for justice.[40] Kimberly Lanegran writes in similar vein about the SCSL's formulation of the legal concepts pertaining to the use of child soldiers, including the meanings of "conscription," and "enlistment." She suggests that disagreements between the Trial and Appeals Chambers of the SCSL over the definition of "enlistment," problems of evidence, as well as controversies over the use of JCE as a mode of liability, demonstrate some of the impediments that remain for future prosecutions of the crime in the SCSL and other courts. Legal controversies also surround ICTR prosecutions for songs as incitement to genocide and/or persecution. This specifically applies to the case against Simon Bikindi which Susan Benesch addresses in her chapter. Benesch focuses on the unresolved issues that remain on this matter particularly in light of Bikindi's acquittal for the majority of charges filed against him.

Additional problems generally associated with the international criminal justice model include the slow pace of justice in international courts which, as some suggest, "undercuts the incentive for states to hold their own trials."[41] For example, since its inception in 1993, proceedings for only 126 persons have been concluded in the ICTY.[42] The pace of justice in the ICC is equally as slow. To date there are only sixteen ongoing cases based on referrals from three states (Central African Republic, Democratic Republic of the Congo, Uganda), from the UNSC, and the Office of the Prosecutor.[43] The ICC is also conducting preliminary investigations regarding allegations of human rights atrocities perpetrated in only eight other countries.[44]

Moreover limitations on the temporal scope of crimes considered by the ICC has meant that victims of human rights atrocities perpetrated *before* 2002 in the DRC, Uganda and elsewhere will not get their day in court. Similar problems are encountered by *ad hoc,* hybrid and domestic courts.[45] As Mitchell, Herman, and Olga Martin-Ortega discuss in their chapters, the failure to bring all relevant parties to justice seriously hampers the truth-telling function of courts (part of the "expressivist" function of institutions of justice).[46] Yuki Takatori addresses this issue with respect to the International Military Tribunal for the Far East (IMTFE); specifically addressing the impact that a failure to hold the Japanese emperor accountable for war crimes; geopolitical considerations that shielded members of the infamous Unit 731 from justice; and the exclusion of cases involving forced labor and prostitution, had on the truth-telling function of the tribunal, as well as its overall legitimacy.

International courts have also been faulted for their detachment from the victims of atrocity crimes,[47] which limits their ability to achieve the goals of strengthening rule of law, and achieving reconciliation in post-conflict societies. This is a topic taken up in the chapter by Adam Smith. Smith specifically examines perceptions of the work of international courts—the ICTY, ICTR, Nuremberg, Tokyo—by the effected societies and explores the ways in which future courts (the ICC) can "bridge" the existing gap.

Overall the perceived decline in legitimacy strengthens critics' charges that these courts are merely imposing "selective justice" which may de-legitimate or undermine international criminal justice as a whole.[48] Aspiring to universal jurisdiction was always part of the original rationale for the creation of a permanent criminal court, yet, the actions of the ICC in response to self-referrals demonstrates that it is not necessarily immune from charges of selective justice.[49]

As indicated previously a number of authors in this volume focus their analysis on the work of hybrid tribunals. These chapters help to close a gap in the existing literature, the bulk of which has focused largely on *ad hoc* tribunals and the ICC.[50] Hybrid tribunals embody a mixture of international and domestic law and are staffed by international and domestic jurists, lawyers, and other personnel. As such, they are believed to administer justice in a more "un-biased and even-handed manner,"[51] consistent with international principles of justice. Moreover because of their location they help to provide greater domestic ownership of the justice process. As Kathleen Barrett argues in her contribution to this volume, hybrid tribunals can therefore partially overcome charges of political bias and Western influence commonly leveled against international tribunals. At the same time she and others contend that enthusiasm for the hybrid justice model should be tempered somewhat by practical considerations including, but not limited to, the need for political stability, the status of ongoing peace processes, a lack of qualified legal personnel, and the role of mass media.

Moreover transitional justice is about more than achieving retribution for the perpetration of human rights atrocities. Trials—domestic, international, hybrid—are also expected to contribute to reconciliation for societies effected by mass conflict. In other words mechanisms of justice are expected to contribute to both negative and positive peace.[52] The pursuit of justice and conflict resolution can foster peace in divided countries by, among other things, marginalizing and stigmatizing extremists and violators of international criminal law.[53] However others contend that trials are useful only when they occur well after peace negotiations have transpired, thus avoiding disruption of peace negotiations or post-pact implementation of agreements.[54]

This is a problem in particular when it comes to live indictments issued by the ICC. As Peter Stoett discusses in his contribution to this volume, live indictments have been selective, largely political, and consequently counterproductive in that they have not achieved their objectives: there has been no deterrence; no end to cultures of impunity. For reasons such as these Candace H. Blake-Amarante suggests in her chapter that an alternative litigation model, such as the domestic tort litigation model proposed by Anthony D'Amato, may provide a suitable alternative; one which preserves both sovereignty and the interests of the parties involved. In any event, as Mahmood Monshipouri discusses, any application of international law standards to ongoing conflicts has become increasingly difficult given the changing nature of warfare and the advent of transnational terrorism.

In some cases amnesties may be the preferred solution to prosecution, particularly from the point of view of the aggressors. Werle suggests: "a waiver of punishment may be essential in certain situations to restore peace and facilitate national reconciliation."[55] As a general rule, however, amnesties face a number of serious problems, especially when they are considered for crimes that violate *jus cogens* norms.[56]

The issue of amnesties is taken up in this volume by Quinn and Burt. Quinn's contribution about the process of transitional justice in Uganda makes it clear that the voluntary amnesties granted prior to the conflict's conclusion may be insufficient for reconciliation and deterrence in Uganda. Amnesties met with far stiffer resistance in the case of Peru. As Burt discusses this resistance laid the foundation for future prosecutions of perpetrators of grave violations of human rights in Peru. However Peru's is a cautionary tale. Despite the success of the Fujimori trial the push for amnesties in Peru has not necessarily disappeared.

As the chapters in this also volume indicate, norms induce a desire for justice whether by formal or informal means. It is also important that domestic justice mechanisms conform to existing normative standards. This latter theme is addressed by Quinn, Mitchell, and Burt among others who address the consequences of integrating (or failing to integrate) the justice process within a culturally accepted normative framework. In most cases domestic judicial institutions ensure greater ownership of the justice process for post-conflict societies. However whether or not adherence to internationally accepted standards of due process ensures for greater legitimacy (as in the case of Peru) or is an obstacle to achieving justice (e.g. Rwanda) must be assessed on a case-by-case basis.

The chapters in this volume contribute to the body of literature that examines the link between norms and international criminal justice, including Addis' work about the mutually constitutive function of the concept of universal jurisdiction, Sikkink's analysis about Argentina's influence on the diffusion of human rights norms and transitional justice practices in other Latin American countries, and studies which examine the evolution of the R2P concept.[57] In one way or another all of the contributors to this volume demonstrate that the diffusion of international human rights norms has influenced and continues to influence the decision-making processes of political leaders and societies with regard to holding past leaders accountable for grave violations of international criminal law.

Organization of the Book

As stated previously, the purpose of this volume is to contribute to the growing discussion and debate about the effectiveness of the international criminal justice model. Similar to the studies by Drumbl, Mani, Fichtelberg, and many others, the contributions to this volume assess the variety of factors that continue to impede the ability of international courts to achieve their mandates.[58]

This volume is divided into two sections. Part I examines thematic approaches about the impact the prosecution of perpetrators of extraordinary crimes has on the development of international criminal law, as well as on the legitimacy and effectiveness of the international criminal justice model more broadly. The chapters by Taulbee, Pease, Lanegran, and Benesch examine the impact court decisions have on substantive aspects of international criminal law. Other authors, such as Smith, Stoett, and Blake-Amarante suggest that enthusiasm for the work of the *ad hoc*, permanent, and hybrid international tribunals should be tempered by the challenges these courts continue to face; challenges that likely inhibit them from fully realizing their respective mandates.

Many of these challenges have to do with the political willingness of powerful actors in the domestic and international community to prosecute wrongdoers. The chapters included in Part II address the impact of political will and other influential factors on the work of specific tribunals and trials. Dougherty evaluates the general political problems of arresting indicted war criminals by focusing on the case of Charles Taylor. Quinn addresses the impact of President Yoweri Museveni's heavy-handed policy-making style on the process of transitional justice in Uganda; focusing on the relationship between politics and a multitude of justice mechanisms. The other chapters in this section consider specific criminal tribunals such as for Cambodia by Herman, Bosnia by Martin-Ortega, and Lebanon by Barrett, as well *gacaca* by Mitchell and Prisca Uwigabye, and Burt's thorough examination of the factors that contributed to the prosecution and conviction of former Peruvian president Fujimori and the implications his trial has for justice and the rule of law in Peru.

We are grateful for the research assistance of Julio Perez-Bravo and Benjamin Kweskin, students at Georgia State University, for their indispensable help in helping to research and prepare this book. We also greatly appreciate the kind assistance of Justin Race and Sabah Ghulamali, wonderful editors at Lexington Books, who helped initiate, encourage and guide this project in such a careful, responsive manner.

Notes

1. R.W. Smith, "Human Destructiveness and Politics: the Twentieth Century as an Age of Genocide," in *Genocide and the Modern Age: Case Studies of Mass Deaths,* ed. I. Wallimann and M. N. Dobkowski (New York: Greenwood Press, 1987), 22.

2. Mark Drumbl, *Atrocity, Punishment and International Law* (Cambridge: Cambridge University Press, 2007), 3-6.

3. Drumbl, *Atrocity*, 24.

4. Werle also includes wars of aggression as a core crime. Gerhard Werle, *Principles of International Criminal Law,* 2d ed. (Hague, The Netherlands: T-M-C Asser Press, 2009), 29.

5. Antonio Cassese, *The Human Dimension of International Law: Selected Papers* (Oxford: Oxford University Press, 2008), 422.

6. David Wippman, "Exaggerating the ICC," in *Bringing Justice to Power? The Prospects of the International Criminal Court,* ed. Johanna Harrington, Michael Milde and Richard Vernon (Montreal: McGill-Queen's University Press, 2006), 123.

7. Werle, *Principles of International Criminal Law,* 34-35.

8. Drumbl, *Atrocity*, 149. See also William A. Schabas, *The UN International Criminal Tribunals: The Former Yugoslavia, Rwanda and Sierra Leone* (Cambridge: Cambridge University Press, 2006), 67-73.

9. Adam M. Smith, "International Organizations and Criminal Justice," *The International Studies Encyclopedia,* Robert A. Denemark (Blackwell Publishing, 2010), 27-28. http://www.isacompendium.com/subscriber/tocnode?id=g9781444336597_chunk_g9781 44433659711_ss1-41 (accessed November 15, 2010). Schabas points out that domestic courts are the preferred venue for addressing these types of cases. William A. Schabas, *Genocide in International Law: The Crime of Crimes,* 2d ed. (Cambridge: Cambridge University Press, 2009), 400-401.

10. Werle, *Principles of International Criminal Law*, 35; also Payam Akhavan, "Are International Criminal Tribunals a Disincentive to Peace?: Reconciling Judicial Romanticism with Political Realism," *Human Rights Quarterly* 31, no. 3 (August 2009): 624-654.

11. Cassese, *Human Dimension*, 422.

12. Schabas, *UN International Criminal Tribunals*, 68-69. Sometimes the UNSC will condition its resolutions by insisting on international and domestic prosecutions and/or other types of investigation and accountability.

13. Schabas, *UN International Criminal Tribunals*, 8.

14. Aaron Fichtelberg, "Criminal Tribunals," *The International Studies Encyclopedia,* Robert A. Denemark (Blackwell Publishing, Blackwell Reference Online, 2010), http://www.isacompendium.com/subscriber/tocnode (accessed November 15, 2010).

15. Fichtelberg, "Criminal Tribunals."

16. Fichtelberg, "Criminal Tribunals."

17. ICTR, *Prosecutor v. Jean-Paul Akayesu,* Case No. ICTR-96-4.

18. The subjective standard of group identification was developed further in subsequent cases; see Antonio Cassese, *International Criminal Law*, 2d ed. (Oxford: Oxford University Press, 2008), 138-140.

19. ICTR, *Prosecutor v. Jean Kambanda,* Case No. ICTR-97-23.

20. ICTY, *Prosecutor v. Kristić*, Case No, IT-98-33.

21. ICTY, *Prosecutor v. Tadić*, Case No. IT-94-1. For further discussion see Malcolm N. Shaw, *International Law*, 6th ed. (New York: Cambridge University Press, 2008), 397-443; also Cassese, *International Criminal Law*, 141-142.

22. For more on this point, see Schabas, *UN International Criminal Tribunals*, 44-46.

23. Werle, *Principles of International Criminal Law*, 48, 498-546.

24. ICC, *All Cases*, http://www.icc-cpi.int/Menus/ICC/Situations+and+Cases/Cases/ (accessed March 10, 2012).

25. This was demonstrated recently by indictments issued by the Extraordinary Chambers of the Courts of Cambodia (ECCC) in October 2010. Beth Van Schaak, "Closing in on the Khmer Rouge: The Closing Order in Case 002 Before the Extraordinary Chambers of the Courts of Cambodia," *ASIL Insights* 14, no. 31 (October 13, 2010), http://www.asil.org/insights101013.cfm. For further criticisms of the UNGC see P. Royane, *Never Again? The United States and the Prevention and Punishment of the Crime of Genocide Since the Holocaust* (Boulder, CO: Rowman and Littlefield, 2001).

26. David Sheffer, "State Parties Approve New Crimes for International Court," *ASIL Insights* (June 22, 2010), www.asil.org/insights100622.cfm and Barbara Crossette, "Judging the War Crimes Tribunal," *The Nation* (November 27, 2010), www.thenation.com/article/155621/judging-war-crimes-tribunal?page=full.

27. Wippman, "Exaggerating," 108.

28. Wippman, "Exaggerating," 108. On this point, see also Cassese, *Human Dimension*, 418.

29. Cassese, *Human Dimension*, 426.

30. Smith, "International Organizations," 20-25. For Smith's analysis of similar problems faced by the ICTR and ICTY, see "International Organizations," 9-16.

31. Adero Addis, "Imaging the International Community," *Human Rights Quarterly* 31, no. 1 (February 2009): 129-162.

32. Cassese, *International Criminal Law*, 403. For a good discussion about the ICC's "surrender regime" see Goran Sluiter, "The Surrender of War Criminals to the International Criminal Court," 25 *Loy. L.A. Int'l & Comp. L. Rev.* 605 (2003).

33. Cassese, *Human Dimension*, 425. By contrast member states of the UN are required to comply with the ICTY and ICTR.

34. Cassese, *Human Dimension*, 430. For a more positive view on the manner in which the ICC has dealt with the "trial for cooperation" see Victor Peskin, "Caution and Confrontation in the International Criminal Court's Pursuit of Accountability in Uganda and Sudan," *Human Rights Quarterly* 31, no. 3 (August 2009): 635-691.

35. Gareth Evans, *The Responsibility to Protect: Ending Mass Atrocity Crimes Once and for All* (Washington, DC: Brookings Institution Press, 2008).

36. Trial Chambers of the ICTY and ICTR are not bound by the decisions of other Trial Chambers; they are however bound by the decisions of the Appeals Chamber which ensures for legal consistency. Schabas, *UN International Criminal Tribunals*, 107-112. In terms of the ICC, Article 21(2) of the Rome Statute states: "The Court *may* [italics added] apply principles and rules of law as interpreted in its previous decisions. The ICC is also not bound by the decisions of other international courts, as clearly demonstrated by the ICC's position on JCE. See Werle, *Principles of International Criminal Law*, 176-177. Nevertheless the precedents set by the *ad hoc* tribunals and other courts are of course still extremely influential. Schabas, *UN International Criminal Tribunals*, 44.

37. Werle raises the issue of precedent in regards to the ICTY and ICTR. Werle, *Principles of International Criminal Law*, 57.

38. Schabas, *UN International Criminal Tribunals*, 80-84.

39. For more on the topic of flexible interpretation of the law, see also Schabas, *UN International Criminal Tribunals*, 74-120.

40. It is worth noting that some of the issues associated with joint liability have been dealt with by the ICC. As Werle notes individual involvement in a joint crime has to make an essential contribution to the crime and participants have to meet all of the *mens rea* elements of that crime. The Pre-Trial Chamber of the ICC in *Lubanga* and other casers has reached a similar conclusion. Werle, Principles *of International Law,* 176-178.

41. Wippman, "Exaggerating," 112. Although he made this statement in reference to the ICC as others contend it also applies to the *ad hoc* tribunals. See Goran Sluiter, "Atrocity Crimes Litigation: Some Human Rights Concerns Occasioned by Selected 2009 Case Law," 8 *Nw. U. J. Int'l Hum. Rts.* 248, 249-252 (2010). A separate issue concerns the financial costs of the tribunals; a point also addressed by Wippman (see "The Costs of International Justice," 100 *Am. J. Int'l. L.* 861 (2006).

42. International Criminal Tribunal for the former Yugoslavia, *ICTY Key Figures*, at http://www.icty.org/sections/TheCases/KeyFigures (accessed September 3, 2012).

43. ICC, *All Cases*.

44. These countries include Afghanistan, Colombia, Georgia, Guinea, Honduras, Korea and Nigeria. See ICC, *Situations and Cases,* http://www.icc-cpi.int/Menus/ICC/Situations+and+Cases.

45. For an excellent assessment of the weakness of domestic courts in the DRC and elsewhere see Ivo Aertsen, Jana Arsovska, Holger-C Rohne, Marta Valinas and Kris Vanspauwen, eds., *Restoring Justice after Large-Scale Conflict* (Portland, OR: Willan, 2008),

46. Drumbl, *Atrocity*, 149. The expressivist function of courts more generally is to engender a normative shift in a society.

47. Cassese, *International Criminal Law*, 332. The ICC has made greater efforts to reach out to victim communities. See Human Rights Watch, *Courting History: The Landmark International Criminal Court's First Years* (July 2008): 99-208..

48. For a discussion of selective justice in the *Milosevic* trial, see Michael P. Scharf, "The Legacy of the Milosevic Trial," in *Bringing Justice to Power? The Prospects of the International Criminal Court,* ed. Johanna Harrington, Michael Milde and Richard Vernon (Montreal: McGill-Queen's Univ. Press, 2006), 25-46.

49. On this point see also Wippman, "Exaggerating," 119 and William Schabas, "First Prosecutions at the International Criminal Court," 27 *Hum. Rts. L. J.* 25 (2006); in reference to the perception of bias in Uganda see, Human Rights Watch, *Courting History*, 41-42.

50. Fichtelberg, "Criminal Tribunals."

51. Cassese, *International Criminal Law*, 333.

52. For more on this distinction see Rama Mani, *Beyond Retribution: Seeking Justice in the Shadows of War* (Cambridge, UK: Polity Press, 2002). Another venue in which victims can achieve some measure of reconciliation is through civil courts. See Rachel Irwin, "Civil Actions Offer some Closure for Bosnian Victims," *Institute for War and Peace Reporting, Tribunal* Update 689, (April 26, 2011), Tribunal_update_english@mailman.iwpr.net (accessed April 26, 2011).

53. Akhavan "International Criminal Tribunals"; on the importance of international law in the conflict resolution process see Richard Falk, "International Law and the Peace Process," 28 *Hastings Int'l & Comp. L. Rev.*331 (2004-2005); also Holger-C. Rohne, "Opportunities and limits for Applying Restorative Justice in the Context of the Israeli-Palestinian Conflict," in *Restoring Justice after Large-Scale Conflict*, ed. Ivo Aertsen, Jana Arsovska, Holger-C Rohne, Marta Valinas and Kris Vanspauwen (Portland, OR: Willan, 2008), 279-320.

54. Jack Snyder and Leslie Vinjamuri, "Trials and Errors: Principle and Pragmatism in Strategies of International Justice," *International Security* 28, (2003/2004): 5-44. See also Chandra Lekha Sriram, Olga Martin-Ortega and Johanna Herman, "War, Conflict, and Human Rights," *The International Studies Encyclopedia*, Robert A. Denemark (Blackwell Publishing, Blackwell Reference Online, 2010), 9-10. <http://www.isacompendium.com/subscriber/tocnode?id=g9781444336597_chunk_g978144433659721_ss1-1> (accessed November 15, 2010); Wippman "Exaggerating," 109. For a discrediting of these arguments see Akhavan, "International Criminal Tribunals."

55. Werle, *Principles of International Criminal Law*, 77.

56. When the violence in Sierra Leone continued unabated after the UN-mediated amnesty, the amnesty was subsequently withdrawn by then-Secretary General Kofi Annan. See Schabas, *UN International Criminal Tribunals*, 34-35.

57. See, for example, B. Welling Hall, "International Law and the Responsibility to Protect," *The International Studies Encyclopedia*, Robert A. Denemark (Blackwell Publishing, 2010), www.isacompendium.com (accessed January 1, 2011). On norms and humanitarian intervention more broadly see Martha Finnemore, *The Purpose of Intervention: Changing Beliefs about the Use of Force* (Ithaca, NY: Cornell Univ. Press, 2003), and Kathryn Sikkink, "From Pariah State to Global Protagonist: Argentina and the Struggle for International Human Rights," *Latin American Politics and Society* 50, no. 1 (Spring 2008): 1-29. For further information on the influence of the "justice cascade," and the "norms cascade" see Ellen Lutz and Kathryn Sikkink, "The Justice Cascade: The Evolution and Impact of Foreign Human Rights Trials in Latin America, 2 *Chi. J. Int'l L.*1 (Spring 2001): 1-34 and Thomas Risse, Stephen Ropp, and Kathryn Sikkink, *The Power of Human Rights*, (New York: Cambridge University Press, 1999), respectively.

58. Fichtelberg, Aaron, *Crimes beyond Justice: Retributivism and War Crimes. Criminal Justice Ethics* 24, no. 1 (2005): 31-46; also Drumbl, *Atrocity* and Mani, *Beyond Retribution.*

Part I

Thematic Studies

Chapter 1

Customary Law and the *Ad Hoc* International Criminal Courts

James Larry Taulbee

The *ad hoc* international criminal tribunals have provided cases, debates, and decisions which provide insights into discovering and defining customary international law. Missing are external controls on these courts. Nonetheless, the legal community's expectations about certain relationships and processes should form the equivalent in providing a consensus about methods and a baseline against which to test results. This article simply asks: *does the use of customary international law by these tribunals reflect the requirements specified by legal authorities?*

International criminal law (ICL) has evolved through conventions, but only with the advent of the *ad hoc* courts, can we identify a significant body of legal practice. The principal problem for these courts stems from the fact that ICL does not constitute a coherent legal code; instead "it has developed in bits and pieces through different experiences which may or may not be linked to one another."[1] Treaties and customary law are often vague and incomplete because they lack specificity regarding the objective and subjective elements that determine criminality, along with unprecedented factual applications.

ICL has traditionally been derived from international humanitarian law. However, some human rights treaties mandate prosecutions, reparations or other remedies, even if most provisions do not. In most cases, the conventions fail to define what consequences should follow from specific violations or to elaborate the important procedural elements necessary for prosecution.[2] The Statutes of the *ad hoc* courts marked a step forward in terms of guidance; yet they lack a section that defines the constituent behavioral elements of the crimes within their mandates in any detail.

Much of ICL lacks "legislative" specificity in terms of procedural law as well. This means the *ad hoc* courts have often had to resort to domestic law While judges routinely deny they "legislate,"[3] the lack of specificity means that ICL contains a large element of judge-made law because of the need for detail to meet both the substantive and procedural requirements of application in practice.

The problem is easily illustrated by reference to the "general principles" in the statutes setting up the three *ad hoc* UN courts: the International Criminal Tribunal for the former Yugoslavia (ICTY), the International Criminal Tribunal for Rwanda (ICTR), and the Special Court for Sierra Leone (SCSL). All three contain almost identical language defining general principles, including criminal responsibility.[4] Unfortunately the Statutes do not contain specific answers to many of the potential problems that arise when trying to define the context in which criminal acts occur nor do they contain guidance for judges for developing such rules.[5]

Treaties and Custom as Sources

ICL treaties lack a uniform approach to the problems addressed. This is partially a consequence of the disjointed and lengthy process of development. Progress in the international milieu requires a productive interaction of idealism and pragmatism. Without idealism to set goals that transcend the demands of the immediate defined by the narrow self-interests of particular states, essential exchanges in political interaction would remain on the most elemental level. Without a leavening dialectic with the "art of the possible" ideals would remain undeveloped and isolated from political experience. The tension between the two ensures that the mix at any specific time never fully satisfies advocates of either position. Yet any idea of progress must take both into account. The practical statesman will attempt to adapt news ideas and approaches to changing circumstances by grafting them to rootstock gleaned from useful and successful practices. It is not surprising that political circumstances generate attempts to deal with perceived threats.[6]

The Vagaries of Custom

In the absence of sufficient specificity in relevant treaties and constituent Statutes, customary law would play a central role. The requisite elements of custom are:

a) concordant practice by a number of states;
b) continuation/repetition of the practice over a reasonable period of time;
c) a belief that the practice is required by, or consistent with, prevailing international law (*opinio juris*); and,
d) general acquiescence in the practice by other states[7]

The problem posed is one of finding and applying rules that fit these simple principles of definition to specific contexts. The International Court of Justice (ICJ) defined the process of determining a customary rule in the *Nicaragua* case:

> It is not to be expected that in the practice of States the application of the rules in question should have been perfect . . . The Court does not consider that, for a rule to be established as customary, the corresponding practice must be in absolutely rigorous conformity with the rule . . . T]he Court deems it sufficient that the conduct of States should, *in general* be consistent with such rules, and that instances of state conduct inconsistent with a given rule should *generally* have been treated as breaches of that rule, not as indications of the recognition of a new rule. (emphasis added)[8]

The decision came under some severe criticism from scholars. By focusing upon *opinio juris* the ICJ found a rule of custom coinciding with that of UN Charter 2(4) "without any reference whatsoever to the ways in which governments actually behave."[9] One normally expects that practice creates obligation, not the converse.

The converse position has found support among contemporary scholars, however. Roberts argues that new customary law is derived by a deductive process that "begins with general statements of rules rather than particular instances of state practice."[10] It emphasizes *opinio juris* rather than overt action. Scholars have argued the importance of this perspective in terms of the evolution of human rights law.[11]

This position has been implicit in some dialogues over customary laws. No better example exists than the *Caroline* case. Most take *Caroline* as the paradigm which defines the elements necessary to establish a claim to self-defense. On closer examination *Caroline* raises as many questions concerning its relevance to modern practice as it answers. For example, Jennings offers no systematic analysis of practice before or after settlement of the 1837 incident to validate the assertion that this established a customary rule governing self-defense.[12] No writer prior spoke of self-defense. Jennings acknowledges this, but rather than providing systematic evidence, dodges the issue by asserting that once the phrase was introduced, "it was possible for lawyers of a later day to give it a legal content."[13]

Following WWII, when it became evident that the collective security system would *not* function as planned, some scholars argued this meant that "customary law" of self-defense remained intact.[14] This begged the question: Can one make a viable argument that a single defining instance in a period of one hundred years has the power to create a binding rule if enough *lawyers* believe in it?

Given the above discussion I hypothesize:

1. Judges on *ad hoc* courts have followed the "modern" deductive approach in reaching decisions that require reliance on customary law in that they will emphasize *opinio juris* rather than practice;
2. *Opinio juris* will be less important than practice because judges have had to draw heavily on "general principles" of domestic law for which there is no *opinio juris*.

This analysis focuses primarily on the ICTY and the development of Joint Criminal Enterprise (JCE) as a mode of individual liability. JCE does not appear in the ICTY Statute, yet it became a staple of ICTY judges who sought a rationale to assign individual responsibility for incidents involving large numbers of people. This should be sufficient to establish a pattern as later panels have relied on precedent. In this sense the tribunals' decisions, regardless of the sources used, became important in defining customary ICL, no matter the rationale or evidence used. Although future courts may revisit the decisions, the weight of "practice" will heavily influence future decisions.

Customary Law and the *ad hoc* Tribunals

Established by the UNSC with Resolution 827,[15] the ICTY immediately faced the challenge that it was an *ex post facto* court. Given the firm establishment of the *nullum crimen* principle in customary international law, tribunals are obligated to apply law extant at the time of commission of the alleged offenses.[16]

The mandates and Statutes of the *ad hoc* Tribunals clearly anticipate that they would rely primarily upon customary law. Baxter explains: "The advantage of the employment of a treaty as evidence of customary international law as it was at the time of the adoption of the treaty or as it has come to be, is that it provides a clear and uniform statement of the rule to which a number of States subscribe."[17] The problem early on was that the international jurists were hunter-gatherers in a legal wilderness,[18] or alchemists seeking to transform common elements into something more valuable. The Nuremberg Tribunal noted for example: "The law of war is to be found not only in treaties, but in the customs and practices of states which gradually obtained universal recognition, and from the general principles of justice applied by jurists and practiced by military courts."[19] The problem with this statement is that it exists in isolation. Other than a suggestion that domestic military courts could perhaps provide evidence of "customs and practices of states," Nuremberg never suggests a method to determine exactly *what* these may be.

Fifty years later, the Secretary-General's report about the ICTY Statute would address the same question with an interesting set of arguments.[20] "While there is international customary law which is not laid down in conventions, some of the major conventional humanitarian law has become part of international customary law."[21] He further identified several sources of law that may be open to the ICTY, including the the Geneva Conventions (1949).[22]

The method of determination here remains somewhat opaque. He later refers to the "grave breaches" provisions in these latter documents, [23] stating "The Security Council has reaffirmed on several occasions that persons who commit or order commissions of grave breaches of the 1949 Geneva Conventions in the territory of the former Yugoslavia are individually responsible for such breaches as serious violations of international humanitarian law."[24] Note UNSC Resolutions are expressions of general community *legal* obligations.

The Secretary-General also indicated that the Charter and decisions of the International Military Tribunal (IMT) clearly form part of customary law. As Zahar and Sluiter ask, in what sense then are crimes against peace part of international customary law?[25] The ICC Statute left this open for a time as the conferees could not agree on definitions and specifications.

Tadić: on Whose Authority?

In retrospect, beginning with low-level participants proved fortuitous because it helped the ICTY work out some important questions of procedural and substantive law. In addition to the issues raised concerning the use of *Geneva Additional Protocol I*, *Tadić* raised the issue of the relationship of customary law to treaty law. The defense challenged the applicability of *Geneva Additional Protocol II*. The Appeals Chamber maintained many provisions of the convention were declaratory of customary international law; others had "crystallized" emerging rules.[26] The problem here is the method used to establish *opinio juris*. The decision rests upon only *two* instances of "practice": the first from interaction of Guatemala with the UN, the second from a single statement by a US State Department lawyer. The standard defining practice seems severely degraded here in favor of the broader idea that the international community embraced the rules in *Protocol II* as declarative of customary law.[27]

Customary Law and Individual Criminal Liability

Grounded in domestic criminal justice systems, the concept of individual criminal liability for international crimes was established by the Nuremberg trials. However the Nuremberg Charter (like the Tokyo Charter) merely listed possible rationales for liability, including command responsibility.[28] The Statutes of the ICTY and ICTR utilize the principle, but lack any references to rationales that might be used to impute the degree of individual liability.[29]

Prosecutors must first connect the individual's behavior with the broader context that defines the crimes. Just because a crime or genocidal massacre occurs during a war does not mean it necessarily forms part of the broader pattern. Moreover, because of the *nullum crimen* principle, to obtain a conviction prosecutors have to prove that the forms and degree of criminal participation underlying these charges actually have a firm basis in prior practice in *international* law. The prosecution must then determine whether the elements of the particular crime have been satisfied.

For ICL the principal focus is on those who plan, organize or order the events that define the broader context because of the presumption that they bear the greatest responsibility; their actions form an essential component in facilitating the activities of the actual perpetrators. Normally the person who commits the act is regarded as the primary perpetrator, while those who plan, instigate etc., are regarded as secondary perpetrators.[30]

Various conventions refer to commission, planning, instigating, ordering, aiding and abetting, JCE, superior/command responsibility, and complicity as principles that prosecutors may use to define liability. These rationales do not represent sharply defined categories and overlap in many cases.

In case law these principles primarily serve a descriptive purpose, defining the modality of participation, not degree of culpability.[31] Although intuitively one might try to assign a hierarchy in terms of degree of guilt, the charges carry little weight with respect to penalties if found guilty. The *degree of participation* stands apart from the charge itself. The degree of culpability is a question of fact to be determined at trial.

The issue of how best to characterize the idea of "joint participation" has generated considerable controversy. The definitions leave many important issues open, depending on circumstance:

1. Can a "common plan" arise extemporaneously? If so, what criteria define the threshold level of participation in the sense of determining "agreement?"
2. What does "jointness" mean? Does the doctrine permit one to determine primary and secondary levels of participation?
3. In determining "foreseeability," what should a person know and when?

Joint Criminal Enterprise as a Form of Liability

Neither the IMT nor the courts authorized under Control Council Law No. 10 utilized JCE.[32] The Statutes of the ICTY and ICTR do not explicitly refer to JCE. Judges have inferred its applicability from Article 7(1) of the ICTY Statute.

The Appeals Chamber for the *ad hoc* Tribunals resisted developing the idea of co-perpetration, relying instead upon JCE.[33] The utility of JCE is that all of those included may be guilty of the crime *regardless* of the specific part each played in the crime's commission. The search for an applicable standard came from a twofold concern: the need to concentrate on the roles of others who in some way made it possible for perpetrator(s) to carry out the act(s); and, the view that "aiding and abetting" might understate the degree of criminal responsibility.[34] The Appeals Chambers developed three levels of participation.[35]

1. All participants share the same intent and purpose and act upon that intent;[36]
2. Crimes committed by individuals as part of the joint criminal enterprise that contribute to the overall "intent and purpose" in that they contribute to a pattern of "ill-treatment."[37]
3. Crimes that fall outside the common design if they result from "a natural and foreseeable consequence of the effecting of that common purpose."[38]

All share a common *mens rea*: "joint criminal enterprise requires: 1) a plurality of individuals; 2) the existence of a common plan or purpose that involves commission of a crime under the Statute; and 3) participation of the accused in the common effort in the sense of committing a crime defined in the Statute."

The ICTY Prosecutor has used JCE as a basis for indicting senior military and political leaders.[39] The SCSL Prosecutor also used JCE as the principal basis for assessing criminal responsibility.[40]

Interestingly, the Trial Chamber in *Tadić* did not discuss any form of common purpose as a separate form of criminal responsibility. The Prosecutor appealed the decision of the Trial Chamber that no proof existed linking Tadić to the actual killing. Tadić had participated in the attack as part of an armed group but the defense had argued that no evidence existed to show that he killed or intended to kill. The Prosecution argued that he bore responsibility because the killings were a foreseeable consequence of the actions of the group.[41] The Appeals Chamber embraced this position in reversing the Trial Chamber's decision.

In developing the idea of JCE, the Appeals Chamber went to great lengths to separate JCE from "conspiracy" and "organizational liability." Despite the distinction, the panel still insisted that JCE had a firm foundation in customary law. The reasoning fails to convince with respect to the extended form of JCE which clearly bears very close kinship to the organizational liability concept.[42] On this issue the Trial Chamber in *Stakiċ* held that because organizational liability was not mentioned in the Statute, its use would violate the *nullum crimen* principle.[43] Moreover, questions arise concerning the reluctance to develop and rely upon "conspiracy," which does have an established provenance in customary law. Nonetheless, the important question becomes, upon what sources did the ICTY draw in their search for a customary rule?

The Search for Relevant Customary International Law

In addressing the problem of sources, the Appeals Chamber in *Tadiċ* characterized possibilities as "chiefly case law and a few instances of international legislation."[44] The panels drew from the series of trials held by Allied military courts authorized by CCL No. 10.[45] The question here involves the extent to which the circumstances of the cases and materials used to develop a rule match the circumstances of contemporary cases.

The Nuremberg trials present an interesting difficulty. Neither CCL Nc. 10 nor the trial proceedings clearly defined particular forms of liability or elaborated rules of application. Those who drafted CCL No. 10 did this as a conscious omission because they wished to avoid making precise legal categories that might have bogged down trials in technical legal arguments.[46] However this presented a problem for future prosecutors and judges.

The principal cases utilized by the *Tadiċ* Appeals Chamber fall into three categories: 1) participation in the activities associated with concentration camps;[47] 2) the *Einsatzgruppen* cases;[48] and 3) the killing of small groups of Allied POWs by German soldiers and others, usually with German soldiers present.[49] In analyzing these cases one finds clear support for the first two specifications of JCE despite the vague definitions in CCL No. 10.

The first two cases provide easy referents. In terms of weighing the contribution of each of the accused to the overall enterprise both involved closed systems that had a clearly defined purpose, assigned roles, and definitive boundaries. A position within the system implied that an individual had performed positive acts in accordance with assigned duties. In both set of cases, the tribunal had access to detailed records kept to confirm the nature and extent of their work.[50]

The ICTY Appeals Chamber built the third form of JCE almost exclusively from the captured POW killing cases.[51] These cases present an enormous difficulty. No literal transcripts exist. Analysts have to rely upon inference with respect to the elements of law and facts that guided the court.[52] In this case on what basis did the panel find a rationale that supported the idea of "foreseeability?" Unlike *Tadić* the factual elements were not contested. The question centered instead on the tests used to determine the degree of culpability of the accused.[53]

One suspects that as the first case, the Appeals Panel might have wished to establish as many precedents as possible. This proved difficult given that Tadić was a "foot soldier," not a leader. The prosecutor could not establish "aiding and abetting." The difficulty associated with the absence of clear evidence of participation drove the search for a rationale that would go beyond mere membership. In this respect, the Appeals Panel ignored the "not guilty" verdicts in the *Einsatzgruppen* cases.

The inconsistencies emerged in the *Vasiljević* case.[54] The factual situation parallels that of *Tadić*. The Trial Panel found Vasiljević guilty using JCE. The Appeals Panel reversed the conviction, relying instead upon "aiding and abetting." More importantly, the Appeals Panel looked at intent and argued that the participation of the appellant failed *to reach the same level* as cases previously heard.[55]

The Trial Chamber in *Brđanin* also disregarded the *Tadić* argument.[56] *Brđanin* was accused of participating in a JCE that forcibly removed Bosnian Muslims and Croats from territory. The Trial Chamber stated that to establish a JCE, the prosecutor must establish "between the person physically committing a crime and the accused, there was an understanding or an agreement to commit that particular crime."[57] The prosecutor must go beyond providing proof of a common plan to establish that the linkages among the accused involved an agreement to commit specific acts.[58] The *Brđanin* standard raised the bar particularly for Form 3 of JCE. Indeed, the Trial Panel in *Milutinović* stated the requirement as:

> In such a case, the accused may be found responsible for such crimes or underlying offences provided that he participated in the common criminal purpose with the intent to further it, and that, in the circumstances of the case, (a) it was reasonably foreseeable to him that the crime or underlying offence would be perpetrated by one or more of the persons used by him (or by any other member of the joint criminal enterprise) in order to carry out the *actus reus* of the crimes or underlying offences forming part of the common purpose and (b) he willingly took that risk (*dolus eventualis*).[59]

Despite citing *Tadić*, the ICTY over time seemingly moved toward a more narrow and conservative definition of JCE. Critics have long asserted that the doctrine is amorphous and overly broad.

The SCSL Appeals Panel has generated a storm with its verdict in the Revolutionary United Front (RUF) cases.[60] According to the majority decision, JCE liability would *not* require that an accused share the intent of the other participants to commit the crimes that are said to be within its common purpose. A defendant charged could be held criminally responsible for all the natural and foreseeable consequences of a JCE. The reasoning seems to eliminate the necessity to prove any degree of causality between the acts of the accused and criminal liability for those acts. Membership in the enterprise seems sufficient for individual responsibility for all or most of the consequences of the actions attributable to the enterprise.[61]

A Note on General Principles of Law as a Source of Custom

The problem with using "general principles" stems from reconciling the differing approaches to liability used by national legal systems. Bogdan suggests: "the principles differ between the national legal systems of the world, and sometimes even within the subcategories of a given national legal system."[62] One legal system may assign responsibility to non-perpetrators for all criminal acts related to the commission of a crime. Other jurisdictions limit their responsibility to acts which are foreseeable. Presumably while the general principle that individuals may be held accountable for the acts of others may be established as part of international customary law, a survey of "general principles" of law in the ICJ Statute sense does not yield consistency in terms of standards of imputability necessary to construct a principle at the international level.

The Appeals Chamber in *Tadić* took these observations into account, noting "reference to national legislation and case law only serves to show that the notion of common purpose upheld in international criminal law has an underpinning in many national systems."[63] However it interjected an important caveat:

> [N]ational legislation and case law cannot be relied upon as a source of international principles or rules, under the doctrine of the general principles of law recognized by the nations of the world: for this reliance to be permissible, it would be necessary to show that most, if not all, countries adopt the same notion of common purpose....Nor can reference to national law have, in this case, the scope and purport adumbrated in general terms by the United Nations Secretary-General in his Report, where it is pointed out that "suggestions have been made that the international tribunal should apply *domestic law* in so far as it *incorporates* customary international humanitarian law.[64]

Considering the *Nicaragua* argument, this seems a curiously conservative position. It ignores the conclusions of the ICJ concerning the necessary "fit" required for determining a principle of customary law. Second, when one examines other case law, this point has not bothered other panels.[65] Judges on *ad hoc* courts have seemingly reversed the normal mode of search in emphasizing differences rather than similarities. Finally, if domestic laws reflect principles gleaned from international law, one would not have to look at domestic law. The fact of incorporation would indicate that the relevant principles are well enough developed at the international level to provide sufficient guidance in constructing a relevant set of rules with respect to liability without reference to "general principles." The panels wished to find sufficient precedent to root the principles firmly in international norms.

Conclusion

I advanced two propositions concerning the ICTY's use of customary law based upon discussions in contemporary literature. These could be summarized as practice versus aspiration. The evolution of the first two forms of JCE fit the "practice" mold. Form 3 reflects neither hypothesis. Consequently subsequent ICTY panels explicitly narrowed the requirements under which Form 3 would apply. However, even as trial panels narrowed the requirements for application, prosecutors still found JCE a useful tool. It has played a very minor role in convictions despite prosecutorial enthusiasm.[66]

To return to an earlier point, the Appeals Panel generated Form 3 out of whole cloth. The bombshell came in the SCSL judgment in *Sesay*. So, to what extent will this case form a solid precedent for future courts? Could it become the *Lotus*[67] or the defining case? Considering the level of criticism in the international legal community, I would see this case as "*Lotus*," much in the way that *Tadić* has assumed *Lotus* status.

Still, a major part of the problem comes from the simple fact that successive panels have failed to provide explicit guidance in terms of rules of discovery and application. Article 25.3(d) of the ICC Statute clarified the meaning of JCE, somewhat however its language encompasses Forms 1 and 2 only. While open to interpretation, it sets a very low level of participation as the trigger. Forms 1 and 2 of JCE now seem well established and rooted in customary law and based upon traditional reasoning. The question now is how useful is JCE as a principle in assessing liability?

Notes

1. M. Cherif Bassiouni, *Introduction to International Criminal Law* (Ardsley, NY: Transnational, 2003), 23.

2. Antonio Cassese, *International Criminal Law* (Oxford: Oxford University Press, 2003), 17.

3. Sir Robert Jennings argued: "This provision I understand as a necessary recognition that judges, whether national or international, are not empowered to make new laws." Jennings, "The Judiciary, International and National, and the Development of International Law," 45 *Int'l & Comp. L. Q.* 1, 3 (1996).

4. William A. Schabas, *The UN International Criminal Tribunals: The Former Yugoslavia, Rwanda and Sierra Leone* (Cambridge: Cambridge University Press, 2006), 289-290. Statute of the International Tribunal for the former Yugoslavia, www.icls.de/dokumente/icty_statut.pdf (accessed May 10, 2011).

5. Schabas, *International Tribunals*, 290-91. For a good summation of this point see the judgment of the Appeals Chamber in the *Galić* case. ICTY, *Prosecutor v. Galić*, Case No. IT-98-29-A, Judgment, paras. 83-85 (November 30, 2006).

6. James L. Taulbee, "Governing the Use of Force: Does the Charter Matter Anymore?" *Civil Wars* 4, no. 2 (2001): 1-58. See also Robert D. Putnam. "Diplomacy and

Domestic Politics: The Logic of Two-Level Games," *International Organization* 42 (Summer 1988): 427-460.

7. Manley O. Hudson, *Article 24 of the Statute of the International Law Commission*, 2 Y.B. Int'l L. Commn. 24, 26, U.N. Doc. A/CN.4/SER.A/1950/Add.1; also Michael Akehurst, "Custom as a Source of International Law," 47 *BYIL* 1, 53 (1974-75).

8. *Nicaragua v. United States,* 1986 I.C.J Reports of Judgments 98 (Merits para. 186) (June 27, 1986).

9. Frederic L. Kirgis, Jr. (Comment), "Custom on a Sliding Scale," 81 *AJIL* 146, 147 (1987); see also Anthony D'Amato (Comment), "Trashing Customary International Law," 81 *AJIL* 101, 101-105 (1987).

10. Anthea Elizabeth Roberts, "Traditional and Modern Approaches to Customary International Law: A Reconciliation," 95 *AJIL* 757, 758 (2001); see also Koskenniemi, *From Apology*, 388-473.

11. Jean-Marie Henckaerts and Louise Doswald-Beck, *Customary International Humanitarian Law* (Cambridge: Cambridge University Press, 2005); Theodor Meron, *Human Rights and Humanitarian Norms as Customary Law* (Oxford: Oxford University Press, 1999).

12. R. Y. Jennings, "The *Caroline* and *McLeod* Cases," 32 *AJIL* 82 (1938).

13. Jennings, "*Caroline*," 91-92.

14. Robert W. Tucker, (Comment), "Reprisals and Self Defense: The Customary Law," 66 *AJIL* 586, 586-596 (1972).

15. "Secretary-General's Report on Aspects of Establishing an IT," 32 *ILM* 1163, 1192 (1993); International Tribunal, "Rules of Procedure and Evidence," 33 *ILM* 484 (1994).

16. James Larry Taulbee, *International Crime and Punishment: A Guide to the Issues* (Praeger, 2009), 49-85.

17. Richard R. Baxter, "Multilateral Treaties as Evidence of Customary International Law," 41 *BYIL* 275 (1965).

18. Alexander Zahar and Göran Sluiter, *International Criminal Law* (Oxford: Oxford University Press, 2008), 80.

19. 22 Judgment of the International Military Tribunal, 463-464, The Avalon Project (Yale University Law School), http://avalon.law.yale.edu/subject_menus/judcont.asp (accessed May 10, 2011).

20. Report of the Secretary-General Pursuant to Paragraph 2 of UN Security Council Resolution 808, (1993), S/25704, May 3, 1993.

21. Report of the Secretary-General, para. 33.

22. Report of the Secretary-General, para. 35, see also paras. 37-38.

23. Report of the Secretary-General, paras. 37-38.

24. Report of the Secretary-General, para. 35; see also para 39.

25. Zahar and Sluiter, *International Criminal Law,* 85.

26. ICTY, *Prosecutor v. Tadić*, Case No. IT-95-16-AR72, Decision on the Defense Motion for Interlocutory Appeal on Jurisdiction, para. 117 (October 2, 1995).

27. The decision in *Tadić* caused a split among judges in the Court (Zahar and Sluiter, *International Criminal Law,* 89-91). The issues also concern application of parts of Geneva Additional Protocol I as well. Compare ICTY, *Prosecutor v. Kordić and Čerkez*, Case No. IT-95-14/2-A, Appeals Judgment, para. 165-169 (December 17, 2004) with *Prosecutor v. Blaskić*, Case No. IT-95-14-A, Appeals Judgment, para 141 (July 29, 2004).

28. *Report of the International Law Commission to the General Assembly, Part III: Formulation of the Nürnberg Principles,* "Principles of International Law Recognized in

the Charter of the Nürnberg Tribunal and in the Judgment of the Tribunal, with Commentaries," 2 *Y.B. Intl L. Comm.* 374, 374-378, U.N. Doc. A/1316.

29. Guénaël Mettraux, *International Crimes and the ad hoc Tribunals* (Oxford: Oxford University Press, 2005), 270.

30. Schabas, *International Tribunals*, 297.

31. Cassese, *International Criminal Law*, 179-180.

32. "Principles of International Law Recognized in the Charter of the Nürnberg Tribunal and in the Judgment of the Tribunal, with Commentaries."

33. The Trial Chamber in *Furundžija* used "co-perpetration." ICTY, *Prosecutor v. Furundžija,* Case No. IT-95-17/1-T Judgment (December 10, 1998). The Appeals Chamber in *Tadić* first referred to responsibility arising out of the execution of a "common criminal plan." Later it used a number of terms interchangeably with common criminal plan. Alison Marston Danner and Jenny S. Martinez, "Guilty Associations: Joint Criminal Enterprise, Command Responsibility and the Development of International Criminal Law," 93 *Cal. L. Rev.* 75, 104-112 (2005).

34. ICTY, *Prosecutor v. Tadić,* Case No. IT-94-1-A, Appeals Chamber Judgment, para. 192 (July 15, 1999).

35. ICTY, *Prosecutor v. Tadić,* Appeals Judgment, paras.195 -196, 204. For an extended discussion see, Danner and Martinez, "Guilty Associations," 104-107.

36. ICTY, *Prosecutor v. Multinović,* Case No. IT-99-37-AR72, Appeals Chamber Decision on Drojliub Ojdanić's Motion Challenging Jurisdiction-Joint Criminal Enterprise, para. 23 (May 21, 2003).

37. ICTY, *Prosecutor v. Tadić*, Appeals Judgment, para. 196.

38. *Prosecutor v. Tadić*, Appeals Judgment, para. 204. This formulation is extremely controversial because of the broad net it casts. It lowers the standard of liability (Danner and Martinez, "Guilty Associations," 109).

39. ICTY, *Prosecutor v. Brdjanin and Talić,* Case No. IT-99-36-PT, Corrected Version of the Fourth Amended Indictment (December 10, 2001); ICTY, *Prosecutor v. Krasjśnik and Plavśić*, Case Nos. IT-00-39 & 40, Consolidated Amended Indictment (March 7, 2002); ICTY, *Prosecutor v. Milošević*, Case No. IT-02-54-PT, Second Amended Indictment (Croatia) (October 23, 2002). JCE probably came of age in the *Krajišnik* case; see ICTY, Prosecutor v. *Krajišnik,* Case No. IT-00-39-T, Trial Chamber I, Judgment (September 27, 2006).

40. Special Court for Sierra Leone (SCSL), *Prosecutor against Charles Ghankay Taylor,* Case No. SCSL-03-01-PT, Pre-Trial Chamber, Second Amended Indictment (May 29, 2007); SCSL, *Prosecutor against Alex Tamba Brima, Brima Bazzy Kamara, and Santigie Borbor Kanu,* Case No. SCSL-2004-16-PT, Pre-Trial Chamber, Further Amended Consolidated Indictment (February 18, 2005).

41. ICTY, *Prosecutor v. Tadić*, Appeals Judgment, para. 175.

42. The concern is understandable, particularly with the "organizational liability" principle. The potential reach would have included two million individuals.

43. ICTY, *Prosecutor v. Stakić*, Case No. IT-97-24-T, Judgment, para. 433 (July 31, 2003).

44. ICTY, *Prosecutor v. Tadić,* Appeals Judgment, para. 194.

45. For the text, see *The Avalon Project*, http://avalon.law.yale.edu/imt/imt10.asp (accessed May 10, 2011).

46. M. Cherif Bassiouni, *Crimes Against Humanity in International Criminal Law* (The Hague: Kluwer Law International, 1999), 383, 386-388.

47. *The Dachau Concentration Camp Trial, Trial of Martin Gottfried Weiss and Thirty-Nine Others*, General Military Government Court of the United States Zone, XI

Law Reports of Trials of War Criminals, 5, 12; *Trial of Gustav Alfred Jepsen and others,* War Crimes Trial held at Luneberg, Germany (13-23 1946), Judgment of 24 August 1946.

48. *United States v. Otto Ohlendorf (Einatzgruppen case*), IV Trials of War Criminal before the Nurnberg Military Tribunals under Control Council Law No. 10 (Hein, 1997); for discussion, see *Prosecutor v. Tadić,* Appeals Judgment, para. 200.

49. *The Essen Lynching Case, Trial of Erich Heyer and Six Others*, British Military Court for the Trial of War Criminals in *Law Reports of Trials of War Criminals*, United Nations War Crimes Commission; *The Almelo Trial, Trial of Otto Sandrock and Seven Others*, British Military Court for the Trial of War Criminals in 1 *Law Reports of Trials of War Criminals*, United Nations War Crimes Commission; *Trial of Franz Schonfeld and Nine Others*, British Military Court for the Trial of War Criminals in 9 *Law Reports of Trials of War Criminals*, United Nations War Crimes Commission; *Kurt Goebell et al.* (also called the *Borkum Island* case), discussed in ICTY, *Prosecutor v. Tadić,* Appeals Judgment, para. 210.

50. Critics have asserted that the Appeals Chamber read too much into the *Einsatzgruppen* cases because the decisions were based on established principles of liability. See Zahar and Sluiter, *International Criminal Law*, 228-230.

51. Zahar and Sluter, *International Criminal Law*, 223-257; Attila Bogdan, "Individual Criminal Responsibility in the Execution of a 'Joint Criminal Enterprise' in the Jurisprudence of the *ad hoc* International Tribunal for the Former Yugoslavia," 6 *International Criminal Law Review* 63, 77-90 (2006).

52. Web Genocide Documentation Centre, "Case No. 8. The Essen Lynching Case," http://www.ess.uwe.ac.uk/wcc/essen.htm (accessed May 10, 2011).

53. In the *Essen* case the principal defendant Heyer incited a mob to mistreat the prisoners and thus committed a war crime. Straightforwardly, this does not require an element of foreseeability in order to assess liability. *Trial of Erich Heyer and Six Others* (December 22, 1945), 89.

54. ICTY, *Prosecutor v. Vasiljević,* Case No. IT-98-32-T, Judgment (November 29, 2002).

55. ICTY, *Prosecutor v. Vasiljević,,* Case No. IT-98-32-A, Judgment, 131 (February 25, 2004).

56. ICTY, *Prosecutor v. Brđanin,* Case No. IT-99-36-T, Trial Judgment (September 1, 2004).

57. ICTY, *Brđanin,* Trial Judgment, para. 344.

58. ICTY, *Brđanin,* Trial Judgment, paras. 352-355.

59. ICTY, *Prosecutor v. Milutinović, et al.*, Case No. IT-05-87-T, Judgment, para. 96 (February 26, 2009); ICTY, *Prosecutor v. Brđanin,* Case No. IT-99-36-A, Judgment, paras. 365, 411 (April 30, 2007); and ICTY, *Blaškić* Appeal Judgment, para. 33; ICTY, *Tadić* Appeal Judgment, para. 204.

60. SCSL, *The Prosecutor against Sesay, Kallon and Gbao (RUF Case)*, Case No. SCSL-04-15-A, Appeals Judgment (October 26, 2009).

61. Guénaël Mettraux, "Joint Criminal Enterprise" Has Grown Another Tentacle!" International Criminal Law Bureau (November 18, 2009).

62. Bogdan, "Individual Criminal Responsibility," 77; also Danner and Martinez, "Guilty Associations," 108-110 and sources cited; and Bogdan, "Individual Criminal Responsibility," 74-76 and sources cited.

63. ICTY, *Prosecutor v. Tadić*, Appeals Judgment, para. 224 and accompanying notes.

64. ICTY, *Prosecutor v. Tadić*, Appeals Judgment, para. 225 (emphasis added).

65. Zahar and Sluiter, *International Criminal Law*, 234-255.

66. For an exception, see ICTY, *Prosecutor v. Krajišnik,* Case No. IT-00-39-A, Appeals Judgment (March 17,2009).

67. *The Lotus Case (France v. Turkey)* PCIJ, Ser. A., No. 10, 1927.

Chapter 2

The Joint Criminal Enterprise Debate and the Case of Charles Taylor: The Politics of International Criminal Tribunal Law

Kelly-Kate Pease

International criminal law is developed by international treaties and statutes, as well as cases tried by international and internationalized domestic courts (hybrids). A widely debated development is the application of "joint criminal enterprise" (JCE) as a way to assign individual liability for group criminality. The case against Charles Taylor, former president of Liberia, for war crimes and crimes against humanity in neighboring Sierra Leone is based almost entirely on the JCE. The final outcome of the Taylor trial is significant because a conviction means that JCE has another important precedent for a legal theory that holds those in leadership positions accountable for their criminal associations with the physical perpetrators of war crimes and crimes against humanity. However, it may also undermine the legitimacy of international criminal law. The extent to which the accused is afforded a fair trial is impaired by the manner in which JCE was discovered and developed in international criminal case law and further expanded by the Special Court for Sierra Leone (SCSL).

The blending of legal traditions to create and inform international and internationalized courts is arguably necessary in order to enhance their legitimacy.

Ultimately, however, the legitimacy of the international criminal regime will be based on whether or not defendants receive a fair trial. The JCE doctrine and its application in international criminal law are problematic because JCE, and its variants, are not found in many domestic legal systems, especially in developing countries.

Joint Criminal Enterprise

JCE applied to international criminal law fully emerged from a case before the International Criminal Tribunal for the Former Yugoslavia (ICTY): *Prosecutor v. Tadić.*[1] *Tadić* has been extensively analyzed by legal scholars because it involves the "discovery" of JCE as mode of liability in international criminal law.[2] Dusko Tadić, a relatively low ranking soldier in a Serb militia, was charged with a variety of crimes including war crimes and crimes against humanity. The original Trial Chamber convicted Tadić on several counts, but acquitted him of the more serious count of crimes against humanity for the killing of five men in Bosnia. The Trial Chamber reasoned that while he was on the scene of the crimes, no direct evidence linked him to the actual commission of the crime. The Prosecutor appealed the acquittal and the ICTY Appeals Chamber ruled that Tadić could be convicted because he was a member of the group that committed the crime and he was part of common criminal plan or purpose.

According to the Appeals Chamber, the objective elements of JCE involve:

1. A plurality of persons.
2. The existence of a common plan, design, or purpose which amounts to or involves the commission of a crime provided for in the statute.
3. Participation of the accused in the common design involving the perpetration of the one of the crimes provided for in the statute.

The Chamber also identified three distinct categories of JCE where the *mens rea* (intent) differs.[3] The first category is a basic form "where all co-defendants possessing the same intent pursue a common criminal design."[4] The second refers to the notion of the systemic form of JCE or the "concentration camp" cases. The objective element of this category is active participation in a system of repression. Intent is established with the defendant's knowledge of the system and desire to further the repressive nature of the system. The third category, under which Tadić was ultimately convicted, is an extended form of JCE and involves cases where "one of the perpetrators commits an act which, while outside the common design, was nevertheless a natural and foreseeable consequence of the effecting of that common purpose."[5] This category is controversial because "it allows the prosecution to impute criminal liability to individuals for crimes they neither committed nor knew were taking place."[6]

Tadić marks an important legal precedent because it provides prosecutors with a theory of legal liability for large scale violations of international human rights and humanitarian law. It has become the principal mechanism for trying defendants before the ICTY, the International Criminal Tribunal for Rwanda (ICTR), the SCSL and the hybrid court in Cambodia. It is important to note that JCE is a mode of liability that allows individuals to be convicted of the actual crimes, as opposed to lesser offense of "aiding and abetting."

JCE is controversial because the Appeals Chamber "discovered" the doctrine. It is not specifically mentioned in the ICTY statute. However the court found that JCE had become part of customary international law. The Appeals Chamber reasoned that "common criminal purpose" was embedded in the Nuremburg Trials, implied in Article 7(1) of the ICTY Statute, included in Article 25 of the Rome Statute for the International Criminal Court (ICC), and is part of the domestic legal system of many states.

Several scholars have pointed out that JCE risks becoming a mechanism for convicting individuals based on their associations.[7] Moreover, the concept of JCE is not widely accepted in the domestic systems of many countries with a continental code law tradition. The Appeals Chamber was imprecise in its discovery in that it referred to "common criminal plan," "common design or purpose," "common criminal design," and "common concerted design" and used them interchangeably.[8] These terms are found in code or common law traditions, but are interpreted differently depending on the context of the code or case law. The chamber used these terms indiscriminately which made it seem like JCE was *more* widely accepted in domestic legal systems than it really was. It is questionable that the Appeals Chambers provided sufficient evidence of state practice and *opinio juris* to support the detailed categories articulated in the *Tadić* appeal decision.[9]

Regardless of the controversy, JCE has become one of the more important instruments in a prosecutor's tool box when trying cases involving gross violations of human rights or humanitarian law. Most of the important convictions in the ICTY and the ICTR were the result of the JCE and JCE was at the heart of the indictments against the late Slobodan Milosević and currently against former President of the Serbian Republic of Bosnia and Herzegovina Radovan Karadžić. Several other cases are important for clarifying JCE and understanding its application in international criminal trials. However, *Prosecutor v. Brđanin* discussed below, has insights for understanding the controversies surrounding the Taylor trial before the SCSL.

Rodslav Brđanin was the president of the Crisis Staff of the Autonomous Region of Krajina andwas charged with crimes ranging from persecution, to torture, to genocide. According to the prosecutor, Brđanin's responsibility for these crimes rested on basic JCE.[10] In 2004 the Trial Chamber ruled that Brđanin was not guilty because the prosecutor needed to "prove that between the member of the JCE physically committing the material crime charged and the person held responsible under JCE for that crime, there was a common plan to commit at least that particular crime."[11] The Trial Chamber essentially required proof of an agreement between the physical and nonphysical perpetrators of a crime.[12] By this reasoning, JCE is not appropriate "as a liability theory for prosecuting and convicting those defendants that are involved in large-scale enterprises and who are structurally remote for the commission of the crimes."[13]

The Appeals Chamber ultimately rejected the Trial Chamber's reasoning, but recognized and shared its concern that JCE might be inappropriate to impose liability on the accused when the links between the physical perpetrators are tenuous.[14] The Appeals Chamber rejected the notion that "express agreement" forms an additional objective element for JCE. *Brđanin* was just one of a series of cases where ICTY judges found the application of JCE problematic.[15] Others include *Prosecutor v. Stakić, Prosecutor v. Simić,* and *Prosecutor v. Krasjišnik* where judges sought to reject or restrain the application of JCE.

The Case of Charles Taylor

The trial of Charles Taylor stems from Taylor's involvement in the Sierra Leone civil war (1991-2002). This complicated violent conflict was distinguished by the depth of its brutality.[16] The violence began in earnest when the Revolutionary United Front (RUF) invaded Sierra Leone to overthrow the government. Taylor supported and financed the RUF and the corrupt Sierra Leone government was unable to put down the rebellion. The RUF, which recruited despondent Sierra Leone youths, soon controlled Eastern Sierra Leone and began plundering diamond mines and terrorizing the local population.[17] Taylor profited extensively, exchanging arms and supplies for Sierra Leone diamonds.[18]

In 1997, members of the Sierra Leone military led a coup against the collapsing Sierra Leone government and formed the Armed Forces Revolutionary Council (ARFC). ARFC then joined forces with the RUF to control the capital and the country. In 1998, the Economic Community of West African States Monitoring Group (ECOMOG) forcibly intervened and restored the elected Sierra Leone government to power and became the *de facto* Sierra Leone military.[19]

In 1999, a particularly brutal rebel assault on the capital generated international and regional concern and peace negotiations resumed. The Lomé Agreement was signed, granting amnesty to the parties and clearing the way for the deployment of a UN peacekeeping mission (UNAMSIL). In 2000, at the request of Sierra Leone, the Security Council authorized the Secretary General to work with Sierra Leone to create a hybrid court. The court's mandate is to prosecute "persons who bear the greatest responsibility for serious violations of international humanitarian law and Sierra Leonean law." Its temporal jurisdiction dates from 1996 and is designed to prosecute those in leadership positions who contributed to the violent conflict and undermined the peace process.

The SCSL utilizes a mixture of domestic and international law. Moreover domestic and international lawyers work side by side in the pursuit of justice. Such hybrid courts attempt to compensate for the "justice fatigue" that stems from the spiraling cost and slow pace of international criminal prosecutions. The international tribunals also have legitimacy issues in that they are imposed from the outside by the international community, and the trials are conducted far from the scene of the crimes.[20]

The SCSL is funded through voluntary contributions with the United States, Great Britain, and the EU being the largest contributors. Sierra Leoneans participate as judges and lawyers. The location of the SCSL in Freetown permits greater citizen access to the justice process. All of these elements contribute to transitional justice in post-conflict societies.

The first of the thirteen SCSL indictments were handed down in March 2003. One of the more important cases was *Prosecutor v. Bima, Karmara, and Kanu*, (the "AFRC case"). Bima, Karmara, and Kanu were principals in the AFRC and were accused of serious war crimes and crimes against humanity, including recruiting child soldiers. Taylor was also accused in a separate indictment. Since Taylor was still president of Liberia at that time, sealing the indictment was thought to facilitate an easier arrest at a later time and to prevent Taylor from hiding his assets. The indictment was effectively unsealed in June 2003 when Taylor left Liberia to attend a peace conference in Ghana. The prosecutor asked the government of Ghana to arrest Taylor and transfer him to the court.[21] Ghana declined and Taylor returned to Liberia. Through a series of negotiations led by Nigeria, Taylor agreed to resign his presidency and went into exile in Nigeria. With the 2005 election of Liberian President Ellen Johnson Sirleaf international pressure on Nigeria to arrest Taylor grew and in March 2006 he was finally handed over to the SCSL.[22]

The location of the trial was of concern. Holding Taylor's trial in Freetown would likely threaten peace and stability in Liberia and Sierra Leone. After intense behind-the-scene negotiations, the Security Council took the exceptional step of moving the Taylor trial to the facilities of the ICC in The Hague.[23] An agreement was reached whereby the Statute of the SCSL and international human rights and humanitarian law would apply to the case and Taylor would be imprisoned in Great Britain at the conclusion of the trial. Taylor was charged with seventeen counts (later amended to eleven) of war crimes and crimes against humanity, including acts of terrorism; outrages upon human dignity; conscripting or enlisting children under the age of fifteen years to serve in the armed forces, murder, and sexual slavery.[24] The Taylor case is unique because the defendant never set foot in Sierra Leone, swung a machete or physically committed a rape. The prosecution's case hinges almost exclusively on JCE as a mode of responsibility and liability.[25] According to the original indictment:

> The RUF and the AFRC shared a common plan, purpose or design (joint criminal enterprise) which was to take any actions necessary to gain and exercise political power and control over the territory of Sierra Leone, in particular the diamond mining areas. The natural resources of Sierra Leone, in particular the diamonds, were to be provided to persons outside Sierra Leone in return for assistance in carrying out the joint criminal enterprise.
>
> The joint criminal enterprise included gaining and exercising control over the population of Sierra Leone in order to prevent or minimize resistance to their geographic control, and to use the members of the population to provide support to the members of the joint criminal enterprise. [26]

As Rose points out, the prosecution substantially amended the indictment in May 2007 whereby the above paragraphs were eliminated and only the following remained:

> The ACCUSED, by his acts or omissions is individually criminally responsible pursuant to Article 6.1 of the Statute for the crimes referred to in Articles 2, 3, and 4 of the Statute as alleged in the Amended Indictment . . . which crimes amount to or were involved within a common plan, design or purpose in which the ACCUSED participated, or were a reasonably foreseeable consequence of such common plan design or purpose.[27]

The SCSL issued its first decision in June 2007. The judgment involved the *AFRC* case whereby the defendants were convicted of the most serious counts of war crimes and crimes against humanity.[28] The Trial Chamber, however, declined to convict the defendants on the basis of JCE because it had been defectively pled by the prosecutor. The Trial Chamber reasoned that, "actions necessary to gain and exercise political power and control over the territory of Sierra Leone did not amount to a crime within the SCSL statute or international human rights or humanitarian law."[29] Instead the defendants were convicted on the counts which they were found guilty of physically perpetrating (or having superior responsibility).

The Trial Chamber's ruling immediately raised flags for *Taylor* because his case rests almost exclusively on JCE. Fortunately for the prosecution in *Taylor*, the Appeals Chamber rejected that reasoning, stating that while the objective of the JCE was not a crime under the statute, the means contemplated to achieve that objective *were*. The Appeals Chamber restored JCE as a theory of liability and convicted the defendants. The *AFRC case* again raised questions about the appropriateness of JCE in international criminal prosecutions. In 2012, Taylor was found guilty of aiding and abetting but was acquitted of the more serious charges, including war crimes and crimes against humanity. Both the defense and prosecution are appealing the trial court's verdict.

The Controversies

The debates surrounding JCE in general and the *Taylor* case in particular acknowledges that international criminal tribunal law involves a blending of legal systems and practices with domestic and international law.[30] These debates involve detailed nuances and finer points of international statutory and case law, as well as relevant domestic law. They also recognize the political context and consequences of creating international criminal courts, issuing indictments, and obtaining convictions. What they tend to ignore are the values embedded in different legal traditions and how norms inform efforts to prosecute the accused. This research describes the values and norms that are rooted in the construction of the international criminal tribunal regime. It shows that, in attempting to build legitimacy for the regime by blending legal traditions, the blend itself seeks to ensure regime success: obtaining convictions for gross violations of human rights and humanitarian law. However legitimacy ultimately rests on the extent to which the accused are afforded a fair trial. As a result, international criminal tribunal law will be *ad hoc*, politically driven, and illegitimate from the perspective of most outside the relatively small group of international lawyers and jurists.

The international criminal tribunal regime is a mix of two developed legal traditions. Code law tradition is based on comprehensively-written statutory codes. Also known as civil law or continental law, it privileges the interests of society and civil order over the rights of individuals. The principal source of law is the legislature. If a behavior or act is not in the code, it is not illegal. The legal culture accompanying code law reflects specific values and attitudes of society toward the law.[31] One of these values is that judges should apply the law as it is written. The code law tradition is also known as the inquisitorial tradition in that judges and lawyers are expected to work together to discover what happened; to arrive at the truth. Judges function as fact-finders, prosecutors, and jurors, which reflects the value that the guilty should not go unpunished.[32] This is not to say that the presumption of innocence is absent from code law. However, it does suggest that being before the court means that the defendant has done something wrong. The "what and how" is a matter for the court to determine. Another way in which society ensures that the guilty do not go unpunished is that in many civil/code systems prosecutors are allowed to appeal the often rare acquittal. Lastly the interests of the individual are balanced with those of society through the principle of *nullum crimen sine lege*. That is, a person cannot be held criminally responsible for conduct unless it is crime within the law.[33]

By comparison in the common-law system, law is also made by judges through their interpretations of statutes and decisions in specific court cases. Judges determine which laws apply (and why) in a particular case; that case then becomes precedent for subsequent cases. The law is enhanced through court decisions. While this tradition gives judges significant authority, the political culture of the common law tradition places greater value on individual liberty and rights over collective interests. A central value is that the legal system should minimize the likelihood that the innocent are found guilty, hence, the accused are afforded significant substantive and procedural rights.[34] Moreover prosecutors often have only "one bite at the apple." They cannot appeal acquittals as the defendant has a right against double jeopardy. The common-law system is based on the adversarial tradition that pits the defense against the prosecution. While often derided as a system of "whoever tells the best story wins," the underlying norm is that the burden is on the prosecution to prove guilt beyond a reasonable doubt.

The common and code law traditions represent variations of liberal political/legal culture that emphasize different roles for individuals and the state in society. While many of the differences are overstated, what is important is how each balances the interests of the community against the rights of the individual and, when those interests conflict, which are more privileged and why? The legal culture frames the reasons and rationales which inform the legitimacy of the law and legal proceedings.

The lawyers and politicians who are constructing the international criminal regime are from or have been schooled in the Western liberal tradition that espouses either system. Their central dilemma centers on how to construct an international legal framework that will be relevant, sustainable, and accepted as legitimate by most of the international community. Moreover, their primary motive for constructing an international criminal regime is so that individuals can be tried (and convicted) of gross violations of international human rights and humanitarian law. As well-intentioned as this motive is, the trend of international criminal tribunal cases involving JCE is leading to the worst combination of both systems. The Taylor case is therefore instructive for several reasons. The first concerns the development of JCE and its application in Taylor's trial. From a code law perspective, fairness is established by having clear, comprehensive laws that express the intent of community as to what behavior is permissible. At the international level the only place where JCE is found in international statutory law is in Article 25(3)(d) of the Rome Statute. The statutes of the ICTY and ICTR do *not* explicitly include JCE. Rather it was discovered by appellate judges in the *Tadić* case and applied by both in subsequent cases. The statutes of hybrid or internationalized courts are mixed with regard to JCE. The SCSL statute does not refer to JCE, but the Special Panels for Serious Crimes (SPSC) for East Timor explicitly adopts the ICC model in Section 14, as does the Supreme Iraqi Criminal Tribunal (SICT).[35] In terms of domestic law, elements of JCE are found more frequently in common law systems (i.e. RICO in the U.S.). Code law systems recognize some categories of JCE, but not others.[36] While these elements and categories are similar, they are incommensurate, which may explain why many argue that the *Tadić* Appeals Chamber overreached by finding that JCE had become part of customary international law on the basis of "existence" in international and domestic law.

For those from a code law perspective, statutory international law has more legitimacy than customary international law because statutory or convention law reflect the intent and agreement of states. Customary international law ultimately must be pronounced upon by a judge or court. The discovery of JCE and its application in international criminal proceedings is problematic because it is vaguely articulated and sometimes not even recognized in domestic law.[37] In the Taylor case, if Sierra Leone and the UN wanted the SCSL to include JCE as a form of responsibility and liability, it should have been included in the statute. From a code law system, this undermines the legitimacy of JCE as a form of liability in the SCSL.

Second, where JCE is explicitly defined (the Rome Statute), the common purpose must be to commit a crime within jurisdiction of the Court.[38] Yet, in the *AFRC* case, the Appeals Chamber ruled that, while the objective of the JCE was not a crime under the Statute, the means contemplated to achieve that objective *are* crimes within the statute. As Rose points out this conflates the objective elements of the crime with the requisite intent. In essence, the Appeals Chamber expanded the already liberal JCE interpretation from a mode of liability for a crime within a statute to any group activity that results in a crime.[39] From a code law perspective, the Rome Statute effectively is being reinterpreted by judges, which may lead to its inconsistent application in other cases.

The common law legal culture, on the other hand, sees the inquisitorial aspects of international and hybrid courts as providing inadequate protection for the rights of the accused. While more accepting of judicial interpretation of international law and legal principles, common law lawyers are concerned about the presumption of guilt that is embedded in the international and hybrid criminal tribunals. The statutes may claim that the defendants are entitled to the presumption of innocence; however, the defendant is assumed to be guilty of something or they would not be before the court. The very mandate of the SCSL is to bring justice to those who bear the greatest responsibility for atrocities committed in Sierra Leone.

Other rights of the accused are at stake. The right to a fair trial is often compromised by excessive media attention. Many legal traditions (especially outside of the United States) place curbs on the media and restrict the parties from discussing the case publicly so as not to bias potential jurors. Judges are no less susceptible to media coverage than a lay person. According to McNabb and Dresden, the Western media vilified Taylor, and SCSL judges, prosecution, and the registry publicly discussed evidence though the media.[40] The SCSL posted prejudicial materials on its website and the prosecution used inflammatory language about Taylor's alleged atrocities.

The diplomatic wrangling to move the Taylor trial to The Hague centered on who would imprison him at the trial's conclusion, not on what would happen to Taylor if he was found *not guilty* of the allegations. The SCSL includes the

Office of the Principal Defender which is supposed to ensure that the accused receives a fair trial. Taylor was unable to meet or confer with the Principal Defender in part because the Registry thought the meeting was a delaying tactic and expensive because the Principal Defender was in Sierra Leone and Charles Taylor in the Netherlands.[41]

In the *ad hoc* tribunals and the SCSL, JCE was "discovered" by appellate judges while they were reversing acquittals made by the Trial Chambers. Moreover, the appellate judges expanded the notion of JCE to mean almost any group behavior resulting in crime that falls within a particular statute. This has the potential to amount to guilt by association and gut the notion of individual responsibility for crimes.[42]

Additionally in the Taylor trial, the theory and the nature of the charges kept changing. JCE first involved an attempt to take and maintain political and physical control in Sierra Leone. After JCE was rejected by the Trial Chamber in the *AFRC case* because that was not a crime within the statute, the Taylor defense sought to have the indictment dismissed. However the Appeals Chamber then restored JCE for the *AFRC case* because the objective of the plan, although not criminal, involved crimes within the statute. The prosecution in the Taylor case then shifted to a theory that involved a common plan to inflict a campaign of terror on the citizens of Sierra Leone (which is a crime within the statute). The only defense left to Taylor is that he had insufficient notice of the charges and the nature of the common plan.[43]

The states and international lawyers building an international criminal regime have drawn upon two of the more developed legal traditions to help establish its legitimacy. However in blending legal traditions, they drew upon the aspects of each tradition that would ensure that those accused of gross violations of human rights and humanitarian law did not go unpunished: appeal of acquittals, "discovering" modes of liability, and the use of case law to enhance statutory law. In doing so, they undermine the legitimacy of the regime because they do not include the checks that properly balance the rights of the international community and the victims for justice with the rights of the accused.

The technicalities and judicial opinions of the case law involving JCE in international and hybrid courts is of keen interest to lawyers and legal scholars. However, the law's legitimacy ultimately centers on the extent to which the accused are afforded a fair trial. The case law thus far suggests that many judges are uncomfortable with JCE as a mode of liability. The Taylor acquittal is yet another example. If, however, the Appeals Chamber reverses the acquittal and convicts as it did in the *AFRC case*, it sets an important legal precedent that may change the meaning of JCE in Article 25 of the Rome Statute from a mode of liability to any group behavior that amounts to crime within a statute. Moreover, current JCE jurisprudence effectively transfers a great deal of power to the prosecutor because once a person is accused of participating in a JCE,it would be difficult to imagine how someone could *not* be found guilty.[44] JCE will become almost impossible to defend against.

Looking down the road, one of the controversies with the Special Tribunal for Lebanon is that its statute states that Lebanese domestic law is the sole source of crimes yet, at the same time, it also explicitly adopts JCE. Yet, Lebanese law does not recognize JCE or its variants. This would allow for the conviction of persons who could not be held responsible under Lebanese law (a violation of the principle of *nullum crime sine lege*).[45] Moreover, these kinds of prosecutions require Western lawyers, Western theories of liability, Western money and Western consent. This does little to dispel notions that these kinds of trials are biased and politically motivated.

Conclusion

JCE was discovered by international judges and used to convict those who were physically remote from crimes when the crimes were committed. It has since been used by lawyers and jurists as a mode of liability to try high ranking officials for violations of international human rights and humanitarian law. JCE has compromised the legitimacy of international criminal law, legally, by undermining the culpability principle.[46] Its development and application are inconsistent with the way the code and common law legal cultures balance the rights of the accused with the rights of the society and victims for justice. The conviction of Charles Taylor for aiding and abetting and his acquittal of the more serious crimes on the basis of JCE further confuses matters. After the *AFRC case* JCE had become a mode of liability used to criminalize any group behavior, not to commit the crime (as JCE was originally conceived), but that results in a crime. The Taylor verdict creates another inconsistency. If Taylor is convicted on appeal once JCE is alleged, there seems to be no defense, especially against the extended concept of JCE, which is why JCE could be interpreted as a retributive form of victor's justice.[47] The irony is that legal efforts to hold powerful individuals accountable for war crimes through the JCE doctrine are undermining the legitimacy of international criminal law, both legally and politically. Those who see international law as mechanism for the powerful to control the weak and criminal prosecutions as show trials may indeed have a point.[48]

Notes

1. The *Tadić* case represents the first developed articulation. ICTY, *Prosecutor v. Tadić*, Case No. IT-94-1-T; Case No. IT-94-1-A. Gideon Boas, James L. Bischoff, and Natalie L. Reid *International Criminal Law Practitioner Library*. Vol. 1. (Cambridge: Cambridge University Press, 2007), 10.

2. Verena Haan, "The Development of the Concept of Joint Criminal Enterprise at the International Criminal Tribunal for the Former Yugoslavia," *Intl. Crim. L. Rev.* 5, 167 (April 2005); Catherine Gibson,"Testing the Legitimacy of the Joint Criminal Enterprise in the ICTY: A Comparison of Individual Liability for Group Conduct in International and Domestic Law," 18 *Duke J. Comp. & Intl. Law* 521 (October 2008); Elies Van Sliedregt, "Criminal Responsibility in International Law," *Eur. J. of Crime, Crim. L. & Crim. Just.*, 14, 81 (2006); Alison Martson Danner and Jenny S. Martinez, "Guilty Associations: Joint Criminal Enterprise, Command Responsibility, and the Development of International Criminal Law," *Cal L. J* 93, 75 (2005).

3. Van Sliedregt, "Criminal Responsibility," 90; Haan, "The Development of the Concept," 169.

4. Van Sliedregt, "Criminal Responsibility," 90.

5. ICTY, *Tadić.*Appeal Judgement, para. 204, cited in Van Sliedregt, "Criminal Responsibility," 90.

6. Gibson, "Testing the Legitimacy," 528.

7. Allen O'Rourke, "Recent Development. Joint Crimininal Enterprise and Brđanin: Misguided Overcorrection," *Harv. Intl. L. J.* 47, 307 (2006); Danner and Martinez, "Guilty Associations," 75-169; Antonio Cassese, "The Proper Limits of Individual Criminal Responsibility Under the Doctrine of Joint Criminal Enterprise," *J. Intl. Crim. Just.* 5, 109 (2007); Jens David Ohlin, "Three Conceptual Problems with the Doctrine of Joint Criminal Enterprise," *J Intl. Crim. Just.* 5, 69 (2007).

8. Danner and Martinez, "Guilty Associations," 103, footnote 106.

9. Boas et al., *International Criminal Law Practioner Library,* 10.

10. O'Rourke, "Recent Development," 317.

11. O'Rourke, "Recent Development," 318.

12. Katrina Gustafson, "The Requirement of an 'Express Agreement' for Joint Criminal Liability," *J Int'. Crim. Just.* 5, 134 (November 2005).

13. Van Sliedregt, "Criminal Responsibility," 94.

14. Federic Bostedt, and Joakim Dungel. "The International Criminal Tribunal and the Former Yugoslavia in 2007: Key Developments in International Humanitarian and Criminal Law," *Chin.J. Intl. L.* 7, 389, 401 (July 2008).

15. Boas et al, *International Criminal Law Practioner Library,* 132-135.

16. Paul Richards, *Fighting for the Rain Forest: War, Youth and Resources in Sierra Leone* (Oxford: James Curry, 1996).

17. John Hirsch, *Sierra Leone: Diamonds and the Struggle for Democracy* (Boulder, CO: Lynne Reinner, 2001).

18. Douglas Farah, *Blood from Stones: The Secret Financial Network of Terror* (New York: Broadway Books, 2004), 33-35.

19. Funmi Olonisakin, *Peacekeeping in Sierra Leone: The Story of UNAMSIL.* (Boulder, CO: Lynne Rienner, 2008), 810; Gill Wigglesworth, "The End of Impunity? Lessons from Sierra Leone," *International Affairs* 84, no. 4 (2008): 810.

20. Janice Dickenson, "Notes and Comments: The Promise of Hybrid Courts," *Am. J. Intl. L.*97, 295 (2003).

21. William Schabas, *An Introduction to the International Criminal Court,* 3d ed. (Cambridge: Cambridge University Press, 2007), 262.

22. Kimberly Lanegran, "The Importance of Trying Charles Taylor," *Journal of Human Rights* 6, no. 2 (April 2007): 169; Lydia Polgreen, and Lacey March, "Nigeria Will End Asylum for Warlord," *New York Times,* March 26, 2006, www.nytimes.com.

23. Security Council, "The Situation in Sierra Leone," S/RES/1688 (2006).

24. Wigglesworth, "The End of Impunity?," 817

25. Charles Taylor is charged with all forms of responsibility in international criminal law including superior responsibility; complicity, aiding and abetting, and planning, instigating and ordering. However, JCE is the theory that ties Taylor most directly to the crimes.

26. Special Court for Sierra Leone, *Prosecutor against Charles Taylor*, SCSL-2003-01-I, Indictment, para. 23-24 (March 7, 2003).

27. Amended Taylor Indictment par 33 as cited in Cicily Rose, "Troubled Indictments at the Special Court for Sierra Leone: The Pleading of Joint Criminal Enterprise and Sex-Based Crimes," *Social Science Research Network.* January 8, 2008, www.ssrn.com 21.

28. Nolwenn Guibert, and Tilman Blumenstock, "The First Judgment of the Special Court for Sierra Leone: A Missed Opportunity," *The Law and the Practice of International Courts and Tribunals* 6, no. 3 (2007): 367, 391.

29. Guibert and Blumenstock, "The First Judgement," 391.

30. Danner and Martinez, "Guilty Associations," 75-169; Mark Osiel, "The Banality of Good: Aligning Incentives Against Mass Atrocity," *Colum. L. Rev.* 105, 1751 (October 2005); Marko Milanovic, "Domestic Crimes and International Responsibility in the Special Tribunal for Lebanon," *J. Intl. Crim. Just.* 5, 1139 (2007); Ohlin, "Three Conceptual Problems," 69-90; Gibson,"Testing the Legitimacy," 521-547.

31. Henry Ehrmann, *Comparative Legal Cultures* (Englewood Cliffs, NJ: Prentice Hall, 1976), 7-9.

32. Gregory Mahler, *Comparative Politics: An Institutional and Cross-National Approach* (Upper Saddle River, NJ: Prentice Hall, 2000), 128.

33. Kenneth Gallant, *The Principle of Legality in International and Comparative Criminal Law* (New York: Cambridge University Press, 2009), 241.

34. Mahler, *Comparative Politics,* 128.

35. Boas et al, *International Criminal Law Practioner Library*, 132-135.

36. Van Sliedregt, "Criminal Responsibility," 95; Kai Hamdorf, "The Concept of a Joint Criminal Enterprise and Domestic Modes of Liability for Parties to a Crime: A Comparison of German and English Law," *J. Intl. Crim. Just.* 5, 208 (April 2007).

37. Milanovic, "Domestic Crimes," 1139.

38. Schabas, *An Introduction to the International Criminal Court,* 217.

39. Rose, "Troubled Indictments," 17.

40. Douglas McNabb, and C.J. Dresden, "Where is Charles Taylor's Defense?" *International Herald Tribune,* 2006, www.iht.com.

41. Osei Boateng, "Taylor's Trial: Whose Agenda," *New African*, July 2007: 46-48.

42. Danner and Martinez, "Guilty Associations," 75-169.

43. Rose, "Troubled Indictments," 17.

44. Danner and Martinez, "Guilty Associations," 137.

45. Milanovic, "Domestic Crimes," 1139.

46. Danner and Martinez, "Guilty Associations," 75-169.

47. Wigglesworth, "The End of Impunity?" 827.

48. John Laughland, *Travesty: The Trial of Slobodan Milosevic and the Corruption of International Justice* (Ann Arbor, MI: Pluto, 2007).

Chapter 3

Prosecuting Recruitment of Child Combatants by the Special Court for Sierra Leone: Precedents and Problems

Kimberly Lanegran

One area of international humanitarian law (IHL) that is dramatically developing and increasing in significance is the criminalization of recruiting children into armed forces. It is estimated that tens of thousands of children were directly involved in seventeen armed conflicts in 2007; a decrease of ten from 2004. This apparent progress was due more to the end of those wars rather than "the impact of initiatives to end child soldier recruitment and use."[1] This chapter focuses on legal initiatives to shield children from participating in warfare. The campaign to end child recruitment has made substantial progress. The Optional Protocol to the Convention on the Rights of the Child prohibits child soldier recruitment/use and has been ratified by 120 states. Novogrodsky notes codification of the norm against child recruitment "sheds light on the increasing overlap and doctrinal cross-pollination between international humanitarian law and human rights law," and believes that future synchronization between traditions "stands to increase as humanitarian law expands to encompass internal wars and crimes committed outside armed conflicts."[2] The Statutes of the Special Court for Sierra Leone (SCSL) and the International Criminal Court (ICC) established conscription, enlistment or use of youth under fifteen years of age, as criminal violations of IHL. Furthermore, in a series of landmark rulings, the SCSL issued the first convictions for the crime of child recruitment.[3] The ICC has since followed suit, convicting rebel leader Thomas Lubanga Dyilo in March 2012 for child recruitment.

Established in 2002, the SCSL has operated during a period of rapidly evolving IHL. When it began its work considerable controversy, disagreement, and murkiness surrounded a number of legal concepts central to the task of prosecuting individuals for child recruitment; specifically, the timing of the criminalization of child recruitment, the definitions of "conscription," "enlistment," and "use," and the new legal doctrine of individual culpability through joint criminal enterprise (JCE).

The SCSL achieved notable success clarifying aspects of criminalization of child recruitment and securing the first convictions for this crime. However some of its rulings remain controversial and reveal the uncertainty surrounding central elements of the crime and the nature of JCE.

New Legal Tools: Child Combatants and JCE

The combatant groups in Sierra Leone's war—the Revolutionary United Front (RUF), the Armed Forces Revolutionary Council (AFRC), the Civil Defence Forces (CDF)—infamously used children as spies, front-line fighters, and sex slaves. Estimates of the total number of children range from eight thousand to fourteen thousand.[4] The SCSL is intended to "prosecute persons who bear the greatest responsibility for serious violations of international humanitarian law" during the war.[5] Sierra Leonean and UN negotiators found the task of deciding how to best treat child combatants a highly emotional issue presenting a number of pressing moral and legal dilemmas.[6] This aspect of the SCSL brought considerable international attention.[7] In the end it embarked on an innovative two-pronged process to address crimes committed by children, as well as those perpetrated *on* child combatants.

Child Combatants

It was widely recognized that children committed atrocities during Sierra Leone's war. Determining how the SCSL would treat these perpetrators was contentious. UN representatives, the Government of Sierra Leone (GSL), and international/domestic NGOs who wrote the SCSL's statute wanted its powers to accord with international humanitarian and human rights law.

The GSL and representatives of Sierra Leone's civil society argued in favor of judicial accountability for combatants younger than eighteen. International NGOs strongly disagreed, fearing that a judicial process would undermine their efforts to build rehabilitation programs.[8] The Office of the Special Representative of the UN Secretary-General for Children and Armed Conflict argued in favor of extending personal jurisdiction to include youth who participated without restraint in the most horrific atrocities.[9] However, it expressed doubt that there would be many persons *under* eighteen who would fall within the SCSL's narrow personal jurisdiction.

The Secretary-General of the UN proposed that the SCSL be empowered to try individuals who were between fifteen and eighteen at the time of their alleged crimes in separate proceedings that would be limited to making determinations of guilt.[10] Human Rights Watch suggested the SCSL follow the ICC model and allow other mechanisms in Sierra Leone to address the issue of juvenile crimes.[11] Amnesty International supported the principle of the SCSL being able to try *some* youth offenders.[12] Representatives on the UNSC repeatedly expressed their belief that it would be extremely unlikely that a juvenile would be regarded as bearing the "greatest responsibility" for human rights atrocities and therefore come before the SCSL. They expected that Sierra Leone's Truth and Reconciliation Commission would "have a major role to play in the case of juvenile offenders."[13] In the end they accepted the argument that there was no international consensus concerning the minimum age for criminal responsibility.

Consequently, the SCSL was given the ability to prosecute children for war crimes and crimes against humanity committed when they were between fifteen and eighteen years of age,[14] although Article 15 of the Statute states: "where appropriate, resort should be had to alternative truth and reconciliation mechanisms, to the extent of their availability."[15] Before trying any juvenile, the Prosecutor would have to demonstrate that he/she has explored other alternatives to prosecution and "for justifiable reasons" rejected them.[16]

In the end, no former child soldier was indicted by the SCSL. As SCSL Prosecutor David Crane stated: "I am not interested in prosecuting children. I want to prosecute the people who forced thousands of children to commit unspeakable crime."[17] Former child combatants have provided statements to the Truth and Reconciliation Commission concerning the crimes perpetrated against them, and the atrocities they themselves committed.[18]

Prosecuting Recruiters of Child Combatants

Defining child recruitment in the SCSL Statute was also controversial. The Rome Statute criminalized all conscription or enlistment, forcible or not, of youth under fifteen years of age. However, then UN Secretary-General Kofi Annan shared the opinion that that crime's place in customary law at the time of

Sierra Leone's war was "doubtful."[19] Although negotiators agreed that the criminalization of *forced* recruitment was firmly part of customary international law at the time of the civil war, [20] there was disagreement over whether it was a crime to enlist a willing fighter less than fifteen years old *prior* to 1998. In offering a draft statute, the UN Secretariat proposed that the SCSL prosecute people for the "[*a*]*bduction and forced* recruitment of children under the age of 15 years into armed forces or groups for the purpose of using them to participate actively in hostilities (emphasis added)."[21]

In the end, the SCSL's final statute identifies "[*c*]*onscripting or enlisting* children under the age of 15 years into armed forces or groups or using them to participate actively in hostilities (emphasis added)"[22] as a violation of IHL under its jurisdiction. The crime need not include the use of force.

Prosecutor Crane quickly made use of his powers to charge people with child recruitment. Among the many charges made against them, all ten individuals brought to trial faced one count of conscripting, enlisting, or using children under the age of fifteen in hostilities.[23] The indictments against three RUF rebel leaders, former Liberian President Charles Taylor, and three members the AFRC alleged that "throughout the Republic of Sierra Leone, AFRC/RUF routinely conscripted, enlisted and/or used boys and girls under the age of 15 to participate in active hostilities. Many of these children were first abducted, then trained in AFRC/RUF camps in various locations throughout the country, and thereafter used as fighters."[24]

Joint Criminal Enterprise

The SCSL Prosecution had another new and controversial tool in its arsenal: JCE doctrine. JCE was developed by the ICTY and ICTR as a means of assigning individual responsibility for group offenses. The three categories of JCE were first established by the ICTY. Type 1 applies to situations in which all participants in a criminal enterprise possess the same criminal intent while individuals might play different roles in the crime. Type 2 applies to situations like concentration camps in which all members of the JCE act according to a plan and the accused were in positions of authority over the individual who personally executed the act. "Extended" JCE, (Type 3) is one in which all participants were part of a common purpose where "one of the persons carrying out the agreed object of that design also commits a crime which, whilst outside the 'common design,' was nevertheless a natural and foreseeable consequence of executing 'that common purpose'."[25]

Since its emergence JCE has been controversial. Some regard JCE as essential in bringing to justice those most responsible for human rights atrocities.[26] Others fear that prosecutors have used it *too* liberally and are in danger of encouraging convictions through guilt by association.[27]

Challenges notwithstanding, the SCSL prosecution eagerly employed JCE in all of its cases. In the indictments, the prosecution asserted that the accused were personally liable for the crimes listed through three alternative ways: 1) their personal planning, instigating, ordering, or aiding and abetting in the crimes, 2) their responsibility as command superiors over the direct perpetrators and/or 3) their participation in a joint criminal enterprise that encompassed the crime.[28] In its indictment of AFRC leaders the prosecution claimed the accused:

> shared a common plan, purpose or design (joint criminal enterprise) which was to take any actions necessary to gain and exercise political power and control over the territory of Sierra Leone, in particular the diamond mining areas . . . The crimes alleged in this Indictment . . . were either actions within the joint criminal enterprise or were a reasonably foreseeable consequence of the joint criminal enterprise.[29]

Precedents and Problems

The SCSL's landmark convictions of the first five men for child recruitment received well-deserved attention.[30] In June 2007, the Trial Chamber found AFRC leaders Alex Tamba Brima, Brima Bazzy Kamara and Santigie Borbor Kanu guilty of planning the conscription of children into their group and using them in hostilities.[31] Judgments in the CDF's trial were more controversial. In October 2007, Allieu Kondewa was found guilty of conscripting or enlisting or using child combatants, while Moinina Fofana was found not guilty of this crime. In May 2008, the Appeals Chamber overturned Kondewa's conviction and upheld Fofana's acquittal. Although the SCSL determined hundreds of children fought or participated in hostilities for the CDF, no CDF leader was personally culpable for this crime. In February 2009 RUF leaders Issa Sesay and Morris Kallon were found guilty of using children in hostilities.[32]

These trials reveal a number of important achievements and shortcomings, the lessons from which are of great significance to future trials of those accused of child recruitment. The SCSL established the criminalization of child recruitment in IHL. Secondly, it made notable progress defining key elements of the crime. Thirdly, it set precedents concerning the types of evidence required to secure a conviction. However judges disagreed about the appropriate use of circumstantial evidence. Finally, the prosecution's mixed record in securing convictions based on guilt through JCE offers a cautionary tale to future prosecutors seeking to employ this doctrine.

Establishing the Criminality of Child Recruitment

Sam Hinga Norman, the most prominent member of the CDF, directly challenged the court's ability to prosecute him for recruiting persons under fifteen into the armed forces.[33] His defense team filed a Preliminary Motion in 2003 arguing that recruiting or enlisting youth under fifteen was not a crime entailing individual criminal responsibility under customary international law in November 1996 (the time acts alleged in the indictments occurred).[34] In a landmark ruling, the Appeals Chamber answered that question by finding that: "[c]hild recruitment was criminalized before it was explicitly set out as a criminal prohibition in treaty law [in the 1998 Rome Statute] and certainly by November 1996, the starting point of the time frame relevant to the indictments."[35]

Norman and all other defendants could be tried on the charge of child recruitment. This decision was upheld. This ruling may become the SCSL's single most lasting legal legacy as it established the exact time frame in which it became a criminal act to make a child less than fifteen years a combatant.[36]

Defining Elements of Child Recruitment

Two sets of Trial Chamber justices needed to clarify aspects of the law prohibiting child recruitment, and demonstrate how central terms would be operationalized. In convicting Brima, Kamara, and Kanu of child enlistment, Trial Chamber II partially clarified some terms and concepts inherent in the crime. The judgments by Trial Chamber I of the RUF and CDF accused more extensively identify the parameters of the crime. Yet, the initial conviction of Kondewa by Trial Chamber I and its subsequent overturning by the Appeals Chamber demonstrates that definitions remain contested.

Particularly important are findings concerning: 1) definitions of "conscription" and "enlistment" and how they can be applied to informal armed groups, 2) what is entailed in "using" children "to participate actively in hostilities."

Conscripting or Enlisting

Article 4 of the Statute states: "conscripting or enlisting children under the age of 15 years into armed forces or groups or using them to participate actively in hostilities" is a violation of IHL.[37] In considering the *actus rea* of "conscripting," the justices in the *AFCR* judgment noted that it "implies compulsion, in some instances through the force of law,"[38] and thereby traditionally applies to government policy. Conscription can include acts by rebel and government forces. The justices also found the "'[e]nlistment' entails accepting and enrolling individuals when they volunteer to join an armed force or group"[39] thereby setting the precedent that a child's consent is *not* a valid defense.

Details about CDF operations and the Kondewa case necessitated that Trial Chamber I consider whether initiation into a traditional society was an act of conscription or enlistment. The prosecution alleged that Kondewa was the leader of the CDF and the Kamajor hunter society that was part of the CDF. He was responsible for all initiations within the CDF.[40] It alleged that hundreds of children under fifteen years became fighters through initiation under Kondewa into Kamajor society. Finally, the prosecution argued that by initiating youth into the Kamajors, Kondewa enlisted or conscripted them into a fighting force.

The Chamber found Kondewa was indeed the senior initiator in the CDF, and performed initiations on boys to make them powerful fighters.[41] The justices found that in such initiations, "the initiates had taken the first step in becoming fighters."[42] Therefore, they concluded "[i]t is beyond reasonable doubt that Kondewa, in these circumstances, when initiating boys, was also performing an act analogous to enlisting them for active military service."[43] Trial Chamber I expanded the definition of enlistment to include initiation into traditional societies.

Kondewa's conviction, however, was overturned by the Appeals Chamber in a surprising way that revealed challenges that may arise when courts apply too broad a definition of "use." Kondewa had appealed his conviction arguing, that the Trial Chamber had erred in conflating initiation and enlistment.[44] The justices seemed to hold sympathy for Kondewa's appeal, writing: "it is apparent . . . that there is a paucity of jurisprudence on the question of how direct an act must be to constitute 'enlistment' . . . as well as the possible modes of enlistment."[45] The Appeals Chamber declined to determine whether the nexus between initiation by Kondewa and a child becoming a CDF fighter was present.

The Appeals Chamber "regards 'enlistment' in the broad sense as including any conduct accepting the child as a part of the militia."[46] A majority of the justices concluded Kondewa's proven subsequent initiations of the one witness who testified against him, when that witness was eleven and thirteen years old, could not have been the witness's enlistment because the child had already been enlisted when he was pressured to carry loot for the militia. The Chamber asserted that some unknown CDF fighter's act forcing the witness to carry loot enlisted the child into the armed group.

Justice Winter's dissenting opinion offers arguments that may guide other benches out of similarly problematic rulings. Her opinion reveals that "enlistment" needs clarification. She suggests that, in some situations, enlistment may be a process of acts, not a single event. This would allow for recognition of the criminal nature of more than just the first step taken in the making of a child soldier. Furthermore, she states, "where the evidence demonstrates the existence of a process that contributes to the enrolment and acceptance of a child into an armed force or group, logic dictates that 'use' of a child cannot constitute enlistment."[47] Perhaps courts in the future will seek to clarify the nature of enlistment and determine whether or not there is a hierarchy in which more regular or formal means of enlistment supersede the criminal act of using child soldiers.

Determining Culpability

Regarding Brima and Kamara, justices ruled the prosecution had proved beyond a reasonable doubt that they had personally planned to recruit children under fifteen and use them in hostilities. Furthermore they held command responsibility over those who directly perpetrated the crime. The prosecution successfully proved that the AFRC's Kanu and the RUF's Sesay and Kallon were guilty of planning the recruitment and use of children in armed groups. The SCSL thus established important precedents concerning the type of evidence and arguments needed to prove such a case. In finding Gbao, and Fofana and Kondewa not guilty of child recruitment, the SCSL shed light on evidence that is inadequate to secure a conviction.

None of the accused, however, was found guilty of this crime through his participation in a JCE. Trial Chamber II ruled the prosecution's JCE argument in *AFRC* was fatally flawed, and refused to consider any evidence of their culpability on JCE grounds. Trial Chamber I found Sesay and Kallon guilty of other crimes via their participation in a JCE but did not rule on whether they were also guilty of child recruitment under the doctrine.

Evidence Concerning Age of Combatants

The prosecution's cases relied on testimony from former combatants, witnesses to the conscription and/or use of child combatants, and experts who gave evidence about child soldier use.

One serious problem with the evidence was the difficulty in proving the age of alleged child soldiers at the time of their enlistment. Defence counsels exploited the fact that many witnesses had to estimate the age of alleged child soldiers due to the lack of documentation. They sought to shed doubt on the assertion that the combatants were actually under fifteen at the time they joined the hostilities. Justices in both Trial Chambers essentially shared the Defence counsels' concern. In *AFRC* the justices explicitly "excluded all evidence related to child soldiers where it was not clear that the evidence referred to soldiers under the age of 15."[48] Trial Chamber II similarly, "exercised caution in determining the ages of children associated with the rebel factions in its findings."[49]

Evidence of Planning Child Recruitment and/or Use

In all trials the testimony of a small number of child soldiers and/or insider witnesses was found to be credible. The Trial Chamber in *AFRC* noted that the testimonies of two former child combatants and two insider witnesses were particularly powerful in proving that Brima, Kamara, and Kanu were personally responsible for child enlistment/use. Two brothers, who testified under protection as witnesses were found to be reliable and credible. Both were taken into the AFRC when they were less than fifteen years old. They testified about their military training at Camp Rosos where all the accused, at various times, were present in supervisory capacities at their training.[50] The insider witnesses George Johnson aka "Junior Lion" and witness TF1-334 also testified that small boys received military training at Camp Rosos under the defendants' leadership. The judges found convincing TF1-334's testimony that during the 1999 invasion of Freetown, Brima had ordered the abduction of youths, and ordered that all soldiers who had a young boy with them should provide the child with basic military training.[51]

The justices in *RUF* heard a broader range of testimony from a larger number of witnesses who gave evidence that Sesay and Kallo engaged in child recruitment. The testimonies of two former child soldiers, TF1-141 and TF1-263, are illustrative of broader patterns in the evidence. Both gave problematic testimonies riddled with inconsistencies. Yet the Trial Chamber found them to be credible witnesses particularly when testifying about their own experiences; their evidence referring to the actions of others would require corroboration from other credible witnesses.[52] Their evidence about Sesay's and Kallon's calls for the training of Small Boys Units was crucial in proving that the accused planned the enlistment/use of children under fifteen. Both witnesses testified that they were abducted and trained at several camps.[53] TF1-141 testified that Sesay was among the senior RUF commanders who addressed recruits at the camp at Bunumbu telling them that they would be sent to the front lines of the battle. On one occasion, Sesay threatened them with execution if they disobeyed.[54]

Ultimately, the Trial Chamber found that the RUF "routinely used persons under the age of 15 to actively participate in hostilities" and that Sesay and Kallon "made substantial contributions to the design and planning of the commission of these crimes."[55] Both were guilty of planning the use of child soldiers in the RUF. In their sentencing, the justices found the "inherent gravity" of that crime was "exceptionally high,"[56] and the gravity of each man's criminal conduct reaches "the highest level."[57] The Chamber found that the "offences relating to the use of child soldiers" were committed "on a large scale and with a significant degree of brutality."[58] Children were abducted from their families, "subjected to cruel and hard military training," forced to mount ambushes, go on armed patrol, serve as bodyguards for commanders, and perpetrate "gruesome crimes."[59] As a result, those who survived the war were profoundly damaged. The convictions and sentences of both Sesay and Kallon were upheld by the Appeals Chamber.

Evidence Insufficient to Secure Conviction

One serious problem that arose in the CDF trial concerned whether circumstantial evidence was sufficient to secure conviction. The Trial Chamber found that Fofana was "Director of War" for the CDF, served in its High Command, and was regularly present at Base Zero where children were initiated and trained. However because there was no direct evidence linking Fofana to planning or using child soldiers, the majority concluded that Fofana could not be found guilty beyond a reasonable doubt.[60]

Gbao was found not guilty of child enlistment, although he was found guilty of eleven other counts. Although the prosecution appealed, the Appeals Chamber noted that it was "unclear if the persons Gbao removed were under the age of 15 years."[61] The prosecution had not eliminated all reasonable doubt concerning the children's ages.

Treatment of JCE Arguments

As noted above, in all cases, the prosecution sought to prove that the accused were guilty of the charges against them by virtue of either personally planning or aiding and abetting the crime, holding command responsibility and/or participating in a JCE. The prosecution has a mixed record in securing convictions under the JCE argument. In the CDF and AFRC trials it failed to convict anyone accused on this ground. In 2009 the three accused RUF leaders were convicted of eleven to thirteen crimes based on their participation in a JCE. Sesay's and Kallon's convictions did not fall under the JCE doctrines. Although the prosecution did eventually win some of its JCE arguments in *RUF*, this tale of contentious disagreements within an evolving interpretation of the doctrine reveals that it remains a highly contested area of IHL and human rights law. However, SCSL precedents regarding the use of JCE are informative for other prosecutions of child recruitment.

The majority CDF ruling does not provide much insight into the justices' reasoning. They simply found that there is "no evidence upon which to conclude beyond reasonable doubt that [the accused acted] to further a common purpose, plan or design to commit criminal acts. There is no evidence proving beyond reasonable doubt such a purpose, plan or design."[62] In his partially dissenting opinion, however, Justice Thompson, seeing a "lack of judicial consensus on the scope of the [joint criminal enterprise] doctrine and the unsettled state of the law,"[63] opines that it is simply too flawed a doctrine to apply in its present state.

The Trial and Appeals Chambers in *AFRC*, in contrast, issued powerful and diverging judgments about the prosecution's JCE argument. The Trial Chamber determined that this entire aspect of the prosecution's case was fatally flawed and refused to consider any part of the case that depended on a JCE argument. The justices reasoned: "The principle of the JCE doctrine is to hold an individual accountable for all his actions that fall within, or are a foreseeable consequence of entering into a criminal agreement."[64]

The justices found that the prosecution failed to plead a case that demonstrated the presence of an agreement or a common plan involving international crimes at its inception. The common criminal purpose alleged in the indictment was, "to take any actions necessary to gain and exercise political control over the territory of Sierra Leone." That, they argued, is not an international crime over which the SCSL has jurisdiction. They noted: "Whether to prosecute the perpetrators of rebellion for their act of rebellion and challenge to the constituted authority of the State as a matter of internal law is for the state authority to decide. There is no rule against rebellion in international law."[65]

In February 2008 the Appeals Chamber overruled the Trial Chamber's interpretation of the prosecution's use of JCE. Based on the Appeals Chamber's own reading of the jurisprudence of international criminal tribunals and the ICC Statute, they determined that "the Trial Chamber erred in law when it concluded that JCE was not properly pleaded in the Indictment."[66] They found that "the requirement that the common plan, design or purpose of a joint criminal enterprise is inherently criminal means that it must *either* have as its objective a crime within the Statute, *or* contemplate crimes within the Statute as the *means* of achieving its objective (emphasis added)."[67] In support of this they referred to the ICTY Appeals Chamber Judgment in *Tadić* which identifies elements of the *actus reus* for JCE liability as "the existence of a common plan, design or purpose which amounts to or involves the commission of a crime provided for in the Statute; [and] participation of the accused in the common design involving the perpetration of one of the crimes provided for in the Statue."[68]

Conclusion: Whither International Humanitarian Law on Child Recruitment?

The first trials before the SCSL blazed a trail for future prosecutions for the use of child soldiers. The Appeals Chambers ruling, confirming the criminal nature of child recruitment in customary and treaty law, will be a lasting landmark in IHL. The legal definitions of the central elements of this crime established by the SCSL will be foundations used in future cases.

These achievements are particularly important to the immediate work of the ICC. The first man tried before the ICC was Thomas Lubanga Dyilo, the alleged founder of the Union des Patriotes Congolais and its armed wing. He was charged with and convicted of the crime of enlisting and using children under the age of fifteen. Two other alleged leaders of armed groups in the Democratic Republic of Congo, face a total of ten charges, one of which is the use of children under fifteen in hostilities. Three of the four leaders of Uganda's Lord's Resistance Army have also been charged with enlisting children into armed groups.

The SCSL's work highlights obstacles inherent in trying persons accused of child recruitment. Each conflict has its own unique attributes, and future courts trying crimes from specific armed conflicts will need to refine operationalization.

The legal achievements discussed here are part of the development of international law, policies, and programs concerning child combatants. Cohn notes there is a "gap between law and reality on the ground."[69] She sees evidence that "in spite of stronger laws and advocacy, the situation of these children has deteriorated in important respects."[70] Of course the deterrent power of these trials has yet to be seen.

Ultimately, international norms and laws contribute to the broader campaign to rid the world of these atrocities. If military leaders must reach a standard of behavior—to toe the line and refuse to enlist youth—then that standard must be identifiable.

Notes

1. The Coalition to Stop the Use of Child Soldiers, "Child Soldiers Global Report 2008: Introduction," www.childsoldiersglobalreport.org (accessed June 1, 2011), 1.

2. Noah B. Novogrodsky, "Litigating Child Recruitment Before the Special Court for Sierra Leone," 7 *San Diego Intl. L. J.*, 421, 425 (2005-2006).

3. "Child recruitment" is popularly accepted as the term for making children under fifteen years combatants and/or using them in armed hostilities.

4. Approximately seven thousand child soldiers were officially disarmed and demobilized via UN-affiliated education programs. "Child Soldiers in Sierra Leone," *Morning Edition*, National Public Radio, September 1, 2003.

5. Security Council (UNSC), Agreement between the United Nations and the Government of Sierra Leone on the Establishment of a Special Court for Sierra Leone, Appendix 2, S/2002/246 at 1 (March 8, 2002).

6. UNSC, Report of the Planning Mission on the Establishment of the Special Court for Sierra Leone, Annex, S/2002/246 (March 8, 2002).

7. Diane Marie Amann, "Calling Children to Account: The Proposal for a Juvenile Chamber in the Special Court for Sierra Leone," 29 *Pepp. L. Rev.* 167 (2001-2002); Ilene Cohn, "The Protection of Children and the Quest for Truth and Justice in Sierra Leone," *Journal of International Affairs* 55, no.1 (2001); Michael Hoffmann, "May We Hold

Them Responsible? The Prosecution of Child Soldiers by the Special Court for Sierra Leone," *International Children's Rights Monitor* 14, no. 2 (2001); Stephanie H. Bald, "Searching for a Lost Childhood: Will the Special Court of Sierra Leone Find Justice for its Children?" 18 *Am. U. Intl. L. Rev.* 537 (2002); Michael Corriero, "The Involvement and Protection of Children in Truth and Justice-Seeking Processes: The Special Court for Sierra Leone," 18 *New York Law School Journal of Human Rights* 337 (2001-2002); Ismene Zarifis, "Sierra Leone's Search for Justice and Accountability of Child Soldiers," *Human Rights Brief* 9 (2002); Joshua A. Romero, "The Special Court for Sierra Leone and the Juvenile Soldier Dilemma," *Northwestern University Journal of International Human Rights* 2 (2004); Sarah L. Wells, "Crimes Against Child Soldiers in Armed Conflict Situations: Application and Limits of International Humanitarian Law," 12 *Tul. J. Intl. & Comp. L.* 287 (2004); Kathryn Howarth, "The Special Court for Sierra Leone–Fair Trials and Justice for the Accused and Victims," 8 *Int'l. Crim. L. Rev.* 399 (2008); Pilar Villanueva Sainz-Pardo, "Is Child Recruitment as a War Crime Part of Customary International Law?" *The International Journal of Human Rights* 12 (2008); David M. Rosen, "Who is a Child, The Legal Conundrum of Child Soldiers," 25 *Conn. J. Int'l. L.* 81 (2009-2010).

8. UNSC, Report of the Secretary-General on the Establishment of a Special Court for Sierra Leone, S/2000/915, para. 35 (October 4, 2000).

9. Cohn, "Protection."

10. UNSC, [Draft] Statue of the Special Court for Sierra Leone, Art. 7, S/2000/915 (October 4, 2000).

11. Cohn, "Protection."

12. Amnesty International, "Sierra Leone: Recommendations on the Draft Statue of the Special Court," AI Index AFR 51/83/00, (London, Amnesty International, November 14, 2000), 13.

13. UNSC, Letter dated 22 December 2000 from the President of the Security Council addressed to the Secretary-General, S/2000/1234 (December 22, 2000).

14. UNSC, Statute of the Special Court for Sierra Leone, Attachment, Art. 7, S/2002/246 (March 8, 2002).

15. UNSC, Statute, Attachment, Art. 15, S/2002/246.

16. UNSC, Report, Annex, S/2002/246, para. 28.

17. Quoted in IRINNEWS, "Sierra Leone: Special Court will not Indict Children-Prosecutor," November 4, 2002, www.irinnews.org.

18. Sierra Leone Truth and Reconciliation Commission, *Final Report* Vol 3B, Chapter 4, www.trcsierraleone.org (June 6, 2011).

19. UNSC, Report, S/2000/915, para. 18.

20. Cohn, "Protection."

21. UNSC, Report, S/2000/915, para. 15.

22. UNSC, Statute of the Special Court, Art. 4, S/2002/246.

23. The Special Court originally indicted a thirteen people. Sam "Mosquito" Bockarie and Johnny Koroma are believed to be dead. RUF leader Foday Sankoh and Sam Hinga Norman (CDF) died in custody.

24. Special Court for Sierra Leone (SCSL), *Prosecutor against Issa Hassan Sesay, Morris Kallon and Augustine Gbao (RUF)*, Case No. SCSL-2004-15-PT, Indictment, para.68 (August 2, 2006); SCSL, *Prosecutor against Alex Tamba Brima, Brima Bazzy Kamara and Santigie Borbor Kanu (AFRC)* Case No. SCSL-2004-16-PT, Indictment, para. 65, (February 18, 2005).

25. ICTY, *Prosecutor v. Milan Milutinović, Nikola Šainović and Dragoljub Ojdanić*, Case No. IT-99-37-AR72, Separate Opinion of Judge David Hunt on Challenge by Ojdanic to Jurisdiction Joint Criminal Enterprise, para. 6 (May 21, 2003).

26. Carla Del Ponte, "Investigation and Prosecution of Large-scale Crimes at the International Level: The Experience of the ICTY," 4 *J. Int'l. Crim. Just.* 539 (2006); Rebecca L. Haffajee, "Prosecuting Crimes of Rape and Sexual Violence at the ICTR: The Application of Joint Criminal Enterprise Theory," 29 *Harv. J. L. & Gender* 201 (2006).

27. Allison Marston Danner and Jenny S. Martinez, "Guilty Associations: Joint Criminal Enterprise, Command Responsibility, and the Development of International Criminal Law," 93 *Cal. L. Rev.* 75 (2005); Tom Briody, "Defending War Crimes in Africa: The Special Court for Sierra Leone," *The Champion* 29 (2005).

28. SCSL, *AFRC*, Indictment, para. 35-36.

29. SCSL, *AFRC*, Indictment, para. 33-34.

30. Howarth, "The Special Court"; Villanueva Sainz-Pardo, "Child Recruitment," Rosen, "Who is a Child."

31. SCSL, *AFRC*, Case No. SCSL-2004-16-T, Judgment Trial Chamber 2 (June 20, 2007). The convictions were upheld by the Appeals Chamber in 2008.

32. SCSL, *RUF*, Case No. SCSL-2004-15-T, Judgment Trial Chamber 1 (February 25, 2009).

33. There was no ruling concerning Norman's guilt. He died in custody.

34. SCSL, *Prosecutor against Sam Hinga Norman, Moinina Fofana and Allieu Kondewa (CDF),* Case No. SCSL-2004-14-AR72(E), Decision on Preliminary Motion Based on Lack of Jurisdiction (child recruitment), (May 31, 2004). 3.

35. SCSL, *CDF*, Decision on Preliminary Motion, para. 53.

36. Villanueva Saniz-Pardo calls these judgments "historic" and "extraordinary."

37. UNSC, *Statute of the Special Court, Attachment*, S/2002/246.

38. SCSL, *AFRC,* Trial Judgment, para. 734.

39. SCSL, *AFRC,* Trial Judgment, para. 735.

40. SCSL, *CDF*, Case No. SCSL-2004-14-PT, Indictment (February 5, 2004).

41. SCSL, *CDF*, Case No. SCSL-2004-14-T, Judgment Trial Chamber 1, para. 968, (August 2, 2007).

42. SCSL, *CDF*, Trial Judgment, para. 970.

43. SCSL, *CDF*, Trial Judgment, para. 970.

44. SCSL, *CDF*, Case No. SCSL-2004-14-AR72(E), Judgment Appeals Chamber, para. 136, (May 28, 2008).

45. SCSL *CDF*, Appeals Judgment, para. 141.

46. SCSL, *CDF,* Appeals Judgment, para. 144.

47. SCSL, *CDF,* Judgment Appeals Chamber, Annex B: Justice Renata Winter Partially Dissenting Opinion, para. 13 (May 28, 2008).

48. SCSL, *AFRC*, Trial Judgment, para. 1246.

49. SCSL, *RUF,* Trial Judgment, para 1628.

50. SCSL, *AFRC*, Trial Judgment, para. 1252-1256.

51. SCSL, *AFRC*, Trial Judgment, para. 1271-1272.

52. SCSL, *RUF*, Trial Judgment, para. 580-587.

53. SCSL, *RUF*, Trial Judgment, para. 1636-1637.

54. SCSL, *RUF*, Trial Judgment, para. 1643.

55. SCSL, *RUF*, Judgment Summary, Trial Chamber I, para. 51, 52 (February 25, 2009); also paras. 53-54.

56. SCSL, *RUF*, Sentencing Judgment, Trial Chamber I, para. 187 (April 8, 2009).
57. SCSL, *RUF*, Sentencing Judgment, para. 212, 236.
58. SCSL, *RUF*, Sentencing Judgment, para. 180.
59. SCSL, *RUF*, Sentencing Judgment, para. 180, 181.
60. SCSL, *CDF*, Judgment Trial Chamber 1, para. 959.
61. SCSL, *RUF*, Appeals Judgment, para. 1177.
62. SCSL, *CDF*, Judgment, para. 732.
63. SCSL, *CDF*, Judgment Trial Chamber I, Annex C: Justice Bankole Thompson Partially Dissenting Opinion, para. 24.
64. SCSL, *AFRC*, Trial Judgment, para. 70.
65. SCSL, *AFRC*, Trial Judgment, para. 67.
66. SCSL, *Prosecutor against Alex Tamba Brima, Brima Bazzy Kamara and Santigie Borbor Kanu (AFRC)*, Case No, SCSL-2004-16-A, Judgment Appeals Chamber, para. 87 (February 22, 2008).
67. SCSL, *AFRC*, Appeals Judgment, para. 80.
68. SCSL, *AFRC*, Appeals Judgment, para. 75.
69. Ilene Cohn, "Progress and Hurdles on the Road to Preventing the Use of Children as Soldiers and Ensuring their Rehabilitating and Reintegration," 37 *Cornell Int'l. L. J.* 531, 540 (2004).
70. Cohn, "Progress," 531.

Chapter 4

Song as a Crime Against Humanity: The First International Prosecution of a Pop Star

Susan Benesch

Simon Bikindi's trial for genocide and crimes against humanity had a lilting soundtrack, since the Rwandan pop star was accused of helping to cause the 1994 Rwandan genocide by means of his music. Convinced that speech in many forms—as public harangues, newspaper articles, radio broadcasts, and even songs—was an important catalyst of the genocide,[1] prosecutors at the International Criminal Tribunal for Rwanda (ICTR) charged Bikindi and others with speech as an international crime,[2] giving rise to a jurisprudence that is one of the tribunal's principal contributions to international criminal law.

This chapter examines that new body of law through the lens of the Bikindi case and his songs, with their elliptical lyrics and melodious tunes. I argue that speech crimes should indeed be a major feature of international criminal law, since inflammatory speech is a catalyst of grave international crimes, including genocide. At the same time, international speech crimes must be defined carefully, lest this young law be misused in ways that impinge on freedom of expression. As Bikindi's songs illustrate, even when words inspire killing, they may not constitute crimes. Although the tribunal found that his songs had inspired killing, Bikindi was acquitted of responsibility for them, and convicted only for shouting an explicit order to exterminate people.

Long before the 1994 catastrophe, other genocides and politicides were also preceded by inflammatory speech.[3] Hateful, inflammatory language and images were famously employed by the Nazis to persuade Germans that they faced a mortal threat from Jews and other "undesirables" and many artists took part, producing anti-Semitic songs, posters, texts, films, and even children's games.[4] In Rwanda, the best-known outlet for such language was the radio station *Radio Télévision Libre des Milles Collines* (RTLM) which began broadcasting nine months before the genocide and was quickly nicknamed "Radio Machete"[5] for the import of its anti-Tutsi broadcasts. The station functioned as "the voice of God," according to Roméo Dallaire, the Canadian general who led the UN mission to Rwanda before and during the genocide.[6] Simon Bikindi's songs were familiar staples of RTLM programming.

The ICTR decided several other speech cases (and accepted some guilty pleas for speech[7]), before grappling with Bikindi's music. It handed down its first conviction for criminal speech in 1998 in the case of Jean-Paul Akayesu,[8] a former *bourgmestre* (township mayor) found guilty of incitement to genocide for delivering an angry speech to a crowd just before massacres began. In its next landmark speech decision five years later, known as the "Media" case, the tribunal convicted two of RTLM's executives for incitement to genocide disseminated over airwaves (and a newspaper publisher, for articles he had printed).[9] Bikindi's is the last case in the new body of law on speech as an international crime that the Rwanda tribunal created almost entirely on its own. Already other courts have begun to follow this lead.

In January 2012, the International Criminal Court (ICC) confirmed charges against a broadcaster from another radio station, this time in Kenya. Joshua arap Sang is one of only four defendants the ICC chose to prosecute for their alleged role in bringing about Kenya's post-election violence of 2007-2008, in which more than 1,000 people were killed and hundreds of thousands were displaced.[10] By selecting Sang among hundreds of potential defendants, the ICC signaled its agreement with the theory that inflammatory speech is a catalyst of mass violence, though it is difficult to prove a causal link in individual cases.

Bikindi's indictment suggested for the first time that songs can constitute the heinous and grave crimes to which the jurisdiction of international criminal tribunals is limited. Because of the new question it raised—whether a song can constitute an international speech crime such as incitement to genocide or a crime against humanity—it drew keen interest from many quarters.[11]

Sweet Songs to Kill By

Bikindi was a skilled musician as a young child, like Michael Jackson, for whom he was later nicknamed.[12] He quickly learned to play traditional Rwandan stringed instruments, and went on to become one of Rwanda's most popular singer-songwriters, combining old-style Rwandan folk music with new words. Even when the lyrics were understood as encouragement to kill, Bikindi's sound remained oddly gentle and melodic.

Bikindi was charged by the ICTR for three songs that were played at anti-Tutsi rallies and on radio stations, before and during the genocide. None of the songs explicitly calls for killing, however, and one dates back almost a decade before the genocide. Bikindi testified that he wrote the song *Twasezereye* in 1986 and entered it in a competition, on July 1, 1987, to commemorate the twenty-fifth anniversary of Rwandan independence. *Twasezereye* won, chosen by a jury of six including Gamaliel Mbonimana, who served as an expert witness at Bikindi's trial almost 20 years later—for the prosecution. Mbonimana alleged that he had had reservations about the song back in 1986, but was outvoted.[13] The song's words, "*twasezereye ingoma ya cyami,*" mean "We said goodbye to the monarchy."

The defense described this song as "a celebration of independence for all Rwandans,"[14] but prosecution witnesses including Mbonimana testified that although the song ostensibly celebrated freedom from Belgian colonial rule, most of its lyrics referred to the cruel domination of Tutsi Rwandans over Hutus, before and during the colonial period.[15]

In 1993, Bikindi became one of fifty founding shareholders of a new radio station. RTLM soon became famous for its anti-Tutsi rants, and once the genocide began, for broadcasting names of Tutsis who had not yet been killed, together with their license plate numbers, to prevent them from escaping by car.[16] RTLM listeners could hardly have understood *Twasezereye's* lyrics to refer to Belgian colonial rule by the time they were broadcast on March 21, 1994 (only weeks before the genocide started), since an RTLM announcer introduced the song with a warning about "the enemy" and "his plan to shed blood." The unnamed announcer "therefore" dedicated *Twasezereye* to the Rwandan Armed Forces.[17] Bikindi did not introduce his own songs when they were broadcast over RTLM, however, so at trial he distanced himself from the way they were used by the station and emphasized that, without interpretation, his lyrics were ambiguous.

Bikindi testified that the other songs were composed between March and June of 1993,[18] just a year before the genocide. Like *Twasezereye,* neither contained any language directly calling for Tutsis to be killed—or even criticizing them explicitly. But numerous prosecution witnesses testified that Rwandan listeners understood them this way. *Bene sebahinzi,* they said, referred to Hutus who had suffered at the hands of the Tutsi. Once again, the Trial Chamber received transcripts of RTLM broadcasts demonstrating that RTLM announcers interpreted this song over the air as Bikindi's exhortation to the "children of *Sebahinzi* (children of Hutus)" to defeat the Tutsi.[19]

Finally, *Nanga abahutu* was described by the prosecution as a song intended to unite Hutus by provoking hatred of other Hutus who associated with Tutsis. Of the three songs, it contains the most bellicose language, but Bikindi testified that it was "akin to smacking a small child to stop him from misbehaving,"[20] and both his wife and ex-wife testified that the song was in favor of peace and against conflict.[21] In translation, some of its lyrics are:

> I hate these Hutus, these de-Hutuized Hutu, who have renounced their identity, dear comrades.
>
> I hate these Hutu, these Hutu who march blindly, like imbeciles, this species of naïve Hutu who join a war without knowing its cause.
>
> I detest these Hutu who can be brought to kill and who, I swear to you, kill Hutus, dear comrades.
>
> And if I hate them, so much the better.[22]

The three judges who made up the Trial Chamber in Bikindi's case[23] listened to days of testimony from linguists and other experts, and to Bikindi's songs themselves, sometimes sung into the record live by the defendant. It was no small challenge for judges from Argentina, Cameroon, and the Czech Republic to deconstruct the meaning of songs in the Kinyarwanda language.

After twenty-six months of trial, the judges reached striking answers. In general a song can indeed constitute incitement to genocide, or persecution as a crime against humanity, according to the Trial Chamber's December 2008 judgment.[24] Also, the tribunal stated that song lyrics need not incite violence in order to qualify as a crime against humanity, since hate speech may constitute persecution.[25]

The Trial Chamber concluded that although the songs featured metaphors and imagery subject to multiple interpretations, "their message was clearly understood" in the context of increasing ethnic tensions—the social climate in which they were composed and disseminated.[26] Moreover, the tribunal found that "the songs inspired action,"[27] based on testimony of *genocidaires* themselves (two of whom testified that the songs incited them to kill) and of others who observed the apparent influence of the songs on *genocidaires* and other Rwandans.[28]

Yet, in spite of the ICTR's unprecedented judicial finding that his musical expression provoked or at least amplified the atrocities, Bikindi was acquitted of all charges related to the three songs. The Trial Chamber found insufficient evidence to conclude that he had specific intent when he wrote the songs "to incite such attacks and killings, even if they were used to that effect in 1994."[29] The prosecution had failed to demonstrate that Bikindi played a role in disseminating his songs (over the radio, for example) in 1994, the year to which the ICTR's temporal jurisdiction was restricted.[30]

These conclusions are sound but frustrating, since it is difficult to believe Bikindi's assertion at trial that he did not listen to RTLM and did not have influence over its broadcasts, given his position as a founding shareholder of the station. However, without evidence of controlling influence, a singer or author cannot be held responsible for criminal uses to which others put his or her intellectual property. In its indictment of Bikindi, the prosecution suggested the singer-songwriter should have affirmatively tried to prevent RTLM from using his songs, stating that under Rwandan law, Bikindi "had a right to forbid or enjoin public broadcasts of his compositions." In fact, Bikindi may have had a right to exercise such control, but he had no legal obligation to do it, no matter how much harm the songs may have caused.[31]

The Trial Chamber also stated, based on its factual findings on the meaning of the songs, that it did not consider the songs to constitute direct and public incitement to genocide *per se*.[32] It did not clarify, unfortunately, exactly why not. The legal requirements for this crime were explained by the ICTR in its first, landmark speech case: the 1998 incitement to genocide conviction of Jean-Paul Akayesu.[33] According to that decision, the speech must be direct,[34] public,[35] and committed with specific intent to commit genocide by creating a genocidal state of mind in the audience.[36]

Bikindi, who lent his celebrity to the "Hutu Power" political cause by speaking at rallies, may well have committed incitement to genocide at a 1993 rally in Kivumu, Rwanda. There, the Trial Chamber found "beyond reasonable doubt" that Bikindi addressed the audience advocating that they must kill Tutsi, to whom he referred as "serpents," and his music was played on cassette.[37] This suggests that the speech may have been incitement to genocide, but the Chamber did not say so. Yet in another leading case on incitement to genocide, the Canadian Supreme Court found that the Rwandan politician Léon Mugesera committed incitement to genocide by giving a speech at a 1992 rally in Rwanda, using elliptical language to encourage the crowd to kill Tutsi.[38]

The Trial Chamber seems to have discounted Bikindi's Kivumu rally speech because "it has not been established that anti-Tutsi violence occurred in the vicinity of the rally either immediately before or after it."[39] This should have been irrelevant, since incitement to genocide is an inchoate crime—a crime in furtherance of another, like attempted murder—and is punishable whether or not it actually leads to genocide.[40]

Since the ICTR has temporal jurisdiction for 1994 only, it would have been unable to convict Bikindi for incitement to genocide at the rally. The Trial Chamber might nonetheless have given legal guidance that would have been useful in future cases. And it seems to have declined to scrutinize evidence from rallies in 1994, when it did have jurisdiction, to determine whether Bikindi's speech at those events constituted incitement to genocide.[41]

Therefore the Trial Chamber missed an opportunity to interpret Bikindi's speech uttered *before* the genocide—which may have been catalytic of genocide and therefore should be of greater interest than speech that came only in the wake of the slaughter. Bikindi left Rwanda just before the carnage started on April 4, 1994, and did not return until it was almost over.[42] It is only happenstance that the ICTR was able to convict him for a speech act after his return, and in the end Bikindi was convicted for a few words shouted over a loudspeaker, without music, although the ICTR clearly selected him from among hundreds of possible defendants because of his songs.

Bikindi was found guilty and sentenced to fifteen years for driving along a road between the towns of Kivumu and Kayove in his native prefecture of Gisenyi in late June 1994, near the end of the three-month-long genocide, calling out to Hutus to exterminate any Tutsi still left alive, and referring to the Tutsi as snakes.[43] He was said to have shouted over a public address system mounted on his vehicle: "The majority population, it's you, the Hutu I am talking to. You know the minority population is the Tutsi. Exterminate quickly the remaining ones."[44]

That speech is a straightforward case of incitement to genocide, in contrast to Bikindi's ambiguous songs. It was delivered publicly, on a road and over a loudspeaker. Bikindi's intent is evident, since he must have been aware both of the context of ongoing Tutsi slaughter and of the impact his words would have on the audience, who revered him not only as a popular artist, but as an anti-Tutsi political leader and an "authoritative figure" to the *Interahamwe* militiamen who committed much of the killing during the genocide.[45]

The Criminalization of Music

The special characteristics of songs give rise to arguments both for and against prohibiting them. On the one hand, one might argue that songs must never be banned if they constitute art, an especially valued form of expression in many societies. On the other hand, words can be more powerful, and therefore more dangerous, when set to music. "[T]he capacity of music to create a group out of a mass of single people is in no doubt," writes Louise Gray. "A heaving crowd at a stadium concert, the choir singing in a church, marching soldiers, a bunch of sports fans celebrating their team with their chants and songs, are in this respect no different. Music motivates."[46]

Songs have been prohibited in several countries for their propensity to spark violence—under national, not international law. For example, the Horst-Wessel-Lied was an anthem of the Nazi party and the Nazi regime used it as an alternate national anthem from 1933 to 1945. Following World War II the song was banned under Section 86 of the German Criminal Code, which prohibits the dissemination of propaganda of unconstitutional organizations.[47] The song remains so notorious, and the prohibition so robust, that in 1987 a German appeals court overturned the acquittal of a group of men who sang the tune of the Horst-Wessel-Lied with different words, finding that singing or playing the melody alone constituted a violation of German law.[48]

In a more recent case, "Get Out," a song by Zimbabwean-born hip-hop artist Zubz, was the center of controversy in South Africa in 2008. The song was featured in a music video showing the artist as a military commander instructing a group of black soldiers, "Understand I'm gonna get this *panga* [machete] to your neck. . . . Tell my people fight, and tell the oppressor get out." After a political party filed a complaint with the South African Broadcast Corporation calling the airing of the video "not only inappropriate but also irresponsible and inexcusable" given the history of racially motivated murders in South Africa, the Corporation banned the video and song from the country's airwaves.[49]

South African authorities have prohibited other music on the grounds that it is hateful, such as "*Dubulu iBhunu*" (shoot the Boer), a chant made famous in 2010 by the African National Congress' then youth leader, Julius Malema.[50] Indeed, many bodies of national law prohibit some form of hate speech, whether musical or not, even if it does not seem to incite violence.[51]

International criminal law, as one might imagine, focuses on extreme forms of inflammatory speech such as incitement to genocide—speech that may inspire an audience to harm others. The UN Convention on the Prevention and Punishment of the Crime of Genocide (and the Statutes of the ad hoc international criminal tribunals and the International Criminal Court) prohibit five acts or modes of liability: genocide itself, conspiracy, attempt and complicity in genocide, and "direct and public incitement to commit genocide."[52]

Under national laws, songs may be outlawed either because they might disturb public order or because they are "merely" offensive. Since the end of the Rwandan genocide, it has been a crime under Rwandan national law to listen to any of Bikindi's music.[53]

Hate Speech as a Crime against Humanity

As noted above, hate speech may also constitute an international crime as a form of persecution, which in turn can constitute a crime against humanity, according to the Bikindi trial chamber.[54] The International Criminal Tribunal for the former Yugoslavia (ICTY) rejected this approach in the case of Dario Kordić in 2001, finding that hate speech "does not by itself constitute persecution as a crime against humanity," that it is not enumerated as a crime elsewhere in the Statute of the ICTY, and "most importantly, it does not rise to the same level of gravity as the other acts enumerated in Article 5."[55] Yet in 2003, in the ICTR's landmark "Media" case against two RTLM executives and a newspaper editor, all three defendants were convicted of crimes against humanity, for the broadcast and publication of words. The Trial Chamber in that case had stated, "It is evident that hate speech targeting a population on the basis of ethnicity, or other discriminatory grounds, reaches this level of gravity and constitutes persecution."[56]

Before the ICTR was established in 1994, no court had decided a case of incitement to genocide or hate speech as a crime against humanity. The ICTR has handed down other convictions for speech,[57] including several guilty pleas,[58] decisions which form nearly all of the world's jurisprudence on incitement to genocide and speech as a crime against humanity.

The ICTR began wrapping up its work after nearly two decades in operation, aiming to close by the end of 2014,[59] so the Bikindi case will likely supply its last words[60] on the difficult questions surrounding speech as an international crime.

And since the tribunal convicted Bikindi only on one unambiguous charge of incitement to genocide, this case left much work undone. Even in light of the ICTR's body of jurisprudence on speech, it remains difficult to distinguish rigorously between speech that is "merely" hateful, repugnant, or discriminatory, and speech that is criminal—and dangerous to restrict or punish speech. It is critical for courts to determine, and explain well, how to draw the line.

The Next Step: The ICC's Kenya Case

At this writing, the ICC was poised to take the baton by hearing the next landmark case on international speech crime, against the Kenyan radio broadcaster Joshua arap Sang. Since the ICC prosecution did not bring any counts related to genocide in the Kenyan cases, the case turns on hate speech as a crime against humanity.

Arap Sang faced trial, together with his three co-defendants, for charges related to the Kenyan post-election violence of 2007-2008. The other three, Uhuru Kenyatta, William Ruto, and Francis Muthaura, are prominent political figures. (Kenyatta is the son of Kenya's first prime minister and president, Jomo Kenyatta, Ruto is a former MP and government minister, and Muthaura is now deputy minister.) By contrast, Sang is a much younger man, born in 1975, with no national post or reputation. He stands accused of crimes against humanity based entirely on his role as a radio presenter at Kass-FM, a station that broadcasts in the Kalenjin language and is popular among members of the Kalenjin ethnic group. In 2007 and 2008, Sang hosted Kass-FM's morning talk show "*Lene Emet*" (roughly translatable as "what is the world saying?") and broadcast inflammatory language against Kikuyus, the largest ethnic group in Kenya. There are longstanding grievances over land between the two groups, and when fighting broke out after Kenya's disputed presidential vote on December 27, 2007, it was especially vicious between Kalenjins and Kikuyus.

After more than 1,000 Kenyans were killed, both candidates who claimed to have won the election (Raila Odinga and Mwai Kibaki) agreed to form a government together (under international pressure), and Kenya achieved a fragile peace. Tensions persisted among the country's forty-two ethnic groups, however,[61] and Kenyan leaders, including the defendants facing trial at the ICC, continued to use inflammatory speech so often that presiding judge Ekaterina Trendafilova warned the defendants on April 7, 2011 that they would face consequences if they did not watch their language. "It came to the knowledge of the chamber by way of following some articles in the Kenyan newspapers that there are some movements towards retriggering the violence in the country by way of using some dangerous speeches," Trendafilova told the defendants: "[S]uch type of action could be perceived as a sort of inducement which may constitute the breach of one of the conditions set out in the summonses to appear. . . . Accordingly, this might prompt the chamber to replace the summonses to appear with warrants of arrest."[62]

The warning came after two suspects delivered speeches "hurling all manner of invective against the ICC and local political opponents they accuse of putting them in the dock," according to the Kenyan newspaper *The Nation.*[63] It is to be hoped that as the case goes forward, the ICC will provide clarification so that its jurisprudence may, in future, help to prevent violence without infringing on freedom of expression.

Notes

1. Alison Des Forges, *Leave None to Tell the Story: Genocide in Rwanda* (New York: Human Rights Watch, 1999), 1, 14-15.

2. International Criminal Tribunal for Rwanda (ICTR), *Prosecutor v Simon Bikindi*, Case No. ICTR-2001-72-I, Amended Indictment Pursuant to Decisions of Trial Chamber III of 11 May 2005 and 10 June 2005 (Hereinafter Amended Indictment). para 14. Bikindi's songs were played "several times a day" before April 1994 and broadcast "repeatedly throughout the day" from April to July 1994.

3. For example Serbia. See Sonja Biserko, "Reporting from the Writing Fields, or How to Prepare Genocide in Five Years," (speech at the *Reporting from the Killing Fields* conference at the University of California, Berkeley, Apr. 11, 2007), http://balkansnet.org/biserko.html (accessed May 25, 2012).

4. See *der ewige Juden* ("the eternal Jew") and other examples in Jeffrey Herf, *The Jewish Enemy: Nazi Propaganda during World War II and the Holocaust*, (Cambridge: Harvard University Press, 2006); and the United States Holocaust Memorial Museum Artifacts Gallery, http://www.ushmm.org/propaganda/archive/ (accessed May 25, 2012).

5. See ICTR, "Three Media Leaders Convicted for Genocide," *Press Release*, December 3, 2003, http://www.unictr.org/tabid/155/Default.aspx?id=226 (accessed May 25, 2012).

6. Romeo Dallaire, *Shake Hands with the Devil: The Failure of Humanity in Rwanda* (Boston: Da Capo Press, 2004), 272.

7. See for example, ICTR, *Prosecutor v. Kambanda*, Case No. ICTR-97-23-S, Judgment and Sentence (Sept. 4, 1998); ICTR, *Prosecutor v. Ruggiu*, Case No. ICTR-97-32-I, Judgment and Sentence (June 1, 2000); and ICTR, *Prosecutor v. Serugendo*, Case No. ICTR-2005-84-I, Judgment and Sentence (June 12, 2006).

8. ICTR, *Prosecutor v. Akayesu*, Case No. ICTR 96-4-T, Judgment (Sept. 2, 1998).

9. See ICTR, *Prosecutor v. Ferdinand Nahimana*, Case No. ICTR-1996-11; *Prosecutor v. Jean Bosco Barayagwiza*, Case No. ICTR-1997-19; and *Prosecutor v. Hassan Ngeze*, Case No. ICTR-1997-27.

10. Hirondelle News Agency, "ICC Must Warn Kenyan Politicians on Incitement to Violence, Says NGO," Jan. 9, 2002, http://www.hirondellenews.org/29879 (accessed May 25, 2012).

11. See Freemuse; Freedom of Musical Expression, "War Crimes Trial Feared to Legitimize New Repression of Musicians Elsewhere," (Nov. 14, 2006), http://www.freemuse.org/sw15535.asp (accessed July 31, 2009).

12. Donald G. McNeil Jr., "Killer Songs," *New York Times Magazine*, March 17, 2002, http://www.nytimes.com/2002/03/17/magazine/killer-songs.html (accessed 14 June 2012). Bikindi was called "the Michael Jackson of Rwanda," a nod to his popularity.

13. ICTR, *Prosecutor v Simon Bikindi*, Case No. ICTR-2001-72-I, Judgment (December 2, 2008), para. 215.

14. ICTR, *Bikindi*, Judgment, para. 214.

15. ICTR, *Bikindi*, Judgment, para. 209, 211.

16. Dina Temple-Raston, "Radio Hate," *Legal Affairs*, 2002, www.legal affairs.org (accessed August 2, 2009)

17. ICTR, *Bikindi*, Judgment, para. 212.

18. ICTR, *Bikindi*, Judgment, para. 193.

19. ICTR, *Bikindi*, Judgment para. 240.

20. ICTR, *Bikindi*, Judgment, para. 229.

21. ICTR, *Bikindi*, Judgment, para. 231.

22. McNeil, "Killer Songs."

23. Judges Inés Mónica Weinberg de Roca, presiding, Florence Rita Arrey, and Robert Fremr.

24. ICTR, *Bikindi*, Judgment, paras. 389, 395; see also ff. 885 ("The Chamber notes the definition of persecution is broad enough to include music, as the *actus reus* of persecution is merely defined as an act or omission which discriminates in fact and which denies or infringes upon a fundamental right.")

25. ICTR, *Bikindi*, Judgment, para. 390; also paras 393 and 394.

26. ICTR, *Bikindi*, Judgment, para. 247.

27. ICTR, *Bikindi*, Judgment, para. 253.

28. ICTR, *Bikindi*, Judgment, para. 253.

29. ICTR, *Bikindi*, Judgment, para. 255.

30. ICTR, *Bikindi*, Judgment, para. 421 and 263.

31. ICTR, *Bikindi*, Judgment, para. 439. ("Mere 'acquiescence' is not sufficient to entail responsibility in international criminal law."), ("The Prosecution has failed to prove that Bikindi had a duty in law to stop the broadcast of his musical compositions.")

32. ICTR, *Bikindi*, Judgment, para. 439.

33. ICTR, *Akayesu*, Judgment.

34. ICTR, *Akayesu*, Judgment, para. 557. ("The 'direct' element of incitement implies that the incitement assume a direct form and specifically provoke another to engage in a criminal act, and that more than mere vague or indirect suggestion goes to constitute direct incitement." Later in the same paragraph, the Trial Chamber went on to note that the language of incitement need not be explicit: "the direct element of incitement should be viewed in the light of its cultural and linguistic content. Indeed, a particular speech may be perceived as 'direct' in one country, and not so in another, depending on the audience.")

35. ICTR, *Akayesu,* Judgment, para. 556. ("According to the International Law Commission, public incitement is characterized by a call for criminal action to a number of individuals in a public place or to members of the general public at large by such means as the mass media, for example, radio or television.")

36. ICTR, *Akayesu*, Judgment, para. 560 ("The *mens rea* required for the crime of direct and public incitement to commit genocide lies in the intent to directly prompt or provoke another to commit genocide. It implies a desire on the part of the perpetrator to

create by his actions a particular state of mind necessary to commit such a crime in the minds of the person(s) he is so engaging.").

37. ICTR, *Bikindi*, Judgment, para. 141.

38. See *Mugesera v. Canada* (Minister of Citizenship and Immigration), [2003] S.C.C. 40, paras. 179-180.

39. ICTR, *Bikindi*, Judgment, para. 183 ("The Prosecution has not proven, however, that this meeting led to anti-Tutsi violence immediately thereafter.")

40. William A. Schabas, *Genocide in International Law: The Crime of Crimes*, (2000), 266; see also ICTR, *Prosecutor v. Nahimana*, Case No. 99-52-A (Nov. 28, 2007) ("[D]irect and public incitement to genocide is...punishable even if no act of genocide results from it. This is confirmed by the *travaux preparatoires* of the Genocide Convention, from which we can conclude that its drafters wished to punish direct and public incitement to genocide even if no genocide is committed, in order to prevent its occurrence.")

41. ICTR, *Bikindi*, Judgment, para. 185. ("Given its conclusions above, the Chamber has not found it necessary to address the issue of whether the meetings that allegedly took place in 1994 not specifically alleged in the Indictment could have formed the basis for a conviction.")

42. ICTR, *Bikindi*, Judgment, para. 26.

43. ICTR, *Bikindi*, Amended Indictment, para. 422.

44. ICTR, *Bikindi*, Amended Indictment, para. 39.

45. ICTR, *Bikindi*, Judgment, para 425, para. 107.

46. Louise Gray, *The No-Nonsense Guide to World Music*, (Oxford: New International Publications, 2009), 78.

47. George Boderick, "Das Horst-Wessel-Lied: A Reappraisal," *International Folklore Review*, vol. 10 (1995): 100-127, sec 1.

48. Boderick, "Das Horst-Wessel-Lied," sec 5.3.

49. Freemuse: Freedom of Musical Expression, "Rap Song Banned for Incitement to Violence," (May 7, 2008), http://www.freemuse.org/sw27698.asp (accessed May 25, 2012).

50. Susan Benesch, "Words as Weapons," *World Policy Journal* 29:1 (Spring 2012).

51. For examples, see chapter 1 of Jeremy Waldron, *The Harm in Hate Speech*, (Harvard University Press, Cambridge, MA, 2012).

52. UN Convention on the Prevention and Punishment of the Crime of Genocide, 78 UNTS 277 (Dec. 9, 1948), Art. III(c).

53. Hirondelle News Agency, "Musician Pleads Not Guilty to Genocide Charges," Apr. 4, 2002, http://www.hirondellenews.org/18779 (accessed May 25, 2012).

54. Antonio Cassese, *International Criminal Law*, 2d ed. (Oxford University Press, 2008), 113.To be sure, Julius Streicher was convicted of speech as a crime against humanity, but that came before all of the ICTY and ICTR's jurisprudence , as well as scholarly commentary, elucidating crimes against humanity.

55. Internal Criminal Tribunal for the former Yugoslavia (ICTY), *Prosecutor v. Kordic & Cerkez*, Case No. IT-95-14/2-T, Judgment, para. 209 (Feb. 26, 2001).

56. ICTR, *Prosecutor v. Nahimana*, Nahimana Judgment, Case No. ICTR-99-52-T, Judgment and Sentence, para. 1072 (December 3, 2003).

57. ICTR, *Prosecutor v Niyitegeka*, Case No. ICTR-96-14-T, Judgment and Sentence (May 16, 2003); ICTR, *Prosecutor v. Muvunyi*, Case No. ICTR-2000-55A-T, Judgment and Sentence (Sept. 12, 2006); and ICTR, *Prosecutor v. Nahimana*, Judgment and Sentence.

58. ICTR, *Prosecutor v. Kambanda*, Judgment and Sentence; ICTR, *Prosecutor v. Ruggiu*, Judgment and Sentence; and ICTR, *Prosecutor v. Serugendo*, Judgment and Sentence.

59. UN Security Council, Resolution 1966, S/RES/1966 (2010), www.unhcr.org/refworld/docid/4d270e432.html (accessed 14 June 2012).

60. The Trial Chamber's judgment in the Bikindi case has been appealed by both sides, however, and that decision is pending at the time of this writing.

61. Institute for Peace and War Reporting, "Fears of Tension Grow in Kenya," (May 24, 2012), http://iwpr.net/report-news/fears-tension-grow-kenya (accessed May 27, 2012).

62. *UN News Centre,* "International Criminal Court Judge Warns Kenyan Suspects on Incitement," April 7, 2011, http://www.un.org/apps/news/story.asp?NewsID=38041 (accessed May 27, 2012).

63. *The Nation,* "Hague Suspects Must Heed Court Warnings." April 7, 2011, http://www.nation.co.ke/oped/Editorial/Hague+suspects+must+heed+court+warnings+/-/440804/1140758/-/31iavkz/-/index.html (accessed May 27, 2012).

Chapter 5

Seeking Justice and Accountability: The Dilemmas of Humanitarian Law and Human Rights NGOs

Mahmood Monshipouri

The conflicts of the 1990s illustrate that the simultaneous provision of relief to victims of armed conflicts and the protection of their human rights constitutes a complicated task. The changing nature of warfare, along with the political consequences of action or inaction, brought into question traditional humanitarian principles of neutrality and impartiality.

The International Committee of the Red Cross (ICRC) underscored the paramount value of humanitarian action: "respect for the fundamental principles of humanity, impartiality, neutrality, and independence . . . for the sake of all victims of armed conflict."[1] These principles have been called into question by those who espouse a shift toward a vision of human solidarity.[2] Some observers have called traditional operating principles obsolete, given the evolving intersection of politics and humanitarian action.[3] Others have viewed neutrality as "a form of moral bankruptcy."[4]

The use of military force to resolve conflicts has only led to the proliferation of human rights abuses. Respect for laws and customs of war, particularly regarding the protection of civilians, has drawn international human rights law

(HRL) and humanitarian law (IHL) closer together. Increasingly, human rights NGOs have relied on IHL standards to prevent the most flagrant violations of human rights in combat zones.[5]

This chapter addresses dilemmas of securing justice and accountability, as well as protecting victims of inter/intrastate conflicts. Despite conceptual and legal differences between human rights NGOs and IHL, the latter provides a useful framework and valuable tool for the former in their mutual attempt to safeguard human rights.[6] After examining the dilemmas of seeking justice and accountability for victims of armed conflicts, this chapter outlines a forward-looking approach toward preventing deadly conflicts and egregious human rights violations.

The Problem: Civil Wars and Genocide

Domestic armed conflicts have been waged around the issue of autonomy for minority ethnic groups and are largely identity driven. They represent a backlash to fears of group marginalization and/or constitute a group's attempt for regional or national autonomy.[7] Some of the more well-known conflicts have ethnic dimensions, but are not essentially ethnic conflicts.[8] Others have been fought by groups aimed at controlling the state. Other conflicts have taken place within the context of "failed states."[9] Moreover the proliferation of conflicts in which new techniques of warfare blur distinctions between combatants and non-combatants, has added new dimensions.[10]

Some experts argue that certain countries are more prone to civil wars than others and that distant history and ethnic tensions are hardly the most plausible explanations for conflict. Collier contends once a country has reached a certain per capita income its risks of civil war are negligible. "At risk" nations with poor and declining economies are more prone to conflict. Collier argues that in countries like these the most solid defense against war is economic growth.[11]

Rich nations could take actions to cut rebel financing and cushion the adverse shocks these countries face when their commodity exports plunge. In exchange these countries could more effectively govern their revenues from natural resources. The fact remains that around 95 percent of the global production of hard drugs are located in civil war zones. Such lawless areas have provided safe havens and training grounds for international terrorists.[12]

Throughout the twentieth century genocides and mass killings were driven by ideological and/or political reasons. In the 1990s, the prevalence of genocide, crimes against humanity, and armed interventions reached epic proportions.[13] In the cases of Rwanda, Bosnia and Kosovo the absence of a prompt international response demonstrated that the world was only minimally committed to intervention.[14]

From a structural perspective inter-group conflicts in modern societies over scare resources and political power create conditions conducive to genocide. Through its control of ideology, the modern nation-state manipulates technology and bureaucracy.[15] Financial contributions and other forms of support given to these states by the international community only makes the potential for genocide greater.

Linking Humanitarian Law with Human Rights Law: Toward Establishing Individual Criminal Responsibility

IHL and HRL are principally concerned with respect for human life and dignity. IHL is the law of armed conflict. The central instruments of IHL are the four Geneva Conventions and the two Additional Protocols.[16]

These Conventions were buttressed by several developments in IHL during the 1990s that further upheld the legal framework for the protection of civilians. These include new laws on landmines and chemical-biological weapons, along with the Rome Statute of the International Criminal Court (ICC), the *ad hoc* Tribunals for Rwanda (ICTR) and the former Yugoslavia (ICTY), and the Special Court for Sierra Leone (SCSL).[17] Despite these developments, the moral argument in favor of civilian immunity continues to be disputed in most contemporary wars.[18]

In recent years, conflicts of different kinds have raised a myriad of legal and political questions ranging from application and accountability to enforcement issues. Because of these new realities, the central principles of IHL—neutrality, impartiality—have come under siege by humanitarian advocates who have called for replacing neutrality with human solidarity.[19] Weiss reinforces this newly emerging idea: "Humanitarian principles are no longer sacrosanct,"[20] calling our attention to the "dark side" of humanitarian actions.

While underscoring the importance of a cross-pollination between HRL and IHL, some draw attention to basic differences between the two. According to HRL, human rights are inalienable and universal.[21] IHL is centered on the imposition of obligations from the individual.[22] Protection granted the individual is typically derived from membership in a group. In the human rights sphere a right is not normally granted on the basis of group membership.[23]

Whereas HRL imposes obligations generally on states rather than individuals, IHL seeks to directly regulate both.[24] IHL is premised on the notion it is inappropriate to insist on the application of a rights-based approach in times of emergency and armed conflict.

In the realm of responsibility, we have witnessed a shift in humanitarian law from states to individuals for violations of customary and conventional humanitarian law. Additional Protocol I and more recently the creation of the ICTY and

ICTR have underlined the significance of individual criminal responsibility for grave breaches of HRL and IHL. With respect to the ICTY its mandate is confined to rendering decisions on the criminal responsibility of specific individuals. In this regard, the ICTY can only disregard an amnesty law or issue non-binding comments about it.[25] Despite these limitations, the ICTY accomplished many goals, including affirming applicability of IHL to internal armed conflicts.[26]

It is important to recognize the role of NGOs in shaping an international climate of support for the ICTY. Eyewitness testimony gathered by women's advocacy NGOs exemplifies the way in which NGOs assist female victims of sexual traumas committed during wartime.[27] These NGOs demonstrated that sexual crimes were part of a broader campaign whose ultimate purpose was ethnic cleansing. Because of their systematic efforts the subject matter jurisdiction of both *ad hoc* international courts included "rape as a crime against humanity."[28]

Despite their accomplishments, for many Security Council representatives and international NGOs, the *ad hoc* nature of the Tribunals was problematic. The growing interest in a system of universal jurisdiction and justice encouraged UNSC members to push for the creation of a permanent international court. NGOs' "worked constantly to create a sense of urgency among state delegations in order to move the process forward."[29] These and many other related efforts led to the creation of ICC.[30]

In most human rights conventions "we find no requirement or power to criminally sanction perpetrators of serious human rights violations similar to what was incorporated in humanitarian law conventions."[31] Cassese echoes a similar sentiment by pointing out that, as long as states retain some crucial aspects of their sovereignty and fail to provide an effective mechanism to enforce arrest warrants and judgments, international criminal tribunals may have little more than normative impact.[32] That said, "the most effective means of enforcing international humanitarian law remains the prosecution and punishment of offenders within national or international criminal jurisdictions."[33]

Paradoxically, the existence of a strong state is key to safeguarding human rights. Protection of human rights requires the establishment of legal mechanisms to investigate violations and prevent abuses. IHL, by contrast, tends to act as a constraint on the conduct of belligerents. Consequently, IHL permits a certain loss of personal freedom without convictions in a court of law. It allows an occupying power to constrain the appeal rights of detained persons, as well as other civil liberties.[34] It is permissible to cause physical and mental pain, deprivation of freedom; even death. Human rights laws, by contrast, preserve physical integrity and human dignity. While HRL applies to rights possessed by all individuals in all situations, IHL applies only in specific cases.

It should be noted, however, that in the case of armed conflict, the application of one does not necessarily exclude implementation of the other. As we move toward establishing global standards, like individual criminal liability, individual rights will also be protected by both sets of standards.[35] This is inevitable, given that the "third generation" of human rights—right to peace, right to food, right to development—has made it possible to claim human rights by individuals or peoples against other states. This expanded scope has also led to a measure of overlap between the two fields of law.[36]

Furthermore, the UN has in recent years relied on IHL when considering the issue of rights in certain cases. The World Conference on Human rights proclaimed in paragraph 29 of the Vienna Declaration a serious concern with the violations of human rights during armed conflicts.[37] Incorporating these two laws is crucial to protecting and promoting human dignity and freedom from violence. This intersection has dramatically affected the interpretations of IHL.[38]

The relief systems in armed conflict and complex emergencies have traditionally been carried out by the ICRC. In recent years, many NGOs have become active in relief, including Worldvision, and Doctors without Borders. These agencies have found it extremely difficult to neutralize and humanize civilian relief, in part because private relief agencies must negotiate access to those in need of assistance. In the process, NGOs have become increasingly subjected to manipulation by political elites.[39] As Forsythe notes, "it is exceedingly difficult to get the protagonists to elevate assistance to civilians to a rank of the first order."[40] Increasingly, these NGOs have raised serious concerns about the implications of the increasing presence of military forces in humanitarian work and the increasing dependency on government funding.

The nature of humanitarian involvement in politics has generated sharp disagreements among humanitarian actors. Some members of Doctors without Borders have argued that they are not concerned with resolving conflicts. Rather, they wish to advocate against injustice, assert basic human rights, and provide quality assistance for the vulnerable.[41] The involvement of humanitarian agencies in conflict resolution initiatives risks undercutting their primary responsibility to alleviate suffering. The responsibility for conflict resolution and the observation of international legal conventions should be left to political institutions. The politicization of humanitarian action is deemed counterproductive by most relief and development NGOs.[42]

A significant convergence between IHL and HRL has helped in cases of IDPs, child soldiers, and limiting the use of certain weapons. Particularly problematic are weapons that fail to discriminate between civilians and combatants.[43] Regarding child combatants in Sierra Leone, NGOs continue to differ regarding how to handle their prosecution. The Coalition to Stop the Use of Child Soldiers urged that juvenile offenders under eighteen be handled according to the international principles of juvenile justice. Others including AI, however, supported prosecution in accordance with international guarantees and standards.[44] This dilemma "illustrates the complexity of balancing culpability, a community's sense of justice, and the best interests of the child."[45]

The emphasis on the repatriation of refugees, and the status of vulnerable groups has also drawn human rights laws and humanitarian norms closer.[46] The

1998 UN's "Guiding Principles for the Protection of Internally Displaced Persons" points to an integrative approach toward recognizing a right not to be unlawfully displaced, the right to access to assistance and protection during displacement, and a right to a secure return.[47]

Presently there are many examples of parallelism of content between humanitarian and human rights standards: the right to life; the prohibition of torture; arbitrary arrest; discrimination on grounds of race, sex, language, or religion; and due process of law. Moreover, HRL, especially its nonderogable core—the right to life, freedoms from torture, slavery, extra-judicial killing—continues to apply in times of armed conflict.

Limits to Wars: Discrimination and Proportionality

Warfare's changing nature has affected and continues to influence the existing understanding of IHL. More specifically, technology has dramatically altered geopolitical contexts, bringing to forefront discussions regarding the principle of discrimination and the effects of warfare on civilians and their property.[48] Restrictions on "method or means" of warfare have come to be known as "Hague Law." Limitations on targeting civilians and civilian objects, the protection of medical personnel and facilities, and norms concerning the treatment of prisoners of war are generally referred to as "Geneva Law."[49]

NATO intervention in Kosovo raised the question of the extent to which war as a means of restoring rule of law and protecting civilians is justified. The aerial bombardment of Kosovo caused considerable human suffering. It is impossible to determine how the scale of suffering NATO intervention sought to prevent, compares with that actually caused.[50] Additionally, the long-term effects of these raids must be taken into consideration, as well as what could have resulted had NATO *not* acted.[51]

Another similar difficulty is that intrastate conflicts heavily target civilian populations. The low-cost, low-tech methods of asymmetrical warfare pose grave risks to the principle of discrimination.[52] Bioterrorism represents the archetypal example of this non-discriminatory form of warfare. In response to these threats, legal experts suggest an international criminal court raises the cost of perpetrating such violations.[53] The growing focus on crimes against humanity and the establishment of individual criminal responsibility for such crimes represent a major step toward the universal enforcement of a specific set of international human rights norms.[54]

Armed Opposition Groups

Under Common Article 3 of the Geneva Conventions, certain acts remain prohibited under all circumstances. Protocol II of the Geneva Conventions provides minimum standards for the conduct of rebel groups in intrastate armed conflicts. International human rights treaties and IHL have nonetheless treated the state as the *sole* legitimate holder of the right to use force and protect the basic rights of its citizenry. Human rights NGOs, properly speaking, have no international legal mandate to condemn non-state actors.[55]

As noted earlier, NGOs have traditionally considered *impartiality* and *neutrality* prerequisites for the provision of humanitarian activities.[56] Increasingly humanitarian activists and NGOs, such as AI and Human Rights Watch (HRW), have called for the substitution of *solidarity* for *neutrality*.[57] No longer can humanitarians deny political realities: "in the post-Cold War era, governmental interpretations of vital national interests and of international conventions have been present along with notions of human solidarity."[58]

Additionally, NGOs have to simultaneously protect the human rights of militants *and* citizens in order to maintain impartially. It is difficult to distinguish between activities of armed opposition groups that should be tolerated as legitimate, and those whose indiscriminate acts of violence should be banned.[59] The issue of class violence adds another difficulty in critiquing armed opposition groups and the nature of the violence in which they engage. Nair poignantly asks: "Given that the main revolutionary class struggles are directed against an inequitable social order that systematically violates human rights, how should human rights NGOs react when militant groups, ostensibly working for the poor and oppressed, also violate human rights?"[60]

Should NGOs make public a state's abuse of human rights perpetrated in the midst of the war? Some experts note that whistle-blowing may risk an agency's operations and endanger its staff.[61] Others question the extent to which humanitarian norms can be expanded, arguing that egregious abuses may not be rectified by humanitarian action alone. Rieff points out that there are no humanitarian solutions to humanitarian problems and that it is *unclear* whether humanitarianism is the appropriate vehicle to advance human rights objectives.[62] NGOs have become "militarized" in that their cooperation with Western armies now seems normal.[63]

Another difficulty is that NGOs are heavily dependent on state power, the UNSC, and regional organizations without which they cannot carry out their operations, or promote/ensure for the enforcement of new laws. Rieff sees this dependency as a major weakness: "A Slobodan Milosevic in Belgrade or a Mullah Omar is not going to permit NGOs to operate as anything but purveyors of charity."[64] Others acknowledge the limits of what NGOs can accomplish on the basis of their resources and their dependency on external funding. They nevertheless argue that "solutions" for problems such as high infant mortality rates, IDPs, and so forth should be sought by governments. Rather, the central tasks of

NGOs are to "document and publicize problems and to press for an open political process through which the issues could be addressed."[65]

Some have pointed out that the issue of humanitarianism must be reframed as an argument about the "responsibility to protect" (R2P) that all sovereign states owe their citizens. This responsibility must be undertaken by the international community if the state lacks the ability to do so.[66] In relation to crises in Darfur and Syria the principle has become part of the debate about how the international community should respond to imminent or actual incidents of mass atrocities. In the case of North Korea R2P has been invoked by civil society actors to draw international attention to lingering human rights crises.[67]

NGOs have also made striking contributions to generating support for the creation of a strong and independent court.[68] The NGO Coalition for an International Criminal Court (CICC) effectively spearheaded the legalization of an international criminal system. The CICC had a truly global reach, represented by hundreds of NGOs, including ICRC, AI, Lawyers Committee for Human Rights, and the International Federation for Human Rights.[69]

Another example of NGOs' efforts at criminalization concerns rape in civil conflicts. Rape was first defined as a crime against humanity by the ICTY. Human rights NGOs and women's' groups argued that the category of "crimes against humanity" entailed difficult questions of proof. They successfully pushed for listing rape in the category of "genocide."[70] As a result, in 1998 the ICTR held rape to be both an act of genocide *and* a crime against humanity. Although the Geneva Conventions have condemned rape, they have not deemed it a war crime.[71]

The general consensus holds that the ICC represents a key step in the direction of promoting just law and deterrence.[72] However, opposition from the United States, China, and India weakens the Court's effectiveness. Some, however, raise a central question: will the ICC be as active in the years to come as its champions assume, given the lack of cooperation from the most powerful state in the world, such as the United States?[73] The *ad hoc* international criminal tribunals have certainly set new benchmarks. Yet the debate rages on about their effectiveness in other situations including the prosecution of international terrorism cases. Moreover, the growing number of States Party to the ICC, which is based on the principle of national court complementarity, is making national courts the front line for international criminal accountability.[74]

There has been gigantic growth in the number and types of judicial mechanisms for the enforcement of IHL. Many have been established to deal with historical traumas, hold accountable those accused of atrocities during civil war, fill the vacuum created by the withdrawal of national authorities, and replace the international community for national authorities following a military defeat.[75] These judicial mechanisms may turn out to be problematic in obtaining justice, rule of law, and promotion of international criminal justice norms. One view holds that a consistent implementation of criminal justice might interfere with other worthwhile goals, including peace, and consolidation of liberal democracy. Well-crafted diplomatic and legal steps also have their role to play in promoting a liberal international order.[76]

Terrorist Threats

Postmodern terrorism appears "to be a way from attacking specific targets like the other side's officials and toward more indiscriminate killing."[77] A more alarming type of violence, terrorism perpetrated against noncombatant civilians by subnational or transnational networks (such as al-Qaeda), poses several challenges to the moral and political imagination, and the interpretation/application of IHL. The September 11 attacks were directed mainly at civilians and clearly aimed at exposing US vulnerability. Although there was a consensus on the illegality of these attacks, no such consensus existed about the legality of the use of US military force against al-Qaeda and the Taliban, the subsequent conduct of war, and the status and treatment of prisoners held by the United States at Guantanamo Bay and elsewhere.[78]

These attacks raised the issue of whether or not terrorism is an act of war. To some, terrorists violate the law, but they are not *criminals* in the general sense of the term. Nor can they be viewed as guerrillas or revolutionaries.[79] To others addressing terrorism requires a paradigm shift in terms of how best to deal with the problem.[80] Members of al-Qaeda have deliberately killed innocent noncombatants and their attacks on military targets are also illegal in that they are executed in civilian disguise. Al-Qaeda members familiar with its criminal purpose can therefore be arrested for conspiracy to commit war crimes.[81]

Still others argue that the September 11 hijackings and killings were crimes under US law and that the United States has jurisdiction to prosecute.[82] There is no general agreement as to what constitutes terrorist activity. Some observers have asked: why are Palestinian suicide bombings and the Bali assault (Indonesia) called terrorist acts, whereas Russia's intentional bombing of Chechen civilians, and the Guatemalan army's massacre of hundreds of thousands of Mayan villagers are not similarly labeled?[83]

Modern security challenges have raised several fundamental questions for the traditional and strictly legalistic interpretation of the theory of self-defense: are restrictions on the use of preemptive force rational and realistic in light of the threats posed by global terrorism? Will terrorism give a victim state the right to invoke self-defense just as the UN Charter recognizes the "right of unilateral humanitarian intervention" whenever a large-scale violation of human rights unfolds?

Moreover although a natural right of national self-defense has long been recognized under international law, this does not apply to anticipatory self-defense. Some experts noted that the intensity, immediacy, and magnitude of terrorist activities have legitimized the notion of anticipatory self-defense and a new interpretation of the Article 51 of the UN Charter, that is the defensive use of force in response to an "armed attack."[84]

Others note that the "Bush Doctrine" of preemptive war, anticipatory self-defense, and proactive counter-proliferation efforts have dubious legal validity. Article 51 does not advocate a free and unbridled use of force in self-defense and confines anticipatory self-defense to situations of "imminent attack." The requirement of "imminent attack" has historically been a requirement for self-defense under customary international law.[85] There is no consensus as to whether or not the totalitarian nature of the Iraqi regime under Saddam Hussein persuasively established a case of imminent threat, especially in light of the false assumption of nuclear weapons production.

Regarding which rules apply in this new war, some have argued that responding forcibly to acts of megaterrorism is legitimate. It is indeed desirable to adopt an adequately flexible approach to self-defense so that states can effectively respond to terrorist acts, even if this means acting outside the letter of international law.[86] One difficulty is the interplay between the right of self-defense and the non-territorial extension of al-Qaeda. The target of military action in Afghanistan had a necessary "connection to both the harm inflicted and the continuation of the capability and threat to inflict future harm."[87]

In the context of the war in Afghanistan, it is important to recognize that compliance with IHL is separate from requirements of self-defense. Both Afghanistan and the United States are parties to the four Geneva Conventions.[88] The holding of captured al-Qaeda members at the Guantanamo Naval Basc under the label of "unlawful combatants," and not considering them as prisoners of war, has invited controversy. Experts argue the detainees were subject to customary international law requirements of humanitarian standards and that some of them may have been entitled to prisoner of war status.[89] US hesitancy to designate a clear legal status for these detainees fell outside the guidelines of the Geneva Conventions.[90]

Another problem that added to the complexity of the war against terrorism was that US relief agencies fiercely debated the nature of their involvement in Iraq. At issue was the extent to which emerging humanitarian-military relations would alter the context of humanitarian response. During the 2003 annual meetings of Inter-Action Forum, NGOs raised numerous concerns about redefining the relationship between soldiers and aid workers in such contexts: "we are struggling with the terrorism dimension of these new wars, in which NGOs are trying to learn how to operate side-by-side with combat activity. NGOs certainly feel less secure in places like Afghanistan and Iraq."[91]

Conclusion

The quintessential justification of IHL and HRL lies in their shared intent to prevent massive abuses that endanger humanity.[92] Resort to minimum humanitarian standards is imperative, especially in the cases of protracted conflicts. This chapter has attempted to answer a key question: What can governments and multilateral institutions do to lessen the probability of armed conflicts? If the incidence of civil wars is to be reduced, governments and multilateral organizations must work together to contain rebel financing and armament, expedite economic development of the countries at risk, and provide an effective presence in post-conflict settings. The costs of such operations are *less* than those of long-term continued conflict and neglect.[93]

The international community has increasingly relied on holding individuals accountable for criminal responsibility rather than commit troops. War crimes tribunals offer a rare opportunity to hold individuals accountable for crimes against humanity. Tribunals also give victims and their families an opportunity to stand up in a court of law and identify those who perpetrated human rights abuses.[94]

There are no simple and definitive answers to the problem of enforcement of international law standards in the age of transnational terrorism. Adapting the rules of warfare to the "war against terrorism" may dictate a fundamental shift in legal thinking. Meanwhile it is important to not lose sight of the fact that internal institutional reforms are the key to preventing arms conflicts.

The two categories of international law provide different ways of seeking justice and accountability. Just as ICRC succeeded in prescribing what was "appropriate behavior" for civilized states involved in armed conflicts,[95] so did many NGOs. These NGOs play a crucial role in the process of norm diffusion and framing the discourse regarding criminal justice and individual criminal responsibility, while influencing both state policies and those of intergovernmental organizations. It is worth remembering the extraordinary role of NGOs in the drive toward the creation of the ICC. It is equally important to bear in mind the limits under which IHL and HRL operate in internal disturbances, and the possibilities for NGOs to hold both governments and armed opposition groups accountable.

Notes

1. Cornelio Sommaruga, "Humanity: Our Priority Now and Always," *Ethics and International Affairs* 13 (1999): 28.
2. Sommaruga, "Humanity," 28.
3. Thomas G. Weiss, "Principles, Politics, and Humanitarian Action," *Ethics and International Affairs* 13 (1999): 1-23.
4. Weiss attributes this statement to a Norwegian research group ("Principles," 8).

5. "Violation of Human Rights and International Humanitarian Law During Armed Conflict in the Chechen Republic," http://amina.com/article/humr_viol.html (accessed June 25, 2011).

6. Rachel Brett, "Non-governmental Human Rights Organizations and International Humanitarian Law," *International Review of the Red Cross* 324 (September 29, 1998): 531-536.

7. Nader Entessar, *Kurdish Ethnonationalism* (Boulder, CO: Lynne Rienner Publishers, 1992).

8. Joseph R. Rudolph, Jr. ed., *Encyclopedia of Modern Ethnic Conflict* (Westport, CT: Greenwood Press, 2003), xxiii.

9. Charles W. Kegley, Jr. and Eugene R. Wittkopf, *World Politics: Trend and Tranfromation* (New York: Bedford/St. Martin's Press, 2001), 440-441.

10. Alan Munro, "Humanitarianism and Conflict in a Post-Cold War World," *International Review of the Red Cross* 835 (September 30, 1999): 463-475.

11. Paul Collier, "The Market for Civil War," *Foreign Policy*, 136 (May/June 2003): 38-45. See also *The Economist*, "Special Report: Civil Wars," May 24, 2003, 22-25.

12. Collier, "Market," 43-45.

13. In the 1990s armed interventions in the political affairs of the state was common. In many developing democracies, the military continues to have enormous political and economic power. UNDP, *Human Development Report 2002: Deepening Democracy in a Fragmented World* (New York: Oxford University Press, 2002), 87.

14. Darren J. O'Byrne, *Human Rights: An Introduction* (New York: Longman, 2003), 309.

15. O'Byrne, *Human Rights*, 317.

16. Geneva Convention (I) for the Amelioration of the Condition of the Wounded and Sick in Armed Forces in the Field (1949); Geneva Convention (II) for the Amelioration of the Condition of Wounded, Sick and Shipwrecked Members of Armed Forces at Sea (1949); Geneva Convention (III) relative to the Treatment of Prisoners of War (1949); Geneva Convention (IV) relative to the Protection of Civilian Persons in Time of War (1949); Protocol Additional to the Geneva Conventions of 12 August 1949, and relating to the Protection of Victims of International Armed Conflicts (1977); and Protocol Additional to the Geneva Conventions of 12 August 1949, and relating to the Protection of Victims of Non-International Armed Conflicts (1977).

17. Hugo Slim, "Why Protect Civilians? Innocence, Immunity and Enmity in War," *International Affairs* 79, no. 3 (May 2003): 496.

18. Slim, "Why Protect," 496.

19. A.M. Johannes, "Neutrality and Impartiality of the UN Peacekeeping Forces," http://amjohannes.wikidot.com/neutrality-and-impartiality-of-the-united-nations-peacekeeping (accessed on June 23, 2011).

20. Weiss, "Principles," 12.

21. Rene Provost, *International Human Rights and Humanitarian Law* (Cambridge: Cambridge University Press, 2002), 13.

22. Provost, *International Human Rights*, 13.

23. Provost, *International Human Rights*, 42.

24. Provost, *International Human Rights*, 58.

25. Mark Freeman, *Necessary Evils: Amnesties and the Search for Justice* (New York: Cambridge University Press, 2009), 50.

26. Bartram S. Brown, "International Criminal Tribunal for the Former Yugoslavia (ICTY)," in *Encyclopedia of Human Rights*, ed. David P. Forsythe, vol. 3 (New York: Oxford University Press, 2009), 137.

27. Jean H. Quataert, *Advocating Dignity: Human Rights Mobilization in Global Politics* (Philadelphia: University of Pennsylvania Press, 2009), 254.

28. Quataert, *Advocating Dignity*, 254.

29. Michael J. Struett, *The Politics of Constructing the International Criminal Court: NGOs, Discourse, and Agency* (New York: Palgrave Macmillan, 2008), 104-105.

30. Quataert, *Advocating Dignity*, 255-256.

31. Provost, *International Human Rights*, 107.

32. Antonio Cassese, "On the Current Trends Toward Criminal Prosecution and Punishment of the Breaches of International Humanitarian Law," 9 *Eur. J. Int'l L.* 2 (1998).

33. Cassese, "Current Trends."

34. Theodor Meron, "The Humanization of Humanitarian Law," 94 *Am. J. Int'l. L.* 239, 240 (2000).

35. Hector Gros Espiell, "Humanitarian Law and Human Rights," in *Human Rights: Concepts and Standards*, Janusz Symonides, ed. (Burlington, VT: Ashgate, 2000), 353.

36. Provost, *International Human Rights*, 7.

37. Provost, *International Human Rights*, 354.

38. Meron, "The Humanization," 244.

39. David P. Forsythe, *Human Rights in International Relations* (Cambridge: Cambridge University Press, 2000), 180-181.

40. Forsythe, *Human Rights*, 184.

41. Joelle Tanguy and Fiona Terry, "Humanitarian Responsibility and Committed Action," *Ethics and International Affairs* 13 (1999): 34.

42. Tanguy and Fiona Terry, "Humanitarian Responsibility," 34.

43. Meron, "Humanization," 247.

44. Ilene Cohn, "The Protection of Children and the Quest for Truth and Justice in Sierra Leone," *Journal of International Affairs* 55, no. 1 (Fall 2001): 15-16.

45. Quoted in Cohn, "Protection of Children," 34.

46. Claude Bruderlein and Jennifer Leaning, "New Challenges for Humanitarian Protection," *British Medical Journal* 319, no. 7270 (August 14, 1999): 433.

47. Bruderlein and Leaning, "New Challenges," 433.

48. Michael N. Schmitt, "The Principle of Discrimination in 21st Century Warfare," 2 *Yale Hum. Rts. & Dev. L. J.* 143 (1999).

49. Schmitt, "Principle of Discrimination," 145.

50. Francois Bugnion, "The Geneva Conventions of 12 August 1949: From the 1949 Diplomatic Conference to the Dawn of the New Millennium," *International Affairs* 76, no. 1 (January 2000): 49.

51. Bugnion, "Geneva Conventions," 49.

52. Bugnion, "Geneva Conventions," 155.

53. Bugnion, "Geneva Conventions," 178.

54. Hans Peter Schmitz and Kathryn Sikkink, "International Human Rights," in *Handbook of International Relations*, ed. Walter Carlsnaes, Thomas Risse, and Beth A. Simmons (Thousand Oaks, CA: Sage Pulications, 2008), 526.

55. Ravi Nair, "Confronting the Violence Committed by Armed Opposition Groups," 1 *Yale Hum. Rts. & Dev. L. J.* 1, 2 (1998).

56. Uwe Kracht, "Human Rights and Humanitarian Law and Principles in Emergencies," http://www.nutrition.uio.no/iprfd/Encounterdocuments/Doc05-G11.html (accessed on May 15, 2003),

57. Kracht, "Human Rights."

58. Thomas G. Weiss, "Principles, Politics, and Humanitarian Action," http://hwproject.tufts.edu/publications/electronic/e_ppaha.html (accessed May 15, 2003).

59. Nair, "Confronting," 11.

60. Nair, "Confronting," 11

61. Hugo Slim, "To the Rescue: Radicals or Poodles?" *The World Today* 53, nos. 8-9 (August/September 1997): 212.

62. David Reiff, "Humanitarianism in Crisis," *Foreign Affairs* 81, no. 6 (November/December 2002): 111-112.

63. Reiff, "Humanitarianism," 113-114.

64. Reiff, "Humanitarianism," 117.

65. Claude E. Welch, Jr., *Protecting Human Rights in African: Roles and Strategies of Nongovernmental Organizations* (Philadelphia: University of Pennsylvania Press, 1995), 284-285.

66. Gareth Evans and Mohamed Sabnoun, "The Responsibility to Protect," *Foreign Affairs* 81, no. 6 (November/December, 2002): 101.

67. Alex J. Bellamy, *Global Politics and the Responsibility to Protect: From Words to Deeds* (New York: Routledge, 2011), 51.

68. Janet E. Lord, "On the Possibilities and Limitations of NGO Participation in International Law and Its Processes," *American Society of International Law: Proceedings of the Annual Meetings* (Washington, D.C., 2001): 295-299.

69. Coalition for the ICC, http://www.iccnow.org/?mod=coalition (accessed on June 24, 2011).

70. UNDP, *Human Development Report 2000: Deepening Democracy in a Fragmented World* (New York: Oxford University Press, 2002), 107.

71. UNDP, *Human Development 2000*, 107.

72. William R. Pace, "Globalizing Justice: NGOs and the Need for an International Criminal Court," *Harvard International Review* (Spring 1998): 26-29.

73. David P. Forsythe, "The United States and International Criminal Court," *Human Rights Quarterly* 24, no. 4 (November 2002): 974-991.

74. Sandra L. Hodgkinson, "Are Ad Hoc Tribunals an Effective Tool for Prosecuting International Terrorism Cases?" 24 *Emory Int'l L. R.* 515, 521(2010),

75. Daryl A. Mundis, "New Mechanisms for the Enforcement of International Humanitarian Law," 95 *Am. J. Int'l L.* 934, 951 (October 2001).

76. David P. Forsythe, *Human Rights in International Relations*, 2d ed. (New York: Cambridge University Press, 2006), 115.

77. Walter Laqueur, "Postmodern Terrorism," *Foreign Affairs* 75, no. 5 (September/October 1996): 4.

78. Christopher Greenwood, "International Law and the War against Terrorism," *International Affairs* 78, no. 2 (April 2002): 301.

79. Thomas M. Magstadt, *Understanding Politics: Ideas, Institutions, and Issues,* 6th ed. (Belmont, CA: Wadsworth/Thomson Learning, 2003), 465.

80. Ruth Wedgwood, "The Law's Response to September 11," *Ethics and International Affairs* 16, no. 1 (2002): 10.

81. Wedgwood, "Law's Response," 12.

82. Greenwood, "International Law," 317.

83. Marcus E. Ethridge and Howard Handelman, *Politics in a Changing World: A Comparative Introduction to Political Science*, 3d ed. (Belmont, CA: Wadsworth/Thomson Learning, 2004), 513.

84. Mikael F. Nabati, "Anticipatory Self-Defense: The Terrorism Exception," *Current History* 102, no. 664 (May 2003): 222-232.

85. Frederick Tse-shyang Chen, "The Planned Preemptive Strike by the United States Against Iraq and the International Law of Self-Defense," 5/6 Ch*uo L. R.* 23, 32 (March 2003).

86. Richard Falk, "Identifying Limits on a Borderless Map," *Ethics and International Affairs* 16, no. 1 (2002): 3.

87. Falk, "Identifying Limits," 3.

88. Greenwood, "International Law," 314.

89. Greenwood, "International Law," 317.

90. George A. Lopez, "The Style of the New War: Making the Rules as We Go Along," *Ethics and International Affairs* 16, no. 1 (2002): 26.

91. Nick Cator, "U.S. Agencies Debate Divisions over Iraq," *Alertnet*, May 19, 2003.

92. David Hamburg, "Human Rights and Warfare: An Ounce of Prevention is Worth a Pound of Cure," in *Realizing Human Rights,* ed. Samantha Power and Graham Allison (New York: St. Martin's Press, 2000), 336.

93. Collier, "Market," 45.

94. Chris McMorran, "What International War Crimes Tribunals Are," *Beyond Intractability* (July 2003).

95. Robert Jackson and Georg Sorensen, *Introduction to International Relations: Theories and Approaches* (New York: Oxford University Press, 2010).

Chapter 6

Peace vs. Justice: The Strategic Use of International Criminal Tribunals

Candace H. Blake-Amarante

In the 1990s, international criminal tribunals (ICTs) emerged to redress the violence perpetrated against civilians during civil wars. Their goal was to establish justice and peace by punishing those most responsible for violating international humanitarian and human rights law.[1] The design of ICTs has been inspired by various legal and political views. In this chapter, I explore the problem of designing an ICT from a strategic point of view; specifically, I consider whether or not an ICT can provide warring parties with the right incentives to end violence and successfully negotiate for peace.

The main idea is that an ICT can be viewed as a device which imposes costs and provides rewards for warring parties. Thus the problem of this chapter becomes that of assessing whether or not there exists a feasible system of costs/rewards which would induce the desired outcome. A key idea is that the determination of which systems of costs/rewards are feasible depends on the political and legal views underlying the design of the ICT.

D'Amato's Proposal

A very instructive debate took place during the Yugoslavian war. International lawyer Anthony D'Amato[2] cautioned the international community not to issue indictments for complicit leaders in tandem with ongoing peace talks. Once leaders were indicted, it would be more profitable for them to take their chances and keep fighting. The measures proposed by the international community posed an *incentive problem.* To remedy this situation, D'Amato proposed a model of an international criminal tribunal based on the principles of the *domestic tort litigation model* (DTL) which is centered on the notion that culpable parties would not be prosecuted once they settle *inter se.* The DTL model creates the right incentive for opposing parties to bargain for a mutually beneficial agreement in order to avoid one of the parties calling the court.

The novelty of D'Amato's proposal is that the DTL model be applied to the international management of civil wars. This is a far reaching extension of the classical DTL model for two reasons: (1) the DTL would operate in an international setting, and (2) the DTL would operate in a *criminal* setting rather than a *civil* one. Yet, the basic logic would be same: the court stands as a potential threat only. The parties' threat of calling the court determines their "outside options" of the bargaining process; that is what they would obtain if they did not settle among themselves.

Applying the DTL model to the international management of civil wars raises several concerns. The most common is a moral one. One of the outcomes of the DTL model is that perpetrators might go unpunished. Unlike civil law, where parties are encouraged to settle disputes before resorting to legal procedures, in criminal law it is generally held that the state has an obligation to punish perpetrators to deter future transgressions. This idea finds its application in an international setting with the principle of Human Rights law (HR).

The general idea is that analogies can be drawn between domestic criminal law and HR law but not between civil law and international HR law. This criticism does not seem sound. First, recent history shows that states often given up their obligation to punish perpetrators for certain crimes to achieve goals that appear more advantageous.[3] Second, a system that causes more atrocities by punishing perpetrators leads to severe moral concerns.

Another concern regarding the applicability of the DTL model stems from the (international) legal status of the parties involved in the conflict. Parties in a domestic civil dispute have the same legal rights. Under the current international legal system, the right to petition an international court is a right that is not afforded to rebels. Given the *modus operandi* of the DTL model, one might fear that these asymmetries in status might severely limit the effectiveness of the model in the international setting.

This chapter explores the validity of D'Amato's idea. Its aim is to introduce a formal setting where the performance of alternative legal regime models—the State Sovereignty (SS), Human Rights (HR), Cosmopolitan Rights (CR), DTL—

can be evaluated on the basis of their ability to alter combatants' incentives from fighting to bargaining for peace.

After examining how the specific design features of each regime might exacerbate or mitigate combatants' incentives to fight or bargain for peace, I provide some general considerations regarding the formal study of civil wars, as well as the impact that different legal regimes might have on the outcomes of wars. These considerations, along with the findings of the literature on bargaining for peace, allow me to identify a set of assumptions that describe civil wars as games. I then provide an example of a civil-war game which formalizes some of the problems in the bargaining for peace literature. I study the possible outcomes achievable in this game under alternative legal regimes. I demonstrate that *under certain circumstances*, the DTL model may be the most efficient model for achieving peace during civil wars.

The State Sovereignty Model

According to the traditional idea of state sovereignty (SS), it is the prerogative of states to decide how to govern their territory and citizens. External entities like ICTs can get involved in a state's affairs *only if* that state calls for intervention. In situations of civil conflict the SS regime produces an asymmetry because only the state has the right to call an ICT. Consequently, the ICT becomes an "instrument" used by states in order to secure their interests. Justice is one-sided and is likely to be fully rendered only in two circumstances: 1) when the state is not culpable but other parties are; or 2) when the state's interests are aligned with those of the ICT.

A similar conclusion can be drawn regarding the ability of this regime to induce opposing parties to bargain for peace. Since the state is the only entity that can call the court, this regime generates a bias towards the government and makes insurgents more susceptible to prosecution. This is extremely problematic because the state: 1) will have an incentive to commit crimes as part of their military strategy;[4] and 2) will not have an incentive to bargain with insurgents. Moreover, since insurgents cannot call the court, and other states are unlikely to do so, the SS regime increases government's incentives to go to war.

Current Interpretations of the Principle of SS

Over the years, the concept of SS has evolved from a very strict interpretation of non-interference to a more permissive stance, whereby external entities can interfere to a certain extent in the domestic affairs of a state. Only the state can request outside interference and if any other entity does so, it is because the state has allowed it to do so. A case in point is the ICC which entered into force on July 1, 2002.[5] It is the first permanent treaty-based international criminal court whose main objective is to end impunity for the perpetrators of the most serious violations of international criminal law.[6]

While the ICC can attempt to intervene, the state is under no obligation to cooperate with the Court. According to Article 87 of the Rome Statute creating the ICC, if a state fails to cooperate, the Court may make a finding to this effect and can then only refer the matter to the Assembly of States Parties or the United Nations Security Council (UNSC).

There is no enforcement power to make states cooperate by way of acts or countermeasures put forth by the Assembly of States, or by way of the UNSC stepping in and imposing sanctions. Cassese questions why the UNSC should not act under its Chapter VII powers especially when a state's refusal to cooperate could constitute a threat to peace and security. The ICC does not exclude such possibilities, but it does not explicitly specify them in the statute either.[7] Moreover, the principle of complementarity gives priority in the exercise of jurisdiction to national courts making the ICC a subsidiary to national courts. This hinders the ICC's ability of rendering justice.

Uganda is a case in point. The Ugandan government (UG) solicited the assistance of the ICC to prosecute members of the rebel group, the Lord's Resistance Army (LRA) for war crimes and crimes against humanity. While the ICC acknowledged that UG also committed crimes, it claims that those of the LRA are more serious than the crimes committed by UG, thus prosecuting the LRA only.

The Human Rights/Cosmopolitan Rights Models

Two monumental events changed the face of SS in the eyes of international law: the human rights movement, which heralded the notion of crimes against humanity (CAH), and the prevalence of civil wars after WWII. With the notion of CAH,[8] how a state treats its own citizens is a matter of international concern. At present CAH are punishable without reference to the circumstances under which they were committed. State officials are duty bound to: (1) refrain from committing CAH; (2) prosecute violations of CAH; and (3) submit to the international community's authority in the event that the state fails to prosecute violators.

Consequently, the idea of sovereignty has been completely redefined. International law imposes obligations not only on states but also individuals. Individuals also have rights under international law. Any individual from any country, irrespective of where the atrocities take place, can petition an international body to intervene on behalf of victims and prosecute perpetrators without necessarily securing states' consent. This is very much in line with the idea of global cosmopolitan rights (CR).[9]

The chief example of an ICT designed according to the principles of HR/CR is the International Criminal Tribunal for Yugoslavia (ICTY). The ICTY has the ability to automatically intervene upon any infraction of the law. To ensure that state perpetrators are brought to justice, such legal regimes are endowed with the necessary powers and jurisdictions to constrain any state from derogating from the duty to prosecute or obstructing the tribunal's work. The problem under HR/CR is that if leaders needed to negotiate for peace are to be prosecuted, they will have no incentive to bargain and will continue to fight. Thus it appears that HR/CR regimes are more likely to ensure the goal of justice rather than peace.

The Domestic Tort Litigation Model

The DTL model shares with the SS model the feature that ICTs cannot intervene without the request of one of the parties directly involved in the conflict. It departs from the SS model in that *all* parties involved in the conflict are given the right to petition ICTs.

The application of the DTL model to the sphere of international law is quite novel. To appreciate its potential, it is necessary to reverse the usual approach to civil wars. The main goal during civil struggles is to either prevent the onset of armed conflict or to end it. Ideally, one would like opposing parties to settle their disputes at the bargaining table. Usually, this is pursued by trying to provide opposing parties with the right bargaining incentives. This is done *within a given institutional context.* Extending the principles of the DTL model to the international management of civil wars flips the terms of this approach: given the goal of achieving peace, one wants to create an institutional environment that would lead opposing parties to bargain rather than to fight.

This motive is the essence of the DTL model in domestic disputes. Under DTL, an injured party claims redress for injuries caused by another person. The legal rules regarding claims for damages by accident victims are found in the law of negligence.[10] The salient features of this system are that: (1) The terms of the law of negligence determine the parties' bargaining opportunities by determining what they would get if they did not settle; (2) The potential enforcement by a court of the law of negligence creates incentives for the parties to bargain; and (3) The court is an external entity with respect to the opposing parties, a set-up guaranteeing that the court would serve the purpose of the law rather than the interests of any of the parties. The last feature has an important implication: if the DTL has to be extended to the management of civil war, then *a court has to be managed by the international community* in order to guarantee its impartiality.

D'Amato looks specifically at the DTL procedure and the law of negligence for guidance in applying these ideas to civil wars. The feature that a court cannot intervene unless solicited by one of the parties involved provides the structure for negotiations. It is under the threat of court proceedings that settlements are ultimately concluded. Without this threat there are little to no incentives for complicit parties to respond to claims of damages.[11] Cases are settled by means of compromise rather than adjudication because the interests of both parties are best served by avoiding the court. Genn argues that the act of compromise is an efficient solution to protracted court proceedings in domestic litigation.[12] Unlike criminal law, there is no element of "punishment" for negligent parties in the award of damages. This feature might lead some to claim that a system based on these principles might not serve the purpose of deterrence. Genn argues that both deterrence and retribution are important and legitimate functions of the law of negligence.[13] D'Amato's proposal follows the same logic and takes into account the international interest of deterring future war criminals when arguing for the use of procedures based on the law of negligence.

The effective transposition of DTL principles to civil wars requires that the same rights would be afforded to *all* warring parties. This implies: 1) both parties can call the court to intervene when either one or both commit international crimes, and 2) if the court should intervene, both parties will be prosecuted and penalized commensurate to the crimes committed.

The DTL model is symmetric. It has the potential of addressing all of the problems stemming from the asymmetries of the SS model. Moreover, by its very design, DTL aims at creating an environment that enhances parties' ability to peacefully settle their disputes. The exact quantification of this feature depends on the exact quantification of the penalties the court can impose and its ability to carry out punishments. *Under certain circumstances,* DTL is likely to outperform the HR/CR model. This outcome is likely when the penalties imposed by the HR/CR model excessively reduce the potential gains from negotiations.

General Considerations on the Formal Study of Different Regimes

A Formal Model for Civil Wars

The actors involved in a civil war are the government (G) and one or more rebel groups. For simplicity, I assume that there is only one of these groups and will denote it by R. G and R fight to seize control of the territory, resources, and assets of their country.

The set of decisions available to G and R, as well as the potential outcomes associated with these decisions, are modeled as a game. It is convenient to think of such a game as being constituted by two interrelated parts, *W* and *B*, each a game in and of itself. *W*, is a *war game*. The players in game *W*are G and R. The actions available to them correspond to the possible ways each player has to fight the war. A coarse description of these options—fighting without committing CAH, fighting by committing CAH—will suffice. The payoffs associated with the players' choices are determined by the underlying structural conditions of the war.

B is a *bargaining game*. The players are still G and R. The actions available to them consist of the possible proposals each can make regarding the division of a "pie." The pie represents the worth of the country's resources, territory and assets. It is allowed that the two parties will value the pie differently.

W and *B* are interrelated. The players' decisions in one game depend on the possible outcomes in the other game. An important ingredient of *B* is the specification of what happens if the players fail to agree (e.g. specification of the players' outside option). In actual situations, when G and R fail to agree one of the available options is war. This corresponds to the players "exiting" the bargaining game and "entering" the war game. Thus, *the players outside options in the bargaining game B correspond to the players' expected outcomes in the war game W.*

Asymmetries in Information

In *W* each player has private information about its own military capabilities and resolve, and can only make an imperfect assessment about the other player's capabilities and resolve. It is possible that players entertain views that are at odds with each other.

In *B*, there are two sources of private information. The first stems from each party's possession of private information about its own assets and resolve. This determines the concessions each party has the potential to make at the bargaining table. The second source of private information comes from *W*. *W* determines each player's outside options in *B*. Since *W* is a game with private information, it follows that the outside options in *B* are also private information. Just like above, this produces the feature that the players' evaluation of their outside options might be at odds with each other and their sum might even exceed the size of the pie.

Modeling Courts under Different Legal Regimes

The presence of a court alters the options available to the warring parties, as well as the potential outcomes each might obtain. *Formally, the introduction of a court appears as a device that alters games W and B.* It does so by modifying the actions available, as well as the players' payoffs. Moreover, the modification to *W* and *B* produced by a court will be different under different legal regimes. It is precisely this feature that renders possible a comparison of the various regimes.

To get an idea of how this works, let us begin by observing that a court can be seen as a mechanism that sanctions the players in game *W* for the use of certain actions. A court may impose a cost for playing the action "fight by committing CAH." By doing so, the court alters the payoffs achievable in *W*. The important point is not that the court changes the players' payoffs *per se,* but rather the court has the ability to alter the *relative profitability* of the various actions. As such, it has the ability to alter the outcomes of *W*. By virtue of what was said above, this is tantamount to altering the players' outside options in game *B*. *The ability of imposing costs on certain actions in game W ultimately translates into the ability of altering the relative profitability of bargaining with respect to going to war.*

Notice that different legal regimes may have a different impact on *W* and *B*. The easiest way to demonstrate this is to consider the action "call the court to intervene." This action is not available to any of the players in a situation of international anarchy, is available to only one player (G) under the SS regime, to both players under the DTL regime, and can be activated independently of the players' will under the HR/CR regime.

A Set of Reasonable Assumptions for Modeling Civil Wars

In this section, I list a set of empirical regularities identified in the literature on bargaining for peace during civil war. Each finding has a formal counterpart in the form of an assumption made on the games *W* and *B* discussed above.

1). R is at a military disadvantage relative to G's forces and will fight indirect, unconventional wars. This translates into the feature that (all other things being equal) R's payoffs for engaging in direct battle are lower than R's payoffs for resorting to indirect battle.[14]

2). Though G is at a military advantage, it is unlikely to engage in direct battle with R. As such, it will be unable to garner information on R's strength, capabilities, and resolve.[15] Formally, this corresponds to the feature that G has only partial information about R's military capabilities. G may obtain more information by engaging R in direct battle than by resorting to indirect methods of warfare.

3). G is more likely to resort to unlawful methods of warfare to defeat R[16] instead of negotiating with R. Formally, given its lack of information about R's military capabilities, G's expected payoff for fighting unconventionally is higher than both the payoffs achievable through conventional warfare and the payoff achievable from negotiating.

4). Both parties are unaware of each other's strength and resolve. They are likely to overestimate their own strength and underestimate that of their opponent's.[17] Formally, the sum of the parties' outside options in the bargaining game exceeds (at least at the onset of the war) the size of the pie.

An Example of the Relative Performance of Different Regimes

In this section, I outline an example of a *W/B* game, and analyze the relative performance of different legal regimes. Without any pretense of being descriptive, the example is suggestive of the phenomena that took place during the war in Yugoslavia,[18] which led D'Amato to foresee both the failure of the negotiations, and the fact that the court would have exacerbated the conflict under the HR/CR legal regime.

A Basic War/Bargaining Game

The players are G and R. In *B*, G and R bargain over a pie worth 100 in total. The actions available to each player consist of the possible proposals of how to split the pie. If they fail to agree, then they will enter the game *W*. *W* is a game with incomplete information. Each player is one of two possible types: Weak or Strong. That is, G has two possible types, $\{G_W, G_S\}$, and so does R $\{R_W, R_S\}$. Each has two possible actions in *W*: fight conventionally (C) or fight unconventionally (U). I assume that war crimes are committed when players fight unconventionally (see Figure 6.1 below).

The War Game

G_W vs. R_W:

	C	U
C	20,15	-10, 55
U	45, 0	30, 20

G_W vs. R_S:

	C	U
C	0, 35	-40,75
U	20,20	5, 65

G_S vs. R_W:

	C	U
C	60,0	10, 30
U	95, -20	80,15

G_S vs. R_S:

	C	U
C	30, 20	0, 40
U	65, 0	20, 45

Figure 6.1. The players' payoffs are determined according to the above tables, where R is the column player and G the row player

I assume that fighting unconventionally is a dominant strategy for both players independently of the other player's type. Moreover, I assume both players are strong, G= G_S and R= R_S. I assume G thinks that R is weak (with probability 1), that R thinks that G is weak with probability x□ (0,1), and that G is strong with the complementary probability 1-x. One might assume that the probability x, the probability that R assigns to G being weak, is close to 1. The assumption that G is absolutely certain that R is weak (while R is, in fact, strong) is only a simplifying assumption, and the analysis below would be essentially the same if one were to assume that G places great weight on the hypothesis that R is weak. The assumption that players are quite "off the mark" in assessing their opponent's strength is motivated by the literature's findings reported above. The equilibrium outcomes of *W* constitute the outside options of *B;* also a game of incomplete information.

The Basic Game in a Situation of Anarchy

If there is no court in the picture, then at the bargaining table, G is willing to offer at most 20 to R because from G's viewpoint the value of going to war (i.e., G's outside option in the bargaining game) is 80, while R is not willing to accept anything less than 65 (R's value of going to war). Thus, no bargaining is possible, and both parties will decide to go to war.

Enriching the Basic Game: a Preemptive Strike

Now, we are going to enrich the previous description by allowing player R an additional action: R can strike before the negotiations begin. We assume the cost of this action for R is 10. If R does strike, this would convince G that R is strong, that is by striking R would reveal its true type. I assume that crimes are committed by R when striking.

In order to examine the outcomes of this game, the first step is to determine whether or not R will strike.

1). If R does not strike, then everything is just like before (because G still perceives R as weak): the parties will go to war and R will get 65.

2). If R strikes G knows that R is strong and is never willing to concede more than 55, because G knows that under no circumstance can R achieve more than this amount.

We conclude that R decides not to strike, that both parties decide to go to war, and that crimes against humanity are committed.

Introducing a Court

Now a court is introduced. This might allow players an additional action ("call the court"). Depending on the legal regime and the players' actions, the court may also potentially reduce the payoff a player might achieve by using action U (unconventional fight), as well as the payoff R can achieve by striking (as war crimes are committed by R when striking.). The costs that the court imposes on the players for committing war crimes are as follows: a penalty of 40 on R for striking, an additional penalty of 10 on each party for using action U (if this follows a strike from R), and a penalty of 20 on each party for using action U (if no strike from R takes place). I stress these are only *potential costs*. They become *actual costs* only when the court is allowed to intervene, which is going to depend on the legal regime in place. In order to complete the description of the game, I must specify which players have the options of calling the court and when they have the option to do so. This varies with the legal regime in place.

The DTL Model

The DTL model requires the court only intervene if one of the parties requests its intervention. Both players have the option of calling the court if war crimes have been committed. If one party calls the court, all players, including the one that called the court, will be punished if they have committed crimes. In order to examine the outcomes of this game, we have to consider several new scenarios.

First, we have to determine if: (1) R strikes or (2) R does not strike. If R strikes, we have to determine if (1a) G calls the court or (1b) G does not call the court. In each of these cases, we will need to determine whether or not one or both players decide to go to war. Finally, if in case (1b) players decide to settle, we will have to determine whether or not G would renege on the agreement and call the court to intervene ("credible commitment problem").

Suppose R does not strike. Then G thinks that R is weak and is willing to concede up to 20. R thinks that by going to war R would get 65 if G does not call the court and 45 if G calls the court. The worst case scenario for R is that it would get 45 from war. It follows that R asks for at least 45 at the bargaining table while G wants to give up at most 20. Hence, no bargaining is possible and both will go to war. Notice that, in this scenario, nobody would call the court, R will get 65 and G will get 20.

If R strikes, we want to find out whether or not G will choose to sit at the bargaining table. We compare three payoffs for G: (i) the payoff that G achieves by not negotiating, not calling the court, and by going to war; (ii) the payoff that G achieves by not negotiating and calling the court; and (iii) the payoff that G achieves by negotiating and not calling the court. We already know that the first payoff is 20 (this payoff would go down to 10 if R calls the court, but this threat is not credible).

Next, suppose that G refuses to negotiate and instead calls the court. What is R going to do? If R does not do anything, R gets -50 (– 40 penalty from the court -10 cost of strike). If R goes to war, R gets 5 (65 gain from going war -10 cost of strike – 50 penalties from court). So, obviously R would choose to go to war. In such a case, G will have to go to war, and G will get a payoff of 10 (20 gain from war -10 penalty from court). Conditionally on R having struck, the value for G of not negotiating and calling the court is 10.

Now, let us examine G's decision of not calling the court and sitting at the bargaining table. Since, R strikes, G knows that the value for R of going to war is 5 (G can credibly threaten to call the court). Thus, any offer greater than 5 that G makes to R would be acceptable. R, on its end, can threaten to go to war, and by doing so would lower G's payoff down to 20 (again, this payoff could go down to 10 if R calls the court, but this threat is not credible). Hence, any offer higher than 20 that R makes to G would be deemed acceptable. If G decides not to call the court and bargain, then there are possibilities of splitting the pie that are mutually beneficial for both parties.

For instance, let us consider the division of the pie (proposed after R strikes), 25 for G and 75 for R. The total payoffs are as follows: R gets 65 (-10 strike plus 75 negotiations) which is equal to 65 (value or not striking preemptively but going to war). Thus, R weakly prefers striking and making the deal of (75 for R, 25 for G) to not striking and going to war. G gets 25 which is more than 20, the value of not negotiating. Summing up, we have found an (Nash) equilibrium of the game where R strikes and the players settle for the division (75 for R, 25 for G).

Finally, if G reneges it is reasonable to assume that the splitting does not take place. Now R can do nothing at all or go to war. It is not profitable for R to do nothing (as the value for R would be -50), so R goes to war and ends up with 5. So G makes R worse off. However, G makes itself worse off, because G's payoff from war is 20 instead of 25. We can conclude that G would not renege on the agreement. Notice that in this equilibrium, war crimes are committed (during the preemptive strike), negotiations take place, and peace is reached without the involvement of the court.

The HR/CR Model

In the HR/CR model the court automatically intervenes when war crimes are committed. The players know that they will face prosecution even if they decide to negotiate for peace. We are now going to determine the equilibrium outcomes that obtain in the *W/B* game when the legal regime in place is the HR/CR model.

We determine whether or not R strikes in a sub-game perfect Nash equilibrium. If R does not strike, the situation is the same as in the DTL model with the only difference being that now the court will definitely impose a penalty of -20 on both for going to war. In the end R gets 45 (65 from war minus 20 from court penalty) and G gets 0 (20 from war minus 20 from court penalty). If R strikes, there are two possibilities: G may or may not go to war. If G goes to war, then R gets 5 (-10 from cost of strike plus 65 from war minus 50 from court penalty) and G gets 10 (20 from war minus 10 from court penalty). If instead G decides to negotiate, then the highest concession that G is willing to make at the bargaining table would be 90 (since by going to war G would get 10). Hence, if R strikes, then it can get at most 90 from bargaining. Thus, in the best case scenario, R will end up with a payoff of 40 (-10 for strike plus 90 from negotiation minus 40 court penalty). We see, then, that for R the value of not striking and going to war (which is 45) is higher than the value of striking (at most 40). Under the HR/CR model, in any subgame perfect Nash equilibrium of the game R does not strike, no information is transmitted, there is no room for negotiation, both parties go to war and war crimes are committed by both parties.

Notes

1. For a distinction between the two see Antonio Cassese, *International Criminal Law* (New York: Oxford University Press, 2003), 65. Nevertheless the ICTY encompassed both international humanitarian and human rights law. See ICTY, *Prosecutor v. Tadić*, Case No. IT-94-1-A, Appeals Judgment, para. 119 (July 15, 1999).

2. Anthony D'Amato, "Peace vs. Accountability in Bosnia," 88 *Am. J. Int'l. L.* 500 (1994).

3. The International Criminal Court refused to indict members of the complicit Ugandan government on the basis that they would assist in the apprehension of more culpable criminals from the Ugandan rebel group, the Lord's Resistance Army.

4. Benjamin Valentino, Paul Huth, and Dylan Balch-Lindsay, "Draining the Sea: Mass Killing and Guerrilla Warfare," *International Organization* 58 (2004): 375.

5. Rome Statute of the International Criminal Court (July 17, 1998).

6. ICC, at http://www.icc-cpi.int/Menus/ICC/About+the+Court/.

7. Cassese, *International Criminal Law*, 360.

8. M. Cherif Bassiouni ed., *Crimes against Humanity in International Criminal Law* (Dordrecht, The Netherlands: Marinus Nijhoff Publishers, 1999), 170.

9. International Commission on Intervention and State Sovereignty, *The Responsibility to Protect* (Canada: IDRC, 2001).

10. For a description see Hazel Genn, *Hard Bargaining: Out of Court Settlement in Personal Injury Actions* (New York: Oxford University Press, 1987), 3.

11. Genn, *Hard Bargaining,* 11.

12. Genn, *Hard Bargaining,* 11.

13. Genn, *Hard Bargaining,* 3.

14. William Zartman, ed., *Elusive Peace: Negotiating an End to Civil Wars* (Washington, DC: Brookings institute, 1995).

15. Darren Filson and Suzanne Werner, "A Bargaining Model for War and Peace: Anticipating the Onset, Duration, and Outcome of War," *American Journal of Political Science* 46 (2002): 819-38.

16. Valentino et al., "Draining the Sea," 375-407.

17. Geoffrey Blainey, *The Causes of War* (New York: Free Press, 1973); James Fearon, "Rationalist Explanations for War," *International Organization* 49 (1995): 379-414.

18. Like D'Amato, I refer to the period in which the War Crimes Commission and ICTY were established (July and September 1992, respectively). I consider further the massacres in Srebrenica, and the ethnic cleansing in Krajina in mid-1995, and Kosovo.

Chapter 7

Understanding the Alienated Constituents of International Tribunals: Bridging the Gap

Adam M. Smith

On April 15, 2011, the International Criminal Tribunal for the former Yugoslavia (ICTY) ruled that a "joint criminal enterprise" made up of much of the senior leadership of wartime Croatia was responsible for violence against the Serb minority in the Krajina region of Croatia during the 1990s.[1] The violence came to a head in 1995 with Operation Storm which catalyzed the departure of the vast majority of Krajina Serbs, solidifying the geography and demography of today's Croatia. The ICTY verdict, rendered in the trial of three Croatian generals involved, ended with Ante Gotovina and Mladen Markač found guilty of crimes against humanity and war crimes.

The *Gotovina* decision is noteworthy both for confirming the complicity of Croatia's senior-most wartime leadership in crimes against Serbs *and* for Croatia's categorical rejection of the judgment. After the verdict, thousands took to the streets in Croatia to protest, celebrating the generals' "heroism" as well as that of other leaders convicted by the ICTY.[2] A survey found that 95 percent of Croats believed the ruling was unfair.[3] Despite the verdict, Croatians remained convinced that Operation Storm was a justified response to Serb hostility.

Croatia's reaction continues an unfortunate trend for international justice. Indeed when *Gotovina* was overturned eighteen months later, it was the Serbs who categorically refused to accept the outcome. International tribunals[4] have had difficulty gaining acceptance for some of their most important decisions by peoples whose acceptance is critical to the success of international justice. While Serbs may have initially felt vindicated by the *Gotovina* decision (and then the Croats after the decision was reversed), the goal of international tribunals has never solely been justice for victims. These tribunals have also sought to make those who "benefited" from crimes recognize their wrongs. Without perpetrators' acknowledging wrongdoing, the ability of international justice to deliver any of its several aims—including truth-telling, reconciliation, or deterrence—is limited.

This chapter provides a brief overview of the history of this particular challenge, analyzes its causes, and provides some thoughts how this shortcoming could be mitigated. The chapter also briefly explores whether the latest iteration of international justice—the International Criminal Court (ICC)—is better situated to overcome this limitation.

The Unseen Aftermath of the Nuremberg and Tokyo Trials

While Nuremberg and Tokyo are rightly lauded as watersheds in history, in neither case was the outcome of the proceedings broadly accepted by average Germans or Japanese.[5]

Evidence of the failure of the Nuremberg trials to capture the "hearts and minds" of Germans comes from opinion polls conducted by the Allied occupation forces in Western Germany. While polls taken in June 1945 revealed a plurality who demanded the "elimination of all traces of the Nazi party,"[6] this did not mean that a plurality also rejected the destructive views promulgated by the party. Indeed in October 1946 surveys revealed that "large numbers of . . . Germans . . . continued to [publicly] express . . . characteristic" National Socialist perceptions.[7] Thirty-three percent of respondents maintained that, "Jews should not have the same rights as those belonging to the Aryan Race"; 37 percent claimed that the "extermination of the Jews and Poles . . . was . . . necessary for the security of Germans," and over half of respondents felt that territories Hitler had annexed should be part of Germany.[8] Throughout the second half of the 1940s, support for National Socialist ideals remained widespread.[9] Surveys in 1947 revealed that more than 60 percent of Germans were "deeply imbued" with anti-Semitic "feeling," and only "a very small fraction" of the population clearly opposed "race hatred."[10] The strength of these views *increased* over time, such that during the 1950s a "declining percentage of . . . respondents, averaging only about a third . . . rejected National Socialism outright. An increasing percentage, averaging about half, thought it merely a good idea badly carried out."[11] At that time, only one in ten Germans supported the prosecution of war criminals.[12]

In Tokyo, the impact of postwar justice was also disconcerting, with the public putting little stock in guilty verdicts and refusing to come to terms with troubling findings. For instance, two years after Mamoru Shigemitsu, the Japanese foreign minister at the end of World War II, was paroled from his war crimes conviction, the Japanese reelected him to Parliament and two years later he regained his post as Japan's top diplomat.[13] Though members of Unit 731—the infamous Unit that conducted medical experiments on POWs—were left unpunished, it was well known that they had committed unspeakable crimes. Even so, many enjoyed unblemished public support in their postwar careers: one became Governor of Tokyo and another the president of the Japanese medical association.[14]

The Tokyo Trials also failed to persuade Japanese of the truth of many of the central crimes committed by the Empire. For instance, the Trials found that during the Japanese occupation of Nanking, China horrific "atrocities" were committed. Despite the amount of evidence provided, the seriousness, even *existence* of, the "Rape of Nanking" remained "debatable" in Japan for a generation.[15]

The "Second Wave" of International Justice and Continued Alienation

At the time of the two post-World War II trials some recognized the difficulties in persuasively communicating their findings to their target populations. However, the rise of the Cold War and international justice's forced fifty-year hibernation meant that many problems experienced by Nuremberg and Tokyo had faded from view by the time international tribunals were reestablished in the early 1990s.

The founders of the ICTY and International Criminal Tribunal for Rwanda (ICTR) paid limited attention to how their tribunals' messages were to be communicated to the belligerent parties. And, similar to their predecessors, these modern tribunals have, on the whole, been largely unsuccessful in changing views on the ground, especially with respect to critical determinations of fact and guilt. Both Croats and Serbs, for example, have been recalcitrant on key judicial verdicts. For the Croats it is Operation Storm; for the Serbs accepting the existence of, let alone culpability for, the genocide at Srebrenica has been similarly fraught, despite overwhelming evidence.

Condemnation for Srebrenica was swift and nearly universal. One month after the event, in August 1995, the US provided the UN evidence of mass graves,[16] and in November 1995 the ICTY indicted Ratko Mladić, the Bosnian Serb general responsible for the action. In the 2001 trial of Radislav Krstić, the ICTY concluded: "the Prosecution has proven beyond all reasonable doubt that genocide [was] . . . perpetrated . . . at Srebrenica;[17] a finding confirmed in 2004,[18] and reaffirmed by the International Court of Justice in 2007.[19] Despite this, in a survey conducted fourteen years after Srebrenica, fewer than half of Serbia's population stated that they knew of or believed that genocide occurred.[20]

Some argue that Serbia finally accepted responsibility in March 2010 when its Parliament passed a resolution "apologizing" for the events. However, the resolution fell short of adopting the view that Serbia was really responsible.[21] In fact, the Parliament refused to use the word "genocide." Serbia's "apology" did not concede complicity—a shortcoming that led many to reject it out of hand. At worst the resolution noted guilt by omission; apologizing for Serbia's inaction to mitigate atrocities. Even going this far was controversial. Serbian legislators debated the matter for thirteen hours and it barely passed: 127 votes in the 250-seat Parliament.[22] Moreover, some believe that many of the resolution's supporters cast their vote due to EU pressure, rather than remorse.[23]

In Rwanda, the ICTR has had similar difficulties convincing Rwandans to accept the international community's determinations of fact and guilt. Just months after the violence ended in July 1994, a UN Expert Committee reported that "individuals from both sides to the armed conflict [Tutsi and Hutu] . . . perpetrated . . . crimes against humanity."[24] However post-genocide, Tutsi-led Rwanda has refused to accept any Tutsi responsibility, successfully preventing ICTR investigations of Tutsis and leaving Hutus as the sole defendants. Hutus, meanwhile, "vehemently reject . . . [the] generalized guilt" implied by their status as the only defendants before the court.[25]

How Serious is the Rejection of International Judicial Decisions?

That participants in or beneficiaries of crimes refuse to accept judicial determinations of wrongdoing is arguably expected and perhaps irrelevant to the prospect of justice. After all, the same sort of denial is seen in domestic trials. Yet there are two aspects of this phenomenon in the international context that set it apart from the domestic and make it particularly concerning.

First, stakeholder rejection of international judicial decisions is strikingly widespread. For example, it is remarkable that in the face of judicial pronouncements and substantial evidence a large segment of the Serbian public remain unwilling to accept Serb involvement in Srebrenica. In contrast, rejections of judicial determinations in the domestic realm are usually limited to persons directly associated with a defendant and/or incorrigible extremists. In the international context, such a direct connection is unneeded and such denials are regularly mainstream.

Second, while reconciliation is seldom a central goal of domestic processes, it is a primary aim of international justice.[26] That large segments of target populations do not accept the truth of judicial verdicts hinders the potential for reconciliation. How can the various peoples of the former-Yugoslavia or the African Great Lakes live peaceably among one another when they have such dissonant views about defining moments in their shared histories—views that directly implicate their neighbors in recent tragedies?

The Causes of Alienation in Target Countries

One of the primary reasons international mechanisms of justice have been unable to persuade target populations concerns the mismatch between the methodology by which international courts operate, and the types of issues upon which they most often rule. Concerning methodology, international tribunals pride themselves on being "distant" from the crimes over which they exercise jurisdiction. The practice of international justice is shorn of emotional, historical, and personal connection with the underlying events or societal mores. The often unstated theory that accounts for this is that it is only by asking dispassionate, disinterested jurists to examine the complex facts of a situation can a truth emerge that could be universally embraced.

However this "scientific" approach is incongruous with the emotional manner in which people treat the matters that so often appear before international tribunals: issues that challenge central, enduring beliefs people have about themselves, their communities, and histories. For instance, in Croatia, it is hard to overstate the role Operation Storm, and the wider war for independence, continue to play in the nation's *Zeitgeist.* That the operation, parts of which the ICTY deemed illegal, was in fact a "noble endeavor" is a central, enduring plank in the country's historical narrative. Every August 5 (the day the operation ended) Croatia observes the "Victory and Homeland Thanksgiving Day and the Day of Croatian Defenders." This is an occasion for political speeches which invariably recount the unblemished glory of Operation Storm. In her 2010 speech Prime Minister Jadranka Kosor recalled "with pride the most brilliant victory of the Croatian army over the [Serb] policy of aggression and occupation,"[27] noting Operation Storm "crowned years of attempts to beat the aggressors."[28] In their remarks, Interior Minister Tomislav Karamarko argued that "if it hadn't been for Operation Storm, there would be no Croatia,"[29] and Croatian President Ivo Josipović noted that the operation was clearly legal and credit should be given to all who . . . participated.[30]

The *Gotovina* decision demanded that Croatians not just question Operation Storm, but accept that the decisive victory that "sealed its independence . . . was . . . criminal."[31] As a corollary the verdict demanded that Croatians accept that leaders of their fight for freedom were themselves criminals. In short, the decision asked Croatians to question their values, their accepted notions of history, and the meaning of modern Croatia. Evidently, the ICTY's detached, scientific justice failed to speak persuasively to Croatians on these core elements of their identities.

Unfortunately, this detached model has permeated the international justice system, from the tribunals' structure, to their procedures. This has served to create more distance between the tribunals and their target populations and made it even *harder* for international courts to be persuasive on difficult issues.

Judges and prosecutors, for instance, have never been from the regions affected. Balkan citizens have rarely been even allowed to be employed in "their" ICTY. *Gotovina* was prosecuted by a team led by an American, and decided by a panel of three non-Balkan judges.[32] The ICTR staff has a similar foreign appearance.

The tribunals' law is likewise largely alien. The ICTY and ICTR have adopted a motley approach to finding applicable legal principles, with some claiming that their international status means that they can legitimately find precedent in any domestic jurisdiction.[33] In the ICTY, this has seen the prosecution and judges refer to laws from countries as diverse (from each other as from the Balkans) as Paraguay,[34] Israel,[35] the Netherlands,[36] and Nigeria.[37]

Prosecutorial strategy is also detached from local perceptions. It has been a practice of international tribunals to prosecute only those "most responsible" for crimes. The strategy derives from the belief that by indicting individuals (rather than whole collectives), the system counters the "attribution of collective responsibility for acts committing by individuals."[38] This in turn is thought to foster reconciliation and deterrence.

In practice, however, this theory breaks down. As an initial failing, it does not countenance the fact that local and international communities often differ on who they believe is most responsible. Consequently in the eyes of their local constituents, the courts have often prosecuted the "wrong people."[39] For instance, in the Balkans many victims assert that those "most responsible" for their suffering—and thus who should be in the international dock—were the middle-ranking officials who participated in violence, rather than the "big fish" brought before The Hague.[40]

The theory that focusing on the "most responsible" alleviates feelings of collective guilt also falters due to the emotion-laden nature of the crimes at issue. Especially when dealing with state crimes, history suggests that it is unreasonable to think that citizens are not somehow implicated when their leaders are prosecuted. At Nuremberg, some suggest that having Germans see the limited number of accused in the dock served as a "meaningful instrument in avoiding the guilt of the Nazis being ascribed to the whole German people."[41] However, the surveys discussed above and the fact that many convicted Nazis were released in order to curry favor with the German people suggest that the Allies knew—and, more importantly, the *Germans felt*—that all Germans were implicated in the proceedings.[42]

In Croatia, even if *Gotovina* was limited to the generals' personal roles in anti-Serb violence, every Croat "owns" their war for independence and consequently the guilty verdict is jointly felt. In Serbia the prosecution of former-

President Slobodan Milosević was viewed both within *and* outside Serbia as a clear indictment of the entire state.[43]

Finally, tribunal procedure has been unmoored from national practices, let alone traditions of target communities which has at times led some to completely reject verdicts.[44] For example, while plea bargaining is not formally a part of international judicial practice, it has been used by some prosecutors. At the ICTY, a plea bargain resulted in the conviction of Bosnian Serb Biljana Plavšić on charges of crimes against humanity. Though her plea allowed prosecutors to try more indictees, in Bosnia (where plea bargaining was unknown) many feel that no matter the practical benefits of Plavšić's deal, the shortened sentence she received was a perversion of justice. Sentences should reflect the gravity of the crimes, and not other factors. The vast majority of Croat and Muslim Bosnians—the victims of Plavšić's crimes—do not accept that justice was done in her case.

If people on the ground do not believe that justice has been done, their willingness to accept the decisions of a tribunal in that case, or others, will be limited.

Towards a Solution

People do not live scientifically-detached lives, especially in the wake of mass crimes. What those affected—both victims and perpetrators—often need is decidedly *un*scientific: an understanding of local psychology, not universalist rationality. This does not mean that the international system need give credence to the jingoism that may anchor people's beliefs about Srebrenica or Operations Storm. However, the international community must recognize that if it wishes to convince people to change core beliefs about themselves and their societies, it must speak to people as they are, not as it would like them to be.

To this end, breaking down the distance and scientific detachment between international justice and target populations is critical. In cases in which once-recalcitrant peoples have begun to reconcile their core internal views with external facts that contradict them, it has almost always been due to *local* developments. For example, for nearly thirty years after the Tokyo Trials' findings concerning the Rape of Nanking, most Japanese refused to accept the verdicts.[45] These views started to change in the 1970s when Japanese journalist Honda Katsuichi began investigating the event. Katsuichi's articles in *Asahi Shinbun*, followed by his book, *Journey into China*, were the first exposure most Japanese had to one of their own examining the Empire's exploits during the 1930s and 1940s.[46] Katsuichi's work helped catalyze a shift in public opinion.

Likewise in Germany, the distressing support for National Socialism in the years following Nuremberg was only reversed in the late 1950s. It was then that Germans themselves began to question the actions of the Third Reich and the wider German people's complicity in the regime's behavior.

Although a disturbing number of Serbs still doubt Serb complicity in Srebrenica, an inflection point toward broader acceptance came in 2005 when a Serb human rights campaigner, Nataša Kandić, presented a devastating video showing some of the killings.[47] That Kandić is a Serb made it much more difficult for hardliners to distrust her motives or the video's authenticity. In the wake of the tape's release, Serbia prosecuted several people involved in the genocide.[48]

Some posit that the delayed acceptance by Germans and Japanese, and begrudging acceptance of Serbs regarding Srebrenica, were only possible *because* of the international proceedings. The international trials softened resistance and allowed difficult conclusions to find root.[49] While this may be true, there is limited evidence that international trials are *necessary* to instigate such a domestic reconsideration. Indeed, in Germany's coming to terms, it is hard to isolate the impact of Nuremberg from the pressures imposed by the international community to ensure that Germany face up to the Holocaust. The early Denazificiation Directives and the domestic illegalization of Holocaust denial further muddy causation. In Rwanda there is little reason to think that the ICTR trials have impacted the mindsets of Hutus or Tutsis. And, in contrast, in the Balkans many assert that rather than promoting changed views, the very fact that the UN has allowed the former-Yugoslavs to "outsource" justice to the international community has delayed the domestic reckoning needed for any lasting reassessment of the past.[50]

Given the importance of local developments in catalyzing changes in critical beliefs, if international justice is to be successful it must account for local understandings and the strength of these understandings. Requests that lead people to challenge their own values and reassess their core beliefs about themselves and their communities must be locally cognizable.

There are a few key principles that can guide the organization of judicial processes in the wake of mass crimes that can help produce justice of an international standard *without* the alienation caused by international justice.

Domesticating the Bench

No matter the quality of judges sitting on the *international* bench, there is a limit to how well they can speak to a distressed people whose principal, enduring beliefs are questioned by their rulings. Asking judicial "outsiders" to confront such a sensitive issue is always going to be difficult. Adding domestic judges to the bench would seem a simple way to ameliorate this quandary. Domestic judges may not be as unbiased as "removed" jurists. Yet, in its practice of international law, the international community has long recognized, at times even welcomed, such judicial bias. In nearly all other aspects of international dispute settlement, parties are allowed to appoint some judges to hear their case.[51] Their implicit role is to bring local perspectives into the decision-making process, enlightening non-local jurists of the specific cultural and historical contexts critical to understanding the events at issue and the people those events impacted.[52] The relatively robust compliance received by tribunals with nationally-relevant jurists could be seen as testament, at least in part, to parties having felt heard in the process regardless the outcome.[53]

Expanding Temporally-Relevant Jurisdiction

International tribunals are temporally constrained—their jurisdictions limited to timeframes specified in their statutes. The ICTY's jurisdiction is from 1991 on; the ICTR's limited to calendar year 1994. Though practicalities make such limits understandable, such limits have *a priori* positioned the tribunals outside the frame of reference of many target communities. This is because in many communities undergoing or recovering from mass crimes history is alive in ways that limited temporal jurisdiction fails to accommodate.[54]

In the former-Yugoslavia, taking the 1990s violence out of its broader historical context meant that the ICTY could not examine the full spectrum of crimes that Balkan citizens believed deserving of justice. That some of these crimes were committed decades earlier make them no less raw for victims and their descendants. For instance, while the Serbs were the primary aggressors in the 1990s, in the 1940s Croatia's brutal *Ustasha* murdered hundreds of thousands of Serbs. *Ustasha* members were never prosecuted by the international community, a source of continuing Serb despair. While prior violence does not justify retaliation, there is a distinction between *excusing* violence partly instigated by an aggressor's historic victimization and *including* the past (as deemed relevant by target communities) in the judicial process. In short, Serbs—many of whom who have dismissed the ICTY as "selective justice"—would have found the ICTY more palatable if Croatia's World War II crimes were addressed alongside more recent Serb crimes. The same phenomenon is present in Rwanda where Hutus had clearly been the primary malefactors in 1994 but had been victimized by Tutsis in years prior.

Localizing Trials

The ultimate bridging of distance would be the localization of trials. There are difficulties with such a strategy, especially if justice is to be pursued while conflict continues. There are also concerns that international verdicts could nonetheless be superior to the ersatz justice that often emerges from local judicial action. Though the definitiveness with which many bemoan the potential of local justice is contradicted by many examples of "good" domestic justice in unlikely environments,[55] there are numerous variations of domestic justice that could mitigate such concerns further. For instance, there are a host of recent domestic judicial processes that have operated with aspects of international assistance. The International Judges and Prosecutors Program in Kosovo and the Supreme Iraqi Criminal Tribunal, are domestic processes that have proceeded with international oversight. Trials before such bodies have been imperfect, but they have usually proven to be more acceptable to local communities.

If justice is only pursued after violence, there are even more options. At Nuremberg it would have dulled claims of "victor's justice"—and perhaps eased German acceptance of the decisions—if those prosecuting Nazism were German. While the legal community in Nazi Germany had been co-opted by the Nazis, jurists and prosecutors could have perhaps come from among the dozens of German legal scholars and practitioners who Hitler had driven into exile.

Post-Saddam Iraq actually implemented a model similar to this. After Saddam was removed and the Coalition Provisional Authority (CPA) began to consider prosecuting the regime's crimes, the CPA soon realized that, outside the senior Iraqi judicial leadership, there were some judges and lawyers inside Iraq, and numerous others abroad, relatively free of Ba'athist sympathies.[56] The U.S. State Department developed a committee of expatriate Iraqi attorneys to assist in the redevelopment of Iraq's legal system, and the CPA created a Judicial Review Commission to vet sitting Iraqi judges. The result has been that prosecutions for the former regime's crimes have been conducted using primarily local professionals.[57] While there is debate regarding the conduct of some of the proceedings many observers believe that trials have been "fair."[58] As important, by bringing locals into the fold, these trials have given Iraqis ownership of the justice process and the reestablishment of rule of law. This is a far cry from the marginalization felt by many Balkan legal professionals.[59]

In the former-Yugoslavia, over the past several years Serbia, Bosnia, and Croatia have all developed their own domestic war crimes prosecution capacities, with varying degrees of international support. Unfortunately, the international community has not always allowed these capacities to be deployed. For instance, even as some of these courts have proven ready to stage high-level trials, many such proceedings have nonetheless been held in The Hague. For example, by the time of Bosnian Serb leader Radovan Karadžić's 2008 Belgrade arrest, Serbia had prosecuted several war criminals and was hearing cases against still more.[60] By 2009, even a plurality of the Bosniak minority in Serbia thought that the Serbian state was capable of adjudicating war crimes.[61] This was even more so by 2011 when Mladić was detained in Serbia. Regardless, both men were quickly extradited to The Hague.[62]

Much as if Nuremberg had been "Germanized," a Serb trial of Karadžić or Mladić would have been uniquely powerful. No matter the international results, they are unlikely to have as great an impact in the Balkans as a domestic taking account would have had.

Conclusion

The ICC has incorporated improvements that address some of the difficulties with alienated constituents faced by its predecessor courts. Some advancements are basic yet no less important. For example, for nearly the first decade of ICTY and ICTR operations, neither had budgets for outreach to target communities.[63] Although ICC efforts remain insufficient, it has nevertheless devoted significant resources to such outreach. Additionally, while the ICTY and ICTR have had jurisdictional preeminence the ICC's complementarity provision recognizes that the international system should only serve as a backstop to local proceedings.

While these changes are promising, the ICC is as hamstrung as its predecessors in other key ways.[64] Its temporal jurisdiction, for example, is fixed (limited to crimes committed from July 1, 2002 on) even if the crimes at issue before it—and certainly the roots of the conflicts—extend back decades. As of this writing, the ICC has opened investigations into seven situations, all in Africa: Uganda, DRC, Central African Republic, Sudan, Kenya, Libya, and Côte d'Ivoire. In nearly all of these cases, looking only at post-July 1, 2002, crimes will be viewed as arbitrary and incomplete by many on the ground. Indeed, as in the Balkans, doing so may be a recipe for establishing a perception of bias and perhaps immediately making whole sectors of societies alien to, if not enemies of, the process.[65]

Regarding the makeup of the bench, while in some ICC cases a judge from a country of interest to a case is a part of the appellate bench,[66] this is not true of most situations and is not true of any situations at the trial stage. Even if the ICC prosecutor is from Gambia, she cannot obscure the fact that the majority of judges hail from outside Africa. Concerns voiced throughout Africa about the ICC's supposed "colonial" designs make such a judicial lineup a distinct handicap as the Court seeks to persuade Africans to accept its rulings.[67]

The goal of prosecutions following atrocities is more than truth-telling. It is convincing others that truth has been found and successfully challenging long-held, potentially sacred beliefs people may hold about themselves and their societies. The ICC may yet become good at scientifically deriving truth but, for much the same reasons as its predecessor institutions, it will likely find it difficult to persuade those on the ground to accept it as such. The purposeful "distance" between court and people, and the fact that the ICC will also often be ruling on issues central to people's identities, promises to continue to hamper the ability of the international justice system to speak in a way that will encourage people to listen.

Notes

1. ICTY, *Prosecutor v. Ante Gotovina, et al.*, Case. No. IT-06-90-T, Judgment, para. 15 (April 15, 2011).

2. Anes Alic, "In Croatia, One Step Forward, Two Steps Back," *Radio Free Europe*, May 1, 2011.

3. Davor Butkovic, "Only 23% of Croats to Join the EU! 95% Considered the Verdict Unjust," *Jutarnji List* (Zagreb), April 16, 2011.

4. This chapter concerns the "pure" international tribunals at Nuremberg, Tokyo, the ICTY, the ICTR, and the ICC. These institutions have provided (or continue to provide) completely internationalized justice.

5. Parts of this section borrow from Adam M. Smith, *After Genocide: Bringing the Devil to Justice* (New York: Prometheus, 2009), 93-95.

6. Konrad H. Jarausch, *After Hitler: Recivilizing Germans, 1945-1995* (Oxford: Oxford University Press, 2006), 6.

7. Anna Merritt and Richard Merritt, *Public Opinion in Occupied Germany—The OMGUS Surveys* (Urbana: University of Illinois Press, 1970), 31.

8. Merritt and Merritt, *After Hitler*, 31.

9. Samuel H. Barnes, "The Contribution of Democracy to Rebuilding Post-Conflict Societies," 95 *Am. J. Int'l L.* 86, 90 (2001).

10. *Anti-Semitism in the American Zone: ODIC Opinion Surveys Headquarters*, Report Number 49 (March 4, 1947), UNRAA Archive/RG-17/55, 516.

11. Anna Merritt and Richard Merritt, *Public Opinion in Semi Sovereign Germany—The HICOG Surveys* (Urbana: University of Illinois Press, 1980), 7.

12. Frank Buscher, *The U.S. War Crimes Program in Germany, 1946–1955* (New York: Greenwood Press, 1989), 91.

13. *Judgment of the International Military Tribunal for the Far East*, Chapter VIII (Conventional War Crimes), 1012, 1015.

14. Nicholas D. Kristof, "Unmasking Horror: A Special Report; Japan Confronting Gruesome War Atrocity," *New York Times*, March 17, 1995.

15. Timothy Brook, "The Tokyo Judgment and the Rape of Nanking," *Journal of Asian Studies* 60, no. 3 (2001), 673-700.

16. "Bosnian Survivor tells UN of Mass Execution by Serbs," *Washington Times*, August 11, 1995.

17. ICTY, *Prosecutor v. Krstić*, Case No. IT-98-33-T, Judgment, para. 599 (August 2, 2001).

18. ICTY, *Prosecutor v. Krstić*, Case No. Case No. IT-98-33-A, Judgment, para. 21 (April 19, 2004).

19. *The Application of the Convention on the Prevention and Punishment of the Crime of Genocide (Bosnia and Herzegovina v. Serbia and Montenegro)*, 2007 ICJ General List No. 91, 108, para. 297.

20. Strategic Marketing Research, "Views on War Crimes, the ICTY, and the National War Crimes Judiciary," Organization of Cooperation and Security in Europe (OSCE) (April 2009), 86-88.

21. "Serbia Apologizes for Srebrenica Massacre," *Agence France Presse*, March 31, 2010.

22. Jovana Gec, "Serbia Offers Apology for Srebrenica Massacre," *Associated Press*, March 31, 2010.

23. Robert Marquand, "War Crimes: Is Serbia's Srebrenica Apology Genuine?" *Christian Science Monitor* (March 31, 2010).

24. United Nations, Preliminary Report of the Independent Commission of Experts Established in Accordance with Security Council Resolution 935, UN Doc. S-1994-1125 (1994).

25. International Crisis Group (ICG), "Rwanda at the End of the Transition," (November 13, 2002), 16-17.

26. In establishing the ICTR, the UN Security Council noted that it was "Convinced that . . . the prosecution of persons . . . would contribute to the process of national reconciliation" UNSC, Resolution 955, Preambular Section (November 8, 1994).

27. "Balkans: Croatia and Serbia Celebrate and Mourn a Rebellion," *Adnkronos International*, August 4, 2010.

28. "Make the Balkans an Area of Peace, Croatia tells Neighbors," *Agence France Presse*, August 5, 2010.

29. "Croatian Officials Remark on Serbian Leader calling 1995 Army Operation 'crime'," *HINA* (Croatia), *BBC Monitoring Europe*, August 4, 2010.

30. "Leaders Address Ceremony Marking Croatia's Victory Day in Knin," *HINA* (Croatia), *BBC Monitoring Europe*, August 5, 2010.

31. Alic, "In Croatia, One Step Forward, Two Steps Back."

32. Rachel Levy, "Alphons Orie: The Pragmatic Dutch Judge whom Karadžić Faces," *Deutsche Presse-Agentur*, July 30, 2008.

33. Adam M. Smith, *After Genocide*, 170.

34. Smith, *After Genocide*, 170.

35. Smith, *After Genocide*, 170.

36. ICTY, *Prosecutor v. Kordić et al*, Case No. IT-95-14/2-A, Decision on Appeal Regarding Statement of a Deceased Witness, para. 17, (July 21, 2000).

37. ICTY, *Prosecutor v. Erdemović*, Case No. IT-96-22-T, Joint Separate Opinion of Judge McDonald and Judge Vohrah, Appellate Chamber, 25-33, (October 7, 1997).

38. Cherie Booth, "Prospects and Issues for the International Criminal Court," in *From Nuremberg to The Hague*, ed. P. Sands (Cambridge: Cambridge University Press, 2003), 184.

39. Smith, *After Genocide*, 138-139.

40. Smith, *After Genocide*, 138-139.

41. Richard Goldstone, "Fifty Years After Nuremberg: A New International Criminal Tribunal for Human Rights Criminals'," in *Contemporary Genocides: Causes, Cases, Consequences*, ed. Albert Jongman (Leiden: PIOOM, 1996), 215.

42. Adam M. Smith, "Book Review: From Nuremberg to The Hague," 45 *Harvard Int'l L. J.* 572 (2004).

43. Nebojsa Bugarinovic, "Beograd: 37 Posto Gradana Smatra da Milosevic u Hagu Brani Srbiju I Srpski Narod," *Danas*, February 20, 2002. Cited/translated in: Emily Shaw, "The Role of Social Identity in Resistance to International Criminal Law: The Case of Serbia and the ICTY," Abstract, Berkeley Program in Soviet and Post-Soviet Studies (2003).

44. Patrick Robinson, "Rough Edges in the Alignment of Legal Systems in the Proceedings at the ICTY," 3 *J. Int'l Crim. Just.* 1037 (2005).

45. John A. Tucker, "The Nanjing Massacre: A Review Essay," *China Review International* 7 (2000), 321.

46. See Honda Katsuichi, *The Nanjing Massacres*, ed. Frank Gibney, Karen Sandness trans. (Armonk, NY: ME Sharpe, 1999).

47. Katarina Kratovac, "Video spurs Serbs to Admit Atrocities," *Pittsburgh Post-Gazette*, June 4, 2005, sec. A.

48. Nicholas Wood, "Video of Serbs in Srebrenica Massacre Leads to Arrests," *New York Times*, June 3, 2005, sec. A.

49. Susanne Karstedt, "The Nuremberg Tribunal and German Society," in ed. David A. Blumenthal and Timothy L.H. McCormack, *The Legacy of Nuremberg: Civilizing Influence or Institutionalized Vengeance* (Leiden: Martinus Nijhoff, 2008), 32-33.

50. Romesh Ratnesar, "The End of the Line," *Time*, July 9, 2001, 18

51. This applies to multistate commercial arbitration or state v. state litigation before the ICJ. See Smith, *After Genocide*, 107.

52. *Procès-Verbaux of the Proceedings of the Advisory Committee of Jurists*, 24th Meeting, July 14, 1920, 532.

53. See Aloysius P. Llamzon, "Jurisdiction and Compliance in Recent Decisions of the International Court of Justice," 18 *Eur. J. Int'l L.* 815 (2007).

54. Smith, *After Genocide*, 131.

55. Smith, *After Genocide*, Chapter 8.

56. Seth Stern, "Race for Order in Iraq," *Christian Science Monitor* (April 24, 2003), 11.

57. "Fact Sheet: Department of Justice Efforts in Iraq," States News Service, August 11, 2007.

58. Julia Preston, "The Trial of Saddam Hussein: Flawed but Fair Verdict," *New York Times*, November 5, 2006; Kingsley Chiedu Moghalu, "Saddam Hussein's Trial Meets the 'Fairness' Test," *Ethics and International Affairs* 20 (4) (2006): 517-525.

59. Jack Snyder and Leslie Vinjamuri, "Trials and Errors: Principles and Pragmatism in Strategies of International Justice," *International Security* 28 (2003): 22.

60. Smith, *After Genocide*, 326.

61. Strategic Marketing Research, "Views on War Crimes," 50, 55.

62. Ratnesar, "The End of the Line," 18.

63. A 2002 survey revealed that 87 percent of Rwandans were not well informed or not informed at all about the Tribunal. Eric Stover and Harvey Weinstein, "Conclusion: A Common Objective, a Universe of Alternatives," in ed. Eric Stover and Harvey Weinstein, *My Neighbor, My Enemy: Justice and Community in the Aftermath of Mass Atrocity*, (Cambridge: Cambridge University Press, 2004), 334. See also Smith, *After Genocide*, 148-149.

64. Smith, *After Genocide*, 197-198.

65. Smith, *After Genocide*, 204.

66. International Criminal Court, *Situation in Uganda: In the Case of the Prosecutor v. Joseph Kony, et al.* ICC-02/04 OA, February 13, 2009.

67. David Hoile, "International Criminal Court: Africa Beware of a New Legal Colonialism," *Independent* (Kampala), June 14, 2010.

Chapter 8

Justice, Peace, and Windmills: An Analysis of "Live Indictments" by the International Criminal Court

Peter J. Stoett

Does the International Criminal Court (ICC) contribute to the positive evolution of international law when it issues indictments for alleged war criminals which could cause more harm than good? Can we make an assessment of the utility of such "live indictments" ending the debate for once and all based on existing evidence? This chapter suggests not. It is too soon to make a definitive conclusion regarding the question of whether or not live indictments are making a significant contribution to ending the "culture of impunity." But it may be soon enough to at least suggest that precaution is the wiser part of discretion in such cases, and that live indictments challenge the legitimacy of the ICC, which risks becoming a legal pawn on the geopolitical chessboard, applicable to Libya in 2011 but not Syria in 2012, for example.

One of the more vexing questions is whether international criminal tribunals should pursue the indictment of accused criminals while the latter retain positions of power, or move beyond the goal of facilitating *post bellum* justice.[1] Absolute justice would demand indictments proceed regardless of their immediate consequences; yet if this delays the cessation of violence or increases its intensity, it is not a utilitarian choice unless it can be argued such indictments serve as able deterrents for similar potential crimes. This chapter examines the conceptual dilemma inherent in prosecutorial decision-making by international legal bodies, with brief reference to the case of Slobodan Milosević and more extensive analysis of the extant cases of Joseph Kony of the Lord's Resistance Army (LRA), President Omar al-Bashir of Sudan, and Bosco Ntaganda of the eastern Democratic Republic of the Congo (DRC). I conclude that an acute awareness of and respect for political circumstances *must* accompany judicial principle in order to preserve the legitimate utility of the ICC and avoid increasing human misery. The UN Security Council (UNSC) shares this responsibility.

The ICC is by nature politicized; it is a creature of politics as much as law, assuming the two are separable.[2] Part of its mandate is to seek peace and justice. It has a vital role to play in punishing and publicizing egregious crimes and reinforcing the importance of the principle of the responsibility to protect.[3] However, it is at risk of becoming little more than a paper substitute for stronger international action in cases of urgent threats to human security.[4]

The ICC is at a jurisdictional crossroads. There are genuine fears that extant arrest warrants have not only delayed active peace negotiations, but will compromise their long-term legitimacy. The use of international criminal tribunals to pursue foreign policy ends is nothing new. Yet the UNSC's use of the ICC remains an ongoing issue regardless of the cases it decides to put to trial. Without this structural contingency, however, it is unlikely that any of the permanent members of the UNSC would ratify the Rome Statute. Thus we are stuck in a conceptual bind between justice, peace, and self-interest. Ironically UNSC restraint might prove to be a silver lining.

Selectivity, Deterrence, and Counter-productivity

I do not propose to debate the proposition that former heads of state accused of *jus cogens* violations should be forced to stand trial, that the principle of *ratione materiae*[5] should be revived, or that leaders of rebel groups accused of atrocities should walk free after conflicts end. The focus here is on leaders who retain office or extra-legal power while violent conflict is proceeding or has recently ceased.

Nor is it even reasonable to continue to debate the validity of international legal responses to civil or intrastate wars. By their very nature, crimes against humanity, genocide, and war crimes encompass behavior during intra- and interstate wars. Arguments for the justification of military courts—invariably courts where "victor's justice" is practiced—have been put forth.[6] However, most human rights advocates are firmly in favor of non-military tribunals to deal with mass atrocities, though these tribunals invariably involve external actors. Grodsky believes that, while it is "human rights organizations or victims groups [which] frequently advocate for international trials . . . it is external state actors that are the engine for justice."[7]

The promises of even limited ICC success are enticing. Most notable is the possibility of ending (or mitigating) the infamous culture of impunity that has frustrated the quest to end mass atrocities. But we must also gauge the impact of indictments on the human security of those suffering most from the perpetuation of conflict, as well as their impact on transitional justice for post-conflict societies. Finally, if we are to take seriously the long-term prospects of the ICC's legitimacy, we must ask the political question of whether arrest warrants are increasing or decreasing the international reputational validity (even the very function) of the court itself. Most profoundly, we face a question of *who justice is for?* Is it victim-centered, or need it serve a broader purpose where international actors are involved?[8] While it is obvious that we have limited recourse to empirical evidence it is certainly not too soon to delve into these political questions.

Two opposing schools have formed. One argues that breaking international criminal law is a crime regardless of when it occurs, and justice must be sought immediately. The other argues that peace settlements should precede indictments if the latter threaten to prolong conflicts. It is difficult to escape this dichotomization of the issue. While the question of selectivity will always hound the quest for absolute justice in an asymmetrical system of sovereign states, and there will always be the possibility of counter-productivity in the joint pursuit of justice and peace, the indictment of sitting leaders is an especially thorny conundrum. Members of the international community intent on establishing the permanency and effectiveness of the ICC must face the sharp political limitations to its abilities.

The question of prosecutorial aggression is always a contentious one. Scheffer warned against the dangers of a self-initiating prosecutor who could "embroil the court in controversy, political decision-making and confusion."[9] Of course, there are serious impediments to such a development written right into the Rome Statute. The Pre-Trial Chamber must approve of any investigative course of action. Article 53(2)(a) through (c) permits the Prosecutor to refuse an investigation if it is not "in the interests of justice."[10]

Other stipulations leave little room for the Pre-Trial Chamber to reject a case where an indictment is bound to cause further human suffering, though the Chamber can in fact overrule a Prosecutor's decision *not* to proceed.[11] In effect, only the UNSC has the ability to do this, by its legal right to defer an investigation.[12] Thus the irony: in the absence of flexible thinking by the ICC, the UNSC is the only authority that can save the ICC from following its responsibility to prosecute. Yet the UNSC is obviously driven by the interests of its permanent members and is quite selective in terms of the cases if refers to the Court.

The ICC was conceived largely to dispense justice after crimes had been committed and to act as a mechanism for deterrence.[13] Leonard writes, the "legal precedent for some form of an international criminal court" is found in the Genocide Convention[14] which stipulates the need for punishment and prevention.

The move away from *ad hoc* tribunals was seen as an effort to establish permanency, overcome the stigma of victor's justice, and provide deterrence. The lack of a robust, coercive enforcement mechanism was always recognized as a potential problem, but the ICTY's record indicates a surprising level of compliance, despite complications.[15] Regardless, it would be phantasmal to assume an ICC arrest warrant will always result in an actual arrest. Within national jurisdictions, arrest warrants have a long pedigree. In international law they are rare indeed.

The logic of charging political leaders is sound; under international law leaders must be held accountable.[16] This does not mean indicting acting leaders is necessarily sound logic. Rather, I suggest three general criteria to discuss the legitimacy of live indictments: deterrence, non-selectivity (or impartiality), and the need to avoid counter-productive human security scenarios. I return to the deterrence argument in my conclusion; in brief the threat of international prosecution has certainly *not* put an end to the commission of mass atrocities by leaders during wartime. Akhaven, referring to the ICTY, has suggested that an immeasurable "general" deterrence effect can change the international culture of impunity, even if it fails in specific cases.[17]

With respect to the second criterion, one of the most compelling arguments for the ICC's establishment was precisely that *ad hoc* tribunals are almost by definition the children of victor's justice; their reliance on UNSC approval weakening the cardinal principle of sovereignty since some states are more equal than others.[18] Furthermore: "impartiality is critical in the context of the ICC because its absence constitutes the basis for the charge most frequently levelled at the court: that it will become a source of politicised prosecutions."[19] As with international intervention in general,[20] some selectivity is inevitable regardless of when charges are pressed. But there is also the strong need to counter selectivity at every corner.

The demand to avoid humanitarian counter-productivity is even more important, if we are to take seriously the first principle of intervention which is to do no greater harm than that which has already occurred. An indictment that leads to further harm of civilians is counter-productive. It challenges the legitimacy and accountability of prosecutorial discretion.[21] The temptation to punish the "international community" for issuing an indictment with deleterious consequences should not be ignored, and may construct a situation whereby international timidity about actual intervention is substituted by a legal measure which only invites more violence. This may be an idiosyncratic variable, contingent on the psychology and political support of the leader in question. Intuitively, however, with dictators and warlords it seems best to err on the side of caution.

The most high-profile live indictment from an international war crimes tribunal was most likely that of Slobodan Milosević. His case presents an interesting prelude to future ICC actions. The relative neatness with which the indictment played out probably emboldened the ICC to engage in its equally controversial indictment activity over a decade later. We should recall, however, that even after his forced retirement, there was little domestic support for the Milosević indictment. His transfer to The Hague followed intense American pressure, coupled with Serbia's urge to accede to the demands of the EU.[22] It is an error to view the indictment as a helpful precedent, even if it served the historic purpose of breaking the taboo against publicly indicting acting heads of state.

Northern Uganda and Joseph Kony

The main drama in Northern Uganda has unfolded as a battle between the government of Yoweri Museveni and the LRA, led in recent decades by Kony. The dominant narrative points to a long-standing conflict between north and south: "Broadly . . . all the insurgencies in northern Uganda, including that of the LRA, can be explained as an attempt by the people of that region to regain power that they lost in January 1986 following the victory of Museveni's NRM [National Resistance Movement],"[23] as well as a reaction to the violent aggression of the NRM.[24] The Acholi people have borne the brunt, living in terror of the LRA, a brutal rebel group that has made child abduction, child soldiering, and sexual slavery part of the politico-cultural landscape of Uganda. The Acholi have also been forced into squalid camps by the Museveni government.

Instead of providing adequate humanitarian intervention in the region, the Museveni government looked to the ICC. Museveni ratified the Rome Statute in June 2002,[25] and in December 2003 requested an ICC investigation.[26] It was hoped that an ICC indictment could encourage other governments to turn Kony over. More likely this was an effort to legitimize the Ugandan war against the LRA and justify the abysmal IDP situation, which had attracted international attention. Despite the fact that the Ugandan military is also responsible for a number of egregious crimes,[27] in October 2005 the ICC Chief Prosecutor issued a statement that "the crimes committed by the LRA were much more numerous and of much higher gravity."[28]

Kony's arrest warrant was released on July 8, 2005. Though much of the public version is redacted, it is clear the ICC believes it has an overwhelming amount of evidence against Kony and his top leadership for crimes against humanity and war crimes. Although the indictment did bring needed attention to the plight of the children of northern Uganda, it also prompted fears of LRA entrenchment and, even, retribution. Some expressed concern that the ICC was playing too closely to the government's hand to avoid compromising any post-conflict transitional justice.[29]

Calls for an ICC investigation met strong opposition long before this, especially from the Acholi Religious Leaders Peace Initiative (ARLPI). The ARLPI denounced the LRA indictments as counter-productive and were outspoken about the need to investigate government criminality. An Amnesty Act passed in 2000 offered LRA members amnesty if they lay down their arms. The Amnesty Commission argued that the ICC probe would make settlement impossible.[30] However, the amnesty offer to Kony appeared empty because of the ICC indictment. In June 2007 the government and the LRA reached an "Agreement on Accountability and Reconciliation," which affirmed that Uganda has the necessary formal and traditional justice mechanisms to address the abuses committed. Despite a February 2008 ceasefire and Museveni's public call for the ICC to rescind its warrant, the latter has steadfastly refused to do so.

An extensive debate exists about the legality and morality of the use of general amnesties to end conflicts.[31] Both Bassiouni and Scharf rejected the claim that amnesties should overpower the ICC's jurisdiction, before it was put to the test.[32] In the meantime the United States has sent one hundred armed military advisors to Uganda to help capture Kony, who is certainly not in Uganda. This could well result in a controversial form of summary justice *not* covered by the Rome Statute.

Kony's refusal to sign the Final Peace Agreement is often attributed to his demand that all forms of justice be denied, coupled with the fear that he would likely be killed by government troops if he attended a signing ceremony.[33] Viewed this way the warrant was just another contributing variable in Kony's decision-making process that quashed efforts to pursue the amnesty option. But it remains debatable whether or not the warrant issue prolonged the conflict. This would require irresponsible counter-factual speculation and discount the need to pursue much broader paths to establishing sustainable peace.[34] LRA attacks continue today in southern Sudan and elsewhere.[35] While many close observers predict that the "issuing of the arrest warrants seems to have ended all hopes of resolving the conflict peacefully,"[36] we have no way of knowing such resolution would have been achieved in their absence. But it begs the question: if ICC indictment of rebel leaders is so problematic, what can we expect with the indictment of active state leaders?

Darfur and Omar al-Bashir

April 26, 2010, the Sudanese government released the results of Sudan's first multiparty election in over two decades. Unsurprisingly, al-Bashir's ruling party won with 68 percent of the popular vote. Few observers accepted these results at face value. From the viewpoint of international criminal law, the results are a disaster, since the winner of the election has been publicly indicted by the ICC for years. It may be hyperbole to claim the election makes a mockery of international criminal law, but it certainly puts into comic relief the notion that arrest warrants are a serious threat to the culture of impunity.

The Darfur conflict has generated hundreds of thousands of refugees and IDPs, and resulted in over three hundred thousand deaths. While there are differing opinions about whether or not the government of Sudan and *Janjaweed* forces committed genocide, there is no question about the continued process of ethnic cleansing, rape, and pillage in the region.[37]

Hostilities in Darfur reached critical proportions in early 2003. The Government of Sudan launched a counterinsurgency campaign in March against rebel forces—the Sudan Liberation Army (SLA), the Justice and Equality Movement (JEM)—using air attacks and *Janjaweed* militias. These assaults escalated in frequency and violence during the summer, especially against the Fur, Masalit, and Zaghawa groups. The massacres formed the basis of the subsequent ICC indictment against al-Bashir.

As a consequence of the government's denial of food aid, famine took root in Darfur. In March 2005 the UN Emergency Relief Coordinator estimated that 180,000 had died from hunger and disease. The destruction of villages continued.[38] Widespread accounts of rape and the use of government air assaults have been widely reported. The 2005 International Commission of Inquiry Report on Darfur recommended the UNSC immediately refer the situation to the ICC, which it did in March 2005. The requisite UNSC Resolution was passed 11 to 0. Splintered rebel groups continued the conflict, and a Darfur Peace Agreement (signed in May 2006) further divided them. Sudan initially rejected the idea of a UN peacekeeping force for the region, but eventually accepted a "hybrid" UN-African Union (AU) force (UNAMID).

On July 14, 2008, ICC Prosecutor Luis Moreno-Ocampo submitted to the pre-Trial Chamber a sealed request for an arrest warrant against President al-Bashir. Soon after, the AU Peace and Security Council warned that the warrant's approval would undermine peace efforts and called on the UNSC to defer the ICC process. In August of 2008 the Organization of the Islamic Conference made a similar plea.[39] By February 2009, during talks in Doha between the Sudanese Government and the JEM, JEM leader Khalil Ibrahim promised the JEM would redouble efforts to overthrow the al-Bashir government if the ICC officially indicted him.

On March 4, 2009, four counts of crimes against humanity and two counts of war crimes (with genocide added later when the Appeals Chamber reversed the initial Pre-Trial decision in February 2010) were leveled against al Bashir. Sudan's immediate response was to expel foreign aid agencies from Darfur. Most resumed their work, but the temporary dislocation was disasterous.[40] In July 2009 a group of African parties to the Rome Statute called on AU member states not to cooperate with the ICC regarding the al-Bashir warrant. This nullified the *de facto* travel ban represented by the indictment. On September 16, 2010, the Arab League unsurprisingly announced its rejection of the indictment.

It is difficult to see where the advantage lies in the ICC's aggressive approach. Although its symbolic value may be difficult to measure, its immediate empirical impact was demonstrably counter-productive.

At the time of writing, al-Bashir hardly seems constrained by the indictment: The Sudanese government has begun a campaign of mass violence against the people of the South Kordofan state in the Nuba mountains, Sudan is in league with Kony's LRA in South Sudan and possibly Darfur, and al-Bashir has publicly visited a number of countries. Al Bashir continues to flaunt the ICC's ability to be the flagship for a new norm against impunity.

Eastern DRC and Bosco Ntaganda

The ICC indictment against Bosco Ntaganda may serve as a cautionary tale for those insisting on peace before justice, or it might be taken to indicate that the ICC's authority is really a function of its usefulness for the pursuit of self-interest.

Ntaganda has remained at large since his arrest warrant was unsealed in April 2008. Known as "The Terminator" for his time in Ituri (northeastern DRC), Ntaganda is accused of recruiting child soldiers while he was allegedly the deputy chief of the general staff of the Patriotic Forces of the Liberation of Congo (FPLC).

The Congolese government's political calculations have allowed Ntaganda to live openly in Goma. In 2004 he was offered a government post and a chance to sign a political accord. Ntaganda rejected the offer and instead joined the National Congress for the Defence of the People (CNDP), allegedly becoming its army chief of staff in 2006.[41] In addition to the crimes he has been charged with by the ICC, human rights groups allege he commanded troops responsible for rapes and massacres. He is also accused of killing a UN peacekeeper and breaking an arms embargo.[42] Since the ICC indictment Ntaganda allegedly commanded the massacre of an estimated 150 people in Kiwanja in November 2008. Yet, in a move that has become all too familiar in the DRC conflict, Ntaganda was appointed deputy commander of military operations in January 2009 following a peace agreement reached between the Congolese government and the CNDP. Ntaganda has since been implicated in assassinations and a number of other crimes.[43]

Immediately following the unsealing of the Ntaganda warrant, then-CNDP leader Laurent Nkunda announced that there was no possibility that he would turn him over to the ICC.[44] Despite being a party to the Rome Statute, and its willingness to cooperate with the ICC on other Ituri cases, the DRC government reneged on its legal obligation to arrest Ntaganda and hand him over to the ICC.[45] President Joseph Kabila has publicly defended his decision stating that he was placing peace, stability, and security in eastern DRC before justice.[46] According to Bueno, a decision on the part of the government to arrest Ntaganda could result in a resumption of hostilities with the CNDP.[47] At the same time the Ntaganda case represents an example where short-term peace has been given priority over long-term justice and the fight against impunity.

Kabila may have opted for peace, but it is a peace where accused war criminals continue to command attacks against civilians and pursue a course of intimidation and violence. One could suggest that the threat of the ICC warrant helped the Congolese government obtain a peace agreement since the latter promised Ntaganda immunity from it. However, this is hardly the purpose of the Rome Statute.

Discussion: Questions of Legitimacy

It is of course impossible to isolate the ICTY/ICC variable in the evolution of the conflicts taking place at the time of the issue of arrest warrants in any of the case studies explored in this chapter. Certainly, all four indicted leaders made subsequent reference to the indictments: they were aware of them, and naturally disparaged them; vowed to fight; and in one case immediately deployed a policy which increased abject human suffering. In the DRC case, the arrest warrant was not only denounced but publicly rejected in the name of peace.

While the issue of selectivity is not always raised in connection with these cases, it cannot be ignored. The ICTY has yet to try NATO commanders for bombing raids. The ICC Prosecutor's Office has not seriously investigated the actions of the Museveni government. With Darfur, the ICC did summon a rebel commander in connection with an attack on AU peacekeepers but the Pre-Trial Chamber rejected his prosecution in 2010. No one is under the illusion that the ICC does not have an understandable if counterproductive fixation on the Sudanese leadership. The DRC offers a wide variety of potential war criminal indictments and though it leads the pack in terms of ICC attention the surface has just been scratched. Again any court with such severe resource restrictions and structural constraints will be accused of selectivity. The question remains, however, whether engaging in limited pre-settlement indictments does not demonstrate an especially problematic form of selectivity, one which also presents the moral hazard of the option of a less robust interventional response,[48] or the possibility that the ICC itself plays an unwitting role in local power struggles.

Again, the argument here is not that state or rebel leaders are above international law. Indeed the Nuremberg Tribunal Charter explicitly rejected this defense, as do the ICTY, ICTR, and ICC Statutes. The ICTY made it quite clear in the so-called "Čelebići Judgment" that the doctrine of command responsibility "is ultimately predicated upon the power of the superior to control the acts of his subordinates."[49] Clearly Milosević had a strong hand in events in Bosnia and Kosovo. Nor should the tired debate over universalism and particularism (or relativism) be allowed to shield dictators from personal accountability.[50] They should be indicted by the ICC though, as the principle of complementarity suggests, it might be best to try them in their own states. But to indict them while hostilities are ongoing may be a premature step, one which may only alienate the ICC from the state actors it needs for the realization of its claims to justice.[51]

At the First Review Conference of the Assembly of States to the Rome Statute former Secretary General Kofi Anan's speech touched on the issue of peace versus justice. He suggested: "The Prosecutor's discretion in matters of timing, wisely used, is important. So is the sensitivity of those mediating conflicts to the legal obligations arising from the Rome Statute."[52] His speech goes back and forth on the issue much as most commentary seems to, with the realization that peace is made on the ground, but that justice needs to be as global as possible. While we would of course prefer to have justice and peace at the same time, events on the ground often conspire to make this impossible; tilting at this particular windmill is quite dangerous if it can result in humanitarian harm.

There is an uncomfortable irony at work here for peace and human rights activists. The ICC Pre-Trial Chamber cannot reject arrest warrants based on whether the pursuit of indictments will prolong or worsen conflict, or damage the legitimacy of the ICC. This is left largely to the UNSC, which has the option of indefinitely deferring investigations. Yet it is the UNSC (which includes non-party states) whose members are most likely to use the ICC for their own foreign policy ends, reinforcing the inevitable charges of selectivity. The question of live indictments and the UNSC has direct relevance and should be subject to greater scrutiny and scholarly analysis.

This was demonstrated in June 2011, when the Security Council asked the Chief Prosecutor to examine the case of former Libyan dictator Muammar al-Gaddafi. He in turn announced an arrest warrant for Gaddafi, his son, and his military intelligence chief, in the midst of an ongoing civil war. Though the indictments may have emboldened the rebels fighting his government, it borders on the absurd to assert that they could have induced Gaddafi to do anything but fight on. And the thorny question of selective judicial intervention resurfaces: where is the indictment for Syrian leader Bashar al-Assad? Indeed, one may be coming, but it is clear that political concerns and not criminality play the decisive role.

If the structure of the ICC within the international system produces this frustrating situation, ICC reform seems pragmatically impossible at this stage. Yet the ICC's mandate includes peace and security; it is inherently politicized and accepting this obvious fact may enable us to steer toward a more realistic understanding of its capacity, while building its legitimacy at the same time.[53] UNSC reform might by extension enhance ICC legitimacy but this is an unrealistic expectation. Ultimately we will need to craft creative policy responses to ongoing conflicts and seek to mitigate the potential damage to international justice efforts, which will never be non-political but could be less politicized than they have proven so far. As unpalatable as it may be to those who fight both injustice and the impulses of war and mass atrocities, judicial restraint may be necessary in order to promise a stronger international criminal law regime in the future; or to promote a "new political space for imagining and even concretizing the possibilities of a flexible form of global juridical power."[54]

And there are broader implications for the global human security agenda as well. Even guarded optimists such as Franceschet remind us that if "human security assumes linkages among complex forms of political causality—linkages that can mask the tough political and ethical dilemmas of world politics—legalism provides a solution that on the surface fixes all problems."[55] The argument can be made that justice demands immediate action regardless of the situation on the ground. This is certainly the view of the one Chamber Judge who permitted himself to be interviewed on the topic by one of my students in 2010. From a political perspective, however, it would seem that unless minimal political stability and a cessation of immediate violence is accomplished, justice will be unattainable. It is imperative that those bravely pushing forth the instruments of global justice keep this foremost in mind. The ICC has gained fame for its innovative character, and the strong role played by NGOs in the Rome process;[56] does it now risk assuming the reputation of how Harris-Short believes some regard the Convention on the Rights of the Child: "imperialist, inept, and ineffective"?[57]

Notes

1. I define "power" as authoritative decision-making capacity, regardless of the external legitimacy endowed on the position or entity of governance.

2. Steven Roach, *Politicizing the International Criminal Court: The Convergence of Politics, Ethics, and Law* (Lanham, MD: Rowman & Littlefield, 2006); Eric Leonard, *The Onset of Global Governance: International Relations Theory and the International Criminal Court* (London: Ashgate, 2005).

3. A. Bellamy, *Responsibility to Protect: The Global Effort to End Mass Atrocities* (Cambridge: Polity, 2009).

4. Thomas W. Smith, "Moral Hazard and Humanitarian Law: The ICC and the Limits of Legalism," *International Politics* 39 (2002):179.

5. Dapo Akande, "The Application of International Law Immunities in Prosecutions," in *Bringing Power to Justice? The Prospects of the International Criminal Court* ed. J. Harrington, M. Milde and R. Vernon (Montreal and Kingston: McGill-Queen's University Press, 2006), 51-53. Richard Wilson, "Prosecuting Pinochet: International Crimes in Spanish Domestic Law," *Human Rights Quarterly* 21, no. 4 (1999): 927-979.

6. Cedric Thornberry, "Saving the War Crimes Tribunal," *Foreign Policy* 104 (1996): 72-86.

7. Brian Grodsky, "International Prosecutions and Domestic Politics: The Use of Truth Commissions as Compromise Justice in Serbia and Croatia," *International Studies Review* 11 (2009): 689.

8. Marlies Glasius, "What is Global Justice and Who Decides? Civil Society and Victim Responses to the ICC's First Investigations," *Human Rights Quarterly* 31 (2009): 496-520.

9. David Scheffer, "Development at the Rome Treaty Conference" (transcript of a speech to the Foreign Relations Committee, U.S. Senate), *US Department of State Dispatch* 9 (1998): 3.

10. For more on this point see Claire de Than and Edwin Shorts, *International Criminal Law and Human Rights* (London: Sweet and Maxwell, 2003), 333-334.

11. Rome Statute of the International Criminal Court, Art. 53(3)(b), (1998).

12. De Than and Shorts, *International Criminal Law,* 326.

13. M. Cherif Bassiouni, *The Statute of the International Criminal Court: A Documentary History* (Ardsley, NY: Transnational Publishers, 1998

14. Leonard, *Onset,* 27.

15. However, there is a corresponding dispute over the source of this compliance; see Christopher Lamont, *International Criminal Justice and the Politics of Compliance* (London: Ashgate, 2010).

16. Ratner and Abrams, *Accountability,* 338.

17. Payam Akhavan, "Justice in the Hague, Peace in the Former Yugoslavia? A Commentary on the UN War Crimes Tribunal," *Human Rights Quarterly* 20 (1998): 781-782.

18. Anne Bodely, "Weakening the Principle of Sovereignty in International Criminal Law: The ICTFY," *International Law and Politics* 31 (2001): 417-471. *Ad hoc* tribunals have been established over the post-war years with fairly limited scopes. *Onset*, 47-48.

19. Allison M. Danner, "Enhancing the Legitimacy and Accountability of Prosecutorial Discretion at the ICC." 97 *Am. J. Int'l, L.* 510, 537 (2003).

20. Lori F. Damrosch, "The Inevitability of Selective Response? Principles to Guide Urgent International Action," in *Kosovo and the Challenge of Humanitarian Intervention: Selective Indignation, Collective Action, and International Citizenship*, ed. A. Schnabel and R. Thakur (New York: UN Press, 2000), 405-419.

21. Danner, "Enhancing Legitimacy."

22. Lamont, *International Criminal Justice*, 82-83.

23. Kasaija Phillip Apuuli, "The ICC and the LRA Insurgency in Northern Uganda," in *The Resolution of African Conflicts: The Management of Conflict Resolution and Post-Conflict Reconstruction,* ed. A. Nhema and P. Zeleza (Oxford: James Currey, 2008), 53; and Tim Allen, *Trial Justice: The ICC and the LRA* (London and New York: Zed Books, 2006).

24. Kayunga Simba, "The Impact of Armed Opposition on the Movement System," in *No-Party Democracy in Uganda: Myths and Realities*, ed. J. Magaju and J. Onyango (Kampala: Fountain, 2000), 112; and Frank Van Acker, "Uganda and the LRA: The New Order No One Ordered," *African Affairs* 103, no. 412 (2004): 335-357.

25. Barney Afoka, "Uganda," in *Unable or Unwilling? Case Studies on Domestic Implementation of the ICC Statue in Selected African Countries,* Monograph Series No. 141, ed. M. Du Plessis and J. Ford (Cape Town: Institute for Security Studies, ISS, 2008).

26. The ICC has jurisdiction over crimes committed after July 1 2002. Consequently many of the LRA's crimes fall outside of ICC jurisdiction. Human Rights Watch, "Stolen Children: Abduction and Recruitment in Northern Uganda," 15, no. 12, http://www.hrw.org/reports/2003/uganda0703 (accessed June 2010).

27. Apuuli, "The ICC," 56. Ironically Uganda acceded to the Optional Protocol on the Rights of the Child on the involvement of Children in Armed Conflict of 2000, and is party to the 1984 UN Convention Against Torture.

28. International Criminal Court, Office of the Prosecutor, "Statement by the CP on the Uganda Arrest Warrants," October 15, 2005, http://www.icc-cpi.int.

29. Adrian Di Giovanni, "The Prospect of ICC Reparations in the Case Concerning Northern Uganda: On a Collision Course with Incoherence?" *Journal of International Law and International Relations* 2, no. 2 (2006).

30. Allen, *Trial Justice*, 74.

31. B. Chigara, Amnesty in International Law: The Legality under International Law of National Amnesty Laws (London: Longman, 2002); Garth Meintjes, "Domestic Amnesties and International Accountability," in *Domestic Amnesties and International Accountability in International Crimes, Peace, and Human Rights: The Role of the International Criminal Court,* ed. D. Sheldon (Ardsley, New York: Transnational Publishers, 2000), 83-92.

32. M. Cherif Bassiouni, "Searching for Peace and Achieving Justice: The Need for Accountability," *Law and Contemporary Problems* 59 (1996): 9-28; Michael Scharf, "The Amnesty Exception to the Jurisdiction of the International Criminal Court," 32 *Cornell Int'l. L. J.* 507 (1999).

33. International Crisis Group, "Northern Uganda: The Road to Peace, With or Without Kony," *Africa Report* 146 (December 10, 2008).

34. Van Acker, "Uganda," 354).

35. "Ghosts of Christmas Past: Protecting Civilians from the LRA", Joint NGO Briefing Paper, http://www.oxfamblogs.org (accessed February 2011).

36. Apuuli, "The ICC."

37. Amanda Grzyb ed., *The World and Darfur: International Response to Crimes against Humanity in Western Sudan* (Montreal: McGill-Queen's University Press, 2009). While some described the violence as genocide, the report of the International Commission of Inquiry found that genocide had not occurred. Report of the International Commission of Inquiry on Darfur to the UN Secretary General (January 25, 2005), 4.

38. Julie Flint and Alex de Waal, *Darfur: A New History of a Long War,* 2d ed. (London: Zed, 2008), 145.

39. These events and dates are culled from various websites including www.iccnow.org, and www.timesonline.co.uk. (accessed December 2010.)

40. The UNSC was unable to arrive at a Resolution calling for Sudan to reverse this decision due to Chinese opposition.

41. Olivia Bueno, "Congo-Kinshasa: Lubanga's Missing Co-perpetrator—Who is Bosco Ntaganda?" September 15, 2010, http://allafrica.com/stories/201009170508.html.

42. Bueno, "Congo-Kinshasa"; Katrina Manson, "Exclusive: Congo War Indictee Says Directs U.N.-backed Ops," *Reuters,* October 6, 2010.

43. HRW, "DR Congo: ICC-Indicted War Criminal Implicated in Assassinations of Opponents," October 12, 2010.

44. Jacques Kahorha, "Congo DRC: Rebel Leader Refuses to Hand over ICC Indicted Deputy," Institute for War and Peace Reporting (2008).

45. HRW, "DRC: ICC's First Trial Focuses on Child Soldiers," January 22, 2009.

46. Sara Darehshori and Elizabeth Evenson, "Peace, Justice, and the International Criminal Court," Oxford Transitional Justice Research: Research Article 1, 2010, http://www.csls.ox.ac.uk/documents/DarehshoriandEvenson2010.pdf. (accessed February 19, 2011).

47. Bueno, "Congo-Kinshasa."

48. Smith, "Moral Hazard."

49. International Criminal Tribunal for the former Yugoslavia, *Prosecutor v. Mucić et al.* ("Čelebići"), Case No. IT-96-21-T, Judgment, para. 377 (November 16, 1998).

50. Ruti Teitel, "The Universal and the Particular in International Criminal Justice," 30 *Colum. Hum. Rts. L. R.* 285 (1998-1999).

51. As this problem applies to deterrence see De Than and Shorts, *International Criminal Law*, 341.

52. Kofi Annan, "Address by H.E. Mr. Kofi Annan" May 31, 2010, http://www.icc-cpi.int/iccdocs/asp_docs/RC2010/Statements/ICC-RC-statements-KofiAnnan-ENG.pdf (accessed March 16, 2012).

53. Roach, *Politicizing.*

54. Roach, *Politicizing,* 90.

55. Antonio Franceschet, "Global Legalism and Human Security," in *A Decade of Human Security: Global Governance and New Multilateralisms,* ed. S. MacLean, D. Black, and T. Shaw (Aldershot: Ashgate, 2006).

56. Philippe Kirsch and John Holmes, "The Rome Conference on an ICC: The Negotiating Process," 93 *Amer. J. Int'l. L.*2 (1999).

57. Sonia Harris-Short, "International Human Rights Law: Imperialist, Inept, and Ineffective? Cultural Relativism and the UN Convention on the Rights of the Child," *Human Rights Quarterly* 25, no. 1 (2003): 130-181.

Chapter 9

Should We Press the Victims?: Uneven Support for International Criminal Tribunals

Michael D. Thurston

In 2002, the Chief Prosecutor of the International Criminal Tribunal for Rwanda (the ICTR), Carla Del Ponte, pressured the Rwandan government to disclose files relating to internal investigations of RPF atrocities committed in 1994.[1]

In the summer of 2002, she met with Rwandan President Paul Kagame to discuss the disclosure of internal Rwanda Patriotic Front (RPF) files. Kagame refused to cooperate.[2] A year later, the UN Security Council (UNSC) passed Resolution 1503, officially stripping Ms. Del Ponte of her authority as Chief Prosecutor of the ICTR, unofficially ending this special RPF investigation.[3]

Until Resolution 1503, the Office of the Prosecutor was responsible for effectively prosecuting war crimes committed in both the former Yugoslavia and Rwanda. Resolution 1503 severed the Office of the Prosecutor into two, thereby dividing the Office's authority over the successful prosecution of these two conflicts.

Resolution 1503 is the most powerful example of the tension between international justice and politics. The tribunals have a primary responsibility for securing international justice; seeing that war criminals are efficiently and fairly prosecuted. Tribunals must also be cognizant of the domestic and international political arenas in which they operate. Kagame's refusal to cooperate with the

ICTR in the summer of 2002, and the international community's unwillingness to support the ICTR in its efforts to investigate RPF atrocities, highlights the fragility of international justice in this particular instance. However, the international community has shown surprising resolve in other instances. The ICTY, coupled with international pressure, has often been effective at overcoming Serbian political resistance. The willingness of the international community to back a tribunal in one instance, but to abandon and in fact remove the chief prosecutor in a second instance, is the puzzle that is at the heart of this chapter.

Existing Explanations

Transitional justice scholars tend to view interactions between international criminal tribunals and the societies in which they operate in at least two fundamentally different ways. Some learn toward having an idealistic view of international criminal tribunals. Scholars in this camp generally argue criminal tribunals have a lasting effect on domestic societies.[4] Moreover tribunals hold criminal leaders accountable,[5] strengthen the rule of law, assist in the preservation of the historical record, and contribute to social reconciliation.[6]

Other scholars view the relationship between criminal tribunals and domestic societies in a more complex and pragmatic manner.[7] This second grouping of scholars focus less on normative or desired long-term impacts of tribunals, and more on the dynamic relationships between domestic and international elites and international criminal tribunals.[8] This group emphasizes tribunal limitations, revealing how tribunals must rely on hostile local elites for documentary evidence and access to witnesses.

Exploring this second perspective in more depth, Peskin argues international tribunals must engage in two forms of trials: actual criminal trials and virtual or political trials.[9] The criminal trial is the public legal proceeding the tribunal was originally designed for. The virtual trial is where the tribunal competes for domestic and international support. The ICTY and ICTR engaged in two parallel struggles, convicting criminal defendants in a court of law, while convincing domestic and international actors of the legitimacy of their work and importance of cooperating at international and domestic levels.

Underlying Peskin's conceptualization is the notion the ICTR and ICTY are not simply legal institutions. They are also political institutions in the sense they both rely heavily on domestic cooperation to secure arrests and access to crime scenes and witnesses. International tribunals have no coercive methods for holding resistant domestic elites accountable.

Scholars have focused on how some post-conflict states attempt to interfere with criminal prosecutions. Subotic describes this process as "norm-hijacking." She illustrates how domestic elites in Serbia, Croatia, and Bosnia-Herzegovina make a show of publicly submitting to the ICTY's requests for arrests, documents, and access to witnesses and crime scenes, while these same elites privately foment resistance to the ICTY.[10] The hollow public compliance is a domestic strategy for appeasing international actors like the EU and UNSC while simultaneously creating domestic resistance to international intervention.[11]

Another component of this argument is that of prosecutorial discretion or the process by which a prosecutor selects who to prosecute, and what crimes to charge. This process involves subjectivity, applying the letter of the law to a given set of facts. The prosecutor will consider a number of different criteria when deciding who and what to prosecute, including limited resources, fairness, and the likelihood of securing a conviction.

The office of the Chief Prosecutor of the ICTY and the ICTR enjoys broad prosecutorial discretion.[12] This discretion is crucially important at the international level for at least three reasons. Prosecutorial discretion is synonymous with independence and impartiality, which is especially important for such highly visible trials. Second, resources are scarce, and an international prosecutor must judiciously decide which cases are worth pursuing.[13] Third, an unavoidable mix of political and legal considerations must be weighed, as these tribunals rely on the cooperation of international and domestic audiences.[14]

An alternative explanation is also worth briefly introducing here: EU conditionality and issue linkage. EU conditionality is the method by which the EU attempts to shape behavior of third-party states. Most commonly, conditionality refers to obligations and restrictions third-party states must abide by in order to join the EU. However, "EU conditionality is not limited to enlargement," and can additionally include positive and negative conditions relating to "trade concessions, aid, cooperation agreements, and political contracts."[15] At first, the EU tried to implement political and economic reforms in the Balkans with trade and financial aid.[16] During the late 1990s and into the early 2000s, the United States and the EU slowly began linking (issue-linkage) cooperation with the ICTY to EU membership.[17]

Rwanda: Genocide and the Creation of the ICTR

In April, 1994, the plane carrying Rwandan President Habyarimana was shot down. His death created the spark that ignited an already tense environment in Rwanda. Rumors had been circulating for months that Hutus were preparing to carry out the "final solution" of the ethnic Tutsi minority problem.[18] President Habaryimana's death provoked the Hutu into action.

Within twenty four hours of his death, the extremist Hutu-dominated government mobilized. Sensing the violence that was to come, "a vast majority of Tutsi fled their homes and sought refuge in central gathering places—churches, schools, hospitals, athletic fields, stadiums, and other accessible places."[19] However, Hutu forces, along with the Interahamwe youth militia, had already prepared for the mass killing of Tutsi. The violence affected the entire nation, and resulted in a large exodus of refugees. The exact number of Tutsi deaths is unknown, but scholars estimate anywhere from 800,000 to 1,000,000 Tutsi were slaughtered during the three month period.[20]

With the passage of UNSC Resolution 955 the ICTR was created. The ICTR was given authority over all war crimes that occurred in and around Rwanda from January 1, 1994, until December 31, 1994.[21] It was intended to not only confront atrocities committed during spring and summer of 1994 but was also "a diplomatic mea culpa, an act of contrition by the world's major powers to make amends for their gross failure to prevent or halt the massacres."[22]

Foreshadowing tension between the ICTR and RPF, Rwanda was in fact the only member of the Security Council to veto Resolution 955.[23] While RPF authorities believed an international criminal tribunal was necessary, they disagreed with the scope and strength of the tribunal.[24] Over time, RPF resistance to the ICTR continued to grow.

The ICTR was initially criticized because of its slow pace in indicting and bringing to trial suspected war criminals.[25] Also, the RPF government criticized some of the ICTR's legal outcomes.[26] Perhaps the boldest challenge to a functioning relationship occurred when the ICTR began investigating allegations of atrocities committed by members of the RPF and Rwanda Patriotic Army (RPA) members in the aftermath of the genocide. These investigations held potential to expose members of the RPF. Consequently the international community refused to back Del Ponte's special investigation. On August 28, 2003, the UN Security Council passed UN Resolution 1503, effectively stripping Prosecutor Carla Del Ponte of her authority over the ICTR.

Domestic Political Dynamics in Rwanda

The RPF inherited a decimated country in July of 1994: "In human terms, the toll was horrendous: about 1.1 million dead, 2 million refugees abroad, over 1 million internally displaced, tens of thousands of deeply traumatized genocide survives, and over half a million 'old caseload' (Tutsi) refugees returned in a chaotic fashion."[27] The institutional destruction was equally problematic. Almost the entire public infrastructure needed to be rebuilt.[28] During the period when the RPF was supposed to be putting the country back together, it was also engaging in large-scale reprisal killings. Between April and September, 1994, between 20,000 to 100,000 Hutu civilians were killed by the RPF.[29]

Since reclaiming the capital of Kigali in July of 1994, the RPF has steadily consolidated its political power. The RPA has harassed, intimidated, and even murdered Hutu elites, including teachers, clerics, judges, regional governors and local mayors.[30] Political consolidation continued into the early 2000s, with one human rights reporting: "The RPF wields almost exclusive military, political and economic control and tolerates no criticism or challenge to its authority. The opposition has been forced into exile, and anti-establishment speeches relegated to secrecy.[31]

This period of transformation has also been marked by intense violence. In 1997, for example, the RPA responded to a small insurgency in the northwest region of Rwanda by killing roughly six thousand Hutu civilians and returning refugees.[32] The RPA has also been implicated in widespread violence in the eastern portion of the Democratic Republic of Congo (the RPA was implicated in 1998, for example, in the disappearance of about 200,000 Hutu refugees in the Democratic Republic of Congo-DRC).[33] Systemic violence both inside and outside Rwanda has been conducted with near impunity. The RPF has received almost no international condemnation for its actions. Reyntjens describes the RPF's political strategy in this way: "the 1994 genocide has become an ideological weapon allowing the RPF to acquire and maintain victim status and, as a perceived form of compensation, to enjoy complete immunity."[34] Reyntjens notes the similarity between the pre-genocide and post-genocide regimes in Rwanda. "Both manipulated ethnicity . . . [and] both used large-scale violence to eliminate their opponents."[35]

International Political Dynamics in Rwanda

The United States became one of Kagame's first, and most lasting international partners. The United States was one of the first to recognize the new Government of National Unity on July 18, 1994.[36] The US provided the RPF with military assistance,[37] and financial aid.[38] Reyntjens describes the motivation behind this aid: "the RPF was squarely supported by 'Friends of the New Rwanda,' in particular the US, the UK and the Netherlands. These countries were not burdened by much knowledge of Rwanda or the region, and, driven by acute guilt syndrome after the genocide, they reasoned in terms of 'good guys' and 'bad guys', the RPF naturally being the 'good guys.'"[39]

The US has also made a point of publicly acknowledging its failure to stop the Rwandan genocide. In Addis Abada in December of 1997, Madeleine Albright, US Ambassador to the UN, apologized for the United States' failure to recognize genocide was occurring.[40] Later, on March 25, 1998, at a layover in Kigali, President Clinton also issued a formal apology for the United States' failure "to recognize the events of 1994 for what they were, as acts of genocide."[41] Despite at least one major exception (France supported the Hutu regime before and during the genocide),[42] the international community largely followed the United States' contrition, and support for Kagame.[43]

Implications of Victim Status

The timing of this victim label is difficult to establish. For a three year period, from July of 1994 until well into 1997, there was still doubt about whether the RPF could govern the war-torn nation. During that period, the RPF ruled

Rwanda with a coalition of other Hutu leaders. It was not until 1997 that large numbers of ethnic Hutus began withdrawing from government posts. This was the first wave of the RPF's consolidation of power. 1997 probably also coincides with the period when the international community openly began applying victim status to the RPF.

Many members of the international community were weary of being drawn into an internal conflict in a region of the world with little strategic value. In fact, in one interview, the Under Secretary of Defense for Policy Walt Slocombe was blunt in stating, "Nobody had any doubt as to what was going on in Rwanda, how awful the crisis was, the degree of the horror . . . [and] we believed we could not run around the world knocking off lousy governments."[44]

Simply put, the United States had no vital interests at stake in Rwanda. This still remains the case, and helps explain why the United States has not kept peacekeeping troops in Rwanda (the United States currently still has troops in Bosnia), why the United States has not pushed for electoral changes there, and why the United States had no interest in coercing the RPF regime to cooperate with the ICTR.

In *A Theory of Justice*, Rawls famously wrote, "Justice is the first virtue of social institutions."[45] The international community pursued this "first virtue" when it devoted more than half a billion dollars towards the ICTR. But this attempt by the international community to achieve justice in Rwanda is only partly successful. The atrocities that took the lives of tens of thousands of civilians remain beyond the ICTR's ability to investigate or to prosecute. Consequently, the ICTR's discretion has been significantly constrained.

Historical Background and the Balkan Wars of 1991-1995

The violence in the Balkans erupted as former member states of Yugoslavia declared independence. In the summer of 1991, Slovenia and Croatia declared independence, and a year later Bosnia-Herzegovina followed suit. I hope to illustrate how historical events of the period of 1991 to 1995 shaped the international community's perception of Serbia as an initial aggressor and of Croatia as both a victim and an aggressor.

Serbian aggression was first unleashed in Croatia. On July 26, 1991, "the first mass killing of Croatian civilians and soldiers by local Serb units happened in Kozibrod."[46] Fighting continued in other areas, including Slavonia, Banija, and Dalmatia. In September, the Yugoslav People's Army (JNA) launched a full scale attack in different portions of Croatia.[47] A three month siege of Vukovar, beginning in August of 1991, involved gruesome attacks on wounded prisoners at a farmhouse in Ovarca. Seven Serbian guards were charged and later convicted of killing 260 unarmed wounded soldiers there.[48]

Serbian aggression was also on display in Bosnia-Herzegovina. Violence occurred throughout the summer and fall of 1992. Serbian armed forces moved quickly, and "within a couple of months, hundreds of thousands of people were on the move, and several tens of thousands were killed; a clear majority of the dead and displaced was Bosniaks."[49] Detention camps were set up across Bosnia to house civilians and combatants alike. Entire villages were either destroyed or "cleansed" of their ethnic Bosnian or Croat populations.[50]

Violence continued into the summer of 1995 when Bosnian Serbs overran a UN "safe haven" in Srebrenica, resulting in the murders of approximately 8,000 unarmed Muslim boys and men. Srebrenica was described by one scholar as "a scene from hell, written on the darkest pages of human history," and became the only instance where the ICTY declared that genocide had occurred.[51]

The attempt to partition Bosnia was purposeful. Evidence presented during Slobodan Milosević's trial revealed that Belgrade financially supported the renegade regions of Republika Sprska (RS) and the Republic of the Serbian Krajina (RSK). Testimony during the trial of the former Krajina president revealed the RSK could not exist without financial support from Belgrade.[52] Similarly, a UN official familiar with the RS financial situation reported the RS had virtually no functioning economy and that 99.6 percent of the budget came from Belgrade credits, most of which was used to fund the military and police.[53] All of this reveals the clarity of Serbia's intentions: to establish an ethnically homogenized Serbian State.[54]

Following Bosnia's independence, Croat-backed forces also went on the offensive. In May of 1995 and in August of 1995, Croatia launched two massive counter-offensives (Operations Flash and Storm) against Serbian civilians and military forces still remaining within Croatian boundaries. The principal aim of these two offensives was to eliminate the Serbian population residing in Krajina. By one estimate, between 150,000 and 300,000 Serbians were forced from their Krajina homes in 1995.[55]

Creation of the ICTY and its Operation in Serbia

When the UNSC created the ICTY the international community was in complete confusion about how to respond to the crises unfolding in the Balkans. The United States had been reluctant to provide ground troops. NATO was still trying to find its post-cold war identity. Some scholars are critical of the international community's original intentions for creating the ICTY. Scharf and Williams believe the ICTY was a "public relations device," and the ICTY gave "breathing room for the other approaches of peace-building to succeed."[56] Rudolph argued the ICTY was "an economically and politically inexpensive means of responding to demands for international action."[57] From Rudolph's perspective, "the regime is a success whether or not it succeeds in bringing justice or alleviating ethnic conflict."[58]

During its first few years in existence, the ICTY struggled to survive. Very little money was actually set aside for personnel or equipment. By one account, "The General Assembly had approved a bare-bones $32 million budget that would cover only costs of renting office space, rental and contracting of equipment and services, and salaries and expenses for a staff of 108."[59] Once Richard Goldstone was selected as Chief Prosecutor, and the Tribunal had a space in The Hague, the ICTY struggled with the proper strategy for investigating and prosecuting suspected war criminals.[60] Today, it operates on an annual budget of roughly $100 million, and has a staff of about 1,000 employees,[61] and has evolved from a war crimes commission housed in Depaul Law School in Chicago to an historic institution that has contributed substantially to the development of international criminal law.

Domestic Political Dynamics in Serbia

Slobodan Milosevic and his SPS political party dominated domestic Serbian politics from 1987 until his removal from office in the fall of 2000.[62] He strongly opposed cooperation with the ICTY, while simultaneously creating a national narrative that cast Serbia as a victim of Croatia, Slovenia, and the Western powers (US, NATO, and the EU). Ramet and Matic describe the xenophobic environment when they write, "the entire popular culture, including folk concerts, popular fiction, sporting events, mass rallies, and of course the media, became obsessed with the idea that the Serbs had been wronged by the other peoples of Yugoslavia."[63]

President Kostunica, Milosević's successor, continued with this posturing of victimhood. As Del Ponte writes in her memoirs: "From Kostunica, there is little admission that Serbs ever did anything untoward during the wars, and much insistence that Serbs were, and always will be victims and only victims."[64] Using the claim of victimhood, Kostunica carefully aligned himself with Milosević's inner circle. One example was his protection of two top Milosević security officers: Chief of the General Staff Nebojsa Pavkovic, and the head of State Security, Rade Markovic.[65]

A culture of criminality also pervaded Serbian politics. Concerning civil society and the ICTY, there has been almost no public support for war crimes investigations in Serbia. Part of this is due to the manipulation of the media, and manipulation for political gain. For example, as late as 2005 almost 81 percent of respondents of a poll believed that Serbs were the most victimized ethnic group of the Yugoslav wars.[66] Massive resistance to the ICTY was also due to the wide scope of ICTY indictments in Serbia, including a former president, government ministers, military elite, opposition leaders, and other members of the political elite.[67]

International Political Dynamics in Serbia

The European Union's response to the unfolding crisis in the Balkans in the early 1990s was emblematic of the international community as a whole. According to Williams and Scharf, the EU's approach was "characterized by deep internal rivalries, a general lack of competence necessary to the handle the Yugoslav crisis, and a pull toward moral equivalence."[68]

The United States was equally unwilling to militarily confront Serbian aggression. During the early stages of the violence, the United States did not even devote basic resources to determine what was happening in the Balkans. Sharf and Williams again explain, "Despite a number of public statements condemning the atrocities in the former Yugoslavia, the State Department devoted almost no resources to the actual investigation of crimes and no resources to determining whether the atrocities were part of an attempted genocide."[69]

Implications of Serbia's Aggressor Status

Serbia's status as initial aggressor was probably firmly set in 1998 and 1999 when Serbia violently interfered in Kosovo. During this same time-frame of 1998 and 1999, the international community became much more supportive of the ICTY. For example, the Labor Party in the United Kingdom in 1996, led by Prime Minister Tony Blair, "took seriously the role and value of the Yugoslav Tribunal," and encouraged the ICTY to be more active with its prosecutions.[70] Because of Serbia's repeatedly failures to abide by its international agreements, the international community gave the ICTY free reign to investigate and prosecute Serbian leaders.

The ICTY's Interactions with Domestic Croatian Elites

The struggle between law and politics is also evident in the ICTY's interactions with Croatian authorities. Just like in Serbia, the ICTY faced stiff political resistance in Croatia between 1996 and 1999. This period was marked by the subversion of domestic law, and the exercise of power concentrated in the hands of President Franjo Tudjman and his close advisers. Lamont describes transferring indicted war criminals to the ICTY (during this period) as "arbitrary" and on an "ad hoc basis."[71] Although Tudjman transferred seventeen indicted Bosnian Croats to the ICTY, these were low-level officials "who lacked close political connections with the governing party or the president."[72]

Freedman argues that Croatian leaders exploited these atrocities: "Croatia sought international intervention. To do this it depended greatly on its victim status. In this it was helped by the presence of the international media, who soon picked up on images of distressed people being shelled out of their homes.[73]

Freedman argues Serbia's siege of an undefended Vukovar benefited Croatia's image as a victim. Rather than viewing the violence in a nuanced manner, "the net effect of the Croatian and Bosnian wars was to leave the Serbs stigmatized."[74]

With Tudjman's death in December of 1999, followed by his party's defeat in 2000, the success of ICTY investigations and prosecutions in Croatia changed. Ivica Racan was selected as prime minister of a coalition majority in the Croatian parliament in January. Stjepan Mesic was elected president in February of 2000. Both Racan and Mesic successfully campaigned on developing closer ties with Europe and the United States. This desire to integrate and to partner with the west, over time resulted in greater cooperation with the ICTY.

Relations between the ICTY and Croatian authorities improved significantly in November of 2003 with the election of Prime Minister Ivo Sanander. He favored a dramatic improvement in his country's interaction with the European Union and the United States. Cooperation with the ICTY was one substantial way in which he could he improve these relationships. Immediately after taking office, he contacted Chief Prosecutor Carla Del Ponte to explore ways in which his administration could better cooperate with the ICTY.[75] This cooperation resulted in the arrests of popular Generals Cermak and Markac in 2004, and General Gotovina in December of 2005.[76]

International Political Dynamics in Croatia

Just as in Rwanda, US reluctance to get involved in the deteriorating Yugoslav crisis in 1990 and 1991 only worsened the crisis. Without exploring US foreign policy in depth here, there was a general reluctance by the international community and the United States in particular to commit ground troops to the region.[77] Serbian-backed forces in Croatia and in Bosnia acted with growing impunity. The peacekeeping troops that were deployed in the region were spread too thin. The 15,000 UN peacekeeping forces deployed in Croatia in February, 1992 (with the task of preventing the outbreak of further violence there) failed to prevent further bloodshed. Operations Flash and Storm resulted in widespread killing and exodus of Croat-Serbs previously living in Krajina.

The EU was also generally ambivalent about how actively it should intervene in the Balkans. The EU provided economic aid and peacekeeping troops to the region, but it was not unified on how to stop the fighting. In fact, as a result of Croatia's Operation Storm in 1995, the European Union froze an EU Cooperation Agreement that it was attempting to entice Croatia with as early as 1994. The EU's priority during much of the 1990s was the stabilization of the Balkans, not the development of the ICTY.[78]

The EU benefited from the Croatian public's widespread desire to integrate. By one estimate in 2003, approximately 80 percent of Croats favored EU membership.[79] The EU used this desire to its advantage. Following General Bobetko's death in April, 2003, the EU, led by the UK, became much more explicit in its demands for Croatian cooperation with the ICTY.[80] Conditioning economic aid and EU membership benefits on cooperation with the ICTY proved pivotal. It was largely this conditional arrangement that supported the ICTY's broad investigative and prosecutorial mandate of confronting all war criminals who committed gross violations of international humanitarian law.

Implications of Croatia's Mixed Status

Croatia has benefited from its mixed status as both victim and aggressor. In fact, Serbia's strategy of portraying itself as a victim of Croatian and Bosnian aggression backfired. Not only has the international community had little sympathy for Serbia, but it has resulted in complete support for the rigorous prosecutions of Serbian atrocities. Also, Croatian leaders like Mesic and Sanander were adept at manufacturing international support. When General Bobteko was indicted, for example, Prime Minister Racan publicly denounced the indictment. Privately, Racan worked closely enough with the ICTY to convince the Tribunal to evaluate the General's ability to stand trial. The Tribunal's declaration that the General was physically unfit to stand trial was emblematic of Racan's political effectiveness.

The ICTY also demonstrated political astuteness. After major protests over the domestic indictment of General Norac, the ICTY wisely withdrew its interest in having him stand trial in the Hague. The extradition of the popular eighty-three year old General Bobetko could have been a public relations disaster. In another instance, the ICTY patiently pursued General Gotovina. The Tribunal allowed the Croatian leadership to generate political separation from this indicted war criminal. Eventually, the ICTY's patience paid off.

Conclusion

Certainly EU conditionality and issue-linkage was vital to securing Serbian and Croatian cooperation. Especially in Serbia, there was little public or elite support for cooperating with the ICTY. After years of cronyism and warfare, the Serbia infrastructure was badly in need of financial assistance. Foreign aid was only available if Serbia could in fact demonstrate that it was cooperating with the Tribunal.

One further explanation about the international community's varying support must be considered here. In the eyes of some members of the international community, Rwanda is of little strategic value. To repeat the words of US Under Secretary of Defense Walt Slocombe, "there was the very legitimate issue of we cannot intervene and no matter how nice the idea may have sounded, we believed we could not run around knocking off lousy governments."[81]

A similar calculation occurred in the Balkans in the early 1990s. The United States at first did not believe that it "had a dog in that fight," but then slowly the US became pulled into the conflict. As the Balkans are of significant interest to its European allies, the United States eventually provided air support and ground troops. The difference between Rwanda and Croatia and Serbia, then, is also a difference of American national interests.

But the issue of preordained outcomes must be examined in a different way. Judith Shklar reminds us that "law is a form of political action, among others, which occasionally is applicable and effective and often is not. It is not an answer to politics neither is it isolated from political purposes nor struggles."[82] The tension between realists and liberals ignores the reality that justice is a product of the political process. The fact that ICTR prosecutions were cut short is disconcerting. However, this should not cast doubt on the whole tribunal experience.

Notes

1. Carla Del Ponte and Chuck Sudetic, *Madame Prosecutor: Confrontations with Humanity's Worst Criminals and the Culture of Impunity: A Memoir*, English-language ed. (New York: Other Press, 2009), 224-225.

2. Ponte and Sudetic, Madame Prosecutor.

3. Ponte and Sudetic, Madame Prosecutor, 239.

4. C. L Sriram, "Revolutions in Accountability: New Approaches to Past Abuses," 19 *Am. U. Int'l L. Rev.* 429 (2003).

5. P. Akhavan, "Beyond Impunity: Can International Criminal Justice Prevent Future Atrocities?," *The American Journal of International Law* 95, no. 1, Symposium: State Reconstruction after Civil Conflict (2001): 14.

6. Diane Orentlicher, "Shrinking the Space for Denial: The Impact of the ICTY in Serbia," *Open Society Institute* (2008): 1-137.

7. Jumal Benomar, "Justice after transitions," *Journal of Democracy* 4, no. 1 (1993): 13.

8. Ellen Lutz and Kathryn Sikkink, "Justice Cascade: The Evolution and Impact of Foreign Human Rights Trials in Latin America," 2 *Chi. J. Int'l. L.* 1, 5 (2001).

9. Victor Peskin, *International Justice in Rwanda and the Balkans: Virtual Trials and the Struggle for State Cooperation* (Cambridge University Press, 2008).

10. Jelena Subotic, *Hijacked Justice: Dealing With the Past in the Balkans* (Cornell University Press, 2009).

11. Subotic, *Hijacked Justice.*

12. Hassan B. Jallow, "Prosecutorial Discretion and International Criminal Justice," 3 *J. Int'l. Crim. Jus.* 145, 147 (March 1, 2005).

13. L. Côté, "Reflections on the Exercise of Prosecutorial Discretion in International Criminal Law," 3 *J. Int'l. Crim. Jus.* 162, 175 (2005).

14. Del Ponte and Sudetic, *Madame Prosecutor*, 41.

15. H. Grabbe, "European Union Conditionality and the Acquis Communautaire," *International Political Science Review/ Revue Internationale de Science Politique* 23, no. 3 (2002): 250.

16. O. Anastasakis and D. Bechev, "EU Conditionality in South East Europe: Bringing Commitment to the Process," in *European Balkan Observer*, vol. 1 (presented at the South East European Studies Programme Conference, University of Oxford, 2003), 1-20.

17. Mathias Dobbels, *Serbia and the ICTY: How Effective Is EU Conditionality?*, EU Diplomacy Papers (College of Europe: Department of EU International Relations and Diplomacy Studies, June 2009), 9.

18. Linda Melvern, *Conspiracy to Murder: The Rwandan Genocide*, Revised. (Verso, 2006), 78.

19. A. J. Kuperman, "Rwanda in Retrospect," *Foreign Affairs* 79, no. 1 (2000): 96.

20. Kuperman, "Rwanda," 95.

21. Del Ponte and Sudetic, *Madame Prosecutor,* 69.

22. Del Ponte and Sudetic, *Madame Prosecutor,* 69.

23. P. Akhavan, "The International Criminal Tribunal for Rwanda: The Politics and Pragmatics of Punishment," 90 *Am. J. Int'l L.* 501 504-505 (July 1996).

24. P. Akhavan, "The International Criminal Tribunal for Rwanda." 505.

25. Del Ponte and Sudetic, *Madame Prosecutor*, 132-138.

26. R. Vokes, "The Arusha Tribunal: Whose justice?," *Anthropology Today* 18, no. 5 (October 2002): 2.

27. F. Reyntjens, "Rwanda, Ten Years on: From Genocide to Dictatorship," *African Affairs* 103, no. 411 (2004): 178.

28. Reyntjens, "Rwanda," 178.

29. Reyntjens, "Rwanda," 194.

30. Reyntjens, "Rwanda," 180.

31. *Rwanda at the End of the Transition: A Necessary Political Liberalisation*, Executive Summary and Recommendations (International Crisis Group, November 13, 2002), 3.

32. *Rwanda: Ending the Silence* (Amnesty International, September 25, 1997), 3.

33. F. Reyntjens, "Post-1994 Politics in Rwanda: Problematising 'Liberation'and 'Democratisation'," *Third World Quarterly* 27, no. 6 (2006): 1111.

34. Reyntjens, "Rwanda," 199.

35. Reyntjens, "Post-1994," 1113.

36. Reyntjens, "Post-1994," 97.

37. Reyntjens, "Post-1994," 97.

38. Reyntjens, "Rwanda," 179.

39. Reyntjens, "Rwanda," 179.

40. Waugh, *Paul Kagame and Rwanda*, 117.

41. Waugh, *Paul Kagame and Rwanda*, 118.

42. Andrew Wallis, *Silent Accomplice: The Untold Story of France's Role in the Rwandan Genocide* (I. B. Tauris, 2007), 25.

43. Peter Uvin, "Difficult Choices in the New Post-Conflict Agenda: The International Community in Rwanda After the Genocide," *Third World Quarterly* 22, no. 2 (April 2001): 182.

44. Jared A. Cohen, *One Hundred Days of Silence: America and the Rwanda Genocide*, illustrated edition. (Rowman & Littlefield Publishers, Inc., 2007), 145.

45. John Rawls, *A Theory of Justice: Revised Edition* (Oxford, UK: Oxford University Press, 1999), 3.

46. Marie-Janine Calic, "Ethnic Cleansing and War Crimes, 1991-1995," in *Confronting The Yugoslav Controversies*, ed. Charles Ingrao and Thomas Emmert (Purdue University Press, 2009), 121.

47. Mile Bjelajac and Ozren Zunec, "The War in Croatia, 1991-1995," in *Confronting The Yugoslav Controversies*, ed. Charles Ingrao and Thomas Emmert (Purdue University Press, 2009), 244.

48. Bjelajac and Zunec, "The War in Croatia," 249.

49. Bjelajac and Zunec, "The War in Croatia," 125.

50. Bjelajac and Zunec, "The War in Croatia," 126-127.

51. James Gow, *Triumph of the Lack of Will* (Columbia University Press, 1997), 273.

52. Human Rights Watch, *Weighing the Evidence* (December 13, 2006), 17.

53. Human Rights Watch, *Weighing the Evidence*, 18.

54. Gow, *Triumph of the Lack of Will*, 308.

55. Gow, *Triumph of the Lack of Will*, 129.

56. Michael P. Scharf and Paul R. Williams, *Peace with Justice? War Crimes and Accountability in the Former Yugoslavia* (Rowman & Littlefield Publishers, Inc., 2002), 91-92.

57. Christopher Rudolph, "Constructing an Atrocities Regime: The Politics of War Crimes Tribunals," *International Organization* 55, no. 3 (2001): 683.

58. Rudolph, "Constructing," 683.

59. Scharf and Williams, *Peace with Justice?*, 110.

60. Scharf and Williams, *Peace with Justice?*, 116.

61. John Hagan and Richard Levi, "Crimes of War and the Force of Law," *Social Forces* 83, no. 4 (2005): 1500.

62. Christopher K. Lamont, *International Criminal Justice and the Politics of Compliance* (Ashgate, 2010), 64.

63. Sabrina P. Ramet and Davorka Matic, *Democratic Transition in Croatia: Value Transformation, Education, and Media* (TAMU Press, 2007).

64. Del Ponte, *Madame Prosecutor*, 94-95.

65. *Serbia's New Government: Turning from Europe*, Europe Briefing (ICG, May 31, 2007), http://www.crisisgroup.org/en/regions/europe/balkans/serbia/b046-serbias-new-government-turning-from-europe.aspx.

66. Lamont, *International Criminal Justice and the Politics of Compliance*, 73.

67. Lamont, *International Criminal Justice and the Politics of Compliance*, 69.

68. Scharf and Williams, *Peace with Justice?*, 80.

69. Scharf and Williams, *Peace with Justice?*, 65.

70. Scharf and Williams, *Peace with Justice?*, 73.

71. Lamont, *International Criminal Justice and the Politics of Compliance*, 36.

72. Lamont, *International Criminal Justice and the Politics of Compliance*, 36.

73. Lawrence Freedman, "Victims and Victors: Reflections on the Kosovo War," *Review of International Studies* 26, no. 3 (2000): 343.

74. Freedman, "Victims and Victors," 344.

75. Lamont, *International Criminal Justice and the Politics of Compliance*, 41.

76. Lamont, *International Criminal Justice and the Politics of Compliance*, 41.

77. Gow, *Triumph of the Lack of Will*, 303-304.

78. Gow, *Triumph of the Lack of Will*, 52.

79. Pond, *Endgame in the Balkans*, 133.

80. Lamont, *International Criminal Justice and the Politics of Compliance*, 53.

81. Cohen, *One Hundred Days of Silence*, 145.

82. Judith Shklar, *Legalism: Law, Morals, and Political Trials* (Harvard University Press, 1986), 143.

Chapter 10

The ICC and R2P: Problems of Individual Culpability and State Responsibility

Benjamin N. Schiff

Following a burst of optimism about the institutionalization of international peace and justice norms that flowed from the end of the cold war in the 1990s, grim realization set in that while norms might be coalescing, human behavior wasn't necessarily improving.[1] The civil conflicts of the 1990s provoked efforts retrospectively to serve justice (through criminal tribunals) and to establish a multilateral framework for international efforts to prevent, reduce, or respond to, breakdowns of peace that could or did lead to mass atrocities.

To counter the potential impunity of perpetrators, to separate perpetrators from innocents, and to establish a record of the atrocities and help rebuild the rule of law, the *ad hoc* international criminal tribunals for the former Yugoslavia and Rwanda were empanelled while negotiations for an international criminal court gained momentum. Based on ideas about individual responsibility for war crimes, the Rome Statute of the International Criminal Court (ICC) was completed in July 1998. The Court came into being in 2002 with jurisdiction over genocide, war crimes, crimes against humanity, and the crime of aggression.[2]

Another set of ideas coalesced in an international organizational context, but without the establishment of a new organization. Inconsistent international responses to humanitarian disasters prompted a new conceptualization of justifications for international involvement in such crises. These were developed and articulated in a series of reports and in 2005 in the UN General Assembly Summit Outcome Document that included paragraphs about states' Responsibility to Protect (R2P).[3]

The ICC and R2P are related because both respond to atrocity crimes and the potential for such crimes. Because of different organizational forms, contrasting formal procedures, and different targets, the ICC/R2P relationship may be problematic. This chapter explores their conceptual overlaps and conflicts, contemplating whether there can be a stable division of labor between them. After first describing the development of the two institutions, the chapter considers the role each plays in events such as atrocity crimes. It describes how the ICC and R2P are supposed to be "triggered" and it examines common and unique hazards they face. The chapter then considers the possibilities for an ICC/R2P division of labor, and concludes that R2P is conceptually purer, though less institutionalized; that the ICC is organizationally more developed, though conceptually more problematic; that while R2P functionaries can make use of the ICC, the reverse is *not* the case; and lastly that ICC legitimacy is vulnerable to the Court's misuse by political actors and excessive posturing by its prosecutor.

Development of the ICC and of the Responsibility to Protect

The Rome Statute placed individual culpability for atrocity crimes into a new organizational bottle (the ICC) with a new label (the end of impunity). For R2P, the old wine of popular sovereignty, responsible government, and governments' ability to delegitimate themselves by atrocious behavior and thus warrant external intervention was relabeled but left in its existing organizational bottle (the UN and regional organizations). While the ICC and R2P imply that the international community can judge the legitimacy of states' exercise of sovereignty, they grew from different premises and apply contrasting means to arrive at their determinations.

International Criminal Court

The end of the Cold War and the wave of atrocities in the first half of the 1990s restored momentum to a long struggling international criminal law project. Explanations for the resurrection of the effort range from advocacy by international law enthusiasts and NGO activists to the more abstract idea of international normative convergence toward an identity based on people's agreement about the inhumanity of atrocity crimes.[4] In 1989 the UN General Assembly (UNGA) renewed a request dating back to the early 1950s to the International Law Commission (ILC) to develop a draft ICC statute. The Yugoslavia and Rwanda (1993, 1994) tribunals' statutes reflected the ILC's initial work, and in 1994 it delivered a draft ICC statute to the GA.[5]

At the July, 1998 ICC Statute final negotiations in Rome, the toughest bargaining sought to resolve the clash between Court independence and state sovereignty. In the last two days of the conference, crucial breakthroughs produced a document that commanded the support of the vast majority of participating states. An effort to delay final adoption was defeated and the Statute was adopted without a further vote.[6]

The negotiations produced a court with less than universal jurisdiction and with significant protections for state sovereignty. Nonetheless, the old idea of individual culpability for atrocity crimes was for the first time packaged in a standing operational organization with an explicit mandate to fight impunity. Under certain circumstances, individuals otherwise subject only to sovereign jurisdictions would be turned over to the ICC.

Responsibility to Protect

The concept of sovereignty as responsibility,[7] a notion long present in international discourse but not previously articulated in international declarations is the key idea of R2P. "Humanitarian intervention" was the old label,[8] and both justify what Anne Orford has termed UN "executive action."[9]

Sovereignty as responsibility proposes that sovereignty adheres to populations, not governments. A government's capacity to provide for its populations' welfare is a paramount criterion for recognizing its legitimacy; failures of such responsibility remove the government's right to non-interference and permit, even may compel, external involvement to protect the subject population. This R2P norm was articulated in the 2001 Report of the International Commission on Intervention and State Sovereignty,[10] and "was first seriously embraced in the doctrine of the newly emerging African Union, created in 2002, which. . . placed the emphasis, when it came to catastrophic internal human rights violations, not on 'noninterference' but on 'nonindifference.'"[11] The report delivered to UN Secretary-General Kofi Annan in December 2004 by his High-level Panel on Threats, Challenges, and Change recommended criteria for outsiders' intervention on behalf of victimized populations.[12] Annan then recommended embrace of the Panel's recommendations in his report, *In Larger Freedom: Towards Development, Security and Human Rights for All,*[13] which served as the basis for negotiations at the 2005 UNGA World Summit. The Summit Outcomes document reduced the frontal challenge to sovereignty by removing the intervention criteria, but retained the core idea of sovereignty as responsibility.

In the resolution, states demonstrated their reluctance to cede to international organizations discretion over intervention even while endorsing the potential legitimacy of such interventions. This small step was perhaps significant for articulating a coalescing international norm, but did little to reduce political factors involved in determining when outsiders should intervene in an atrocity situation or to assure availability of resources necessary for successful interventions.

Overlaps and Divisions

The ICC's Statute and R2P's three pillars[14] assert the existence of an international community sharing values that sovereign states are obligated to uphold. The ICC requires member states to investigate and punish individuals responsible for atrocity crimes, with due consideration to victims. The R2P norm requires states to recognize international responsibility when states fail to protect their populations, to ameliorate the conditions that can lead to atrocity crimes, to intervene when they are imminent or underway, and to help prevent recurrence.

ICC and R2P are both expressions of international engagement seeking to prevent and respond to atrocity crimes inside the traditional boundaries of Westphalian sovereignty.[15] Moreover they both establish external arbiters—ICC, UN Security Council (UNSC)—to determine if a government is fulfilling its obligations of sovereignty and thus whether it is legitimate.[16]

Under the Rome Statute the ICC is a permanent, single, legal-judicial organ to investigate, prosecute, and punish individual perpetrators of atrocity crimes when states fail to do so. Technically its judges can determine that a government is not upholding its responsibilities (to investigate and prosecute) upon evidence provided by the prosecutor. Deciding upon the adequacy of a state's justice system can be construed as a highly political act, superseding what has historically been considered an internal function of the state's body politic.[17]

The R2P norm asserts the appropriateness of engagement by external actors in a sovereign jurisdiction when the state has failed to protect its inhabitants. Despite repeated efforts to reorganize and consolidate the UN's role in peacekeeping and related operations from the early 1990s onward, states have avoided giving the UN a coherent, standing intervention capability.[18] Thus R2P does not have unitary organizational form. R2P can be carried out by the UN, regional organizations or other groups of states authorized by the UNSC, or the UNGA acting under the Uniting for Peace resolution.[19]

Once the UNSC or UNGA have authorized action, UN activities under the R2P rubric are coordinated by the Special Advisor to the UN Secretary-General, in collaboration with the Secretary-General's Special Advisor on Genocide. R2P operations are thus explicitly political, diplomatic, developmental, police and military, under the Secretary-General and the UNSC. By implication, the UNSC determines whether a government is legitimate based on fulfillment of its duty to protect its citizens. Unlike the ICC's legal-judicial basis, when the UNSC (or UNGA) acts, its decision is explicitly political. This political aspect can readily be seen in the differential responses to Libya where UNSC resolutions called for sanctions, an ICC investigation, and "all necessary measures to protect civilians under threat of attack" to protect civilians,[20] as opposed to inaction in the case of the Syrian civil war because of divided interests among the UNSC permanent members.

The Atrocity Sequence

The ICC is largely an organization for administering retributive justice. The more effective the ICC, the more it should deter future crimes. Proponents skeptical of the deterrent effect, or at least hoping to make it less necessary, seek to move the Court's focus to strengthening rule-of-law in vulnerable countries ("positive" or "pro-active complementarity"). This would obviate the need for the ICC's exercise of its retributive mission.[21] R2P, in contrast, focuses on a much wider span of the causal chain that ranges from situations in which atrocity crimes threaten to those in which they have taken place.

In their prevention modes, R2P and ICC "positive complementarity," may entail similar tasks: strengthening civil society, improving rule-of-law, and reducing government policies that can lead toward group polarization. R2P seeks to prevent, by political means, the breakdown of civil order. The ICC focuses on deterrence or prosecution of individuals who, in the context of such breakdowns, perpetrate atrocity crimes. Should all else fail, exponents of R2P hope to deter atrocities by threatening or implementing UNSC-authorized intervention. In contrast, the ICC can only deter with threats of prosecution.

R2P and ICC mechanisms are formally very different. R2P hinges on international political mobilization. The ICC depends (at least formally) upon legal judgment. Exponents of R2P might be charged with ineffectiveness, bias or hypocrisy, but cannot be charged with politicization because the relevant UN bodies' judgments are inherently political. The ICC can be charged with ineffectiveness, bias, hypocrisy *and* politicization because *it's not supposed to make decisions on a political basis* although some observers argue that consideration of political factors cannot be (and should not be) precluded from the ICC prosecutor's considerations.[22] Judicial decisions, nonetheless, are supposed to be based on law.

Principles and Triggers

The International Criminal Court

By establishing a court to investigate and try individuals responsible for atrocity crimes, the Statute established the first standing international forum with the authority, if not the power, under limited conditions to seek extraction of individuals from the sovereign jurisdiction of states and subject them to international legal process. The limits are important and are detailed in the Statute.[23] Under its doctrine of complementarity, the Court proceeds only when states with jurisdiction fail to investigate and prosecute an alleged perpetrator. The Court has the authority to decide when states are so failing. Thus, even with the complementarity proviso, it is an international forum that can, at least in theory, reach within the traditional boundaries of state sovereignty to address individual criminal perpetrators of "the most serious crimes of concern to the international community."[24] The process of ICC scrutiny begins when the Prosecutor determines that a "situation" exists in which statutory crimes appear to have been or are being committed. The Prosecutor has articulated various criteria for judging when the ICC should become engaged. These include the "gravity" of a situation. Analysis of the Prosecutor's and Pre-Trial Chambers' statement show that a consistent doctrine of gravity has, however, not yet emerged in Court practice.[25]

To trigger ICC involvement, atrocity crimes need to have taken place, led or commissioned by high-level functionaries of an organization that is or was itself deeply involved in commission of the crimes. Additionally, the Prosecutor has referred to the "impact of the prosecution in prevention of further crimes."[26] Pursuit of cases in a situation in which prosecution would be likely to *stop* ongoing criminality should have priority over a purely retrospective prosecution. Critics charge, however, that the reverse is also possible: prosecution might *increase* the likelihood of continued crimes. This argument has been pressed by critics of the Prosecutor's indictments of Sudanese President Omar al-Bashir,[27] and leaders of the Ugandan Lord's Resistance Army (LRA).[28]

Responsibility to Protect

The further back up the causal chain from actual atrocities that R2P-justified efforts can be initiated, the greater the likelihood of atrocities averted, but the harder it is to motivate international attention and to attribute non-events to R2P-connected action.[29] While some proponents strive to keep the definition of the threatened failures narrow and focus the time for engagement close to the period when atrocities are imminent (or underway),[30] broad and early measures could be undertaken to avert the social polarization that can eventuate in atrocity crimes. Measures could be undertaken to improve the egalitarianism of government development assistance, implement rule-of-law reforms, and develop the inclusionary political processes that are thought to prevent violent conflict. Some R2P advocates criticize detractors' claim that forceful intervention is at the core, arguing instead that prevention, response, and rebuilding must be addressed symmetrically to build a firm basis for peace; however, they also recognize the risk that broadening the concept too far can weaken the R2P norm.[31]

Edward Luck, the first Special Advisor to the Secretary-General on R2P, argues that the crucial first step for the implementation of R2P is "agreeing that something ought to be done when an important international standard has been breached in unacceptable ways."[32] This vision truncates the preventive end of the causal chain, but perhaps reasonably at a point where mobilization becomes possible because need is visible. The practical challenge is to motivate action and then coordinate implementation across relevant organizations. Although some critics worry that R2P could be used as a smokescreen for intervention, the larger problem in practice has been gaining a commitment to action.[33]

Overlap between the ICC and R2P

The ICC Prosecutor can act upon referrals from member states and the UNSC, and upon his/her own authority. The Prosecutor has in practice declared that he was watching events in a particular state or region, having received troubling information from states or non-governmental organizations. His declarations appeared intended to deter potential transgressors from committing or continuing to commit Statute crimes, actions that could be seen as political. The boundaries between legal-judicial actions and political stances are thus fuzzy and maybe unamenable to clarification. If R2P is invoked when atrocity crimes are imminent, it would be sensible for ICC scrutiny to follow. Conversely, when the ICC Prosecutor announces a preliminary investigation, it would seem sensible that the political organs of the international community should also take notice. There appears less a division of labor between R2P and the ICC than overlapping responsibilities triggered in different ways. Moreover, with different temporal focuses, R2P ideally becomes relevant prior to ICC scrutiny.

The ICC Prosecutor has a position and a platform from which to broadcast his concerns, whereas R2P is much more fluidly applied. It can be invoked by anyone, perhaps most significantly by the Secretary-General, the UN High Commissioner for Human Rights, states' representatives and/or NGO spokespeople. There is no formal R2P process, only Chapters VI, VII, and VIII of the UN Charter.

Hazards, Law, and Politics

The ICC and R2P share four hazards that detract from their multilateral efforts to transgress sovereignty. The hazards may be mitigated by wise judgment on the part of international decision-makers and by a division of labor between the implementing organizations of R2P and the ICC.

Moral Hazard

According to some critics, the ICC's involvement in ongoing conflict situations has reduced participants' inclination to make the compromises needed to bring peace, for example in the Sudan. Some observers assert that rebel groups hardened their negotiating positions in the false belief that the warrants issued against Sudanese President al-Bashir would result in international pressures to remove him from office or pressure him to compromise. Incentives to reach agreement were reduced and conflict was prolonged as a result.[34]

Critics also argue that President Yoweri Museveni of Uganda sought to use the ICC to his own advantage when he referred the Uganda situation to the Court, seeking internationai support against the LRA rebels. Consequently, LRA leadership may have become *less* inclined to reach an accommodation with the government because ICC indictments meant that they could not gain immunity from international prosecution.[35] Others argue that the *threat* of ICC warrants motivated some LRA members to accept government amnesties and that ICC pressure partially motivated LRA leaders to engage in negotiations.[36]

In both countries a counter-argument could be made that negotiations were bound to fail or not be respected by the indicted parties anyway. However ICC intervention cannot be shown to have helped resolve either situation. If actors in conflicts believe ICC involvement will aid (or hinder) their positions, their responses will be to manipulate the intervention. In both cases the ICC Prosecutor argued that political considerations were not part of his decision calculus. Unfortunately these claims do not withstand close scrutiny given the range of prosecutorial discretion and the lack of clarity in articulation of decision criteria. Opinions differ on the desirability and range of this discretion.[37]

The same kinds of gaming phenomena can be predicted with R2P, although evidence is as yet lacking. Potential internal opposition to a government may avoid internal conflict resolution efforts in order to bring international weight to its side, or a government might welcome international assistance in response to internal upheavals, due to limited government resources.

Political/Legal Distinction

Prosecutorial discretion is broad and the combination of limited resources and efforts to have the most positive effects mean that some calculus is being applied that is *more than* purely legalistic. Observers can thus argue over whether or not the Prosecutor is taking on too "political" a role in situation and case selection, and if some of his decisions have been taken more with an eye to their effects upon the ICC than on the situations themselves. William Schabas argues that there has so been no consistency in the Prosecutor's case selection, and that the criterion of "gravity" is of recent emergence and inconsistently applied.[38] In contrast, the Prosecutor has explained strategy in terms of a "sequential" process, pursuing individual cases to maximize the focus of resources on the worst suspected offenders.[39] Particularly in the Sudan case, the OTP was criticized by outsiders for an overly cautious approach that failed to pressure the government in ways that might have reduced commission of atrocity crimes.[40]

The problem could be minimized with the plain assertion that the ICC is an inherently political institution. However, this would not resolve the tensions between its legal logic and real implementation. It would place the OTP in a quandary. If situation and case selection is ultimately a question of judgment, and judgment is necessarily political, then the appeal to legal neutrality is spurious. The Court can only be as legitimate as interlocutors are willing to grant that the OTP is making wise choices. The wisdom of the OTP's choices, however, will not be evaluated from a judicial-legal standpoint, since the primary audience is states that will likely judge according to their own political calculi as long as any of their interests are engaged.

The ICC's preoccupation with Africa, and the OTP's decision *not* to pursue alleged crimes in Iraq or in Afghanistan, have led African leaders to question the Court's objectivity. This problem is exacerbated by the UNSC's referral power, exercised in the Sudan and Libya situations despite the fact that three of the five permanent members are *not* ICC parties. This creates the anomalous situation in which they can refer situations to the Court but are not subject to its jurisdiction.[41]

In contrast to the ICC, advocates of R2P make no claims that it is non-political. On the contrary, R2P is based explicitly on what advocates *hope* is a growing international acceptance of norms whose implementation depends upon the agreement of relevant organizations and states in order to trigger timely responses to human security threats.[42] There may be hypocrisy, but there is no direct contradiction. After all it is a legitimate state prerogative to act on political preferences. While the task of the ICC is somehow to accommodate inherently political decision-making with legal principles, the challenge for R2P is not rationale but mobilization.

Power Bias

The patterns of ICC and R2P involvement are uncomfortably shaped by power distribution at the international level. The ICC has been accused of focusing on Africa because of the unlikelihood of a negative international response to its involvement.[43] AU condemnation of the al-Bashir indictment and its quest for UNSC suspension of proceedings against Kenyan suspects demonstrated some states' disaffection for a purportedly neo-imperialist justice mechanism.[44] How an appearance of bias can be altered without basing situation and case selection on political balance considerations is unclear. What *is* clear is that the Prosecutor's judgment needs to inspire confidence among the ICC's interlocutors. One recent commentator suggested that, instead of continuing to hold the hard line regarding active ICC warrants, the Prosecutor should be willing to invoke the "interests of justice" to withdraw from a situation when it appears that involvement is exacerbating conflict.[45]

Responding to the recent conflict in Libya, the UNSC invoked both the ICC and R2P mechanisms; referring the Libyan situation to the ICC,[46] and authorizing the use of force to protect anti-government activists from government attacks.[47] The AU declared its support for the relevant UNSC Resolutions,[48] but then condemned as discriminatory the subsequent issuance of arrest warrants for Col. Moammar Gadhafi and two others.[49] As long as the ICC appears to be working closely in concert with the UNSC in a way that reinforces the international distribution of power, it will be suspected by detractors of being less than independent and another instrument of neocolonial power. R2P faces a similar threat.

Legitimacy Deficit

ICC and R2P legitimacy is in the process of construction. With no enforcement capacity, ICC warrants appear symbolic. States, including member states, have not acted consistently to implement their obligations to cooperate with the Court in arresting individuals subject to its warrants. Although some suspects have been turned over, others remain at large; notably al Bashir.[50]

Despite ICC member state Kenya's and the AU's demands that the UNSC suspend ICC proceedings in connection with Kenya's post-election violence of 2007-2008, the Court issued summonses to six leading Kenyan politicians and government officials.[51] When the UNSC failed to suspend, the Kenyans voluntarily proceeded to The Hague and submitted themselves to the Court.

The AU supported UNSC resolutions regarding Libya, but excoriated the ICC for issuing warrants for Libyan leader Gadhafi, his son Saif al-Islam, and intelligence chief Abdullah al-Sanussi. Despite Gadhafi's death in 2011, ICC Prosecutor Moreno-Ocampo declared his continued intention to gain transfer to the Court of the other two accused.[52] In October 2011, the US military Africa

Command announced deployment of 100 advisors to Uganda to aid in pursuit of LRA leaders.[53] This could be interpreted as support for the ICC's mission; however, it appears more easily explained as a US policy initiative in support of a friendly African government. ICC legitimacy might be enhanced were al-Isam, al-Sanussi, and Joseph Kony and his henchmen turned over to the Court for trial.

As a putatively legal-judicial institution, ICC legitimacy partially rests on its appearance of neutrality. The more the Court is used by the UNSC and/or tied closely to major power political interests, the less it will appear to be an independent judicial body. The Sudan and Libyan referrals could be seen as evidence of the growing legitimacy of the Court as a judicial adjunct to the UNSC. However they could also be seen as exercises of great power control. The more politically selective the Court's decisions appear, the harder it will be to argue that objective justice is being dispensed.[54]

The R2P norm suffers from a similar crisis of legitimacy. Rather than being consistently invoked as a response to evaluations carried out by the Human Rights Council or special representatives of the UNSC, its invocation has been uneven. For example, the UNSC acted quickly to thwart the recent attacks perpetrated by the Libyan government, but did not even put the large-scale killings perpetrated by the Sri Lankan government in 2009 on its agenda.[55]

An ICC/R2P Division of Labor?

Since conditions that lead to questions about the abdication of a state's internal responsibility to protect begin *before* the commission of atrocity crimes, R2P should be invoked *before* ICC announcement of an investigation. In practice, however, ICC scrutiny often *precedes* citation of R2P or takes place in its absence. ICC determination that a conflict "situation" appears to fulfill criteria for jurisdiction implies that individual crimes have taken place that should have been addressed by state authorities. If states have failed in this regard and atrocity crimes have taken place, the ICC should be involved, but R2P should already have been implemented.

If the OTP routinely issues warnings, either R2P is failing at the domestic and international level, or the OTP is overzealous. The milder and earlier form of Court involvement in potential conflict situations would move the ICC into territory that its Statute does not denote. Such assistance would more properly fall into the bailiwick of R2P-stimulated development assistance missions or aid organizations to which the ICC could provide expert advice or codes of best practices.

So far it appears that there is no coordination or division of labor between the ICC and organizations seeking to apply R2P. R2P has been invoked[56] as a direct cause of action, although it is possible that the spirit of R2P is behind more international involvement in domestic upheavals than is apparent from official declarations. Mobilization around R2P remains nascent, its advocates hoping it will be extended with practice and success.[57] But even though it is seldom invoked and faces low levels of institutionalization, R2P has the virtue of logical consistency.

The ICC, in contrast, is formally a non-political organization. The scrutiny of the ICC should be triggered when crimes under its Statute appear to be taking place *regardless* of a separate international determination of the state's legitimacy. Unfortunately, the Prosecutor often has to make political and pragmatic decisions rather than purely legalistic ones. The best the Court can do is to substitute good political judgment for putatively non-political judgment in situation and case selection and public pronouncements. The actions of the Prosecutor are key.

In theory there should always be R2P action before an ICC investigation. R2P initiatives prior to, or obviating, ICC involvement would enhance R2P without undermining the ICC. On the other hand, ICC findings of judicial failures in the absence of actions under R2P will discredit the organizations that should be implementing R2P.

The ICC is a new organization still finding its balance between legal-judicial formalism and the pragmatic requirements of operating in a political arena. R2P is a new normative structure whose proponents seek to bring order to the multiplicity of international efforts to prevent and respond to atrocity crimes, and whose operatives still struggle to mobilize international action. So far there is neither a division of labor nor coordination between the two. They are two institutions with overlapping purviews that both run legitimation risks and have unrealized potential to be mutually reinforcing. They are also newcomers to international society that may yet be brought into coordination as a result of officials' and states' accumulating experience and developing practice.

Notes

1. I thank Ms. Catherine Minall for her assiduous and constructive research assistance.

2. Following agreement on definitions and a set of other agreements at the Review Conference of the Parties to the Rome Statute in June, 2010, jurisdiction may be exercised over aggression at the earliest in 2017. For contrasting views on the outcome, see Claus Kreb and Leonie von Holtzendorf, "The Kampala Compromise on the Crime of Aggression," 8 *J. Int'l Crim Just.* 1179 (2010) and Beth van Schaak, "Negotiating at the Interface of Power and Law: The Crime of Aggression," (September 2010), http://works.bepress.com/beth_van_schaack/2/ (accessed July 27, 2011).

3. Anne Orford, *International Authority and the Responsibility to Protect* (Cambridge University Press, 2011).

4. On NGOs, see Michael Struett, *The Politics of Constructing the International Criminal Court: NGOs, Discourse, and Agency* (Palgrave Macmillan, 2008); on universal jurisdiction and an international cosmopolitan identity, see Adeno Addis, "Imagining the International Community: The Constitutive Dimension of Universal Jurisdiction," *Hu-*

man Rights Quarterly, Vol. 31, No. 1 (February 2009): 129-162; on the role of international lawyers and legal experts in the growth of international criminal law, see Martti Koskeniemi, *The Gentle Civilizer of Nations: The Rise and Fall of International Law 1870-1960* (Cambridge University Press, 2001).

5. ILC, "Draft Statute for an International Criminal Court," in *Report of the Commission to the General Assembly on the work of its 46th session* 1994 Volume II, Part Two (United Nations, 1996) 20-73.

6. Hans Peter Kaul, "Special Note: The Struggle for the International Criminal Court's Jurisdiction," 6 *Eur. J. Crime Crim. L. & Crim. Just.* 364, 373 (1998); Schiff, *Building*, 72.

7. Francis Deng, Sadikiel Kimaro, Terrence Lyons, Donald Rothchild, and I. William Zartman, *Sovereignty as Responsibility: Conflict Management in Africa* (Brookings, 1996).

8. Luke Glanville, "Ellery Stowell and the Enduring Dilemmas of Humanitarian Intervention," *International Studies Review* Vol. 13, No. 2 (June 2011): 241-258.

9. Orford, *International Authority.*

10. ICISS, *The Responsibility to Protect* (International Development Research Centre, Canada, 2001), http://www.iciss.ca/report-en.asp (accessed July 28, 2011).

11. Gareth Evans, *The Responsibility to Protect: Ending Mass Atrocity Crimes Once and For All* (Brookings, 2008), 44, citing the 2000 Constitutive Act of the African Union, article 4(h).

12. *A More Secure World: Our Shared Responsibility*, Secretary-General's High-Level Panel on Threats, Challenges and Change, (2004), http://www.un.org/secureworld/ (accessed July 27, 2011).

13. Secretary-General of the United Nations, *In Larger Freedom: Towards Security, Development and Human Rights for All*, A/59/2005 (2005).

14. (a) States are obligated to protect their own populations, (b) the international community is committed to help states carry out this responsibility, (c) all are responsible to respond when a state is failing to provide such protection. UN General Assembly, *Implementing the Responsibility to Protect, Report of the Secretary General,* A/63/677 (2009), 8-9.

15. Alex Bellamy and Paul Williams, *Understanding Peacekeeping,* 2d ed. (Polity, 2010), 4.

16. On this point, see Orford, *International Authority.*

17. Orford, *International Authority.*

18. Bellamy and Williams, *Understanding Peacekeeping*, chapters 4-5.

19. UN General Assembly Res. No. 377 A (V) (1950).

20. UN Security Council Res. No. 1970, UN Doc S/RES/1970 (2011).

21. William Burke-White, "Proactive Complementarity: The International Criminal Court and National Courts in the Rome System of International Justice,"49 *Harv. Int'l. L. J.* 53 (2008).

22. Kenneth Rodman, "Is Peace in the Interests of Justice? The Case for Broad Prosecutorial Discretion at the International Criminal Court," 22 *Leiden J. Int'l L.* 99 (2009).

23. Rome Statute of the International Criminal Court, Art. 12-13, 15-17, http://untreaty.un.org/cod/icc/statute/romefra.htm (accessed July 27, 2011).

24. Rome Statute, Preamble.

25. For analysis of ICC prosecutorial and judicial criteriain "gravity" determinations, see Mohamed M. El Zeidy, "The Gravity Threshold Under the Statute of the International Criminal Court," 19 *Crim. L. Forum* 35 (2008).

26. "Statement of the Prosecutor of the International Criminal Court, Mr. Luis Moreno Ocampo to the U.N. Security Council Pursuant to UNSCR 1593(2005)," June 14, 2006, 2, cited in El Zeidy, "The Gravity Threshold," 43.

27. See Julie Flint and Alex de Waal, "Case Closed: A Prosecutor Without Borders," *World Affairs* (Spring, 2009).

28. Kasaija Phillip Apuuli, "The ICC Arrest Warrants for the Lord's Resistance Army Leaders and Peace prospects for Northern Uganda," 4 *J. Int'l Crim. Just.* 179 (2006).

29. Alex Bellamy, "The Responsibility to Protect–Five Years On," *Ethics & International Affairs*, 24, No. 2 (2010): 164.

30. Gareth Evans, "The Responsibility to Protect: An Idea Whose Time Has Come and Gone?" *International Relations*. 22, No. 3 (2008): 283-298.

31. Evans *The Responsibility to Protect,* 64-69.

32. Edward Luck, "The Responsibility to Protect: Growing Pains or Early Promise?" *Ethics and International Affairs*, Volume 24, No. 4 (Winter 2010): 5.

33. Luck, "The Responsibility to Protect," 6.

34. Sarah Nouwen, "Complementarity in practice: Critical Lessons for R2P," presentation to symposium The International Criminal Court and the Responsibility to Protect: Synergies and Tensions, University of Helsinki, Dec. 3-4, 2010. On this point see also Jack Snyder and Leslie Vinjamuri, "Trials and Errors: Principle and Pragmatism in Strategies of International Justice" *International Security* Vol. 28, No. 3 (Winter 2003-2004): 5-44.

35. Schiff, *Building,* 201-204.

36. Nick Grono and Adam O'Brien, "Justice in Conflict? The ICC and Peace Processes," in *Courting Conflict? Justice, Peace and the ICC in Africa,* ed. Nicholas Waddell and Phil Clark (Royal African Society, 2008), 14-19.

37. For contrasting views see Margaret deGuzman, "Gravity and the Legitimacy of the International Criminal Court," 32 *Fordham Int'l L. J.* 1400 (2009), and Kenneth Rodman, "Is Peace in the Interests of Justice? The Case for Broad Prosecutorial Discretion at the International Criminal Court," 22 *Leiden J. Int'l L.* 99 (2009).

38. William Schabas, "Prosecutorial Discretion v. Judicial Activism at the International Criminal Court," 6 *J. Int'l Crim. Just.* 731 (September, 2008).

39. ICC, "Statement by Luis Moreno Ocampo to the Press Conference in relations with the surrender to the Court of Mr. Thomas Lubanga Dyilo," The Hague, (March 18, 2006).

40. *Amicus curiae* briefs to PTC from Antonio Cassese and Louise Arbour, 2006, as cited in Schiff, *Building*, 237-239.

41. Ramesh Thakur, "International Criminal Justice: At the Vortex of Power, Norms and a Shifting Global Order," (Pretoria: Institute for Security Studies, 2011, forthcoming) 24-24.

42. International Coalition for the Responsibility to Protect, http://www.responsibilitytoprotect.org. Regarding norm diffusion, see Martha Finnemore and Kathryn Sikkink, "International Norms and Political Change," *International Organization* Vol. 52, No. 4 (Autumn, 1998): 887-917.

43. Ramesh Thakur, "International Criminal Justice,"19.

44. African Union, "On the Decision of the Pre-Trial Chamber of the ICC Informing the UN Security Council and the Assembly of the State Parties to the Rome Statute About the Presence of President Omar Hassan Al-Bashir of the Sudan in the Territories

of the Republic of Chad and the Republic Of Kenya," Press Release No 119/2010, www.africa-uion.org (accessed July 27, 2011).

45. William Schabas, "Britain, France Flirting with letting Gaddafi Avoid Prosecution by the ICC," (July 28, 2011), http://humanrightsdoctorate.blogspot.com/ (accessed July 28, 2011).

46. UN Security Council Res. No, 1970 (2011).

47. UN Security Council Res, No, 1973 (2011).

48. Ban Ki-Moon, "Letter dated 16 May 2011 from the Secretary-General addressed to the President of the Security Council," S/2011/307 (May 17 2011).

49. CBC News, "Gadhafi Indictment Hinders Peace: African Union," July 2, 2011.

50. See for example, Xan Rice, "Omar al-Bashir Tarnishes Kenya's Landmark Day," *Guardian,* August 27, 2010, http://www.guardian.co.uk/world/2010/aug/27/omar-al-bashir-war-crimes-kenya (accessed July 27, 2011).

51. *Daily Nation*, "Kenya Petitions UN Organ to Delay Trials," February 10, 2011.

52. *Reuters*, "ICC Prosecutor May Bring Libya Rape Charges," November 9, 2011 http://af.reuters.com/article/topNews/idAFJOE7A80CK20111109 (accessed November 11, 2011).

53. Africom Public Affairs, "Text and Fact Sheet: US Support to Regional Efforts to Counter the Lord's Resistance Army," October 15, 2011, http://www.africom.mil (accessed November 11, 2011).

54. Louise Arbour, "The Rise and Fall of International Human Rights," Joseph Hotung International Human Rights Lecture 2011 at the British Museum (April 27, 2011), www.crisisgroup.org/en/publication-type/speeches/2011 (accessed July 27, 2011).

55. Louise Arbour, "The Rise and Fall."

56. Bellamy, "The Responsibility to Protect."

57. As Luck argues, R2P may be a less-than-half-full-glass gradually and unevenly filling, "The Responsibility to Protect: Growing Pains or Early Promise?" 5.

Part II

Case Studies

Chapter 11

The Tokyo War Crimes Trial

Yuki Takatori

The Tokyo War Crimes Trial, officially known as the International Military Tribunal for the Far East (IMTFE), was the longest war crimes trial following World War II, opening on May 3, 1946, and concluding on November 12, 1948. The model for the IMTFE Charter was the Nuremberg Charter. Unlike the latter, a product of the 1945 London Conference, the former was drafted by members of the American prosecution team and promulgated as an executive decree by General MacArthur, Supreme Commander for the Allied Powers (SCAP). The tribunal held jurisdiction over (a) crimes against peace, (b) conventional war crimes, and (c) crimes against humanity. Only persons suspected of committing crimes against peace, the so-called "Class A" (or, major) war criminals, were tried in Tokyo.[1]

Shortly after signing of the Instrument of Surrender on September 2, 1945, SCAP ordered the arrest of war crimes suspects. Overall, more than one hundred suspects of eight different nationalities[2] were taken into custody before the year's end. On December 6, 1945, Joseph B. Keenan, head of the American prosecution team, arrived in Tokyo.[3] Two days later, SCAP established the eleven-nation (Australia, Canada, China, France, India, the Netherlands, New Zealand, the Philippines, Soviet Union, the United Kingdom, the United States) International Prosecution Section (IPS), whose primary responsibility was the investigation and prosecution of Class A war crimes suspects. Keenan was appointed head of the IPS.

The criminal law of modern Japan was modeled after Continental (specifically, German) law, and most Japanese defense attorneys were not familiar with the Anglo-Saxon court procedures to be used at the trial. Thus, MacArthur's office requested Washington to select qualified personnel. The Judge Advocate General's office promptly agreed, and on March 19, 1946, the office "advised that arrangements were being made to send fifteen defense attorneys, principally civilians."[4] Naturally, the defendants looked upon the Americans with distrust at first. However, as they later watched them lock horns with the prosecutors and the judges in pursuit of a fair trial, despite being hamstrung by inadequate financial resources, many of them were deeply struck by their defenders' indefatigable and professional advocacy.

The IPS wished to prosecute only those suspects who it had a high likelihood of convicting and to limit their number to a manageable one. To this end, it formed an executive committee whose purpose was to deliberate on whom to indict and on what charges. Within a month, after about a dozen meetings, the committee had drawn up a list of potential defendants and forwarded it to the associate prosecutors for their approval. The final list of twenty-eight defendants was made public on April 29 and the arraignment was held four days later.

During the preliminary hearings, the defense submitted two motions: one demanded that President Webb excuse himself because he had been a member of an Australian team investigating Japanese atrocities in New Guinea; the other challenged the jurisdiction of the tribunal, arguing that, as Japan had surrendered under the terms of the Potsdam Proclamation, which mentioned only conventional war crimes, not "Crimes against Peace," and as SCAP was bound by that Proclamation, it was in consequence exercising a power it did not legally possess.[5]

The trial had begun with twenty-eight defendants: two died during the proceedings due to illness; of the remaining twenty-six, one was acquitted by reason of insanity, one was sentenced to seven years in prison, one to twenty years, sixteen to life imprisonment, and seven to death by hanging. MacArthur upheld every sentence; after an unsuccessful attempt by several of the defense lawyers to persuade the US Supreme Court to issue a writ of *habeas corpus*, the executions of the seven condemned were carried out in the early hours of December 23, 1948.

The Tokyo War Crimes Trial left behind a legacy of controversy in the years that followed, fuelling debates among historians that continue today. In this chapter I address the controversies associated with the following subjects: crimes against peace, crimes against humanity, biological and chemical warfare, the failure to prosecute the emperor, and clemency and parole.

Crimes against Peace

In its spirit and content, the charge of "Crimes against Peace" was a judicial novelty, one which some jurists, national leaders, and participants in the London Conference had misgivings. Traditionally, "war crimes" meant conventional war crimes, that is, any killing in violations of the laws and customs of war. Prior to the tribunal, the general consensus among jurists was that wars were neither just nor unjust, and, whether in self-defense or as a means of conquest, war was a legal exercise of sovereignty. Though some theologists and idealists had long denounced war on moral grounds as the ultimate crime against mankind, the prevailing theory held that political reality could not allow morality to intervene in the pursuit of national interest.

A final point needs to be made in relation to crimes against peace: it cannot be assumed judges, prosecutors, and defense lawyers were in agreement about the definition of "aggressive war." Neither the Nuremberg Charter nor the IMTFE Charter defined "aggression." In passing judgment on Japan's war, the bench circumvented the issue stating: "[w]hatever may be the difficulty of stating a comprehensive definition of war of aggression, attacks made with the above motive cannot but be characterized as wars of aggression."[6] Imagine, in the above passage, the substitution of the phrase "non-consensual sex" for "war(s) of aggression" and "sex" for "attacks made."

Crime against Humanity: Forced Labor and "Comfort Women"

At Nuremberg, the charge of crimes against humanity took center stage as an independent count in the indictment;

> Namely, murder, extermination, enslavement, deportation, and other inhumane acts committed *against any civilian* before or during the war, or persecution on political, racial or religious grounds in execution of or in connection with any crime within the jurisdiction of the Tribunal, whether or not in violation of the domestic law of the country where persecuted. [*emphasis mine.*][7]

In Tokyo, it was almost an afterthought, conjoined with conventional war crimes. In the IMTFE Charter, the phrase "against any civilian" is missing. This omission had the effect of placing outside the jurisdiction of the Tokyo court all Japanese nationals, whose lives and activities had constantly been intruded upon by Gestapo-like *kempeitai* officers empowered to incarcerate anyone upon the slightest provocation, or the mere hint of suspicious conduct. It also meant the exclusion of inhabitants of former Japanese colonies. In the original draft of the indictment, crimes against humanity included crimes committed against the Korean population, which had been a colony of Japan since 1910. However, the IPS soon realized that including colonial subjects as victims of war crimes would breed an enormous peril: four member nations of the tribunal and the IPS (Great Britain, the Netherlands, France, and the United States) were suzerains, and it could not risk the possibility, however remote, of colonization itself becoming the subject of prosecution, thereby implicating several of the organizers of the tribunal in the very crimes that Japan was being tried for.

Consequently, the scope of the indictment had to be narrowed so as to exclude any inhumane acts committed against the "Imperial Subjects" of Korea. While this alteration might have saved the prosecution from a very embarrassing situation, it abandoned many Koreans (and Taiwanese) who had endured bureaucratized slavery and forced prostitution, and conveyed to the Japanese people the impression that what had been done was not criminal. By tampering with the definition of crimes against humanity, the Tokyo War Crimes Trial essentially acquiesced in colonialism.

Most of the victims of forced prostitution, the so-called "comfort women," wished to take their dark secrets to the grave as a consequence of the social stigma attached to the sexual relations they had engaged in against their will. Their long silence was finally broken when a Japanese government official flatly declared for the record, during a diet session in June 1990, there had been no formal involvement in the matter. This denial motivated three former Korean comfort women to come forward and file a lawsuit against the Japanese government, demanding an apology and compensation. Their stories led a Japanese college professor to search archives of the National Institute for Defense Studies, where he uncovered official papers that survived the post-surrender wholesale destruction of documents and proved beyond a reasonable doubt Imperial Japanese Armed Forces directed the establishment of military brothels ("comfort stations") and recruitment of comfort women from Japan, Korea, and China. Faced with irrefutable evidence of crimes against humanity, the government pledged to get to the bottom of the matter, only to find out, to their chagrin, that not only the Army, but also the central government (by its issuance of identification cards and certificates), had a part in the institutionalization of sexual labor.

Gradually, the disgraceful history of government-sponsored sex slavery began to be recognized as part of the larger problem of war-related violence against women. Due partly to the revelations of mass rape and forced pregnancy in the former Yugoslavia, there arose a renewed interest in Japan's comfort women among human rights activists outside East Asia. So serious and significant was the issue, that the UN Special Rapporteur on violence against women, submitted a special report in which it was recommended that the Japanese government (1) acknowledge that comfort stations were set up by the Imperial Army in violation of international law, and make a public apology in this regard, (2) pay compensation to the victims, and (3) make a full disclosure of documents. In response to mounting external pressure then Prime Minister Murayama Tomiichi made a statement expressing the nation's "profound and sincere remorse and apology" and its resolve to "fulfill its responsibility for the wartime comfort women issue." Soon thereafter, the Asian Women's Fund (AWF), a non-profit foundation, was established.[8] While reparation recipients have expressed their gratitude to the Japanese government, and to all those who supported them in their efforts, they are far outnumbered by women who, considering the AWF to be neither appropriate nor adequate, have refused to accept any atonement money to this day. Central to their objection is that, because the AWF is funded mostly by donations from private citizens, not by the government, the latter's legal responsibility is obscured.

There were other equally determined victims, including Chinese civilians and Allied prisoners who had been transported to Japan, against their will or lured by false promises to relieve domestic labor shortages. Consigned to coalmines, construction sites, ports and the like they labored with little respite under the most oppressive working conditions. When those who had been so clearly exploited came forward to claim the compensation they believed to be long overdue, what transpired bore a striking resemblance to the sequence of events that took place in the comfort women case. Initially, the Japanese government denied the existence of a report which the Ministry of Foreign Affairs had allegedly compiled in March 1946, titled *An Investigative Report on the Working Conditions of Chinese Laborers*. However, the Japan Broadcasting Corporation (NHK) located the only existing copy, preserved in the Tokyo Office of the Overseas Chinese Association. The report's meticulous recording of victims' names, birthplaces, work places, causes of deaths, etc., spoke eloquently of the harsh day-in and day-out circumstances of their servitude to Japanese companies. The discovery of this self-incriminating document resulted in a flood of lawsuits, mostly brought by Chinese victims.

Biological and Chemical Warfare

One of the most severe criticisms of the prosecution regarded its decision not to try members of Unit 731, a detachment of the Japanese Army that engaged in biological and chemical warfare in Northern China.[9] The founder of this detachment was Major General Ishii Shirō, who, having toured Europe and America in the late 1920s, returned with the conviction that modern war could not be won without scientific knowledge and that biological and chemical weapons would be the most powerful and effective products of such expertise.

Allegations that the Japanese developed and used biological and chemical weapons had surfaced, and had been reported to the US government, even before the war had come to a close. General Ishii and Lt-General Kitano Masaji, the Unit's second-in-command, were allowed by MacArthur's office to hold discussions with each other prior to being interrogated by Dr. Norbert Fell and Lt-Colonel Arvo T. Thompson of the US Chemical Warfare Service,[10] so that there would be no inconsistency between their stories. Ishii was even allowed to visit Camp Detrick (Fort Detrick) and lecture there on his findings. The installation's researchers, who had been eager to set up a line of communication with his men, embraced him as a "colleague." Far from being disgusted, these scientists heaped lavish praise on Ishii's unethical experiments of the most revolting nature.[11]

All these arrangements were made because the US government, convinced of the likelihood of military confrontation and the possibility of biological warfare with the Soviets, had already decided to grant immunity to Ishii and his men in exchange for the data he could provide on human experiments, some of which had been conducted on American prisoners of war. More than 3,000 Chinese, Russians, Koreans, and Americans suffered at the hands of Unit 731, which destroyed its victims, referred to euphemistically as *maruta*, "logs," by vivisecting them, injecting them with various pathogens, and subjecting them to below-freezing temperatures in frostbite experiments. The Japanese secret police, the *kempeitai*, assisted Unit 731 by rounding up criminals, or even plucking ordinary people from the streets of occupied towns, like so many lab rats, and sending them to the Unit's laboratories.[12]

Incongruously, it was the Soviet Union that chose to pursue the perpetrators of the biological warfare experiments. Among the several hundred thousand Japanese soldiers captured in Manchuria by the Soviet Army were twelve officers involved in the experiments. They were brought to trial in Khabarovsk in December 1949, and sentenced to prison terms ranging from two to twenty-five years. Although Moscow published the transcript of the trial in full the following year, its efforts to get to the bottom of the matter were largely ignored, being viewed merely as propaganda or as a "counter-move to the demand for the return of the Japanese prisoners of war" held in Siberia.[13] One plausible reason for the lack of attention paid is that the many show trials Stalin had conducted to purge his opponents had "discredited the Marxist-Leninist concept of justice."[14]

The immunity deal struck by MacArthur's office and Unit 731 did not put an end to their mutual postwar assistance, as demonstrated by the response to a bizarre incident in which a lone individual from the defunct detachment terrorized his own countrymen. In January 1948, when the Tokyo Trial was wrapping up, a man pretending to be a researcher from the Ministry of Welfare was suspected of poisoning the employees of Teikoku Bank, in the heart of Tokyo. The Tokyo Metropolitan Police were reasonably sure that the suspect was a former Unit 731 member, but they were ordered not to hold him, allegedly because MacArthur's office did not want there to be any embarrassing revelations at a time when it might urgently need the services of former Unit researchers in the event of an armed conflict in Korea. When war did come, and epidemic hemorrhagic fever, which had been virtually unknown in the peninsula, mysteriously broke out among US soldiers, former subordinates of Ishii were said to have been flown in for consultations.[15]

Due partly to hubris arising out of the unprecedented economic prosperity of the 1970s, the Japanese government remained misguidedly and blithely content there was no proof of unlawful activities by Unit 731 (whose official name had been the innocuous-sounding "Epidemic Prevention and Water Purification Detachment"). However, a group of Chinese citizens, armed with evidence found in a year-long, painstaking investigation by historians, sued the Japanese government in Tokyo District Court in August 1987. Other workers injured by the unearthing of remnants of Unit 731's handiwork were to follow; from the late 1960s through the middle of 1990s, numerous poison gas canisters and bombs with chemical warheads, buried in the Chinese soil by the fleeing Japanese Army, ruptured or exploded when disturbed at construction sites and processed at recycling stations.

In one of these cases, the court in 2002 ruled Japan had indeed conducted germ warfare in China. Although the plaintiff's claims for compensation were denied, this was significant. It was the first official determination that such method had been used. A year later, in a different case, the court acknowledged abandoning and concealing chemical weapons was an "exercise of public authority," and ordered the government to pay reparations for its "omission" of any effort to properly dispose of them.[16]

Notwithstanding the court's findings, the Japanese government did not alter its basic stance: reparations were settled by the 1951 San Francisco Peace Treaty and subsequent bilateral treaties. However, the world was not ready to let memories of Unit 731 fade away. On June 25, 1998, two former members of Unit 731 en route, as guest speakers, to an exhibit and a panel discussion about Japan's biological experiments, were prohibited from entering the United States by immigration officers at Chicago's O'Hare Airport. It was the first time the US law, known as the Holtzman Amendment, barring "individuals who, in association with . . . any government that was an ally of Nazi Germany, participated in acts of persecution during World War II," was applied to Japanese nationals, and it was done so to alumni of an organization the United States protected from prosecution.[17] Public opinion on this action was sharply divided.

Rabbi Abraham Cooper of the Simon Wiesenthal Center agreed with the Justice Department, saying, "A week doesn't go by that one of these people doesn't try to have a vacation in the United States." On the other hand, support groups of the victims of Japanese aggression called the action a "miscarriage of law," urging US Attorney General Janet Reno, to give permission to the two deportees to take part in public disclosure of war crimes. Reno and Eli Rosenbaum, the director of the Justice Department's Office of Special Investigations, were unmoved, believing one exception would soon inundate their offices with applications from ex-war criminals to come to America to apologize, and perhaps later partake of fine meals at "the best restaurants in Manhattan and Los Angeles."[18]

The Failure to Prosecute the Emperor

The United States wished to keep the emperor out of court. By protecting him, and using his unequaled prestige and influence, they hoped to follow the path of least resistance in their subsequent occupation. Its desire fortuitously coincided with the Japanese government's; to prevent the prosecution of the embodiment of the nation. The defendants, Japanese defense lawyers, Japanese government officials, and even the American prosecutors coordinated their efforts to achieve this goal. Only the judges were kept completely "out of the loop." It was a prime example of the Japanese custom of *nemawashi*, the holding of informal, behind-the-scenes discussions among the key people involved in making and implementing a decision.

However, in 1989 a stunning discovery was made. In the home of the daughter of Terasaki Hidenari, a pre-war diplomat and the emperor's trusted advisor in the post-war period, was found the emperor's *Monologue*. The *Monologue*, was a summary of his recollection of memorable events during his tenure which he dictated to five members of his entourage, including Terasaki, in the spring of 1946.[19] From the beginning, there were disagreements among readers concerning the motive behind the creation of this document, but the consensus now is the emperor narrated his "autobiography" not out of a nostalgic need to reminisce, but out of a necessity to eliminate the possibility of his prosecution.

In the *Monologue*, the emperor recounted his thinking and his decision-making at pivotal moments both before and during the war. Ironically, in addition to revealing his "human" side, it included many confessions that would unquestionably have caused him to be regarded as an accomplice to the "conspiracy" had Terasaki provided a faithful translation to SCAP.[20]

In light of the situation in the late 1940s, the United States seems to have been not only sincere, but well-motivated, in its efforts to keep the emperor out of court. Furthermore, with communism spreading throughout China, it became of the utmost importance to check the spread of the ideology and, in furtherance of that aim, to nurture Japan as an ally in the Far East.

It was feared that prosecution of the emperor would generate animosity toward the US and create a chaotic situation that would allow homegrown communists an opportunity to gain a foothold. For the United States, the choice was either to hang Hirohito now and risk losing the Cold War in Asia, or protect him and secure Japan as a firm anticommunist bulwark in the future. MacArthur estimated in a cable message to Eisenhower, that, if the emperor was destroyed, "[a] minimum of [a] million troops would be required which would have to be maintained for an indefinite number of years."[21] It appears that this appraisal was based merely on his personal assessment, for there is no record that indicates any analysis of this subject was conducted by his office. To relieve of all legal and moral responsibilities a head of the state who had unleashed unspeakable atrocities had the unwanted by-product of engendering in the popular mind a positive reevaluation of, and a modicum of secret pride in, the "Great East Asia

War," hampering to this day, the restoration of wholesome relationships between Japan and the nations that were its victims. SCAP's decision to leave the emperor untouched had widespread ramifications, and a detailed account of it is beyond the scope of this chapter. What was done was done because it was thought the circumstances required it, but the question must still be asked: Did America knowingly let the highest-ranking Japanese war criminal escape unpunished?

Clemency and Parole

After the San Francisco Peace Treaty came into force on April 28, 1952, the Allied Powers (minus the Soviet Union, the People's Republic of China, and the Philippines) needed to settle various matters regarding procedures for clemency. This was done in preparation for the Japanese government's approach to individual governments with its own interpretation of Article 11 of the Treaty. Article 11 declared that "Japan accepts the judgments of the International Military Tribunal for the Far East and of other Allied War Crimes Courts both within and outside Japan, and will carry out the sentences imposed thereby upon Japanese nationals imprisoned in Japan," and further stipulated that "[i]n the case of persons sentenced by the International Military Tribunal for the Far East, [the power to grant clemency] may not be exercised except on the decision of a majority of the Governments represented on the Tribunal, and on the recommendation of Japan."[22]

The promptness with which Japan made known its desire in this matter was likely a sign of optimism that its wish would be satisfied, a positive attitude that was perhaps fostered by the increasing moderation of some of the Allied powers toward Japan at the end of the trial and beginning of the Cold War.

The eight Allied Powers, quite mindful of the consequences of pursuing an uncompromising hard-line policy, especially in light of the goodwill engendered by the Soviets, who had carried out a mass release of Japanese war criminals from Soviet prisons, continued to give Japan what it wanted. These efforts culminated in a diplomatic note sent to Tokyo on April 7, 1958, announcing their decision to reduce the sentences of Class A war criminals to time already served. A few days later, their embassies received a note from Japanese Foreign Minister Fujiyama Aiichirō, expressing his gratitude for the Allies' "humanitarian decision."[23]

Though most of the Class A war criminal convicts and suspects went on to live private lives after being released, a few reentered the public spotlight. Most notable among the latter was Kishi Nobusuke, a member of the Pearl Harbor Cabinet. After spending two and half years in jail, Kishi made a triumphant return to the political scene: he was rewarded with the premiership in 1957. Equally indicative of the evanescent impact of the Tokyo Trial was the secret deal, struck only ten years after he became a free man, by Kodama Yoshio (former purchasing agent for the Navy and Class A suspect, who the IPS predicted would pursue a "poisonous [course] of action" once released) and Lockheed Corporation,[24] to bribe two of Japan's major air lines (Japan Airlines and All Nippon Airways) to purchase the company's wide-body L-1011 TriStars.[25] When the "Lockheed Scandal," the worst instance of corruption in post-war Japan, was made public in 1976 many who heard Kodama's name could not help thinking that, more than thirty years after the war, a propensity toward criminality continued to thrive within him.

Tokyo, Nuremberg, and Beyond

While there were three acquittals (out of twenty-two defendants) at Nuremberg, all twenty-five defendants at Tokyo were found guilty. Despite these notable features, the trial in the Far East was utterly overshadowed by the one in Germany and was forgotten in the West soon after its conclusion. A variety of hypotheses have been advanced as to why it fell short in both import and impact, but the foremost has to do with its duration. The Nuremberg Trial concluded within a year of its beginning, and within a year and a half of Germany's surrender, when the public desire to mete out justice to its wartime leaders still remained high.

The truly serious criticisms the trial has drawn are for the most part over other problems, including those regarding the IMTFE charter. Unlike in Nuremberg, where all members of the bench had to be present for a quorum, the prerequisite in Tokyo was a simple majority. And under Article 4, a majority vote of that quorum was sufficient in all decisions pertaining to verdicts and sentences; in case of a tie, it was necessary for the president to cast the decisive vote.[26] The consequences of this article were potentially quite grave: as Minear rightly points out, just three out of eleven judges (if the president was among the three) could have held the life or death of each of the twenty five accused.[27]

Despite its excessive length and legal inadequacies, the Tokyo War Crimes Trial was far from a show trial and thus should surely have bestowed a more consequential legacy.[28] The tribunal's President Webb, when questioned about the sluggish pace of progress in his courtroom, replied that it would be more important to "make the trial a fair one than a quick one."[29] True to Webb's intention, the trial kept those procedures necessary for the protection of the rights of the accused: the defendants were represented by defense attorneys of their choice and were shown all prosecution documents, both in English and Japanese, at least twenty-four hours before they were to be submitted in evidence, and each had the opportunity to tell his version of events in open court. By any standard of judicial propriety, the trial exhibited high regard for fair and correct procedure.

The integrity of the trial notwithstanding, it failed to be the significant contributor to international jurisprudence many hoped it would be. Nonetheless, the lack of attention paid to it while it was in progress and its subsequent disappearance from popular memory in no way diminishes its many positive aspects. Unlike the Nuremberg Trial, a virtual monopoly of the "Big Four" (France, the Soviet Union, the United Kingdom, and the United States), the greater inclusiveness of the Tokyo Trial allowed the participation of the less powerful of the Allies. And its importance to historians transcends its results for the details of many events and operations would not have been brought to light in such a thoroughgoing manner had it not been held.

Another important feature must be pointed out in this connection. At Nuremberg, the prosecution chose not to delve into causation, reasoning that to do so would have opened the floodgates for the Nazis to present their views and further spread their propaganda. Fearing more than anything else what Shklar has termed an "open recrimination of who did what to whom in Europe in the interwar years,"[30] the Allies did not allow the defense to state its own viewpoint, only letting it dispute the legality of the charges in the indictment. Fortunately, at Nuremberg, the prosecution was able to prove beyond a shadow of doubt that the twenty-two men in the dock were responsible for the outbreak of war. At Tokyo, on the other hand, the prosecution took the risk of examining the causes of the war. Unfortunately, Chief Prosecutor Keenan handled poorly what should have been the showcase cross-examination of General Tōjō Hideki, the premier of the Pearl Harbor cabinet, allowing him to defend all the main assertions of his affidavit without serious challenge.

As the Tokyo Trial continued to be a subject of debate and criticism, there arose among the revisionists in the 1970s a growing resentment toward and reaction against what was labeled the "Tokyo Trial View of History," or the idea that everything Japan had done between 1928 and 1945 was immoral and malign. For right-wing politicians, it represented a miscarriage of justice. Those who were convicted were scapegoats, not criminals. Therefore, the trial for them was a falsification of the history of modern Japan.[31] From the very inception of their crusade, the revisionists sought to unburden their fellow countrymen of this distorted and self-loathing notion.

While historical revisionists among the Japanese still persist in their effort to whitewash Japan's wrong doings during WWII, the atrocities in Yugoslavia and Rwanda compelled Japan to gradually coordinate with the global community toward the creation of the International Criminal Court, a permanent court that overcomes many of the difficulties encountered by *ad hoc* tribunals, such as the Tokyo and Nuremberg courts.

All in all, Japan's profile in international justice remains low because, domestically, it has allowed questions of war responsibility to remain unexamined and unanswered. By neither squarely confronting nor fully understanding their history, the Japanese have kept alive a profound sense of their victimhood. When the Japanese government and people finally learn the wisdom of doing so and appreciate the benefits that would accrue, Japan's neighbors, upon whom it inflicted far more damage than upon the western Allies, will no longer remain (one may hope) uneasy and mistrustful.

Notes

1. Philip Piccigallo, *The Japanese on Trial* (Austin: University of Texas Press, 1979), 34-208; Patrick Brode, *Casual Slaughters and Accidental Judgments. Canadian War Crimes Prosecutions, 1944 – 1948* (Toronto: University of Toronto Press, 1997).

2. These included Japanese, German, American, Australian, Chinese, Burmese, Dutch, and Filipino.

3. Concerning circumstances surrounding Keenan's appointment, see Robert Donihi, "War Crimes" *St. John's Law Review* 66 (3): 741.

4. Memorandum. February 15, 1946. RG-331/1668/Roll 17, National Archives and Records Administration (NARA), College Park, MD; Letter from MacArthur to Justice E. Northcroft, March 19, 1946. RG-153/Entry 145/Series 118-7/Box 123, NARA.

5. Thirty years later, this argument was exhumed and rehashed as the so-called "Unconditional Surrender Controversy," in which apologists for the "Great East Asia War" insisted Japan's surrender was "conditional." Americans may be surprised to learn the Japanese are still debating whether or not their surrender was unconditional, but this argument has become so influential in Japan that the Ministry of Education used it as leverage to pressure publishers to revise history textbooks.

6. International Military Tribunal for the Far East (IMTFE), The Tokyo War Crimes Trial (New York: Garland Publishing, 1981), 49, 584.

7. Agreement for the Prosecution and Punishment of the Major War Criminals of the European Axis, and the Charter of the International Military Tribunal (August 8, 1945), Art. 6(c).

8. The Comfort Women Issue and the Asian Women's Fund (http://www.awf.or.jp/english/index.html).

9. Sheldon Harris, *Factories of Death: Japanese Biological Warfare, 1932 – 1945, and the American Cover-up* (New York: Routlege, 2002)

10. This facility was set up "as a consequence of Intelligence Service reports on biological warfare activity elsewhere in the world." Peter Williams and David Wallace, *Unit 731: Japan's Secret Biological Warfare in World War II* (New York: The Free Press, 1989), 121.

11. Sheldon Harris, "American Cover-UP of Japanese Experiments," in *Science and the Pacific War: Science and Survival in the Pacific, 1939 – 1945*, ed. Roy McLeod (Dordrecht: Kluwer Academic Publishers, 2000), 260-264.

12. Williams and Wallace, *Unit 731*, 160-162; Hal Gold, *Unit 731* (Tokyo: Yen Books, 1996), 29.

13. Message from Canadian Embassy in Moscow, No. 560. December 31, 1949. RG-25/Volume 6196/File 4060-C-40/Part 4-2. Library and Archives of Canada.

14. Arnold Brackman, *The Other Nuremberg: The Untold Story of the Tokyo War Crimes Trial* (New York: William Morrow and Company, Inc., 1987), 198.

15. Gold, *Unit 731*: 117-123

16. Unpleasant revelations have continued, the most gruesome of was the exhumation in July 1989 of human skulls and bones at a construction site in Shinjuku,

where the Army Medical School once stood. Even to untrained eyes, holes and drill marks on some of them strongly suggested persons buried there had been shot or experimented upon surgically. The bones were at last analyzed, by Sapporo University's Sakura Hajime, who concluded they were belonged to various Asian ethnicities who had been buried between 1890 and 1940. Ultimately, he found no definitive connection to Ishii's activities.

17. US Dept. of Justice, "First time Japanese War Crime Suspects Have been Placed on List," December 1996), http://www.usdoj.gov/opa/pr/1996/Dec96/574crm.htm.

18. *The New York Times*. June 27, 1998.

19. The other four were, Inada Shūichi (cabinet secretary), Kinoshita Michio (Vice Grand Chamberlain), Matsudaira Yoshitami (Imperial Household Minister), and Matsudaira Yasumasa (Kido's secretary).

20. The less than full and accurate English version of the *Monologue* that was furnished is preserved in the Bonner Fellers Papers, RG-44a, MacArthur Archives.

21. Message from MacArthur to Joint Chief of Staff, January 24, 1946, RG-9 Radiograms, Reel 324, WC75, MacArthur Archives.

22. San Francisco Peace Treaty (September 8, 1951), Art. 11.

23. Letter to William Frederick Bull, Ambassador Extraordinary and Plenipotentiary for Canada, April 8, 1958; Letter to the Under-Secretary of State for External Affairs, No. 329, 11 Apr. 1958, RG25/Volume 6854/File 4060-C-40/Part 10-2, External Affairs Series G-2. LAC.

24. "Dangerous Potential in the Release of Certain Class 'A' War Crime Suspects," RG 331/Entry 1294/Box 1434, the National Archives and Records Administration.

25. The acquisition of Lockheed's TriStars caused three DC-10s, wide-body jets made by rival McDonnell Douglas and scheduled to be purchased by a Japanese trading company, to be palmed off on Turkish Airlines. On March 3, 1974, one of them, Ship 29, due to a defective cargo door latching mechanism, crashed outside Paris, killing all 346 on board, including forty-eight Japanese businessmen.

26. To quote for comparison the Rome Statute of the International Criminal Court entered into force on July 1, 2002, Article 74 states that "[a]ll judges of the Trial Chamber shall be present at each stage of the trial and throughout their deliberations" and the "judges shall attempt to achieve unanimity in their decision, failing which the decision shall be taken. by a majority of the judges." Rome Statue of the International Criminal Court (July 2002), Art. 74.

27. Richard Minear, *Victors' Justice: The Tokyo War Crimes Trial* (New Jersey: Princeton University Press, 1971), 89.

28. Gary Jonathan Bass, *Stay the Hand of Vengeance: The Politics of War Crimes Tribunals* (New Jersey: Princeton University Press, 2001).

29. Message to Foreign Office, 25 November 1946, FO371/57429. The National Archives, Kew, England.

30. Judith Shklar, *Legalism: Law, Morals, and Political Trials* (Cambridge: Harvard University Press, 1965), 173.

31. Ian Buruma, *Wages of Guilt* (Farrar Straus Giroux, 1994), 161.

Chapter 12

Arresting Charles Taylor

Beth Dougherty

In April 2012, former Liberian leader Charles Ghankay Taylor was found guilty on eleven counts of war crimes and crimes against humanity for his role in Sierra Leone's brutal civil war. Judges at the Special Court for Sierra Leone (SCSL) sentenced him to fifty years, describing his crimes as of the "utmost gravity in terms of scale and brutality." The United States played a critical role in bringing Taylor to justice. Prominent officials in the administration of President George W. Bush were on record stating Taylor had to be held accountable. The United States successfully exerted pressure on both Liberia and Nigeria to bring about Taylor's arrest, especially during Taylor's disappearance in 2007. When the White House suggested that it might need to cancel a meeting between Bush and Nigerian President General Olusegun Obasanjo, Nigerian authorities suddenly found Taylor and placed him in custody.

At first glance, this appears to be a straightforward success story. But the seemingly consistent nature of US policy in the Taylor case hides a more complex reality. The Bush administration was recalcitrant regarding the SCSL, and nearly squandered opportunities to hold Taylor accountable. It was Congress which drove American policy and which ultimately deserves credit for its success. Unraveling the inside story of the American role in Taylor's arrest highlights the often hidden side of foreign policy-making—the nuances, the bureaucratic and personal rivalries, the tactics, the coalitions, the passions—and offers a detailed account of how the US Congress helped bring a war criminal to justice.

When the SCSL unsealed its indictment against Taylor in 2003, the Liberian president was in Ghana attending peace talks aimed at ending the latest chapter of the Liberian civil war. The flustered Ghanaians bundled Taylor off to Monrovia as the international community scrambled to avert the humanitarian disaster everyone feared would accompany a fight for control of the capital. Although Taylor avoided arrest, the indictment succeeded in pushing him out of power and into exile in Nigeria. In return for offering him asylum, Nigeria prohibited Taylor "from engaging in active communication with anyone involved in political, illegal or governmental activities in Liberia."[1] Before agreeing to take Taylor in, Obasanjo sought assurances from concerned parties that Nigeria would not be criticized for harboring an indicted war criminal.

Taylor's exile threatened the SCSL's efficacy. The SCSL recognized that the *sine qua non* for its ultimate success was the appearance of Taylor before its trial chamber. Its jurisdiction covers "those bearing the greatest responsibility" for the atrocities committed in Sierra Leone, and Sierra Leoneans are generally united in blaming Taylor for the calamity that befell their country. The final report of the Sierra Leone Truth and Reconciliation Commission found that Taylor played a pivotal role in bringing conflict to Sierra Leone.[2] His prosecution was the most critical expectation of the SCSL's local constituency, a fact of which it was well aware. Without Taylor, the SCSL would be at best a partial and at worst an irrelevant contribution to promoting justice and accountability in Sierra Leone. As someone at the SCSL put it before Taylor's arrest, "we (the SCSL) will always be the 90 percent solution if we do not get Taylor."[3]

The SCSL's inability to try its most wanted suspect also threatened to tarnish a promising new model of international criminal justice. Trials as a tool of transitional justice aim to establish a credible system of justice and accountability, end impunity, and help restore and maintain peace. Finding the right institutional structure to effectively translate these goals into achievements on the ground proved challenging. The SCSL was self-consciously designed to address the weaknesses of the *ad hoc* tribunals for Rwanda and the former Yugoslavia: it would provide justice in accordance with international standards within a politically acceptable time frame, on a limited budget, and with greater local ownership.[4] The SCSL's most innovative feature was its "hybrid" nature; it mixed elements of the international and the national, including locating the court in the home country.

One of the most discouraging outcomes of Taylor escaping trial was that it would have confirmed the deep suspicion many ordinary Africans harbor that impunity still rules on the continent. If the SCSL, a court with millions of dollars and international support, could not get a "big man," what lessons might local NGOs and activists draw about their prospects for demanding accountability? Taylor's indictment was intended as a warning that in this new century leaders would be held accountable for their crimes.[5] Allowing Taylor to escape justice in the face of multiple counts of crimes against humanity and war crimes would have been a signal that *realpolitik* continued to prevail over international justice.

Such outcomes also threatened to undermine the significant American commitment to the SCSL and stability in West Africa. The United States was the SCSL's largest donor and was a key member of the Management Committee which oversaw SCSL operations.[6] Although not an official presence, many Americans worked at the SCSL: the prosecutor who indicted Taylor, David Crane, (is an American, and a sizeable contingent of the SCSL's personnel was American. The United States contributed a substantial portion of the $2 billion the UN spent on peacekeeping in Sierra Leone.[7]

Although it had blessed the arrangement that sent Taylor to Nigeria, the Bush administration insisted that it was committed to seeing him stand trial at the SCSL. In June 2004 Ambassador for War Crimes Pierre Prosper told Congress: "it is US policy that Taylor must be held accountable and must appear before the Court."[8] Assistant Secretary of State for African Affairs Jendayi Frazier testified to the House of Representatives in February 2006 that the United States had "consistently maintained that Taylor must be brought to justice before the Special Court" and that his trial would "significantly help to bring closure to a tragic chapter in Liberia's history and help all of West Africa overcome patterns of impunity, illicit trade and civil conflict."[9]

Several members of Congress lobbied to ensure that the SCSL Statute was written in such a way as to allow the prosecution of Taylor. This sentiment reflected a general commitment to bringing an end to impunity in Africa. One staffer recalled that the announcement of the 1999 Lomé accord, which extended a blanket amnesty for crimes committed in Sierra Leone, caused several Congressional members to "go ballistic."[10] Congress also appreciated the possibility that the SCSL would correct the problems of the *ad hoc* tribunals while offering greater local buy-in. For some, this was motivated by opposition to the International Criminal Court (ICC); for others it reflected a more general commitment to international justice.

An early warning sign of the strained relationship that would develop between Congress and the State Department came before the SCSL was even formally constituted. In September 2001 Senator Russ Feingold (D-WI), chair of the African Affairs Subcommittee of the Senate Foreign Relations Committee, pushed legislation to have the State Department's "Rewards for Justice" program expanded to the SCSL.[11] Rewards for Justice offered cash in return for information leading to the arrest of wanted terrorists or war criminals, and it applied to suspects wanted by the Rwanda and Yugoslav tribunals.[12] However, the State Department never announced this extension and never included the SCSL as part of Rewards for Justice on its website. The Department of State's failure to act on this rankled the SCSL's Congressional supporters.

Moreover, Congress wanted to provide an additional $5 million in 2002.[13] The extra money represented a substantial boost to the SCSL. However, the Bush administration strongly opposed the idea, and a heated bureaucratic battle erupted. Several of the major Congressional backers of the SCSL held powerful positions from which to shape policy: Patrick Leahy (D-VT) was chair of the Foreign Operations Subcommittee of the Senate Appropriations Committee; Judd Gregg (R-NH) was chair of the Commerce, Justice, State, the Judiciary and Related Agencies Subcommittee of the Senate Appropriations Committee; and Jack Reed (D-RI) and Mike DeWine (R-OH) were on the Appropriations Committee. The Senate Appropriations Committee inserted mandatory language requiring the State Department to send an additional $5 million to the SCSL in fiscal year 2003.[14] State dragged its feet, and in June four members of the House Committee on International Relations—Henry Hyde (R-IL) (chair), Chris Smith (R-NJ) (vice-chair), Ed Royce (R-CA) (chair, Subcommittee on Africa), and Tom Lantos (D-CA) (the committee's ranking Democrat)—wrote to Secretary of State Colin Powell, urging the administration to obligate and release the $10 million "without delay."[15] To underscore its point, Congress placed a hold on funding for the construction of a new US embassy in Freetown.[16] The State Department capitulated, but it was furious about the Congressional strong-arming.

This incident also contributed to the emerging rift between State and SCSL Chief Prosecutor David Crane. Some in the Africa Bureau could barely disguise their dislike of the SCSL and its prosecutor. The Africa experts resented being lectured to by people it perceived as newcomers who lacked experience and sensitivity to West Africa. They complained that the SCSL's early outreach efforts alienated the local population. Said one person in the Africa Bureau, the SCSL "wrong-footed itself because it doesn't know West Africa."[17] A turf battle developed in Freetown between then US Ambassador Peter Chaveas and the SCSL, which represented an independent center of power also run by an American.[18]

These tensions exploded in June 2003 with the unsealing of Taylor's indictment. Some supporters of the SCSL on the Hill suggested that State seemed to resent such an action from an American, who it insinuated should have taken US foreign policy goals into account.[19] State viewed the timing of the indictment as extremely unhelpful and as threatening the diplomatic efforts to bring Liberia to the desired "soft landing." According to Crane the administration basically stopped communicating with him.[20] Consequently Crane turned to Congress for support. The close relationship between Congress and Crane further damaged the atmosphere, as State was upset that Crane could (and did) go around it to sympathetic members of Congress to get what the SCSL sought.

While the indictment forced Taylor out of Liberia, it introduced a new complication: getting him out of Nigeria. Obasanjo staked out the position that having offered Taylor asylum, Nigeria could not turn him over to the SCSL. To do so would gravely harm Nigeria's honor and reputation. Obasanjo repeatedly pointed out that Nigeria had taken Taylor in as a way to bring peace to the region and that he had done so after wide consultations. He altered his position slightly in late November 2003, by promising to turn Taylor over to the Liberian government if it asked for his return.[21] But Liberia was in no position to make such a request. Obasanjo refused to budge from this position, even as evidence mounted that Taylor was violating the terms of his asylum.

The relationship between Congressional advocates of the SCSL and the administration, especially the State Department, became increasingly tense following the 2003 asylum deal. State considered the arrangement of Taylor's exile a great victory, one that had brought peace to Liberia and avoided a humanitarian catastrophe. Many in Congress did not share this view.[22] They failed to see who benefited from allowing Taylor to escape justice, and focused on the risks he posed to Liberia's transition and to the wider region. According to these members, Taylor was a continuing threat, a threat that they believed State minimized by downplaying his ability to influence events or cause trouble while in exile.[23]

By summer 2004, members of Congress had become impatient with the lack of progress. They had given the administration a full calendar year after the asylum agreement to allow the tensions to settle and to permit quiet diplomacy with Nigeria. Congress wanted the administration to demonstrate some resolve and to either begin pressuring Nigeria or to produce a blueprint for achieving Taylor's extradition to the SCSL.

Unable to discern evidence of either pressure or a blueprint, in July 2004 Congress attached strong conditions on the provision of aid, including funds for debt restructuring, to countries "in which individuals indicted by the ICTR and SCSL are credibly alleged to be living."[24] This provision was clearly targeted at Nigeria. The specific mention of debt restructuring was included to make clear to Nigeria that Congress was serious about seeing Taylor handed over. Nigeria lost $6 million in military aid as a result.[25] Congress included a waiver, but in order for the administration to claim the waiver it had to report to Congress on "the steps being taken to obtain the cooperation of the government in surrendering the indictee in question to the SCSL or ICTR" and "a strategy for bringing the indictee before the ICTR or SCSL."[26] Congress was willing to allow the strategy to be classified rather than public, but it was adamant that there *be* a strategy. The fact that the administration did not apply for the waiver only intensified the belief in Congress that the administration did not have a plan for getting Taylor to the SCSL.

Not without bitterness, staff on Capitol Hill and at the SCSL blamed the State Department for the administration's reluctance to publicly and later forcefully press Nigeria for Taylor's arrest. Its policies were considered to be consistently short-sighted. Lomé was characterized as one of these "lousy" decisions; the Taylor asylum deal was another.[27] State's repeated assurances that it was committed to seeing Taylor brought to justice lacked credibility in Congress because the administration could offer little evidence of any actions it had taken in support of its rhetoric.

Careerists in the African Bureau came in for scathing criticism from the SCSL and its Congressional backers.[28] They were "co-opted," too fearful of rocking the boat or of risking diplomatic ramifications with Nigeria. The Africa Bureau "didn't give a damn about international justice," according to its critics, it cared only about keeping Africa out of the headlines so that the administration would not have to intervene. While the Special Office of War Crimes (SOWC) said all the right things, it lacked "fire in the belly" when it came to Taylor. Its critics alleged that the SOWC was too preoccupied with securing Article 98 agreements to circumvent the ICC to advocate forcefully for Taylor's arrest.[29] Ambassador for War Crimes Prosper was "terrible," "ineffectual," and "a major impediment" on the Taylor case, and "inconsistent" in his support for the SCSL. The SOWC itself saw the Africa Bureau as too cautious in its approach to Nigeria, to the point that some in the SOWC felt the Africa Bureau was actively impeding its efforts to pressure Obasanjo.[30] But institutionally, the Africa Bureau was the more powerful of the two when it came to shaping policies toward Africa.

On the other hand, State resented being told what to do by people whom it believed had no understanding of West Africa, and who stubbornly refused to consider diplomatic realities. By early 2005, there were certainly members of the administration who found Obasanjo's position to be illogical and untenable. However, based on past experiences with the Nigerian leader, the State Department argued that pressure on Obasanjo would backfire, and that quiet diplomacy was the correct course of action.

Moreover, the State Department viewed Nigeria as an important ally. It was a regional peacekeeper, having participated in missions in Liberia, Sierra Leone, and Darfur. The arrival of Nigerian troops in Monrovia in 2003 had relieved the intense pressure on the administration to deploy the Marines floating off the Liberian coast. Nigeria was a major oil producer, and the United States' fifth largest supplier.[31] Obasanjo was a leader in key African organizations, including the African Union (AU). As chair of the AU from 2004 to 2006, Obasanjo had taken the lead on Darfur, overseeing the peacekeeping mission and hosting negotiations. All these considerations were accorded a higher priority than bringing Taylor to account.

In the first half of 2005, the SCSL launched a carefully coordinated diplomatic and media campaign to secure Taylor's extradition.[32] The SCSL and its supporters viewed this push as its best chance to gain custody of the former Liberian leader. As part of this campaign, the SCSL highlighted several charges against Taylor which reinforced the difficulties between the State Department on one side and the SCSL and its Congressional backers on the other. SCSL investigators had been alleging that al-Qaeda had benefited from the illegal diamond trade organized by Taylor, and members of Congress and the press voiced this accusation repeatedly.[33] In early 2005, Crane claimed Taylor had been behind the attempted assassination of Guinean President Lansana Conte, which the SCSL cast as part of wider efforts by Taylor to destabilize Liberia through Guinea.[34] State believed that these accusations were not supported by the available intelligence information.[35] It had sent the FBI to West Africa twice to investigate Taylor's connection with al-Qaeda, and both times the FBI reported that the sources relied upon by the SCSL investigators were not credible. The State

Department also found evidence that demonstrated the SCSL's claims about the Conte assassination attempt were thin.

However at this time, some movement was forthcoming on the part of the administration. Both Bush and National Security Advisor Condoleezza Rice discussed Taylor with Obasanjo. A senior administration official said "I think we made clear our desire to find a way forward. Nigeria basically understood that the status quo would no longer hold and it is time to find a solution to the matter."[36] But neither the White House nor the State Department would say that Obasanjo had been told that Taylor must go to the SCSL.

After his meeting with Bush, Obasanjo insisted that Nigeria would not surrender Taylor without "absolute evidence" he had violated the terms of his asylum deal, although it would consider returning Taylor to Liberia if an elected government there requested it. Obasanjo claimed that the allegations related to Taylor's activities were unproven.[37] Although State had "no doubt" that such allegations were true, it would not show its evidence to Obasanjo, fearful of revealing its intelligence sources.[38] That of course only heightened the indignation towards State expressed by its Congressional critics.

Despite the orchestrated campaign by the SCSL and its supporters, Taylor remained free in the summer of 2005. Disappointment and frustration ran high. But Congressional supporters firmly believed that their steady pressure on the administration had forced it to alter its position. Frazier had assured key Congressional offices that the administration would move more aggressively on the Taylor issue, Prosper indicated that a plan to get Taylor to the SCSL had been drafted, and Rice and Bush had at least raised the issue with Obasanjo.[39] Congress had kept the issue alive and in the administration's direct line of vision, although it remained unconvinced that the administration was willing to bring any genuine pressure to bear on Nigeria.

Determined members of Congress continued to push the administration. In June 2005, Leahy and Barack Obama (D-IL) had an exchange on the Senate floor in which they both explicitly linked debt relief for Nigeria to Nigeria turning Taylor over to the SCSL. Such a provision had been included in the 2005 appropriations bill, and Leahy made clear that the provision was very likely to be reauthorized for fiscal year 2006.[40] Not only was this provision reauthorized, Congress inserted an additional $13 million in funds for the SCSL into the 2006 appropriations bill.[41]

Liberia's election was scheduled for October 2005. Given Obasanjo's frequently repeated promise to hand Taylor over to an elected Liberian government, it appeared that the best chance of getting Taylor to Freetown was to hope that the new government would "do the right thing," as one staffer put it.[42] This was by no means a sure thing. Taylor had supporters in Liberia, and was funding as many as nine parties contesting the elections.[43] The new government might decide it was too dangerous to risk angering Taylor's followers by asking Nigeria to send him to the SCSL. But if Taylor did return to Liberia, UN Resolution 1638 gave the UN peacekeepers in Liberia the authority to apprehend him and to transfer or facilitate his transfer to the SCSL. Moreover, signals from the SCSL to members of Congress led them to strongly suspect that a Taylor trial would be moved to The Hague, thereby relieving fears about what could happen in the region if Taylor was tried in Sierra Leone.[44]

Ellen Johnson-Sirleaf won election as president of Liberia in November 2005, and arrangements were quickly made for her to visit the United States in March 2006. Much to the dismay of the SCSL and its Congressional backers, she indicated during her inauguration that a trial for Taylor was not a top priority of her government. While she may have hoped that her status as the first elected leader of post-conflict Liberia and Africa's first woman president would earn her a honeymoon period in Washington, some members of Congress saw her new government as a critical opportunity. Their calculus was simple. The new Liberian government would desperately need money. Congress could provide that funding, but it wanted Taylor arrested. So if Liberia wanted $50 million in aid, it needed to ask Obasanjo to hand Taylor over to the SCSL.

With Johnson-Sirleaf and Obasanjo scheduled to visit Washington in March, the SCSL's Congressional backers had ample opportunity to make their wishes clear to all concerned parties. They did not hesitate to use their leverage. Royce sent Johnson-Sirleaf a letter about Taylor immediately following her victory. He followed this with a letter to Rice on December 13, co-signed by thirteen colleagues, calling on Rice to make Taylor "a paramount concern of the United States" in conversations with Johnson-Sirleaf, and to "strongly recommend" that Taylor be handed over.[45]

The necessity for Taylor's arrest was a prominent theme at a House hearing on the Liberian elections held in February 2006. Frazier told the committee that "now is the right time" for Taylor to be handed over to the SCSL, and stated that Rice had told Johnson-Sirleaf and Obasanjo that the United States wanted "to make sure" Taylor went to the SCSL, and "the sooner the better."[46] Royce also pressed Frazier on the $13 million appropriated to the SCSL, which the State Department wanted to significantly reduce as part of a reprogramming of economic support funds. He pointedly told her: "Congress, which controls the purse strings, passed a bill emphasizing a specific amount to go, in this case to the Special Court in Sierra Leone. The bill was signed into law, and so we expect that to happen."[47]

There were loud rumblings coming from the House, and especially from Royce's office, that aid to Liberia in the supplemental spending bill should be conditioned on Johnson-Sirleaf's cooperation. Other prominent members of Congress let the Liberians know that while they would not push the Taylor issue on the March trip, they would soon after. Privately, well-placed individuals told the Liberians that Congress would not let up on this issue.

Confirmation came on March 17, when Obasanjo's office issued the following statement: "In keeping with his commitment to give due consideration to any formal request from a democratically elected government of Liberia for the return of former President Charles Taylor, President Olusegun Obasanjo has duly notified the chairmen of the African Union . . . and the Economic Community of African States . . . that President Johnson Sirleaf has made such a request."[48]

Nigeria did not submit to the request gracefully. Johnson-Sirleaf wanted Nigeria to send Taylor directly to the SCSL, but instead Obasanjo informed the Liberian government on March 25 that it was "free to take former president Charles Taylor into custody," and did not otherwise offer any details about when and how the handover would take place.[49] The SCSL urged Nigeria to arrest Taylor in the interim, "to avoid the possibility of him using his wealth and associates to slip away, with grave consequences to the stability of the region."[50]

On March 27, such fears were realized. Taylor disappeared. The uproar was immediate. Obasanjo was scheduled to meet with Bush at the White House on March 29, and the highly irregular circumstances of Taylor's disappearance finally brought Congress, the Africa Bureau, and the SOWC together, as all three agreed that the Bush-Obasanjo meeting should not go ahead unless Taylor was caught. Several members of Congress placed phone calls to the administration, demanding action. Royce told the *New York Times* that Bush should not meet with Obasanjo unless Taylor was apprehended. Obama publicly concurred. Representative Diane Watson (D-CA) issued a press release blaming Nigeria for Taylor's disappearance, adding "We here in Congress expect that President Obasanjo will fix this problem by the time he meets with President Bush tomorrow. Otherwise, it will be difficult to predict what damage will be done to US/Nigeria relations."[51] At a Senate Appropriations Committee hearing, Leahy told Rice that under the circumstances it would be inappropriate for Bush to meet with Obasanjo.[52] While Rice agreed that Taylor's disappearance was a matter of concern, she would not comment on whether Bush would refuse to see Obasanjo.

By March 28, Rice was warning of "consequences" if Nigeria did not hand Taylor over, and the White House itself was suggesting Obasanjo's visit was in jeopardy.[53] A *New York Times* editorial called Taylor's disappearance "a diplomatic disaster" for Obasanjo, and the *Washington Post* labeled it a "catastrophe."[54] In the face of this intense pressure, the administration quietly informed Obasanjo that unless Taylor was apprehended, Bush would not meet with him.[55] With Obasanjo already in Washington, a cancellation of this meeting would represent a very public humiliation for him.

Hours before Obasanjo was scheduled to meet with Bush, Nigerian police caught Taylor trying to cross into Cameroon. With Taylor officially in Nigerian custody, the Bush-Obasanjo meeting went ahead as scheduled. Taylor was flown to Monrovia on a Nigerian presidential jet, and once in Monrovia he was immediately transferred to a UN helicopter and flown to the SCSL compound in Freetown. On March 29, 2006, three long years after his indictment, Charles Taylor was finally led into a jail cell to await trial before the SCSL.

Conclusion

Without the efforts of a dedicated, bipartisan group of Congressional members, Charles Taylor might still be enjoying his exile in Nigeria. Throughout the three years of Taylor's exile, Congress demonstrated a consistent commitment to bringing him to justice. With their very blunt calls for Bush to cancel his meeting with Obasanjo, Congressional members made clear that they considered the Taylor issue important enough to risk publicly embarrassing Obasanjo. The Bush administration by contrast was always willing to subordinate Taylor's fate to other interests. Congress used all the tools at its disposal. It secured a total of $35 million for the SCSL and offered the SCSL valuable moral and political support. It placed steady and at times intense pressure on the Bush administration to take more assertive positions. It sent Nigeria a stern message by restricting its access to US funds. Most importantly, it played the pivotal role in pushing Johnson-Sirleaf to ask Nigeria to hand Taylor over to the SCSL.

Finally, Congressional pressure was successful because in the end Liberia, which could end the stalemate by requesting Taylor's arrest, also happened to be the actor over which Congress exerted the greatest leverage. Congress did push the administration to adopt more forceful rhetoric on the Taylor issue, but it could not compel the administration to take more forceful actions. It could also inflict some punishment on Nigeria but there were limits. Unlike Nigeria, Liberia was peripheral to US interests and Liberia desperately needed US funding. The choice was simple and stark: ask Nigeria to turn over Taylor and get access to $50 million, or risk having Congress limit or condition or refuse the funding.

Lacking Chapter VII powers, the SCSL had no power of its own save moral suasion; it could exert steady rhetorical pressure when it needed something, but it could not compel the UN, the Bush administration, or Nigeria to cooperate with it. Moreover, most of the SCSL's efforts to secure cooperation from the international community were of necessity focused on raising funds. By building and maintaining a network of supporters on Capitol Hill, and at times coordinating strategy with them such as in the summer of 2005, the SCSL gained the powerful ally it required to bring Charles Taylor to justice.

Notes

1. "Taylor Meddling in Liberian Politics, Diplomats Say," *UN Integrated Regional Information Networks*, September 17, 2003.

2. Sierra Leone Truth and Reconciliation Commission, *Final Report*, 2, chap 2, finding 28, www.trcsierraleone.org/drwebsite/publish/index.shtml (accessed November 14, 2011).

3. Member of the Office of the Prosecutor, interviewed by author in Freetown, Sierra Leone, October 19, 2004. On a more general note, much of the information in this paper is drawn from over twenty interviews I conducted between 2005 and 2007 at the State Department (Africa Bureau and SOWC) and the US Embassy in Freetown, Sierra

Leone; with Congressional staffers; and with personnel at the SCSL. Because of the sensitive nature of many of these conversations, I agreed to only identify people by where they worked.

4. Beth K. Dougherty, "Right-sizing International Criminal Justice: The Hybrid Experiment at the Special Court for Sierra Leone," *International Affairs* 10, no. 2 (March 2004): 311-328.

5. SCSL Prosecutor David Crane, interviewed by author in Freetown, Sierra Leone, June 8, 2005.

6. The US donated $35 million from 2002 to 2007. UN Security Council, "The Situation in Sierra Leone," S/PV.5690 at 8, (June 8, 2007), www.daccessdds.un.org/doc.

7. The United Nations Mission in Sierra Leone (UNAMSIL) cost nearly $2 billion between July 1999 and June 2003; its total cost (1999-2006) is estimated at $2.8 billion.

8. *Confronting, Ending, and Preventing War Crimes in Africa: Hearings before the House Committee on International Relations, Subcommittee on Africa,* 108th Cong. 2d sess. (June 24, 2004) (testimony of Pierre Prosper).

9. *The Impact of Liberia's Election on West Africa: Hearings before the House Committee on International Relations, Subcommittee on Africa,* 109th Cong. 2d sess. (February 8, 2006), (testimony by Jendayi Frazier).

10. S. Res. 315 asserted that Lomé rewarded the RUF leaders, and resolved that the US "should not condone, support or be a party to, any agreement that provides amnesty to those responsible for the crimes and abuses in Sierra Leone."

11. The provision was included in Foreign Relations Authorization Act, Fiscal Years 2002 and 2003, S. 1401, sec. 776, (introduced on September 4, 2001). The provision was part of Foreign Relations Authorization Act, Fiscal Year 2003, Pub. L. No. 107-228, sec. 697, 107th Cong. 2d sess. (September 30, 2002).

12. Rewards for Justice Program, www.rewardsforjustice.net/index.cfm.

13. PL107-228 provided $5 million for the SCSL in fiscal year 2002 and fiscal year 2003. The State Department also provided $5 million in start-up funds in 2001.

14. A total of $10 million was authorized for the SCSL in fiscal year 2003. Omnibus Appropriation Bill, Pub. L. No. 108-7, 108th Cong. 1st sess. (February 20, 2003), http://www.gpo.gov/fdsys/pkg/PLAW-108publ7/pdf/PLAW-108publ7.pdf.

15. "Hyde, Lantos Urge Powell to Release Funds for Sierra Leone Court Facing Security Threats," June 13, 2003, Press Release, www.foreignaffairs.house.gov..

16. According to interviews with SCSL personnel and Congressional staffers, Judd Gregg was responsible for the hold.

17. State Department officer, interviewed by author in Washington, DC, April 20, 2005.

18. US embassy officer, interviewed by author in Freetown, June 6, 2005; SCSL personnel, interviewed by author in Freetown, June 2005; and Congressional staffers, interviewed by author in Washington, DC, April 20, 2005.

19. Lansana Gberie, "Special Court for Sierra Leone," *African Affairs* 102, no. 409 (October 2003); Congressional staffer interviews April 20, 2005; SCSL personnel interviewed by author in Freetown, June 8, 2005; June 14, 2005.

20. Crane, interview June 8, 2005.

21. Somini Sengupta, "Nigerian Says He May Return Liberia's Ex-Leader for Trial if Liberia Asks," *New York Times,* November 26, 2003.

22. Senators Feingold and Leahy both put statements on the record on June 5, 2003, praising the unsealing of the Taylor indictment, and the June 13, 2003, letter to Powell signed by Hyde, Smith, Royce and Lantos stated "exile for Mr. Taylor is not a sound option."

23. *US Policy Toward Liberia: House International Relations Committee, Subcommittee on Africa,* 108th Cong. 1st sess. (October 2, 2003). Colin Powell, "Roundtable on African Issues," February 4, 2004, www.state.gov.

24. Consolidated Appropriations Act, 2005, H.R. 4818, sec. 585, 108th Cong 2d sess, http://www.gpo.gov/fdsys/pkg/BILLS-108hr4818enr/pdf/BILLS-108hr4818enr.pdf. It was introduced on July 13, 2004 and became Pub. L No. 108-447 on December 8, 2004 (at http://www.gpo.gov/fdsys/pkg/PLAW-108publ447/pdf/PLAW-108publ447.pdf). This provision was co-authored by Patrick Leahy and Judd Gregg.

25. Congressional staffer, interviewed by author in Washington DC, May 5, 2005.

26. Congressional staffer interview, May 5, 2005.

27. Congressional staffer interview, April 20, 2005.

28. All quotes come from interviews with Congressional staffers and SCSL personnel in 2005 and 2006.

29. Article 98 agreements are "bilateral non-surrender agreements protecting American citizens from the International Criminal Court (ICC)." US State Department, www.state.gov/t/pm/98.

30. Former State Department official interviewed by author in Washington, DC, July 17, 2007.

31. Ibrahim Mshelizza, "Nigeria Deports Fugitive ex-Liberian Warlord Taylor," *Washington Post,* March 29, 2006.

32. Interviews with David Crane and member of the OTP, Freetown, Sierra Leone, June 2005.

33. See for example, Ryan Lizza, "Charles at Large," *New Republic,* April 25, 2005, 10-11.

34. Special Court for Sierra Leone, *SCSL Press Release: Prosecutor Welcomes Resolution on Charles Taylor and Calls for Leadership From US President Bush,* (Freetown: SCSL May 4, 2004), www.sc-sl.org/Press/prosecutor-050505.pdf.

35. US Embassy officer interview, June 6, 2005; State Department personnel, interviewed by author in Washington, DC, April 20, 2005.

36. Bryan Bender, "US, Nigeria Step Up Bid to Bring Taylor to Trial," *Boston Globe,* May 6, 2005.

37. Michael Fletcher, "Nigerian Leader Says He Won't Turn Taylor Over for Trial," *Washington Post,* May 6, 2005.

38. State Department interviews, April 20, 2005.

39. According to Congressional staffers, Frazier denied a memo drafted by Prosper had reached her desk. This incident helps explain the especially negative feelings towards Prosper displayed by the staffers I interviewed. Interview, September 8, 2006.

40. US Senate, "Charles Taylor and Nigerian Debt Relief," *Congressional Record,* (June 15, 2005), www.thomas.loc.gov/cgi-bin/query/D?r109:21:./temp/~r109zHFs59.

41. The insertion was requested in October by a bipartisan group drawn from both Houses, and became part of Foreign Appropriations, Export Financing, and Related Programs Appropriations Act, 2006, Pub. L. No. 109-102, 109th Cong. 1st sess. (November 14, 2005). Royce, Smith, Obama, and Watson were the key movers of this effort.

42. Congressional staffer, interviewed by author in Washington, DC, September 8, 2006.

43. Global Witness, *Timber, Taylor, Soldier, Spy,* June 15, 2005, 33, http://www.globalwitness.org/library/timber-taylor-soldier-spy (accessed November 15, 2011).

44. UNAMSIL was drawing down throughout 2005, and its mission ended in 2006.

45. Senators Chafee, Leahy, Obama, Reed, and Feingold and Representatives Hyde, McCollum, Wolf, Snyder, Kelly, Watson, and Smith also signed. Text of letter available at http://democrats.foreignaffairs.house.gov/archives/109/news121405.htm (accessed November 15, 2011).

46. Frazier, *Liberia's Election.*

47. *The Impact of Liberia's Election on West Africa: Hearings before the House Committee on International Relations, Subcommittee on Africa*, 109th Cong. 2d sess. (February 8, 2006), (Ed Royce).

48. "'Time to Bring Taylor Issue to Closure,' Says Sirleaf," *IRINnews.org*, March 17, 2006, http://www.irinnews.org/report.aspx?reportid=58474 (accessed November 15, 2011).

49. Lydia Polgreen and Marc Lacey, "Nigeria Will End Asylum for Warlord," *New York Times*, March 26, 2006

50. Office of the Prosecutor, Special Court for Sierra Leone, *Press Release*, (Freetown, Sierra Leone, March 26, 2006), www.sc-sl.org/Press/prosecutor-032606.pdf.

51. *Press Release*, (Washington, DC: Office of Diane Watson, March 28, 2006), www.house.gov/list/press/ca33_watson/060328.html.

52. George Gedda, "Bush May refuse to Meet Nigerian President," *Associated Press*, March 29, 2006.

53. Craig Timberg, "Taylor Said to Vanish in Nigeria," *Washington Post*, March 29, 2006.

54. Editorial, "The Least Surprising Jailbreak Ever," *New York Times*, March 29, 2006; Editorial, "A War Criminal Escapes," *Washington Post*, March 29, 2006.

55. Former State Department official interview.

Chapter 13

Hybrid Tribunals and the Rule of Law: War Crimes Chamber of the State Court of Bosnia and Herzegovina

Olga Martin-Ortega

Until recently the relationship between peacebuilding and transitional justice has been depicted as a contentious one.[1] There are however growing efforts to highlight the complementarities between justice and peace.[2] The analysis undertaken in this chapter is framed by this debate. I address the relationship between hybrid courts, and an essential aspect of the peacebuilding process: reconstruction of the rule of law.[3] Rebuilding rule of law and the pursuit of retributive and restorative justice in post-conflict societies are interlinked processes.[4] All are meant to contribute to the peaceful resolution of group conflicts and the deterrence of violent behavior.

Hybrid tribunals are considered to be an excellent mechanism for the achievement of these aims. They are defined by the Office of the High Commissioner of Human Rights (OHCHR), "as courts of mixed composition and jurisdiction, encompassing both national and international aspects, usually operating within the jurisdiction where the crimes occurred.[5] They have proliferated over the last decade as a response to the costs and distance of *ad hoc* tribunals, and the impunity or bias perpetuated by domestic prosecutions.[6]

High expectations are placed on hybrid tribunals to achieve not only retributive and restorative justice but wider goals of and institutional reform.[7] It is hoped that the mixture of international and domestic elements in a hybrid tribunal has a positive impact on the domestic justice system of the affected country and its human rights compliance.[8]Among the main expectations are that trials contribute to broader programs of legal reform and the development of the domestic justice system through the capacity building of national staff.[9] Moreover the "demonstration effect" of hybrid courts may increase public trust in justice and national institutions,[10] and contribute to social reconciliation.[11]

It is important to bear in mind however that a standard hybrid tribunal model does not exist or, for that matter, a consistent set of hybrid tribunal practices. The experimentation with hybrid courts has been conducted on an *ad hoc* basis;[12] their primary objective to carry out criminal prosecutions. The expectations about the capacity of hybrid courts to influence peacebuilding processes through their impact on the rule of law are not explicitly mentioned and as such do not tend to be reflected in the financial provisions for these courts or the functions and competences of their bodies and personnel. Thus it is important to be aware of the limitations of hybrid courts and what could be unrealistic goals or expectations,[13] at the same time to acknowledge their special role in the post-conflict reconstruction process.

Establishment of the War Crimes Chamber

Background

The Bosnian conflict, which had horrific human consequences,[14] including genocide,[15] ended in 1995 with the Dayton Peace Accords (DPA). Brokered by the United States, the DPA established the Office of the High Representative (OHR) to monitor its implementation. The powers of the OHR include powers to make binding decisions related to the removal of elected officials, impose legislation, amend entity constitutions, and create new institutions.

The DPA established a new political structure: the Federation of Bosnia and Herzegovina and *Republika Srpska*; each with its own government, parliament, and judiciary. The DPA also established a third separate political entity with autonomous status: the Brčko District. These entities remain ethnically distinctive. Bosniaks and Croats primarily reside in the Federation; Serbs in *Republika Srpska*. The DPA also established a tripartite shared presidency composed of a Bosnian Croat, a Bosniak, and a Bosnian Serb representative at the state level. This complex administrative structure and tripartite system of government—

necessary at the time for the achievement of peace—has become an obstacle for governance and the administration of justice. As for the judicial system, during the war it suffered from misuse. After the war new courts were created,[16] a massive backlog of cases generated, and the judiciary became an instrument of ethic discrimination.[17]

The promotion of rule of law had been on the international agenda since 1998. That year the UN Judicial System Assessment Programme was created. In 2002 the OHR presented its strategy for reform of the judicial sector.[18] Among the most important reforms included the vetting and reappointment of judicial staff, domestic passage of new criminal codes, the establishment of the State Court and the State Prosecutor's Office, and the creation of the High Judicial and Prosecutorial Council (HJPC).[19]

The State Court became operational in 2003. It comprises three divisions: criminal, administrative, and appellate. It has jurisdiction over the whole country and was created to permit the centralized exercise of judicial power and guarantee rule of law.[20] The War Crimes Chamber (WCC) is a section of the State Court; the Special Department for War Crimes (SDWC) part of the State Office of the Prosecutor.

WCC Establishment and Competence

Prosecution of atrocity crimes in Bosnia and Herzegovina (referred here generically as "Bosnia") has taken place in three venues: the International Criminal Tribunal for the former Yugoslavia (ICTY), the WCC, and national courts. The ICTY was established in 1993 and scheduled to cease operations in 2013. Part of its completion strategy involves the transfer of cases to the national courts. Thus far, cases dealing with lower-level perpetrators have been transferred to Bosnia, Croatia, and Serbia. Eight cases have been transferred to national jurisdictions under Rule 11 bis,[21] with six of these going to the WCC.

The WCC was created as part of the Criminal Division of the State Court. The WCC, the Organised Crime Chamber, the SDWC and the Special Department for Organised Crime were composed of national and international staff.[22] The establishment of the WCC and SDWC was a direct result of the agreement reached in January 2003 between the OHR and the ICTY which created the Registry.[23] They were established, in part, to counter the destabilization arising from national prosecutions.[24] The WCC's main objective is to provide the justice system with the tools and capacity necessary to prosecute and carry out war crimes trials pursuant to international justice standards.[25] By doing so it is believed the WCC will contribute to rule of law efforts in Bosnia.[26] Therefore, the WCC and the SDWC were created, not only as part of the completion strategy of the ICTY, but also as part of the wider rule of law reform.

Accompanying the WCC and the SDWC are the Defence Office (OKO), the Victim Support Office, and the Public Information and Outreach Office (PIOS). All were to have international components at the time of their establishment. These international components were to be replaced as the State Court became a fully national institution financed by the Bosnian budget in December 2009. This makes the WCC unique compared to other hybrid tribunals. However although the presence of international staff has diminished, the WCC is still not fully national

The WCC has jurisdiction over crimes against humanity, genocide, and war crimes.[27] The majority of cases heard by the WCC involve crimes against humanity; including murder and persecution.[28] By May 2011 the WCC concluded thirty-five cases in second instance and a similar number in first instance.[29]

Since 2004 SDWC has had chief responsibility for classifying cases to be tried by the WCC. However, a more systematic prosecutorial strategy was established in 2008.[30] The National War Crimes Prosecution Strategy was approved by the Council of Ministers under pressure from the international community.[31] The Strategy states that the WCC's objective is to prosecute the most serious war crimes cases within seven years of its adoption; lesser priority cases within fifteen years.[32] The Head of the SDWC specifically expressed disagreement with this ambitious new strategy, opting instead to continue the procedures he had put in place in 2007.[33] Even with a consolidated, effective, and well-resourced judicial system, completing this number of complex cases is unrealistic.[34]

The State Court's Registry was tasked with overseeing the transition from a hybrid to fully national court. In March 2006 a Bosnian took charge and by December the Registry was run with only national staff and financed through the national budget. To assist in the phasing out of international staff and financial support, the Registry was supported by a Transitional Council, composed of domestic and regional representatives.[35] Although the phasing out of international staff happened relatively smoothly in certain bodies, the transition phase for international judges and prosecutors has been another matter altogether.

The WCC originally had six trial panels and one appellate panel. The panels were composed of two Bosnian judges and one international judge. Even if their mandate had been extended at the end of 2009, only Bosnian judges sat on first instance panels. A shortage of judges made it necessary to reduce the number of first instance panels to four (even as the number of cases before the WCC increased).[36] By August 2010 one international judge, out of the six judges still remaining, left before his mandate expired.[37] By the end of 2010 the WCC was still waiting for four national judges to be appointed. The four international judges that remain are in the appellate division.[38]

International prosecutors have not been as numerous as international judges. They have always been a minority compared to their national counterparts. Although the Head of the SDWC and Deputy Chief Prosecutor was international, since December 2009 this position has been held by a Bosnian. In 2010 the

SDWC continued to recruit international staff, including three international prosecutors. As of May 2011, four of the nineteen prosecutors at the SDWC are internationals.

Impact on the Domestic Justice System: Capacity Building and Knowledge Transfer

The international community foresaw that through the establishment of the WCC it was contributing to the empowerment of the people and institutions of Bosnia by providing the necessary management and technical tools and financial and material resources to generate capacity to carry out the task of bringing to justice the perpetrators of war crimes.[39] It was hoped that the presence of experienced international judges and lawyers would contribute to the capacity building of domestic legal personnel. The international community has also invested a significant amount of resources into training justice sector staff in the WCC and domestic courts. Most of this training has occurred as part of the ICTY's completion strategy, as well as judicial reform in Bosnia more generally.[40] At the national level, the HJPC is in charge of capacity building and training, which is done through Judicial and Prosecutorial Training Centres in each entity. These centres have also conducted trainings on war crimes prosecutions.[41]

Potentially one of the best practices developed in the WCC is the Judicial College. Prior to the launch of the Judicial College the different training events organised by or for the Court did not appear to be fully accepted by participants and had a negligible impact on the staff's everyday work.[42] The Judicial College, modelled after the Vermont Judicial College,[43] is currently organised by the Judicial Education Committee. Both the Committee and the College were created under the initiative of one international judge, but were welcomed by national and internationals alike.[44] The Education Committee was endorsed by the President and set up in 2008, with international Judge Whalen as its Chair. The Committee, composed of six Bosnians and two internationals, meets regularly to discuss the educational needs of the Court, to screen requests for funding and training offers by donors, and to develop criteria for who should attend training sessions.[45] The Committee also oversees the education of legal officers.

Since 2006 programs have been organised in Sarajevo and throughout the country.[46] Their format permits Bosnian staff to select topics for discussion in an environment that guarantees a free and open exchange of information. It has covered the issues of efficiency, credibility of witnesses, and jurisdiction of the Court. It is also been important as a means to hand over responsibility from international to national staff. In 2009 Bosnians took responsibility for the development and implementation of fifty percent of the program with the goal to have Bosnians totally responsible for the College by 2012. Interestingly, the practice initiated at the State Court is generating sufficient "spill-over" and has the potential to positively contribute to wider knowledge transfer to the domestic judicial system. The OKO has also played a role in capacity building for defence councils acting before the Court,[47] and contributing to rule of law by increasing the equality of arms in criminal prosecutions.[48]

The practice of other tribunals has shown that the structure and institutional design of a hybrid court can either help or hinder the experience of national staff.[49] In Bosnia the fact that the institution was designed from the beginning to give a prominent role to national judges has been important both in terms of increasing the domestic ownership of the justice process, and creating positive interaction between national and international staff. Judges are reported to have good relationships with each other and there is a strong collaborative spirit.[50]

The presence of international staff has been especially important in terms of court management, even if doubts have been raised about the willingness of local staff to fully embrace the new working practices.[51] Very important too has been the role of international judges in the implementation of legal reforms introduced by the legislature.[52] The change from a prosecutorial to an adversarial system, for example, made training and practice in such areas as plea bargaining agreements and cross examination necessary.[53]Although international prosecutors provided some training to their national counterparts, this was not done in a systematic way and there was no strategy for skills building put into place.[54]

The fact that the WCC is a specialised court limits its capacity to engage with the other judicial and legal communities in Bosnia, which in turn limits its ability to contribute to wider capacity building. However, a positive demonstration effect seems to be taking place. The experience of Bosnian staff working alongside international staff, the WCC management and work practices developed during these six years, and the knowledge transfer that has taken place, all benefit the judiciary as a whole. In 2009 the Registry pointed out that an important process was taking place within the larger process of transitioning from an international presence to national counterparts, integration of national staff into national judicial institutions, and building of national capacity. Staff trained in the State Court and the Registry are always among the best candidates for vacancies at other courts.[55] It is expected that this impact will continue and the WCC and the State Court in general continue to act as important sources of professionalism which permeate local justice institutions.

Effects on Public Perceptions of the Rule of Law and Institutional Trust

Advocates of hybrid tribunals also argue that they have a positive impact on the perception of rule of law held by those directly involved with the tribunal, as well as on the wider population; this leading to stability and an increase in public trust in governing institutions. This demonstration effect may also contribute to culture shifts and an increased awareness of human rights which, in turn, may result in increased demands for governmental accountability.[56] The presence of international judges creates an aura of impartiality, which can lead to a greater confidence that fair trials have been conducted. They permit greater participation in the justice process; this ultimately promoting peaceful relations between previously fighting groups.[57]

Bosnia's experience with the WCC demonstrates it necessary to temper the above-mentioned claims. The egregious human rights violations perpetrated during the conflict had a lasting negative impact on Bosnian society. Political discourse remains highly polarized with constant appeals made to underlying resentments. War crimes prosecutions dominate societies' responses to the atrocities; the processes of social repair and the rebuilding of trust have been become inextricably linked with retributive approaches to justice. The divisiveness of prosecutions certainly effects the WCC's work; its capacity to affect social perceptions of the rule of law, and to contribute to wider goals of social reconciliation.

A crucial lesson learned from the work of the ICTY is that for prosecutions to have a positive social impact, knowledge of and engagement with the work of the courts are crucial. Most of the population in Bosnia rely on the media as a source of information about the war trials and form opinions based on the information received.[58] The mainstream media tends to focus more on scandalous aspects of specific cases.[59] The coverage of trials is highly politicised and information on certain trials is silenced or sensationalised depending on the ethnicity of the perpetrator, the victims, and/or the ethnic composition of the population in a certain area.[60]

The specialised media organisation, Balkan Initiative Reporting Network (BIRN), has made a significant contribution to increasing public knowledge about the WCC. Their coverage of every single trial brings the work of the WCC closer to the public. Particularly important have been the efforts of BIRN to train both journalists and civil society organizations on war crimes trials reporting.[61]

Notwithstanding these initiatives, Bosnian society has not demonstrated a pressing interest in following the trials. This lack of interest has been blamed on war-fatigue,[62] and a range of misconceptions and falsehoods about the work of the WCC.[63] In this regard, the WCC is constantly battling accusations on every flank, including to victims associations disappointed and frustrated with the pace of the process and what they perceive to be lenient sentences.[64] Bosnian Serb political leaders have been very vocal about their rejection of the Court, arguing that it has focused more strongly on the prosecution of Serbs.[65] In line with the discourse of Bosnian Serb political leaders, Serb victim associations have led the charge against the Court and several demonstrations have taken place.

In early 2011 the WCC suffered a serious challenge to its legitimacy when the *Republika Srpska's* Prime Minister, Mirolad Dodik, called for a referendum to question the law which established the Court.[66] These challenges make outreach much more pressing. Consequently it is now considered central as a means to guarantee the WCC's legitimacy and legacy.[67]

Both the PIOS and outreach strategy were established at the outset.[68] From the beginning the PIOS has been composed exclusively of national staff.[69] PIOS aims to enable communication with national and international media and with the general public in order to enable a wider understanding of its work and a general awareness of its importance.[70] PIOS not only bears the responsibility of making the prosecutorial and judicial work accessible to the general public, they are also responsible for demonstrating that the new judicial institutions are transparent, independent, and effective.[71]

To complement its work and maximise outreach, the WCC initially relied on the work of NGOs and established a "Court Support Network" of over five hundred organisations with no restrictions placed on membership.[72] The four information centres set up were meant to serve as a link between citizens and the WCC;[73] their purpose to create "such a climate that will be motivating for all citizens across communities and in which citizens will relate to the judicial system in Bosnia with a trust, which this country enormously lacks."[74] Unfortunately this initiative failed due to problems of coordination, lack of institutional support and funding.[75] Moreover, the absence of restrictions on membership meant that a wide variety of organisations were included in the network; organizations ranging from victims associations, to churches, to a football club. Such diversity did not permit the creation of a coherent working strategy and consequently contributed to the network's lack of success.[76]

If prosecutions are to have a positive role in rebuilding rule of law, greater public engagement is necessary. The outreach strategy has failed to reverse the lack of engagement of certain segments of society, the denials and revisionist discourses rampant in certain communities, the disillusionment and apathy of certain victims,[77] and to contain attacks against the WCC and its staff. Additionally there is a risk that certain political elites will obstruct the advancement towards accountability and victim's rights recognition. Improvement of public perceptions of the WCC requires greater understanding of criminal procedure, including plea agreements.[78]

Together with a stronger and improved outreach strategy the WCC requires further and committed protection from political attacks. The OSCE has repeatedly warned of threats to the independence of the judiciary.[79] It is important that other protective measures be taken to preserve the WCC's reputation and shield judges from politically motivated claims of bias or even corruption. In this sense, the HJPC could institute protective procedures against defamation of judges, which would not only preserve their independence, but contribute to public perception of the State Court as an impartial, non-politically motivated institution, and send a message of strength from the judiciary as a whole.

At present the desired impact of rebuilding social trust and social relations is difficult to detect in Bosnia.[80] The work of the WCC is limited in terms of establishing a narrative of the conflict which could serve as a basis for peace and reconciliation, as well as a forum for the recognition of victims' needs beyond retribution.[81] Complementary transitional justice activities, especially truth-seeking ones, have encountered numerous problems in Bosnia until now.[82] The official neglect of restorative justice initiatives contrasts with the number of civil society initiatives.[83] The difficulties in creating other fora for discussion, mechanisms for restoration and reparations for victims, and rebuilding social trust among individuals and within communities may place too much pressure on the WCC.

Conclusions

This chapter has explored the WCC's impact on strengthening the rule of law in Bosnia and Herzegovina. The experience of the WCC thus far could be considered positive. A large number of cases have been prosecuted, cooperation between national and international staff has been fluid, and it is doing important work upholding international criminal standards. It has also managed to withstand political attacks for the past seven years.

An important lesson learned from the WCC's experience is that hybrid tribunals' practice can be further capitalised if they develop their activities within wider processes of judicial and legislative reform. The fact that capacity building and training were taking place as part of a wider rule of law programme has relieved the WCC of some of these pressures. Of course the WCC has advantages that are not replicable in other contexts, such as its link to the ICTY. On the other hand most of the good practices developed in the WCC provide interesting examples for other hybrid or national tribunals prosecuting war crimes.

The tasks remaining for the WCC are still enormous. In order to be successful it will need firm support from the international community and stronger commitment from national authorities. Beyond the WCC, this study demonstrates that hybrid tribunals alone are not able to fulfil all the expectations placed on them with regards to prosecution, strengthening the rule of law and restorative justice needs. In order to maximise their impact, consideration should be given to how other rule of law reform processes and transitional justice mechanisms engage with one another.

Notes

This chapter was written with the support of the British Academy Grant (SG100735) on "The role of hybrid courts in the institutional and substantive development of international criminal justice. A study of the War Crimes Chamber of the State Court of Bosnia and Herzegovina" and the European Union 7th Framework Programme Collaborative Project on "Just and Durable Peace by Piece" (no. 217488). I am grateful to Chandra L. Sriram, Johanna Herman and Iva Vukušić for their comments to earlier versions of this chapter, to Julie Broome for invaluable help in organising my fieldwork, to Stephanie Barbour and Clara Ramirez-Barrat for their generosity in sharing their work and to Jeannette Simpoha-Nylin for her research assistance. This chapter was concluded in May 2011. The data is current up to this date.

1. See for example, Jack Snyder and Leslie Vinjamuri, "Trials and Errors: Principle and Pragmatism in Strategies of International Justice," *International Security* 28 (2003/2004): 5-44.

2. UN Secretary-General, *Rule Of Law and Transitional Justice in Conflict and Post-Conflict Societies* (Report of the Secretary-General), UN Doc. A/2004/61 (August 23, 2004); "Nuremberg Declaration on Peace and Justice," UN Doc. A/62/885 (June 19, 2008);

3. Rule of law is defined as "a principle of governance in which all persons, institutions and entities, public and private, including the State itself, are accountable to laws that are publicly promulgated, equally enforced and independently adjudicated, and which are consistent with international human rights norms and standards." UN Secretary-General, *Rule of Law*, para. 6.

4. Rama Mani, *Beyond Retribution: Seeking Justice in the Shadows of War* (Cambridge: Polity Press, 2002), 3-22.

5. *Rule of Law Tools for Post-Conflict States: Maximizing The Legacy Of Hybrid Courts,* UN Office of the High Commissioner for Human Rights (OHCHR), at 1 (New York; Geneva: United Nations, 2008).

6. Antonio Cassese, "The Role of Internationalized Courts and Tribunals in the Fight Against International Criminality," in *Internationalized Criminal Courts. Sierra Leone, East Timor and Cambodia,* ed. Cesare Romano, Andre Nollkaemper, and Jann Kleffner (Oxford: Oxford University Press, 2004), 7.

7. Laura A. Dickinson, "Notes and Comments: The Promise of Hybrid Courts," 97 *Am. J. Int'l. L.* 295 (2003).

8. OHCHR, *Rule of Law Tools*, 1; Parinaz Kermani Mendez, "The New Wave of Hybrid Tribunals: A Sophisticated Approach to Enforcing International Humanitarian Law or an Idealistic Solution with Empty Promises?," 20 *Crim. L. Forum*, 53, 63 (2009).

9. OHCHR, *Rule of Law Tools*, 5.

10. Jane Stromseth, David Wippman and Rosa Brooks, *Can Might Make Rights? Building the Rule of Law After Military Interventions* (Cambridge: Cambridge University Press, 2008), 258-259.

11. Cassese, "Internationalized Courts," 6.

12. Mendez, "The New Wave," 62.

13. Olga Martin-Ortega and Johanna Herman, "Hybrid Tribunals: Interaction and Resistance in Bosnia and Herzegovina and Cambodia" in *Hybrid Forms of Peace: From the 'Everyday' to Post-liberalism,* ed. Oliver Richmond and Audra Mitchell (Basingstoke: Palgrave, 2011), 73-88.

14. The number killed during the war has been disputed with initial UN estimates of two hundred thousand people, *Report of the Secretary-General the UN Mission in BiH,* UN Doc. S/2002/1314 (December 2, 2002). The recent study, Research and Documenta-

tion Center, *Population Losses in Bosnia and Herzegovina '92-95* (Sarajevo: Research and Documentation Centre, 2007), has documented one hundred thousand deaths.

15. The ICTY considers the acts in Srebrenica to be genocide. ICTY, *Prosecutor v. Krstić*, Case No. IT-98-33-T, Judgement (August 2, 2001), confirmed by Appeals Chamber in April 19, 2004.

16. Michael H. Doyle, "Too Little, Too Late? Justice and Security Reform in Bosnia and Herzegovina," in *Constructing Justice and Security After War*, ed. Charles T. Call (Washington D.C., USIP, 2007), 248.

17. On prosecutions for war crimes at the domestic level, see International Crisis Group, *Courting Disaster: The Misrule of Law in Bosnia & Herzegovina*, Balkans Report No. 127 (Sarajevo/Brussels: ICG, 2002) and Organization for Security and Cooperation in Europe (OSCE), *War Crimes Trials Before the Domestic Courts of Bosnia and Herzegovina. Progress and Obstacles* (March 2005).

18. Office of the High Representative (OHR), *Jobs and Justice: Our Agenda* (Sarajevo: May 2002).

19. The HJPC is in charge of the appointment, development, and discipline of all judges and prosecutors.

20. "Law on the Court of Bosnia and Herzegovina," *Official Gazette* 16/02 and "Law Re-amending the Law on the Court of Bosnia and Herzegovina," *Official Gazette* 3/03. These laws were first approved by decision of the OHR (50/00 and 97/03 respectively) and later by the Parliamentary Assembly.

21. Rule 11 *bis* refers to the provision of the ICTY's "Rule of Procedure and Evidence" which enables the Tribunal to transfer cases to domestic courts.. http://www.icty.org/sections/LegalLibrary/RulesofProcedureandEvidence (accessed May 15, 2011).

22. The Prosecutor's Office of Bosnia and Herzegovina is divided into the Department for General Crimes, the Special Department for War Crimes, and the Special Department for Organized Crime, Economic Crime and Corruption.

23. *Agreement on the Establishment of the Registry for Section I for War Crimes and Section II for Organised Crime, Economic Crime and Corruption of the Criminal and Appellate Divisions of the Court of Bosnia and Herzegovina and the Special Department for War Crimes and the Special Department for Organised Crime, Economic Crime and Corruption of the Prosecutor's Office of Bosnia and Herzegovina* (December 1, 2004). See also Security Council Res. No. 1503, Sec. 5, S/Res/1503 (August 28, 2003).

24. The lack of impartiality had previously led to the creation of a system of ICTY oversight over national prosecutions. OHR, "Domestic War Crimes Trials and the Rules of the Road," Rome Agreement, para. 5 (February 18, 1996), http://www.ohr.int/ohr-dept/hr-rol/thedept/war-crime-tr/default.asp?content_id=5231 (accessed May 15, 2011).

25. OHR, *War Crimes Chamber Project, Project Implementation Plan, Registry Progress Report* (October 20, 2004), http://www.ohr.int/ohr-dept/rule-of-law-pillar/pdf/wcc-project-plan-201004-eng.pdf (accessed October 5, 2010).

26. OHR, *War Crimes Chamber Project*, 44.

27. Court of Bosnia & Herzegovina, "Law on the Court of Bosnia and Herzegovina," http://www.sudbih.gov.ba/files/docs/zakoni/en/Zakon_o_sudu_-_eng.pdf, (accessed May 15, 2011).

28. Bogdan Ivanešević, *The War Crimes Chamber in Bosnia and Herzegovina: From Hybrid to Domestic Court* (New York: ICTJ, 2008), 10.

29. "Statistics," at http://www.sudbih.gov.ba/?opcija=statistike&jezik=e (accessed May 2011).

30. Lara Nettelfield, *Courting Democracy in Bosnia and Herzegovina. The Hague Tribunal's Impact in a Postwar State* (Cambridge: Cambridge University Press, 2010), 262.

31. Peace Implementation Council, *Declaration of the Steering Board* (February 27, 2008), 2-3.

32. National Prosecution Strategy, approved in December 2008 by the Council of Ministers, reproduced in "Annex 2 of the Forum for International Criminal and Humanitarian Law," *The Backlog of Core International Crimes Case Files in Bosnia and Herzegovina* (2009).

33. David Schwendiman, "Prosecuting Atrocity Crimes in National Courts: Looking back on 2009 in Bosnia and Herzegovina," *Northwestern Journal of International Human Rights* 8, no. 3 (2010): 274.

34. Member of the SDWC interviewed by author in Sarajevo in September 2009.

35. The design of mechanisms to support the transition was established in the "OHR-Presidency of BiH Agreement Establishing a Transitional Council on September 26, 2007" and "Attachment A Integration Strategy of the National Staff of the Registry into the Justice Institutions of Bosnia-Herzegovina 2006-2009," *Official Gazette* 3/07, http://www.registrarbih.gov.ba/files/docs/New_Registry_Agreement_-_eng.pdf (accessed May 10, 2011).

36. Registry of the State Court of Bosnia & Herzegovina, *The Registry Annual Report 2009*, http://www.sudbih.gov.ba/?jezik=e (accessed May 10, 2011).

37. Registry of the State Court of Bosnia & Herzegovina, *The Registry Quarterly Report, September 2010,* http://www.sudbih.gov.ba/?jezik=e (accessed May 10, 2011)

38. Court of Bosnia & Herzegovina, "Jurisdiction, Organisation and Structure," http://www.sudbih.gov.ba/?opcija=sadrzaj&kat=3&id=3&jezik=e (accessed May 10, 2011).

39. OHR, *War Crimes Chamber Project*, 4.

40. Alejandro Chehtman and Ruth Mackenzie, *Capacity Development in International Criminal Justice: A Mapping Exercise of Existing Practice*, DOMAC/2 (September 2009); Annex-Section A; OSCE-ODIHR-ICTY-UNICRI, "Supporting the Transition Process: Lessons Learned and Best Practices in Knowledge Transfer," (Warsaw, The Hague, Turin, September 2009).

41. Members of the High Judicial and Prosecutorial Council and the Judicial and Prosecutorial Training Centre of *Republika Srpska*, Sarajevo and Banja Luka, interviewed by author in Sarajevo in August-September 2009.

42. Members of the State Court, interviewed by author in Sarajevo between August and September 2009.

43. The Vermont Judicial College consists of annual week-long, residential gathering of the members of the Supreme Court of Vermont judicial officers, court management and staff. It orients its sessions around a theme, including topics such as new developments in law and practice. For more information see the Vermont Judiciary at http://www.vermontjudiciary.org/JC/masterpages/committee-judicialed.aspx (accessed April 20, 2011).

44. The Judicial College started under the impulse of Judge Fisher and was later taken over by Judge Whalen. Both are from Vermont, USA.

45. International judge, interviewed by author interview in Sarajevo between August-September 2009; email exchange with author in February 2010.

46. The 2007 Judicial College on "Efficiency Takes Time" was attended by over seventy participants; see *Efficiency Takes Time: UNDP Helps Court of BiH to Tackle with Organizational Challenges,* UN Development Programme, http://www.undp.ba/index.aspx?PID=7&RID=434 (accessed February 15, 2010).

47. Member of OKO, interviewed by author in Sarajevo in between August-September 2009; see also *OKO War Crimes Reporter* 4 (Winter 2007) on trainings on joint criminal enterprise, and David Tolbert and Aleksandar Kontić, *Final Report of the International Criminal Law Services (ICLS) Experts on the Sustainable Transition of the Registry and International Donor Support to the Court of Bosnia and Herzegovina and the Prosecutor's Office of Bosnia and Herzegovina in 2009* (The Hague, ICLS, 2008), 24.

48. Martin-Ortega and Herman, "Hybrid Tribunals."

49. Martin-Ortega and Herman, "Hybrid Tribunals."

50. Members of the State Court, interviewed by author in Sarajevo between August-September 2009.

51. International judge, interviewed by author in Sarajevo, August-September 2009.

52. Lilian A. Barria & Steven D. Roper, "Judicial Capacity Building in Bosnia and Herzegovina: Understanding Legal Reform Beyond the Completion Strategy of the ICTY," *Human Rights Review* 9 (2008): 323.

53. Chehtman and Mackenzie, *Capacity Development.*

54. Tolbert and Kontić, *Final Report of the ICLS*, 35.

55. Registry of the Court of Bosnia & Herzegovina, *Annual Report 2009.*

56. OHCHR, *Rule of Law Tools*, 17-18.

57. Mendez, "The New Wave," 74.

58. Refik Hodžić, "Living the Legacy of Mass Atrocities. Victim's Perspectives on War Crimes Trials," 8 *J. Int'l Crim. Just.* 113, 126 (2010).

59. Member of BIRN Sarajevo, interviewed by author in Sarajevo, August-September 2009.

60. Hodžić, "Living the Legacy," 128-129.

61. Nettelfiend, *Courting Democracy*, 256.

62. Ivanešević, *The War Crimes Chamber*, 33.

63. Tolbert and Kontić, *Final Report of the ICLS*, 22.

64. Hodzic, "Living the Legacy," 128-131; Ivanešević, *The War Crimes Chamber*, 34.

65. *Republika Srpska's* Prime Minister Milorad Dodik has been particularly aggressive towards the Court. See for example, http://www.humanrights-geneva.info/Bosnia-future-of-international,6541 (accessed December 11, 2009).

66. EU Inside, "Bosnian Serbs Defy International Community Again," *http//*www.euinside.eu/en/news/serbs-in-bosnia-provoke-again-the-international-community (accessed May 10, 2011).

67. Clara Ramirez-Barrat, *Making an Impact: Guidelines on Designing and Implementing Outreach Programs for Transitional Justice* (New York: ICTJ, 2011), 6-7.

68. The OTP has its own public relations department, the Press Office, whose work is limited to relations with the media, Office of the Prosecutor of Bosnia and Herzegovina, see www.tuzilastvobih.gov.ba/?opcija=sadrzaj&kat=6&id=13&jezik=e (accessed October 15, 2010).

69. Stephanie Barbour, "Domestic War Crimes Processing in Bosnia and Herzegovina," *Internal Case Study, ICTJ Research Project: Making an Impact: Guidance on Designing Effective Outreach Programs for Transitional Justice* (April 2011): 7 (on file with the author).

70. The website of Public Information and Outreach Section states "The main function of this Office is to enable two way communications with the representatives of the BiH public and to provide all public information from the Court of Bosnia & Herzegovina," at http://www.sudbih.gov.ba/?opcija=sadrzaj&kat=7&id=81&jezik=e (accessed May 10, 2011).

71. Barbour, "Domestic War Crimes," 8.

72. Ivanešević, *The War Crimes Chamber*, 36.

73. Barbour, "Domestic War Crimes"; also Ramirez-Barrat *Making an Impact*, 30.

74. Centre for Civil Initiatives, www.ccibh.org/main.php?lang=ENG (accessed November 8, 2010).

75. Barbour, "Domestic War Crimes"; Ramirez-Barrat, *Making an Impact*, 30; Nettelfield, *Courting Democracy*, 255-256; also Ivanešević, *The War Crimes Chamber*, 36.

76. Barbour, "Domestic War Crimes," 9; Ramirez-Barrat, *Making an Impact*, 30.

77. Refik Hodžić, "Living the Legacy," 133.

78. Schwendiman, "Prosecuting Atrocity Crimes," 297.

79. OSCE, *Attempts to Undermine the Court of Bosnia and Herzegovina and the Prosecutor's Office of BiH Harm all People in BiH*, Press Release, http://www.osce.org/bih/76212 (March 25, 2011).

80. The word "reconciliation" is often avoided. At the same time it is constantly suggested that there exists not one truth, but three. Author interviews, Sarajevo, August-September 2009.

81. Martin-Ortega and Herman, "Hybrid Tribunals."

82. See *Transitional Justice Guidebook for Bosnia and Herzegovina,* Executive Summary, UN Development Programme, at 26-28, www.undp.ba (accessed November 8, 2010); also Jasna Dragović-Soso and Eric Gordy, "Coming to Terms with the Past: Transitional Justice and Reconciliation in Post-Yugoslav Lands" in *New Perspectives on Yugoslavia: Key Issues and Controversies,* ed. James Ker-Lindsay and Dejan Djokic (Oxon: Routledge, 2010).

83. At the time of writing the initiative by several hundreds of NGOs for a regional truth seeking body is gaining momentum. Balkan Insight, *Montenegro's PM Endorses Fact-Finding Initiative RECOM*, April 29, 2011.

Chapter 14

A Necessary Compromise or Compromised Justice? The Extraordinary Chambers in the Courts of Cambodia

Johanna Herman

The Extraordinary Chambers in the Courts of Cambodia (ECCC) completed its first trial in 2010. Despite delays in its establishment and criticisms over corruption and political interference, it has been widely accepted that the trial of Kaing Guek Eav ("Duch") was a success. Additionally, the ECCC has led the way in the promotion of victims' rights by permitting participation of civil parties in a hybrid tribunal. However, there are still lessons to be learned and changes required. In addition to issues associated with the reparations process, there are also significant challenges posed by the Royal Government of Cambodia (RGC). This chapter argues the ECCC is at a turning point. It is increasingly likely that its positive impact will be undermined by the RGC. In the period between the conclusion of the Duch trial and the start of the second the government has been very vocal in telling the UN that there should be *no* additional prosecutions.[1] The development of Cases 003 and 004 pose significant challenges for the prosecution and a test of the ECCC's independence.

Background and Establishment of the ECCC

For three decades Cambodia experienced substantial turmoil which included civil war and rule by the Khmer Rouge (KR) and Vietnam. The ECCC focuses solely on the abuses perpetrated by the KR between 1975 and 1978.

Led by Pol Pot the KR aimed to bring about a revolution in Cambodia. The forced evacuation of cities led to several hundred thousand deaths.[2] Approximately two million people died as a result of KR policies, which included overwork, starvation, and political purges.[3] The latter included interrogations and "confessions" in a number of security prisons in Cambodia.[4]

In 1979 Pol Pot and Ieng Sary (former Deputy Prime Minister and Foreign Minister) were tried *in absentia* by a special tribunal. They were found guilty of genocide and sentenced to death.[5] There were a number of reports of low-ranking KR soldiers being held without trial and reports of vigilante justice.[6] After the Paris Agreement and elections, the newly elected RGC took an approach towards political reconciliation. In 1994 it passed a law outlawing the KR and granting a six month amnesty period which resulted in thousands of KR defections and a Royal Pardon for Ieng Sary.[7]

At the request of the Cambodian Prime Ministers, the UN appointed a Group of Experts in December 1997 to consider the options available for bringing KR perpetrators to justice.[8] They discovered numerous problems with Cambodia's judicial system, including an absence of impartiality, which they attributed to official interference and corruption.[9] They concluded that an international criminal tribunal would be the best option.[10]

By the time the Group of Experts delivered their report, Prime Minister Hun Sen had consolidated his position as the sole Prime Minister. He then sought to limit international involvement. This led UN Special Representative of the Secretary-General for Human Rights in Cambodia, Thomas Hammarberg, to state "Hun Sen has obviously seen the international tribunal as an instrument to defeat the Khmer Rouge more than as a means of establishing justice."[11] The RGC did not wish to cooperate with any form of tribunal held outside of the country. Hammarberg then held discussions with the government about a hybrid model.[12]

This broke the deadlock and in June 1999 Hun Sen requested assistance from the UN for a hybrid tribunal. However disagreements between the UN and the RGC persisted primarily over the numbers of Cambodian judges permitted. The RGC wanted a majority of Cambodian judges; the UN a majority of international judges.

Eventually the RGC began preparing a law which permitted the Khmer Rouge Tribunal to have a majority of Cambodian judges. The United States proposed that all decisions be made on the basis of a supermajority; meaning that at least one foreign judge would have to agree with the Cambodian judges. International influence was believed to be necessary as a means to counterbalance any negative external pressures on domestic staff and prohibit political interference and corruption. Although this suggestion moved the negotiations forward it was not done in consultation with the UN, which still had fundamental concerns about the proposed model.[13] After the law establishing the ECCC was passed by the Cambodian Senate in January 2001 (ratified in August 2001), the UN still had significant problems with the law's content and the proposed structure of the ECCC, and withdrew its support from negotiations in February 2002.[14]

Pressure from a number of member states to compromise on the question of the majority of international judges, led the Secretary-General to resume negotiations and a draft agreement was presented to the General Assembly in March 2003. The *Agreement between the United Nations and the Royal Government of Cambodia Concerning the Prosecution Under Cambodian Law of Crimes Committed during the Period of Democratic Kampuchea* was signed by the UN and RGC in June 2003, and approved by the Cambodian National Assembly and Senate in October 2004.

This protracted process demonstrates the problems hybrid models encounter when the question of ownership is unclear and stakeholders are at odds with one another over the tribunal's objectives. The UN had little choice in the matter; it could either accept the compromise or withdraw altogether.

Mandate and Structure

The ECCC has a mandate "to bring to trial senior leaders of Democratic Kampuchea and those most responsible for the crimes and serious violations, international humanitarian law and custom and international conventions recognised by Cambodia that were committed during the period from 1975 to 1979."[15] Both the Pre-Trial and Trial Chambers have five judges (three Cambodian and two international). According to the supermajority rule, agreement of four judges is required for an affirmative vote. The Supreme Court Chamber requires five votes for a "supermajority" from its seven judges (four Cambodian; three international).

Cambodia's legal system is based on civil law; a consequence of its long relationship with France. This makes the ECCC unique because it operates entirely within a civil law rather than a common law system. In addition to two co-prosecutors, (one Cambodian, one international), there are also two co-investigating judges (one Cambodian, one international). After preliminary investigations co-prosecutors file an Introductory Submission. Subsequently, co-investigating judges examine the evidence and decide whether or not to charge the suspects. They then carry out an investigation, after which a case file is transferred to the co-prosecutors who then make a Final Submission. On the basis of such a Submission, the judges decide whether to issue a Closing Order, which sends the accused to trial. Other organs of the ECCC—the Defense Support Section, Office of Administration, Victims Support Section—also have half Cambodian and half international staff.

The ECCC began operating in February 2006. In September 2009, the international co-prosecutor put forward five confidential names, two of which have been leaked out.[16] These latter prosecutions have stalled amidst charges of judicial incompetence and government interference; charges which promoted international co-investigating judge—Siegfred Blunk—to resign in October 2011. The possible implications these recent events will have for the ECCC are well-stated by Executive Director for the Open Society Justice Initiative (OSJI) James A. Goldstone: "The credibility of this court, including its current case against the top four surviving Khmer Rouge leaders, depends on restoring confidence in the independence of its investigations, both past and future."[17]

Lessons from the Duch Trial

Duch was responsible for the torture and murder of thousands of people. He disappeared from Phnom Penh with the retreating KR and was not seen for two decades. In 1999 a journalist tracked him down and found him living in the jungle. Duch admitted who he was and gave himself up to Cambodian authorities.[18] After years of military detention, he was charged in the Prosecution's Introductory Submission in July 2007 and transferred to the ECCC. In August 2008 the Closing Order was issued and he was indicted for crimes against humanity and grave breaches of the Geneva Conventions. The Closing Order stated that, "while DUCH was not a senior leader of Democratic Kampuchea, he may be considered in the category of most responsible for crimes and serious violations committed between April 17, 1975 and January 6, 1979, due both to his formal and effective hierarchical authority and his personal participation as Deputy Secretary then Secretary of S21."[19]

The judgment handed down in mid 2010 found Duch guilty of crimes against humanity, including extermination, enslavement, imprisonment, and persecution on political grounds.[20] He was also found guilty of grave breaches of the Geneva Conventions, including willful killing and torture.[21] He was sentenced to thirty-five years in jail.[22] Due to the illegality of his pre-trial detention, five years were taken off his sentence. The Trial Chamber ruled Duch's detention to be in violation of Cambodian domestic law applicable at the time which guaranteed a defendant's right to a speedy trial. He was therefore entitled to credit for this period.[23] His sentence was reduced a further eleven years because of time served. Both the defense and prosecution appealed in March 2011. The defense wanted an acquittal, the prosecution wanted a maximum sentence of life in prison. In February 2012 the Supreme Court Chamber increased Duch's sentence to life imprisonment.

The Trial Chamber determined that there was an international armed conflict in Cambodia during KR rule,[24] and held that their attacks against civilians constituted crimes under international law according to the customary definition of crimes against humanity during 1975-1979.[25] This is particularly important for Case 002 since the Chamber was unable to reach a decision on whether the charges against Duch for crimes under domestic law were barred by the statute of limitations.[26] The judgment also outlined the hierarchical structure of the KR, its policies of secrecy, and the "smashing" of enemies.[27] Scheffer states: "The Co-Prosecutors now have the means to show why senior leaders used various crimes against humanity to advance their evil intent to discriminate against and extinguish so many politically inconvenient people."[28]

Despite the displeasure of victims and the objections made by the prosecution, the Duch trial demonstrated to Cambodians the importance of fair trial standards. Although the factual and legal findings above are significant, this chapter focuses on other important aspects of the Duch trial that impact the ECCC's work and provide lessons for other tribunals regarding victim participation and outreach.

The Civil Party System

The Cambodian judicial system allows victims to stand as civil parties in criminal proceedings. The ECCC is similar. Anyone who has suffered harm as a direct consequence of the KR regime can apply to become a civil party and is allowed to seek collective and moral reparations. As civil parties they have the same rights as other parties to the proceedings. This makes the ECCC unique compared to other tribunals.

This is not to say of course that the civil party system has not encountered its own share of difficulties. These became apparent during the course of the Duch trial, during which a number of amendments were made to Rule 23. An amendment in February 2010 introduced lead co-lawyers to represent the civil parties as a group for Case 002. Ninety-four civil parties applied to participate in the Duch case[29] and were divided into four groups. Each had a Cambodian lawyer and an international lawyer. Since they had the same rights as all other parties in the proceedings, the questioning of witnesses took a very long time, with four teams of civil party lawyers taking part, in addition to judges, the prosecution, and the defense. For this reason, it was hoped the lead co-lawyer system would support a more efficient trial process. Although there are some concerns about how this system will work in practice, particularly when it comes to the adequacy of victim representation, there really was no other practical solution. Despite these difficulties the participation of civil parties in the Duch trial was significant.[30]

Reparations

The Internal Rules also permit "moral and collective reparations" to be awarded to victims. However, it has been difficult to manage the expectations of civil party applicants. There has been some uncertainty about what these reparations entail. As ordered in the Duch judgment, the ECCC compiled and published all statements of apology made by Duch during the trial. Ten thousand copies were distributed in early 2012.[31] Other requests made by the four groups of civil parties—the publication of the judgment, individual monetary awards, a national commemoration day, construction of pagodas, preservation of archives, access to medical care and education—were considered to fall outside the competence of the ECCC. The ECCC's narrow view of reparations has understandably led to a great deal of disappointment on the part of victims.[32]

The revised Internal Rules state there will now be a single claim for collective and moral reparations on behalf of all civil parties. In addition, the Victims Support Section's mandate includes the development and implementation of programs for non-judicial measures, which can be developed in consultation with NGOs.[33] These programs, are meant to address the broader interests of victims in Cambodia and have an impact beyond the single claim for civil parties.

Outreach

The *ad hoc* tribunals for the former Yugoslavia and Rwanda were criticised for their inadequate outreach. It is here that hybrid tribunals may have an advantage because they are located in the countries where the effected populations live. At the same time the ECCC faces a unique challenge in that the crimes involved were committed thirty years ago. Sixty eight percent of the population has no first-hand knowledge of KR atrocities.[34] It became obvious early on that there was going to be a need for a concerted outreach strategy to ensure that young people would feel engaged with the justice process. If done well, such outreach could not only achieve the important goal of informing the population about the particular crimes in question, but also have an impact on public trust in Cambodia's courts. This in turn could ultimately impact public perception of other governing institutions.

The Public Affairs office of the ECCC has staff working in Public Information, Media Relations and Outreach Departments. Public Affairs issues statements, has briefings, produces publications explaining the ECCC's work, and distributes publicity materials across Cambodia informing the public about, for example, the nature of the supermajority rule. Although attendance was low at the beginning of the Duch trial, by late August 2009 over twenty thousand had attended the hearings.

Low attendance problems in the past were also attributed to the ECCC's location. The ECCC is sixteen kilometres outside of Phnom Penh. In bad traffic it can take up to an hour to get to the ECCC from the city. This obviously made participation difficult for those living in the capital, as well as in the rural areas. A few weeks into the trial, however, Public Affairs made a number of announcements through radio and newspapers that they would arrange for buses to transport people to and from the ECCC. This helped increase attendance. Moreover for the closing statements in the Duch trial 100 seats were allocated to civil parties and arranged by the Victims Unit, 300 to the general public, with the rest divided between national and international NGO representatives, media, and diplomats.[35]

Beyond the work of the Public Affairs office, a number of NGOs and international organisations worked to ensure adequate media coverage of the Duch trial. A weekly television report, "Duch on Trial," was broadcast every Monday at lunchtime, with an estimated audience of two to three million people.

Because of its lack of resources the ECCC Public Affairs section has relied heavily on NGOs to maximise its impact. A number of NGOs have held information sessions and meetings in order to inform and educate the public about the ECCC. This led to some criticism of the ECCC before and during the Duch trial for relying *too* much on external parties for outreach.[36] The Victims Unit of the ECCC also performs outreach activities which inform victims about the reparations process and their right to participate in the trials. This is particularly necessary given the role civil parties play in the process. In this they are supported by a number of NGOs and civil society organizations.[37] NGOs assist victims in filing complaints and acquiring legal representation should they wish to participate in the process. This work has been crucial in achieving the high number of civil party applications.[38]

Impact of the ECCC on Rule of Law in Cambodia

Widespread corruption prevails and impunity exists in Cambodia. Cambodia's human rights situation has deteriorated over the past few years, with the government clamping down on human rights advocates and pursuing high profile cases of defamation to demonstrate its seriousness on the matter. Moreover during UN Secretary-General Ban Ki Moon's visit to Cambodia, Prime Minister Hun Sen spoke out against the Office of the High Commissioner for Human Rights (OHCHR), calling for the head of the office to resign and claiming that if this was not done the OHCHR office in Cambodia would be shut down.[39] A Foreign Ministry spokesman referred to the OHCHR as "unnecessary."[40]

In terms of the justice sector, the Cambodian government has long-been criticised for its poor record on rule of law by successive Special Representatives of the Secretary-General on Human Rights in Cambodia. In 2006 the OHCHR stated that court reform was the area most in need of Cambodia's immediate attention.[41] This is not surprising considering the fact that Cambodia's judicial system was completely devastated by the KR.[42] Although there was willingness to focus on the legal sector once Hun Sen became Prime Minister in 1989, this was tempered by a lack of resources and personnel.[43] Since 1993 a great deal of money has been poured into the rule of law sector. Although judicial independence is enshrined in the constitution, the judicial system has never been able to function independently.[44] The problems within the judiciary can be seen as problems emblematic of post-conflict Cambodia as a whole, where power is based on patronage and "corruption within the judiciary is just a symptom of the problem in the wider political system."[45] This problem is compounded by a severe lack of material and human resources.[46]

With such fundamental problems in the legal and judicial sectors in Cambodia there is a great deal of work to be done in terms of strengthening rule of law in the country. One of the arguments supporting the establishment of the ECCC was that it would have a positive impact on the domestic judicial system. This impact, through the demonstration effect and training, is seen as one of the main advantages of a hybrid tribunal.[47] It is suggested that hybrid tribunals positively affect the human rights compliance of weakened and damaged justice systems.[48] For instance Japan, the largest donor to the ECCC, contends the justice process in Cambodia will promote democracy, rule of law, and good governance.[49]

A number of training sessions have been carried out by the ECCC and organisations including the International Bar Association, and the UN Development Programme (UNDP).[50] Within the ECCC individual departments differ as to the types of training they can provide. The Defense Support Section carries out a number of initiatives, including weekly briefings for all staff on international justice issues, and training sessions for case managers and lawyers.[51] It has also carried out training for lawyers *outside* the institution. This has been especially important in order to inform people about due process rights granted Duch. Although the training of staff within the institution is crucial to the everyday functioning of the ECCC, whether this then feeds back into the domestic legal system depends on whether trained staff stay in the country or leave with their new skills. It also depends on the extent to which they are given support within the domestic system to implement their new skills and ideas.

Other factors also stand as impediments to the ECCC's ability to impact the broader domestic justice system. First, the ECCC and the national judicial system are not comparable. For example the ECCC's case management systems will be difficult to transfer to domestic courts because these systems rely heavily on the availability of computers and other equipment. This is why it is particularly important to focus on good practices that can be incorporated into the wider judiciary. The OHCHR recruited a Legacy Officer in 2010 to promote lessons from the ECCC into the daily practice of domestic courts in order to promote compliance with international human rights standards.

The ECCC may have an impact on some practices, but it is too early to evaluate to the extent these will be adopted *outside* of the ECCC. It is only through long-term commitment to this transfer of skills and knowledge that change will occur. Even if some best practices are transferred and adopted by Cambodian courts, another significant obstacle to progress is the reported lack of political will from the RGC, which has refrained from improving rule of law in Cambodia in an effort to continue its control of the judiciary.[52] The fact that the RGC has little commitment to rule of law activities is compounded by its attitude towards the ECCC and public criticism of additional prosecutions.

The Controversy Surrounding Additional Prosecutions and Political Interference

In December 2008 Cambodian Co-Prosecutor Chea Leang opposed the submission of five additional suspects for prosecution by former international Co-Prosecutor Robert Petit. Leang stated further investigations should not proceed because of past instabilities and the UN and the ECCC's limited duration and budget.[53] Such a disagreement between the international and Cambodian co-prosecutors was foreseen and established procedures exist to deal with the situation. To resolve the matter Petit filed a Statement of Disagreement with the Pre-Trial Chamber. In September 2009 it was announced that the pre-trial judges had failed to reach a supermajority decision on the matter.[54] In a situation such as this the Internal Rules provide that a submission proposed by a co-prosecutor automatically move to the next stage at which co-investigating judges conduct an investigation. The considerations of the Pre-Trial Chamber demonstrate that the three Cambodian judges agreed with Leang, while the two international judges found Leang's reasoning to be insufficient to block the submissions.[55] Following Leang's failure the judicial investigation stage began. Disagreements between the international and Cambodian co-investigating judges persisted amid accusations of political interference.[56]

The ongoing dispute led a number of politicians, including the Prime Minister Hun to openly criticise the ECCC's approach. In 2009 he claimed that any additional prosecutions would lead to civil war.[57] In late 2010, during a meeting with the UN Secretary-General, he said that there would be no more ECCC prosecutions after Case 002.[58] Ban Ki Moon then visited the ECCC and stated that the question of additional prosecutions was up to the court.[59] In response to the newly appointed Co-Prosecutor Cayley's statement regarding the necessity of further investigation, the Information Minister stated: "If they want to go into Case 003 or 004, they should just pack their bags and return home."[60] The fact is that Hun Sen and several members of the RGC are unconcerned about being seen as attempting to direct the work of the ECCC which would undermine judicial independence. The statements by government officials, in tandem with remarks to shut down the Cambodian OHCHR office, demonstrates how little respect there is for both institutions and ultimately rule of law in the country. Despite the investigating judges' contention that they have acted independently, their closure of the investigation into Case 003 led to the resignation of UN staff members and renewed criticism levelled at the ECCC and the RGC.[61] Judge Siegfred Blunk stepped down in early October 2011 as a consequence of the mounting criticism. The reserve international co-investigating judge carried out his duties until he also resigned, stating his Cambodian counterpart was opposed to further investigations.[62] Observers have also been critical of the UN, forcing the Secretary-General to defend his stance regarding the continuance of Case 003.[63]

Even if their views have no substantial impact on the ECCC's work, the public may believe that Cambodian judges are listening more to the RGC than they are to the facts of the cases. The recent actions by long-time Cambodian activist Theary Seng may be an indication that public support and patience for the Tribunal may further diminish.[64] If the public perceives that the UN-backed ECCC is susceptible to political interference, this will likely diminish public expectations for an independent domestic judiciary. In doing so, it actively impedes credibility of the rule of law rather than fostering rule of law in Cambodia by increasing the number of people who believe in the legitimacy of legal institutions.[65]

The Controversy Surrounding Corruption

Allegations of corruption have been rumoured since the ECCC began its work in 2006.[66] In July 2008 a number of Cambodian employees reported to the UN that they had to give a percentage of their salary to their superiors in order to keep their jobs.[67] The OSJI was very active in raising domestic and international awareness of this issue.[68] In August 2009 an ECCC anticorruption package was agreed upon by the UN and RGC.[69] It provided for an Independent Counsellor who would be available to all staff confidentially. When concerns about corruption are raised, staff alleged to be involved are then counselled and the Counsellor can subsequently raise the complaint with the UN and RGC.[70] However ECCC staff were unable to make contact with the appointed Counsellor and the OSJI remained sceptical about the effectiveness of this new anticorruption mechanism;[71] particularly given the fact that it lacks a protection and public reporting mechanism, and has little investigative capacity.[72]

It is clear that corruption allegations undermine the ECCC's integrity and its potential impact as a model for the Cambodian judicial system. They also impact public demand for rule of law. If Cambodians perceive that there is corruption at the ECCC then they will be unlikely to expect or demand anything different at the domestic level. Nevertheless, the actions of the ECCC in response to the allegations demonstrate that corruption does not have to be tolerated. The anti-corruption package could function as an example of how to find a solution to deal with corruption when it occurs.

Conclusion

When considering whether the ECCC has fulfilled its mandate, there are a number of considerations that must be taken into account. Foremost, the ECCC *has* managed to carry out the prosecution of Duch and is now prosecuting Case 002. Carrying out successful trials is its primary objective which is significant. It establishes an official record of the crimes committed by the accused, and an historical record of the conflict. Successful trials demonstrate that there is no impunity for those responsible for perpetrating war crimes. The importance of the Duch trial should therefore *not* be underestimated. This trial holds a great deal of significance for KR victims. Secondly, it is hoped that capacity-building of national staff will ensure that judicial standards are raised *after* the work of the ECCC has concluded.

Nevertheless serious concerns about political interference at the ECCC could prove serious enough to undermine any contribution to building a "rule of law culture" in Cambodia. Even if Cases 003 and 004 proceed without interference, the influence of capacity-building and legacy initiatives are uncertain. It may simply be unrealistic to expect the ECCC to contribute to developing a "rule of law culture" when there is no political will to do so.

Despite the difficulties faced, the ECCC is the only transitional justice process to officially take place in Cambodia. Given the length of time that has passed since these offences were perpetrated, this may be the only opportunity for victims of the KR to achieve some measure of justice. The participation of victims in the ECCC was extremely innovative and meaningful, and will likely continue as such in Case 002. The success of the revisions to the civil party system will determine whether the participation of victims is the lasting legacy of the ECCC, having an important impact in the country and providing an example to other tribunals.

Notes

1. Cheang Sokha and James O'Toole, "Hun Sen to Ban Ki Moon: Case 002 Last Trial at ECCC," *Phnom Penh Post*, October 27, 2010; see also Seth Mydans, "Conflicts Imperil Future Khmer Rouge," *New York Times*, June 16, 2011, www.nytimes.com (accessed July 12, 2011).

2. David Chandler, *A History of Cambodia* (Boulder, CO: Westview, 2008), 256-257.

3. Chandler, *Cambodia,* 259.

4. David Chandler, *Voices from S-21: Terror and History in Pol Pot's Secret Prison* (Berkeley, CA and London: University of California Press, 1999), viii.

5. Suzannah Linton, "Putting Cambodia's Extraordinary Chambers into context," *Singapore Year Book of International Law* 11 (2007): 208-211.

6. Linton, "Extraordinary Chambers," 212.

7. Linton, "Extraordinary Chambers," 213.

8. UN General Assembly, Res. No. 52/135, A/RES/52/135 (December 12, 1997).

9. Group of Experts for Cambodia, *Report of the Group of Experts for Cambodia Established Pursuant to General Assembly Resolution 52/135*, para. 127-129 (1999).

10. Group of Experts, *Report,* paras. 178-179.

11. Thomas Hammarberg, "Efforts To Establish a Tribunal Against the Khmer Rouge Leaders: Discussions Between the Cambodian Government and the UN," (paper presented at a seminar organised by SIDA, Stockholm, Sweden, May 29, 2001), 15.

12. Hammarberg, "Efforts To Establish," 16.

13. Hammarberg, "Efforts To Establish," 22.

14. Office of the UN Secretary General, *Report Of The Secretary-General On The Khmer Rouge Trials*, UN Doc A/57/769 at para. 7 (March 31, 2003).

15. Extraordinary Chambers of the Courts of Cambodia, Law On The Establishment Of The Extraordinary Chambers, With Inclusion Of Amendments As Promulgated on 27 October 2004, chap. 1, Art. 1.

16. James O'Toole, "Sheen Comes off Khmer Rouge Trial," *Diplomat,* July 10, 2011, 1.

17. OSJI, "UN Must Confront Political Interference in Cambodia's Khmer Rouge Court," http://www.soros.org (accessed October 29, 2011).

18. Nic Dunlop, "I Tracked Down a Man Who Killed 14,000 People," *Guardian,* September 4, 2010.

19. ECCC, Office of the Co-Investigating Judges, Closing Order Indicting Kaing Guek Eav alias Duch, Public Redacted Version, Criminal Case File No: 002/14-08-2006 (August 8, 2008).

20. ECCC, *Prosecutor v. Duch,* Case File/Dossier No. 001/18-07-2007/ECCC/TC, Trial Judgment, para. 567 (July 26, 2010).

21. ECCC, *Duch,* Trial Judgment, para. 567.

22. The Prosecution appealed this decision seeking to increase the time Duch was given to life on three grounds: error in the exercise of sentencing discretion; error regarding cumulative convictions, and that Duch should have been convicted for enslavement. See "Co-Prosecutors Appeal Against The Judgment Of The Trial Chamber In The Case Of Kaing Guek Eav alias Duch," October 13, 2010. The Defence asked for an acquittal. Robert Carmichael, "Defense Calls For Acquittal Of Khmer Rouge War Criminal," *VOA Khmer,* March 28, 2011.

23. Robert Petit and Anees Ahmed, "A Review of the Jurisprudence of the Khmer Rouge Tribunal," *Northwestern Journal of International Human Rights* 8, no. 2 (Spring 2010): 175-176.

24. ECCC, *Duch,* Trial Judgment, para. 423.

25. ECCC, *Duch,* Trial Judgment, para. 292.

26. "Recent Development," http://www.soros.org/initiatives/justice (accessed July 31, 2011), 5-6.

27. ECCC, *Duch*, Trial Judgment, paras. 97-102.

28. David J. Scheffer, "Cambodia's Precedent for Humanity," *Wall Street Journal*, July 27, 2010.

29. One applicant was declared inadmissible and three withdrew, so ninety participated in Case 001. Ultimately sixty-six individuals were awarded Civil Party status.

30. Johanna Herman, "Reaching for Justice: The Participation of Victims at the Extraordinary Chambers in the Courts of Cambodia," CHRC Policy Paper 5 (September 2010).

31. Kong Sothanarith, "Court Begins Reparations Campaign," *Voice of America*, February 20, 2012.

32. James O'Toole, "Reparation Remain A Key Issue," *Phnom Penh Post*, July 27, 2010; Sam Rith, "KRT Civil Parties Plan Appeal," *Phnom Penh Post*, August 24, 2010.

33. ECCC, Internal Rules (Rev. 7), February 23, 2011, Rule 12*bis* (2), http://www.eccc.gov.kh/en (accessed August 1, 2011).

34. Phuong Pham, Patrick Vinick, Mychelle Balthazard, Sokhom Hean and Eric Stover, *So We will Never Forget: A Population-based Survey on Attitudes about Social Reconstruction and the Extraordinary Chambers in the Courts of Cambodia*, (Berkeley, CA: Human Rights Center, University of California, 2009), 2.

35. Invitation to attend the Closing Statements in the "Duch"—Trial, November 23-27, 2009.

36. Author interviews in Phnom Penh, September 2009

37. ECCC, www.eccc.gov.kh/en/victims-support/intermediary-organizations-ios-0 (last accessed May 2011).

38. For further information on the important role of civil society in the victim participation process, see Johanna Herman "Reaching for Justice."

39. *Phnom Penh Post*, "NGOs Show Support for UN Rights Office," November 2, 2010 and "Stance on UN Expulsion Flipped," October 31, 2010.

40. *Phnom Penh Post*, "Stance on UN Expulsion Flipped."

41. Yashi Ghai, *Technical Assistance And Capacity-Building, Report Of The Special Representative Of The Secretary-General For Human Rights In Cambodia, Yashi Ghai*, A/HRC/7/42, para. 8.

42. Frederick Brown, ed., *Rebuilding Cambodia: Human Resources, Human Rights, And Law* (Washington, DC: Foreign Policy Institute, 1993), 69.

43. Brown, *Rebuilding Cambodia*, 69-70.

44. Kheang Un, "The Judicial System and Democratization in Post-Conflict Cambodia," in *Beyond Democracy in Cambodia*, ed. Joakim Öjendal and Mona Lilja (Copenhagen: Nias, 2009), 75.

45. Tara Urs, "Imagining Locally-Motivated Accountability For Mass Atrocities: Voices from Cambodia," *Sur. Revista Internacional de Direitos Humanos* 7 (2007): 95.

46. Un, "Judicial System," 75.

47. Laura A. Dickenson, "Notes and Comments: The Promise of Hybrid Courts," 97 *Am. J. Int'l. L.* 295, 307-308 (2003).

48. *Rule Of Law Tools For Post-Conflict States: Maximizing The Legacy Of Hybrid Courts*, UN Office of the High Commissioner for Human Rights at 1 (2008).

49. Embassy of Japan, "Press Release: Japanese ODA News Japanese Assistance For The Project To Enhance Judicial Process of the ECCC," June 17, 2008.

50. Alejandro Chehtman and Ruth Mackenzie, *Capacity Development In International Criminal Justice: A Mapping Exercise Of Existing Practice*, DOMAC/2, Annex—Section E (September 2009) for trainings in Cambodia.

51. For further information, see the Legacy section of the Defense Support Section of the ECCC's website at http://www.eccc.gov.kh/en/dss/legacy.

52. Urs, "Imagining," 66.

53. ECCC, "Statement of the Co-Prosecutors," January 5, 2009.

54. ECCC , "Press Release," September 2, 2009.

55. ECCC, Considerations Of The Pre-Trial Chamber Regarding The Disagreement Between The Co-Prosecutors Pursuant To Internal Rule 71 (August 18, 2009).

56. OSJI, "Political Interference at the Extraordinary Chambers in the Courts of Cambodia," (July 2010), 21.

57. Cheang Sokha and Robbie Corey-Boulet, "ECCC Ruling Risks Unrest: PM," *Phnom Penh Post,* September 8, 2009.

58. *Agence France Presse* (AFP), "Cambodian PM says no Third Khmer Rouge Trial," October 27, 2010.

59. *AFP,* "Cambodia Criticised On Trial," October 29, 2010.

60. James O'Toole and Cheang Sokha, "Prosecutor Speaks Out," *Phnom Penh Post,* May 10, 2011.

61. O'Toole, "Sheen," 2; Mydans, "Conflicts."

62. ECCC, "Press Release from the International Reserve Co-investigating Judge," March 19, 2012.

63. Mydans, "Conflicts"; also O'Toole, "Sheen," 3.

64. Richard Carmichael, "Khmer Rouge Victim Quits Tribunal Saying UN-Baked Court is a Sham," *Deutsche Presse-Agentur,* November 15, 2011, *Cambodia Tribunal Monitor,* http://www.cambodiatribunal.org/ (accessed November 16, 2011).

65. Jane Stromseth, David Wippman, and Rosa Brooks, *Can Might Make Rights? Building the Rule of Law after Military Interventions,* (Cambridge: Cambridge University Press, 2006), 311.

66. Michael Saliba, "Allegations of Corruption at ECCC," *Cambodia Tribunal Monitor,* (2009), http://www.cambodiatribunal.org/blog/2009/09/allegations-of-corruption-at-eccc.html (accessed April 2011).

67. OSJI, "Recent Developments at the Extraordinary Chambers in the Courts of Cambodia: October 2008 Update," 2.

68. For example, Seth Mydans, "Corruption Allegations affect Khmer Rouge Trials," *New York Times,* April 9, 2009; *CNN,* "Cambodian War Crimes Court In Corruption Probe"; *Economist* "Accusations Of Corruption Threaten To Discredit The Trial Of the Khmer Rouges," April 2, 2009.

69. OSJI, "Recent Developments at the Extraordinary Chambers in the Courts of Cambodia: August 2009 Update," 4.

70. OSJI, "Recent Developments August 2009 Update," 4.

71. OSJI, "Recent Developments at the Extraordinary Chambers in the Courts of Cambodia: November 2009 Update," 21.

72. OSJI, "Recent Developments August 2009 Update," 4-5.

Chapter 15

Special Tribunal for Lebanon

Kathleen Barrett

In a national address on November 21, 1989, former Lebanese President Rene Mouawad stated: "There can be no Nation, no State and no entity without the unity of the people. There can be no unity without common agreement, no agreement without reconciliation and no reconciliation without forgiveness and sacrifice."[1] He was assassinated the next day.

On Valentine's Day 2005, former Lebanese Prime Minister Rafiq Hariri and twenty-two of his companions were assassinated by a car bomb in Beirut. The United Nations Security Council (UNSC) and Secretary General (SG) immediately condemned the assassination as an act of terrorism. Factions within Lebanon and across the Middle East were divided on its political implications and those responsible for the crime.

The attack brought about the Cedar Revolution, which demanded an end to nearly thirty years of Syrian occupation and political interference, and resulted in the full withdrawal of Syrian troops from Lebanon pursuant to UNSC Resolution 1559.[2] In the midst of national disarray, the Lebanese nation for the first time in its history called for independence and solidarity and an end to impunity.

The Special Tribunal for Lebanon (STL) is still in a process of development, although it has demonstrated progress. It issued its first indictments in June 2011 against members of Hezbollah. Nevertheless, both internal and regional political barriers will likely continue to hamper the STL's work; much in the same way they impaired the progress of the UN International Independent Investigation Commission (UNIIIC).

The Road to Justice

Primary UN Resolutions

On the recommendation of a UN Fact Finding Mission,[3] the UNSC adopted Resolution 1595 establishing the UNIIIC to investigate the February attacks.[4] Acting with the cooperation of the Lebanese government, the UNSC adopted Resolutions 1644[5] and 1664,[6] which requested official negotiations between the Lebanese government and the SG "aimed at establishing a tribunal of an international character based on the highest international standards of criminal justice."[7]

Nearly two years latter an official agreement between the UN and Government of Lebanon was signed in February 2007, soon followed by UNSC Resolution 1757 which officially authorized the establishment of a tribunal under UNSC Chapter VII authority.[8] It would be "a purely independent judicial body . . . [aimed] at establishing the truth that all Lebanese people want to know and helping in ending impunity of political assassination in Lebanon."[9]

Despite the Lebanese Parliament's refusal to convene to ratify the agreement, the provisions of the Resolution, its annexed document, and attachments entered into force on June 10, 2007.[10] Pursuant to a 2007 agreement between the UN and Dutch authorities the headquarters of the STL were located at The Hague.[11]

UNIIIC—Reports and Findings

UNIIIC officially began operations on June 16, 2005. All told eleven reports were released by the body between October 2005 and the end of 2008; each detailing the results of numerous interviews and crime scene analyses of the crimes in question. These UNIIIC investigations continued despite growing opposition to the UNIIIC's work, and increasing safety concerns stemming from the serious deterioration of conditions in Lebanon.

The first UNIIIC report demonstrated that Hariri's assassination had been pre-meditated for several months by "a group with an extensive organization and considerable resources and capabilities . . . Rafiq Hariri had been monitored and the itineraries of his convoy recorded in detail."[12] The responsible parties included both Lebanese and Syrian actors. Regarding the role of Syrian intelligence community UNIIIC Commissioner Detlev Mehlis stated: "it is difficult to envisage a scenario whereby such a complex assassination plot could have been carried out without their knowledge."[13] Syrian military intelligence had been infiltrating Lebanon over three decades, had and was also "working in tandem with Lebanese intelligence services."[14]

The report also highlighted a tense fifteen minute meeting between Hariri and Syrian President Bashar al-Assad in August 2004 regarding the extension of then President Emile Lahoud's term, which Hariri opposed. The discussion centered on Syria's support of Lahoud and the consequences to Hariri and Lebanon if they opposed this extension.[15] Pursuant to UNSC Resolution 1636,[16] the UNSC called "upon the Syrian authorities to cooperate fully and unconditionally with the commission and to detain any Syrian officials or nationals considered as suspects by the Commission."[17]

Although the second report indicated progress on the confirmation of nineteen suspects and continued communication with the Office of the Prosecutor General of Lebanon regarding evidence and additional information, Mehlis voiced doubt concerning continued Syrian cooperation with the UNIIIC. Expressing dissatisfaction he stated that Syrian authorities were reluctant to provide access to the six Syrian officials the UNIIIC had summoned as suspects and were at times providing "contradictory feedback."[18] Mehlis called for full and unconditional cooperation by Syrian authorities if the provisions of Resolution 1636 were to be abided by and the investigations reported in an "earnest and professional manner."[19] Although in the UNIIIC's third report Commissioner Brammertz expressed optimism regarding cooperation with the Syrian authorities,[20] in the fourth he, like Mehlis, indicated his concern that *full* open cooperation with Syrian authorities was not forthcoming.[21]

The UNIIIC's mandate was soon expanded to investigate fourteen other assassinations, assassination attempts, and explosions that occurred in Lebanon *since* October 2004. The UNIIIC also actively assisted the Lebanese government with its own inquiries into similar crimes while simultaneously evaluating its own progress in preparation for the transition to the STL. Commission organization, communication, and documentation were improved to ensure for a successful transfer of authority, as well as continuity of the investigation progress.[22]

Despite this progress, the STL became a source of contention between political rivals in Lebanon. Pro-Syrian factions of the March 8 Opposition Alliance—namely Hezbollah—considered the STL to be no more than international interference in Lebanese domestic affairs. Anti-Syrian, pro-independence factions—primarily the March 14 Alliance and their supporters—maintained that the STL was essential as a means of achieving truth and justice.[23] In any event, the Commission continued its investigations acquiring evidence to demonstrate that claims of responsibility voiced by an Islamic militant suspect, Ahmed Abu Adass, were most likely a result of coercion.[24] The UNIIIC attributed the motives for Hariri's murder to a number of factors: Security Council Resolution 1559 which called for the withdrawal of foreign troops from Lebanon; the disarming of militias, and free and fair elections;[25] and the extension of Emile Lahoud's term as President, among others.

UNIIIC reports eight through ten were written under similar conditions of internal turmoil. In June 2007 a member of parliament and seven others were killed, followed by an attack on a United Nations Interim Force in Lebanon convoy, and several other bomb attacks.[26] Moreover, in November 2007 Emile Lahoud's term as president expired with no agreed replacement named.

In the eleventh and final report Bellemare indicated progress, while also requesting that the Commission's mandate be extended to ensure a smooth transition to the STL.[27] Politically the situation in Lebanon had improved with the signing of the Doha Agreement, and the election of a new government.[28] However, security was still enough of a concern that Bellemare arranged with other countries to relocate sources to ensure their safety. He also stressed the need for the investigation to continue.[29] At this point the UNIIIC was facing two pressures: expectations that its investigations were complete and indictments ready to be presented at opening of the Tribunal, and decreasing public support for the STL. With regard to the latter, he recognized the need for greater transparency and communication to foster support.[30] With respect to the former he clarifies in the report that indictments were by no means imminent.[31]

UNIIIC Controversies

The eleven reports demonstrate that the trail of assassinations consisted of a series of attacks connected by common motives, that the organized group responsible for the Hariri assassination had been active for months prior to the attack,[32] and that the network of people involved in the attack are Syrian and Lebanese. Of the nineteen suspects mentioned in the initial report, some politically controversial figures were named including Former President Emile Lahoud and Syrian President Bashar al-Assad.[33] Additionally, it implicated four Lebanese Generals whose detention by Lebanese authorities raised international and domestic concerns. They remained in custody absent indictment for almost four years.[34] When asked to justify their arrest, Bellemare replied that the decision to detain the Generals was made "by the Lebanese judicial authorities according to Lebanese criminal law," adding that "it is not for [him] to second-guess their decision."[35]

Leaks of information from the UNIIIC about possible Hezbollah indictments did not ease tensions. A comprehensive report, produced by the Canadian Broadcasting Company (CBC), detailed evidence implicating Hezbollah and accusing the UNIIIC of incompetence.[36] Hezbollah reacted to these speculations by impugning the integrity and impartiality of the STL, as well as threatening retaliation if its members were indicted.[37]

The Special Tribunal

Transition

Despite criticisms of the transition process UNSC members expressed their satisfaction with the UNIIIC's work. Under-Secretary-General for Legal Affairs and UN Legal Counsel Michel Nicolas stated: "the matter of concern is to have an efficient investigation in place," as opposed to a speedy transition lacking in credible evidence and legal substance.[38] By February 2008, the SG had established the STL's Management Committee whose tasks were to "provide advice and policy direction on all non-judicial aspects of [its] operations and review and approve its annual budget."[39] By the end of March, the SG had appointed the Prosecutor and Registrar, the STL's twelve judges, and was in the process of recruiting its Defense Officer.[40] Moreover the projected funds of over $60 million US dollars needed to maintain the Tribunal's first year of operations were collected from donor countries.[41]

Other aspects of the STL's establishment were more slowly resolved. One issue concerned its physical location. According to Article 8 of the Annex to Resolution 1757, the STL was to be located in The Hague.[42] Although this makes victim participation more difficult, strong internal opposition to the STL necessitated its relocation.[43] The SG explained that the Government of Lebanon felt that the political situation would *not* allow timely ratification of such an agreement and therefore a bi-lateral agreement between the UN and The Netherlands would be required.[44]

Tribunal Mandate and Main Features

Consistent with the Lebanese government's December 2005 request and pursuant to Resolution 1757, its Annexed document and Statute, the STL is responsible for the prosecution of the perpetrators of the February 2005 assault on former Prime Minister Rafiq Hariri, and the death or injury of several others. The Tribunal also has jurisdiction over attacks between October 1, 2004, and December 12, 2005 that are connected and similar to the Hariri attack as well as such attacks after December 12, 2005.[45] In August 2011 the Pre-Trial judge established STL jurisdiction over attacks on Marwan Hamadeh, George Hawi, and Elias El-Murr.[46]

The STL is a hybrid court meaning that it combines both national and international aspects.[47] Its main legal features are designed to provide the neutrality of international participation, while respecting state sovereignty and international human rights principles. The applicable law is the Lebanese Criminal Code (with the exclusion of the death penalty otherwise applicable under Lebanese law).[48]

The international character of the STL is also reflected in its mixed panel composition and its reliance on legal precedents established by previous international tribunals.[49] The independence, fairness, and efficiency of the process represents the highest standards of human rights principles.

Victim Consideration

Although the STL's primary focus is the Hariri assassination, over two hundred people were also direct victims of that attack.[50] In an effort to overcome Lebanon's history of general amnesty laws and inattention to the concerns of victims,[51] the STL has made efforts to improve court-victim relations.[52] Article 17 of the Statute addresses victims' rights by allowing victims' "views and concerns to be presented and considered at stages of the proceedings . . . in a manner that is not prejudicial or inconsistent with the rights of the accused and a fair and impartial trial."[53] However this is not an unlimited right. Victims cannot participate in investigations and must abide by restrictions imposed by the judge.[54]

Article 25 of the Statute addresses victim compensation. The STL is responsible for identifying victims and providing the relevant information on convictions. It is victims' responsibility to claim compensation through the national courts. Although this process appears to be time consuming, it does offer victims hope and formal recognition of their suffering.

Lastly, Article 12 of the Statute establishes a unit to "protect the safety, physical and psychological well-being, dignity and privacy of victims."[55] It is a broad effort that applies to victims that will appear before the STL and "others who are at risk on account of testimony given by such witnesses."[56]

Differences from Other Tribunals

Several features make the STL unique compared to other international tribunals. For example, the STL has the ability to try people *in absentia.* Applying international human rights law to the Lebanese Criminal Code, the STL's Statute requires that if the accused is *not* present at trial, he or she will be represented by counsel. Moreover, the STL only adjudicates Lebanese crimes set forth in the Lebanese Criminal Code. The STL mandate excludes international crimes.[57]

The STL also differs from other tribunals in two formative ways. Its creation resulted from a negotiated agreement between Lebanon and the UN. The Chapter VII enactment of the STL occurred at the request, and with the agreement of, at least a segment of the Lebanese government. At the time this showed unprecedented cooperation between the UN and a member state to ensure justice. This soon evaporated with the government's failure to ratify the agreement.

Also, the STL is uniquely funded. Although the UN directly funds other tirubnals, it is *not* funding the STL although it may provide funds should Lebanon be unable to meet its financial commitments.[58]

Significant Decisions

The Tribunal has made a number of significant decisions in its short existence. Some of these concern the rights of detainees while others concern clarification of the law. Arguably, the most controversial concern the indictments issued by the Tribunal in July 2011.

As concerns the rights of detainees, the STL had to address the issue of the four Generals detained since 2005.[59] It soon came to the attention of the Tribunal that the four were being held in a separate facility, not allowed to communicate with other prisoners or each other, and were not able to have confidential communications with their legal counsel.[60] Upon immediate review of their status the Prosecutor petitioned the Pre-Trial judge to release them without prejudice due to lack of evidence.[61] This provides an example of the STL's adherence to internationally accepted standards of due process.

The STL also clarified the definition of terrorism used by the Tribunal. In February 2011 the Appeals Chamber identified elements of the crime of terrorism: it must be an intentional act intended to spread terror, and it must use a means intended to create a public danger. This definition has two notable aspects. First, there must be an intention to spread terror through a means intended to endanger the public. Second, although the definition includes a list of methods that would qualify it is not an exhaustive list. This ensures that the definition will remain viable in the future, as methods of terrorism evolve.[62]

Indictments

On June 28, 2011, the Pre-Trial judge confirmed the release of indictments and associated arrest warrants.[63] STL's Rules of Procedure and Evidence require Lebanon to report on measures taken to arrest the individuals within thirty days of the indictment.[64] If Lebanon does not make reasonable progress toward complying with the arrest warrants the STL can ultimately refer the situation to the UNSC.[65] Alternately, the trials can be held *in absentia* if the accused agrees not to be present or cannot be apprehended.[66]

Despite the Tribunal's efforts to keep the names of the indictees confidential, the *Lebanon Daily Star* announced the four names and their association with Hezbollah.[67] Hariri's son—replaced as prime minister by Hezbollah-backed Najib Miqati following the 2011 collapse of the Hariri government[68]—praised the indictments as a "historic moment in the political, judicial, security, and moral life of Lebanon."[69] Conversely, Hezbollah saw the indictments as politically motivated.[70] Hassan Nasrallah soon clarified Hezbollah's position by stating that Hezbollah members would not be arrested.[71]

The four indicted Hezbollah members are Mustafa Badreddine, a high-ranking member accused of directing the operation to kill Hariri; Salim Ayyah, a senior member accused of co-coordinating activities associated with the attack; and Hussein Oneissi and Assad Sabra both accused of complicity and covering evidence.[72] To date Lebanon has been unable to arrest the accused.[73]

Consequently the Tribunal judge requested a trial *in absentia.*[74] The Tribunal Defence Office requested that the arrest warrants be withdrawn and a trial by videoconference held.[75] The Trial Chamber felt the accused had the right to attend a formal trial and granted additional time to arrest the accused.[76] In February 2012 the Trial Judge established a work plan for holding the trials *in absentia.*[77] A provisional date for the trials was set for March 25, 2013.[78]

Other STL Controversies

A controversy that continues to undermine STL's credibility concerns the method used to establish the STL. The use of Chapter VII authority to establish the Tribunal could be viewed as a violation of Article 51 of the Vienna Convention on the Law of Treaties.[79] Chapter VII obligates member states to abide by UNSC Resolutions, consequently UNSC action in this instance could be interpreted as a form of coercion.[80] Since this is the first time an international tribunal has been established to prosecute a national crime under national law the use of Chapter VII powers to mandate the tribunal *over the will* of the elected Lebanese Parliament remains seriously controversial.

The STL addressed this question when the Defense challenged the legality of the STL.[81] Noting that the UN acted within its capacity, Lebanon never challenged the action, and Lebanon has fulfilled its obligations, the Trial Chamber confirmed the legality of the STL.[82]

It also raises tactical questions. Will the STL set an example of justice that will end the perception of impunity? It is easy to perceive Chapter VII enforcement of the STL in neo-colonial terms.[83] Neo-colonial perspectives are being advanced because the impetus for the UN investigation and subsequent establishment of the STL was the US and France.[84]

There is also the issue raised by Hezbollah MPs regarding the constitutionality of the STL. The Lebanese Constitution mandates proportionality and equal representation between religious groups and geographic regions.[85] When the STL agreement was signed Shi'a ministers had resigned from the government.[86] Consequently, Hezbollah has challenged the notion of equal representation and the validity of the government's action.[87]

A third controversy concerns the STL's ability to try people *in absentia*. It is generally accepted, and supported by ECHR jurisprudence, that the right of an accused to be present at his or her trial as guaranteed in Article 14(3)(d) of the International Convention on Civil and Political Rights, is *not* an absolute right.[88] Arguments indicate that the STL Statute does not even provide the minimum human rights protections for *in absentia* cases because it does not provide for the accused to receive a retrial.[89] In the Tribunal's defense, trials *in absentia* are allowed due to the expectation that states or groups such as Hezbollah will shelter the accused thus delaying and/or preventing justice.

More debilitating are the political controversies surrounding the STL's actual purpose. Some argue it is a tool of Western foreign policy. Hezbollah has blatantly accused the US of using the STL to spur conflict within Lebanon.[90] Syria perceives the STL to be an action against Syria by its enemies.[91] Others see the STL as an effort to discredit Hezbollah.[92] Countering these charges, while still discrediting the competency and impartiality of the UN effort, are the accusations made by the CBC. According to its investigative report the CBC contends that the UNIIIC delayed investigating cell phone records, failed to interrogate a suspect who may also have been compromising the investigation, and overlooked evidence presented by Lebanese police.[93] Such accusations raise questions about the competence and impartiality of the Tribunal.

Hezbollah threatened to boycott the STL,[94] supported attacks against UN investigatory staff,[95] and threatened retaliation for indictments of its members. Hezbollah put the STL in an especially difficult position. One of the justifications for UNSC action is a threat to international peace. Hezbollah's threats are credible as their militia is stronger than Lebanese security forces and army, and are considered to be strategically prepared for a quick reaction.[96] Moreover there are several political options that could effectively undermine the STL's efforts. The simplest would be for the Lebanese government to stop funding the Tribunal. Since Hezbollah is part of the government,[97] this is a distinct possibility as evidenced by the near collapse of the Lebanese government over the 2011 payment.[98] Although the UNSC has the power to solicit additional funds it would be difficult to attract enough foreign contributors to continue the STL for an extended period of time.

An option was proposed by former Prime Minister Saad Hariri. In anticipation of an indictment of Hezbollah members Hariri proposed portraying the accused as rogues in exchange for Hezbollah's cooperation in handing over members to the STL.[99] This could bring justice while distancing Hezbollah from any crimes. However, since high ranking members have been indicted it might prove difficult to portray them as rogues. Such an agreement would also undermine the STL's impartiality since it could be perceived as affording Hezbollah impunity.

Finally, Saudi Arabia and Syria—supporters of rival factions within Lebanon—attempted to forge an agreement to stop the STL.[100] Hezbollah recommended embracing these efforts to prevent conflict within Lebanon.[101] Syria suggested an end to the STL in favor of a Lebanese investigation.[102] Given past assessments of Lebanon's ability to conduct investigations, as well as the current level of posturing by the different actors involved, it is unlikely this solution will actually achieve justice. However, Saudi Arabia abandoned this effort due to lack of progress in the negotiations.[103]

Despite the controversies and attempts to undermine the STL there is one major legal hurdle to stopping the STL. Since it was established under Chapter VII authority the SG has the ability to continue the STL without Lebanon's support. The problem, however, is the enforcement of these legal obligations. If Lebanon ignores its legal commitments, the UNSC could be asked to work with Lebanon.[104] However the UNSC has little other than diplomatic negotiations or sanctions to force Lebanon to abide by its legal obligations.

The STL needs to rebuild confidence in its efforts. A decision to abandon the Tribunal could be seen as bowing to the pressures of Hezbollah. Similarly, the trial of Hezbollah members could lead to reduced STL credibility. Hezbollah's position is that it protects Lebanon and requires arms to defend Lebanon against enemies.[105] A conviction would imply that Hezbollah not only harms its fellow Lebanese, but is willing to throw the country it claims to protect into civil strife to achieve its objectives.

Given the nature and severity of these controversies the STL has a difficult road ahead. Eventual arrest and prosecution of those indicted could still destabilize Lebanon. If Syria is found to be involved, it could further destabilize Syria and affect the entire region.[106]

Will Lebanon Reach the End of the Road?

In his inauguration speech on May 24, 2008, Lebanese President and former Army Commander Michel Suleiman called for national unity and peace, while pledging full support to UN Resolutions and recommendations.[107] His hopeful address came after the bloodiest internal outrage since Lebanon's civil war, led by Hezbollah in response to the government's attempt to dismantle the group's telecommunication network.[108]

The future impact of the STL must be considered in the context of Middle East politics, particularly the "Arab Spring." Syria, who provides considerable support to Hezbollah, is experiencing violent civil conflict that is spilling into Lebanon.[109] This puts both Hezbollah and the UNSC in a difficult position. The outcome of unrest in Syria could strengthen or weaken support for Hezbollah thus impacting their ability to ignore the arrest warrants. If Hezbollah continues to ignore the arrest warrants the UNSC may be unwilling to take action against the Lebanese government for fear of further destabilizing the area. However, this could also be viewed as an international amnesty for Hezbollah and its members. The need to focus on national situations may also reduce regional interest in supporting both the STL and alternates.

To date a number of lessons may be learned from the Lebanese experience, and a number of questions remain unanswered. The UNIIIC has certainly progressed in its investigations and reporting methods despite the security environment. To ensure a smooth transfer of authority to the STL, the UNIIIC's work depended on its level of discretion, a stable security environment, as well as cohesive international cooperation to provide it with needed assistance.

In terms of efficiency and timely completion of tasks, the STL has seen more preliminary progress than the UNIIIC. Indeed, indictments have been issued. The STL made extensive efforts to ensure international cooperation and fair international and domestic representation. It also demonstrated a commitment to the application of human rights as evidenced by the changes to Lebanese legal code applicable to the STL and the release of the four Lebanese generals. If the Lebanese judiciary recognizes the primacy of the STL a demonstration effect may be possible. However, skepticism exists among the Lebanese people regarding the efficiency of both the STL and UNIIIC. Continued attention to human rights as a basis for international justice will increase the credibility of both bodies and hopefully set a legitimate precedent for applied international human rights principles. In any event, the UNIIIC and the STL have shown tremendous success in light of the most tumultuous circumstances.

Notes

1. *Rene Moawad Foundation Website*, "President Rene Moawad, Excerpts from his Speech to the Nation," http://www.rmf.org.lb/aboutus/aboutrm/rmspeech.html (accessed May 24, 2008).
2. UN Security Council Res. No. 1559, S/RES/1559 (September 2, 2004).
3. Peter FitzGerald, "Report of the Fact Finding Mission to Lebanon Inquiring Into The Causes, Circumstances And Consequences Of The Assassination Of Former Prime Minister Rafik Hariri," S/2005/203 (2005).
4. UN Security Council Res. No. 1595, S/RES/1595 (April 7, 2005).
5. UN Security Council Res. No. 1644, S/RES/1644 at para. 6 (December 15, 2005).
6. UN Security Council Res. No, 1664, S/RES/1664 (March 29, 2006).
7. S/RES/1664, para 1.
8. UN Security Council Res. No. 1757, S/RES/1757 (March 30, 2007).
9. UN Press Conference, "Press Conference by United Nations Legal Counsel on Special Tribunal for Lebanon," UN Department of Public Information, News and Media Division (September 19, 2007).
10. Samar El-Marsi, "The Hariri Tribunal: Politics and International Law," *Middle East Policy* (2008): 80-92.
11. Secretary-General, "Special Tribunal for Lebabnon to be Based at The Hague," SG/SM/11347, UN Department of Public Information, News and Media Division (December 21, 2007).

12. Detlev Mehlis, Commissioner, *International Independent Investigation Commission (UNIIIC) First Report* (Beirut, October 19, 2005).

13. Mehlis, *First Report.*

14. Mehlis, *First Report.*

15. Mehlis, *First Report*, paras. 25-27.

16. UN Security Council Res. No. 1636, S/Res/1636 (2005).

17. Detlev Mehlis, *Second Report of the International Independent Investigation Commission established pursuant to Security Council Resolutions 1595(2005) and 1636 (2005)* (Beirut, December 10, 2005).

18. Mehlis, *Second Report,* Preface, para. 9.

19. Mehlis, *Second Report,* Preface, paras. 10-11.

20. Serge Brammertz, Commissioner, *Third Report of the International Independent Investigation Commission established pursuant to Security Council Resolutions 1595 (2005), 1636 (2005) and 1644 (2005),* (Beirut, March 14, 2006), Summary.

21. Serge Brammertz, *Fourth Report of the International Independent Investigation Commission established pursuant to Security Council Resolutions 1595 (2005), 1636 (2005) and 1644 (2005)* (Beirut, June 10, 2006).

22. Serge Brammertz, *Sixth Report of the International Independent Investigation Commission established pursuant to Security Council Resolutions 1595 (2005), 1636 (2005), 1644 (2005) and 1686 (2006)* (Beirut, December 12, 2006), paras. 3, 8.

23. Gary C. Gambill, "Lemons from Lemonade: Washington and Lebanon after the Syrian Withdrawal," *Mideast Monitor Organization* 2, no. 1 (June/July 2007).

24. Serge Brammertz, *Seventh Report of the International Independent Investigation Commission established pursuant to Security Council Resolutions 1595 (2005), 1636 (2005), 1644 (2005) and 1686 (2006)* (Beirut, March 2007).

25. UN Security Council Res. No, S/RES/1559, paras. 2-3, 5 (September 2, 2004).

26. Serge Brammertz, *Eighth Report of the International Independent Investigation Commission established pursuant to Security Council Resolutions 1595 (2005), 1636 (2005) 1644 (2005), 1686 (2006) and 1748 (2007)* (Beirut, July 2007), para. 4.

27. Daniel Bellemare, *Eleventh Report of the International Independent Investigation Commission established pursuant to Security Council Resolutions 1595 (2005), 1636 (2005) 1644 (2005), 1686 (2006) and 1748 (2007)* (Beirut, December 10, 2008).

28. Bellemare, *Eleventh Report*, para. 15.

29. Bellemare, *Eleventh Report*, paras. 5, 62.

30. Bellemare, *Eleventh Report*, paras. 11-12.

31. Bellemare, *Eleventh Report*, paras. 6, 58.

32. Daniel Bellemare, Commissioner, *Tenth Report of the International Independent Investigation Commission established pursuant to Security Council Resolutions 1595 (2005), 1636 (2005) 1644 (2005), 1686 (2006) and 1748 (2007)* (Beirut, March 28, 2008), paras. 23-26.

33. Mehlis, *First Report*, beginning with para. 23.

34. Naharnet (*Al-Nahar News Network*), "Bellemare Seeks Extended Mandate, Says Search for Justice Can't be Rushed," April 9, 2008.

35. Naharnet, "Bellemare Seeks."

36. Neil Macdonald, "CBC Investigation: Who Killed Lebanon's Rafik Hariri?" www.cbc.ca/world/story/2010/11/19/f-rfa-macdonald-lebanon-hariri.html (accessed December 31, 2010).

37. Elias Sakr, "Nasrallah: We will not Allow Arrest of Fighters," *Daily Star*, http://www.dailystar.com.lb/article.asp?edition_id=1&categ_id=2&article_id=121473#axzz16hxmEBGw, (accessed December 31, 2010).

38. UN Press Conference, "Press Conference by United Nations Legal Counsel on Special Tribunal for Lebanon," UN Department of Public Information, News and Media Division (September 19, 2007).

39. Secretary-General, Office of the Spokesperson, "Statement Attributable to the Spokesperson for the Secretary-General on the Special Tribunal for Lebanon," (February 13, 2008).

40. Special Tribunal for Lebanon, "List of Current Vacancies. Head of Defense Office, D-1/D-2," http://www.stleb.org/EN/employment/vacancies.shtml (accessed May 29, 2008). "Factsheet: Organization of the Special Tribunal," http://www.un.org, (accessed May 29, 2008).

41. Thijs Bouwknegt, "Substantial Progress Special Tribunal for Lebanon," *International Justice* (March 28, 2008).

42. UN Security Council, Agreement between the United Nations and the Lebanese Republic on the Establishment of a Special Tribunal for Lebanon: Annex to UNSC Res 1757 (May 30, 2007).

43. UN Security Council, Second Report of the Secretary-General Submitted Pursuant to Security Council Resolution 1757, 2007, S/2008/173 at para 4 (2008).

44. UN Security Council, Second Report, paras. 5-6; also UN Security Council, Fourth Report of the Secretary-General Submitted Pursuant to Security Council Resolution 1757 (2007), S/2009/106 at para. 4 (2009).

45. STL, "Brochure A5" http://www.scribd.com/doc/71265767/Special-Tribunal-for-Lebanon-Brochure-A5-English (accessed November 11, 2011).

46. STL, "Pre-Trial Judge Rules on Connected Cases," at http://www.stl-tsl.org/en/media/press-releases/19-08-2011 (accessed August 31, 2012).

47. David Tolbert, "Introductory Note to the Special Tribunal For Lebanon: Orders Regarding the Detention of Persons and Memorandum of Understanding," 48 *Int'l Legal Materials* 1149 (2009).

48. STL, "Factsheet: Main Features," http://www.scribd.com/doc (accessed May 29, 2008).

49. STL, "Factsheet: Main Features."

50. Marieke Wierda, Habib Nassar, Lynn Maalouf, "Early Reflections on Local Perceptions, Legitimacy and Legacy of the Special Tribunal for Lebanon," 5 *J. Int'l. Crim. Just.* 1065 (2007).

51. Wierda et al, "Early Reflections," 1.

52. Jerome De Hemptinne, "Challenges Raised by Victims' Participation in the Proceedings of the Special Tribunal for Lebanon," 8 *J. Int'l. Crim. Just.* 165 (2010).

53. STL, Statute of the Special Tribunal for Lebanon, http://www.stl-tsl.org/x/file/TheRegistry/Library/BackgroundDocuments/RulesRegulations/Resolution_Agreement_Statute_EN.pdf (accessed December 31, 2010).

54. De Hemptinne, "Challenges," 164-179.

55. Statute of the Special Tribunal for Lebanon.

56. Statute of the Special Tribunal for Lebanon.

57. International Center for Transitional Justice (ICTJ), *Handbook on the Special Tribunal for Lebanon* (2008).

58. ICTJ, *Handbook.*

59. Macdonald, "Who Killed Rafik Hariri?"; also STL, Case No. CH/PRES/2009/01/rev, Order on Conditions of Detention, paras. 5-6 (April 21, 2009).

60. STL, Order on Conditions of Detention.

61. STL, Case No. CH/PTJ/2099/06, Order Regarding the Detention of Persons Detained in Lebanon in Connection with the Case of the Attack Against Prime Minister Rafiq Hariri and Others (April 29, 2009).

62. STL, "Media Advisory on the Appeals Chamber Ruling," February 16, 2011, http://www.stl-tsl.org/sid/250 (accessed February 17, 2011).

63. STL, Confirmed Indictment Submitted to the Lebanese Authorities, 2011, http://www.stl-tsl.org/sid/276 (accessed July 3, 2011).

64. STL, Confirmed Indictment.

65. STL, "Rules of Procedure" STL/BD/2009/01/Rev. 3, http://www.stl-tsl.org, (accessed July 4, 2011).

66. Statute for the Special Tribunal for Lebanon, art. 22 .

67. *Daily Star*, "STL Indicts 4 Hezbollah Members, Seeks Arrests," June 30, 2011.

68. *Associated Press in Beirut*, "Hezbollah Leader Refuses to Hand over Hariri Suspects," July 3, 2011 and Nada Bakiri, "Hezbollah Rejects Charges Over '05 Killing of Hariri." *New York Times*, July 2, 2011.

69. *Reuters* and Oren Kessler, "US Urges Lebanon to Act on Hariri indictments," *Jerusalem Post*, June 30, 2011.

70. *Reuters* and Kessler, "US Urges Lebanon."

71. *Reuters*, "Hezbollah Leader Rejects Hariri Court Indictments." *Jerusalem Post*, July 2, 2011.

72. *BBC News Middle East*, "Hezbollah Suspects to be Tried over Rafik Hariri," August 17, 2011, http://www.bbc.co.uk/news/world-middle-east-14557594 (access December 6, 2011).

73. *BBC*, "Hezbollah Suspects."

74. Drew Singer, "Lebanon Tribunal Judge asks for Trial in Absentia," *Jurist*, October 18, 2011

75. *Washington Post*, "UN-Backed Court won't Immediately Start Trials in Absentia for Suspected Hariri Assassins," November 23, 2011.

76. *Washington Post*, "UN-Backed Court."

77. STL, Case No. STL-11-01/I/TC, Decision to Hold Trial *In Absentia* (February 11, 2012).

78. STL, Case No. STL-11-01/PT/PTJ, Order Setting a Tentative Date for the Start of Trial Proceedings (February 11, 2012).

79. Vienna Convention on the Law of Treaties (1969), Article 51.

80. Bardo Fassbender, "Reflections on the International Legality of the Special Tribunal for Lebanon," 5 *J. Int'l. Crim. Just.* 1091 (2007).

81. STL, "Trial Chamber Rules on Jurisdiction," see article at http://www.stl-tsl.org/en/media/press-releases/30-07-2012-trial-chamber-rules-on-jurisdiction (accessed August 31, 2012).

82. STL, "Trial Chamber Rules on Jurisdiction."

83. Muhamad Mugraby, "The Syndrome of One-Time Exceptions and the Drive to Establish the Proposed Hariri Court," *Mediterranean Politics* 13, no. 2 (2008): 171-193.

84. Omar Nashabe, "The Special Tribunal for Lebanon," Global Governance Lecture at www2.lse.ac.uk/publicEvents/events/2011/20110118t1800vHKT.aspx (accessed December 12, 2011).

85. Constitution, Article 24 at www.servat.unibe.ch/icl/le00000_.html#A024 (accessed July 1, 2011).

86. Gianluca Serra, "Special Tribunal for Lebanon: A Commentary on its Major Legal Aspects," 18 *Int'l. Crim. Just. Rev.* 344 (2008).

87. Mike Corder, "Hariri Assassination Indictment Coming Very Soon," *Associated Press/Real Clear World*, December 9, 2010.

88. Wayne Jordash and Tim Parker, "Trials in Absentia at the Special Tribunal for Lebanon: Incompatibility with International Human Rights Law," 8 *J. Int'l. Crim. Just.* 487 (2010).

89. Jordash and Parker, "Trials in Absentia."

90. Elias Sakr, "Nasrallah."

91. James Denselow, "Lebanon: Justice at What Cost?" *Guardian*, November 20, 2010.

92. Alexander Henley, "Lebanon's International Theatre of War," *Guardian*, December 3, 2010.

93. Macdonald "Who Killed Lebanon's Rafik Hariri?"

94. Neil Macdonald, "Hezbollah Urges Hariri Case Boycott," *Aljazeera*, October 2010, http://english.aljazeera.net/news/middleeast/2010/10/2010102819122690558.html (accessed December 31, 2010).

95. Neil Macdonald, "Can There be Justice as well as Stability?" *Economist* (November 11, 2010), http://www.economist.com/node/17463379 (accessed December 31, 2010).

96. Macdonald, "Can There be Justice?"

97. Corder, "Hariri Assassination,"

98. *Al Jazeera*, "Lebanon in Bid to Avert Government Collapse" November 30, 2011, http://www.aljazeera.com/news/middleeast/2011/11/201111306247312308.html (accessed December 12, 2011)

99. Alexander Henley, "Lebanon's International Theatre of War," *Guardian*, December 3, 2010.

100. Fawaz Gerges, "Lebanon is Staring into the Abyss," *Guardian*, December 31, 2010.

101. Elias Sakr, "Nasrallah."

102. Jay Solomon and Margaret Coker, "U. N. Indictments Near in Lebanon Killing," *Wall Street Journal*, November 8, 2010

103. *BBC News*, "Hariri Tribunal: Saudi Arabia Quits Lebanon Mediation," January 19, 2011, http://www.bbc.co.uk/news/world-middle-east-12226982 (accessed December 8, 2011).

104. ICTJ, *Handbook*.

105. Macdonald, "Can There be Justice?"

106. Joshua Hammer, "Getting Away With Murder," *Atlantic* (December 2008): 69-78.

107. Naharnet (*Al-Nahar News Network*), "Suleiman for Unity, Defense Strategy and Diplomatic Ties with Syria," May 25, 2008.

108. *Al-Jazeera*, "Life Returns to Beirut's Streets," May 22, 2008; also *Al-Jazeera*, "New Lebanon President in Unity Call," May 26, 2008.

109. *CBS News World*, "Syria's Civil war Claims 10 More Lives in Lebanon, As Sectarian Strife Continues to Spread," August 22, 2012, http://www.cbsnews.com/8301-

503543_162-57497963-503543/syrias-civil-war-claims-10-more-lives-in-lebanon-as-sectarian-strife-continues-to-spread/ (accessed August 31, 2012).

Chapter 16

Comparing Formal and Informal Mechanisms of Acknowledgment in Uganda

Joanna R. Quinn

"Acknowledgement" has been identified as a necessary condition for peace-building, reconciliation, the generation of social capital, and the development of democracy in societies torn apart by conflict. This chapter provides a discussion of four mechanisms that have been utilized in Uganda to bring about this kind of acknowledgement: a truth commission, amnesties, the International Criminal Court (ICC), and customary justice mechanisms.

Background and Current Ugandan Conflict

Uganda has a long history of political violence, including that associated with the regimes of Milton Obote (1962-1971) and Idi Amin Dada (1971-1979). Between 1962 and 1986, Uganda underwent a series of coups, culminating in a great concentration of power in the hands of the head of state. Hundreds of thousands of Ugandans were raped, tortured and/or killed during this period.[1] It is a history that has left a lasting legacy on Ugandan politics and society.

Conditions in Uganda began to improve when Yoweri Museveni assumed power in January 1986. Human rights abuses abated and today many Ugandans enjoy a degree of freedom unknown to them under the previous regimes. In 1986, Museveni abolished all political parties except his own, the National Resistance Movement (NRM), although parties were reinstated in 2005.[2]

Consequently not everyone supports Museveni. There have been more than twenty insurgencies since the NRM came to power.[3] One of the most deadly and longest-lasting of these is the twenty-five year rebellion of the Lord's Resistance Army (LRA) in the Acholi sub-region of northern Uganda.[4] At the height of the conflict, it was estimated that thirty thousand[5] children from the region had been abducted by rebels.[6] More than 1.8 million people were forced to flee and live in the internally displaced persons (IDP) camps throughout the region.[7] In 2005 the LRA and the Government of Uganda (GOU) came close to signing a final peace agreement. This agreement was scuttled when leader of the LRA Joseph Kony refused to come out of the bush.[8]

Formal versus Informal Mechanisms

When considering mechanisms of justice it is important to understand the genesis and application of what are often referred to as "traditional" mechanisms. Each of Uganda's many ethnic communities traditionally used different forms of customary mechanisms to deal with conflict. Although some of these traditions have disappeared in other places they remain an active part of community life.

For purposes of clarification I have found the categorization of mechanisms of transitional justice as "formal" or "informal" to be a convenient tool. This taxonomy has the virtue of affording a quickly-accessible conception of the various kinds of mechanisms that are available for use. Mechanisms are considered to be "formal" by virtue of their connection to a domestic or international governing body and their codified practices that assure both procedural fairness and standards of accountability. These codified practices are based on cultural norms. "Informal" mechanisms are not required to meet any of these standards and are not formally codified.

Societies around the world are familiar with "formal" mechanisms of justice. In the West, the trial is the most recognizable of these. Although mostly used to prosecute a citizen of a particular state within that state, permutations of this form have begun to arise. Among these are efforts by a national court of one state to prosecute a citizen of another state for crimes committed elsewhere (e.g., universal jurisdiction).[9] Other efforts in this direction have taken the form of international tribunals, including the ICC. Another formal mechanism implemented in the modern era is the truth commission.

Informal mechanisms are often much less familiar to those who live in the West. In many cases, these mechanisms follow "traditional" practices that were used to keep order within societies and to provide socialization into accepted community norms. These mechanisms are found around the globe, and include a type of traditional psychological healing called *conselho*, practiced by war-affected people in Angola.[10] Holistic purification and cleansing rituals, attended by the family and broader community, are carried out in welcoming ex-combatant child soldiers back into the community in both Angola and Mozambique.[11] In Western Kenya, traditional conflict resolution mechanisms are used by the Pokot, Turkana, Samburu and Marakwet.[12] Ceremonies to "cool the heart[s]" of child ex-combatants upon their return to their communities in Sierra Leone are carried out by the broader community.[13]

Distinctions between "formal" and "informal," though, are problematic. First, it is often the case that customary mechanisms are recognized and adopted by the state apparatus, thereby becoming "formalized."[14]

Second, many customary mechanisms already operate at a level that is highly respected by the community in which they take place. In many parts of Uganda such practices have more *de facto* authority than comparative Western models. This is the case particularly among the Sabiny,[15] and the Karamojong.[16] It was frequently reported to me that councils of elders hold more sway within the community than do law enforcement officials, and that such councils have the authority to override police sentences.

Third, many of these mechanisms are utilized by different groups at different times. They do not remain static in their categorization as formal or informal. The truth commission provides an apt example. In South Africa truth commissions have been both formal and informal. In 1992 and 1993 two commissions were carried out during the era of *apartheid* by members of the African National Congress (ANC).[17] By my own "formality" criteria laid out above, these two commissions were "informal." When the ANC came to power in 1995 it convoked the much-publicized Truth and Reconciliation Commission (TRC), a formal body.

Fourth, it is often the case that mechanisms that are considered "informal" at first glance may actually have codified procedures. Customary mechanisms are built on ceremonies and traditions that have evolved over time into precise instruments that are carried out in an almost "formulaic" manner. This is true among the majority of ceremonies practiced among the ethnic groups within Uganda. Among the Karimojong the *akiriket* meetings are very stratified and "everyone knows his position and where to sit."[18] Likewise, Acholi mechanisms are carried out in a clearly defined manner.[19] "The actual reconciliation ritual [for example] to redress the wrongs of a killing between clans is complex and sophisticated. The ritual involves many people and takes a full day. Before the actual ritual, however, many things must be arranged, discussed and decided upon. The ritual can be preceded by weeks, months or even years of careful negotiations."[20]

The fifth problematic element of the distinction between formal and informal is that the lens often used to decide between the two is culturally biased. So-called international standards are used as benchmarks. Indeed, the inverse might actually be ideal. That is, some of the questions arising from the conflict in northern Uganda and other transitional situations should inform current international law, rather than constantly having to fit these complex situations to "international standards." While the more formalized Western models often allow for only one form of justice—retributive, restorative, reparative—traditional institutions seek to combine these forms in keeping with the community values.

Competing Efforts at Social Rebuilding in Uganda

There have been a number of efforts to deal with the legacies of Uganda's conflict. It is certainly the case that the GOU has paid a lot of lip service to the idea of social rebuilding.[21] Yet government spending in the areas of social and physical reconstruction does not bear this out. In the 2004-2005 budget the GOU allocated only 0.01 percent of its national budget to reconstruction efforts in northern Uganda.[22]

The system of single-party rule implemented by Museveni remained until late 2005 and demonstrated his lack of commitment to reconciliation efforts. Only the NRM was allowed to exist. Some have dismissed the one-party system as "a unique political system to try and prevent the chaos and ethnic conflicts that plagued Uganda throughout the 1970s and early 1980s. Although political parties were allowed to exist, they were severely restricted and could not participate in elections. In a 2005 referendum, Ugandans voted to return to full multiparty politics."[23] However rival politicians are still subjected to arbitrary arrest and detention.[24]

Uganda's Truth Commission (1986-1994)

The Commission of Inquiry into Violations of Human Rights (CIVHR) was inaugurated on June 13, 1986.[25] Until the tabling of the Report on October 10, 1994, the CIVHR worked to gather evidence and testimony relating to the events from 1962 to 1986. Thousands of people completed questionnaires about their recollection of particular events, many of which were then investigated in the hopes of eventual prosecution. In all, 608 witnesses appeared before the CIVHR between 1986 and 1993.[26] The CIVHR travelled to many regions of Uganda, holding hearings, and collecting testimony in seventeen districts.[27] The CIVHR's final report is more than 720 pages, and contains testimony, analysis, recommendations, and lists of names of those who were subjected to torture and abuse.[28]

In seeking to understand this process much more clearly, I spent nearly three months in Uganda in the summer of 2001. While there, I carried out archival research and conducted a series of open-ended interviews that focused specifically on the Ugandan experience of coming to terms with its past. I looked for evidence of acknowledgement, and the social trust which might be expected to result from the process. I spoke with truth commissioners, government and opposition officials, members of the NGO community, and representatives of civil society. In the end, I was able to interview nearly forty people. To date this represents the only study that has ever been undertaken of the CIVHR.

The CIVHR's path was not easy. Despite the best efforts of those who saw the work of the commissions through, the CIVHR ultimately faced political and practical limitations that would prove to be its un-doing.

One of the biggest constraints was funding. Because of the government's financial limitations, the CIVHR was chronically short of staff. The CIVHR was only able to continue its work after receiving several large infusions of cash from the international donor community, along with supplies and expertise.

Similarly, the overall capacity of the Commission was extremely limited. Commissioners frequently faced significant opposition from those within and outside of the very governments that had appointed them. This often translated into death threats and the disappearance of key evidence. Other government agencies, which should have been able to provide support, were themselves in disarray; unable to provide the safeguards necessary to ensure the CIVHR'S success. Moreover the Ugandan public seemed reluctant to talk about what had happened. Many feared retribution for their participation in the CIVHR.

Ultimately, the CIVHR's legacy is small. Most Ugandans appear to be unaware of the CIVHR's work. Those who are aware are critical of its findings, which they see as inherently biased towards the NRM. The CIVHR is believed by many to have been a bureaucratic panacea that was unable to affect real and lasting political stability, let alone foster social capital, in Uganda.[29] Although a modest and nascent civil society has emerged its growth remains stunted. Democracy is not firmly embedded in Uganda and Museveni shows no sign of allowing it to take hold.

Amnesty Act (2000)

In January 2000 the Amnesty Act was enacted by the GOU. Under the terms of the Act,

> An amnesty is declared in respect of any Ugandan who has at any time since the 26th day of January, 1986 engaged in or is engaging in war or armed rebellion against the government of the Republic of Uganda by:

(a) actual participation in combat;
(b) collaborating with the perpetrators of the war or armed rebellion;
(c) committing any other crime in the furtherance of war or armed rebellion; or
(d) assisting or aiding the conduct or prosecution of the war or armed rebellion.[30]

The Act allows rebels to receive amnesty if they voluntarily come "out of the bush" and renounce rebellion. More practically, it provides for the material needs of those who are given amnesty ("reporters"). By July 2008, 22,107 amnesties had been granted.[31]

The Act was enacted within the ongoing context of armed conflict "after a great deal of activism from civil society groups, NGOs and concerned politicians."[32] It is applied equally to all combatants and ex-combatants involved in any of the insurgencies against Museveni's government.[33] It "was conceived as a tool for ending conflict . . . a significant step towards ending the conflict in the north and working towards a process of national reconciliation."[34] The Act claims to address, "the expressed desire of the people of Uganda to end armed hostilities, reconcile with those who have caused suffering and rebuild their communities."[35] As the Chairman of the Amnesty Commission expressed to me: "national reconciliation is especially important and must be promoted."[36]

One study reported early in 2005: "Amnesty was seen to be a mechanism that formalized a process that was already taking place. Many informants [in an RLP study] referred to the fact that they had been 'doing' Amnesty before it had become law, as it was a culturally recognized approach to carrying out justice within the specific context."[37] Consequently, many Ugandans appear to support the process and "there is passionate support for the Amnesty amongst political activists, churches, NGOs and an influential group of 'traditional' leaders."[38]

One of its greatest supporters was a radio station located in Gulu: MEGA FM. One of its most effective programmes, *Dwog Paco* (literally "come back home" in Acholi), was broadcast three times each week. Its programming was specifically tailored to be heard by the rebels. It broadcasted live testimonies of former LRA fighters and others about living in the bush and how they escaped from the LRA. Especially important in each broadcast was an appeal to those still in the bush to come home. Between December 2003 and November 2004, more than 1,200 children had come out of the bush as a result of these broadcasts, thanks in large part to the Amnesty available to them.[39]

Others are more reluctant to embrace the Amnesty. One Christian NGO official said: "The Amnesty Commission must try to redefine its mandate because there are too many loopholes in the system. And there is no element of confession, which is important to add. But at least people will admit to taking part in atrocity. After that, though, they must then confess. Only then will they have healing. The way it is, when they are absolved by the Amnesty, the healing process is destroyed."[40] Another stated: "the Amnesty Commission is returning kids on an Amnesty ticket, but then they are being charged with treason and put into jail."[41]

Others are more forceful in their objections. Some argue that the Amnesty is simply a means of "buying peace." It does not promote "healing" as it is understood in many quarters. Rather, there is mounting evidence that some of those who report for the Amnesty do so for immediate gain.[42]

It has been said that, "[s]ince coming to power, the government has had a policy of buying rebels out of the bush in order to end conflict, creating a culture of entitlement that has only been reinforced by attaching a package to the Amnesty process."[43] However, "[t]he President['s] . . . attitude to the Amnesty is more equivocal. Museveni was always rather reluctant to accept it for the LRA, and he has stated that he wants the Act to be amended. . . . He, like his military officers, continues to assert the need for a military solution."[44] Although it is clear that Museveni intended the Amnesty to be a mechanism to end the conflict, he is pleased with neither the process, nor the speed with which the conflict is ending.

International Criminal Court

The ultimate expression of Museveni's displeasure with the amnesty process came in December 2003 when he formally requested that the ICC investigate the LRA actions in northern Uganda.[45] This effectively means "the ICC is in [a] sense acting on behalf of the Ugandan state, even though the Ugandan government is itself involved in the conflict. . . . [This] has certainly created an awkward impression."[46]

The ICC Chief Prosecutor determined that there was a reasonable basis to open an investigation. In July 2004 warrants were issued for the arrest of Kony and four other senior LRA members. Each warrant details atrocities attributed to the LRA and the accused. Kony is charged with twelve counts of crimes against humanity and twenty-one counts of war crimes.[47]

The fact that the Rome Statute and ICC have not yet been tested in any real way with regard to the issues of admissibility and complementarity has garnered much debate in Uganda. While aid agencies and human rights groups were enthusiastic about the ICC announcements, some "Ugandan organizations tended to be rather more assertive, even openly hostile. Those promoting the Amnesty and negotiating a ceasefire made it plain that they viewed the ICC as a liability, and argued that prosecution could well make circumstances even worse."[48] More specifically it was feared that the arrest warrants would prolong the conflict.[49]

There is also the issue of the ICC's impact on extant amnesties. Understandably, many granted amnesty are afraid they may have to face justice in the ICC. However the Court has issued warrants for top LRA leaders only, and shows no interest in prosecuting lower level actors. Yet ICC investigations have implications for others, including Brigadier Sam Kolo (alleged "second-in-command" of the LRA) who sought and received amnesty in March 2005.[50]

Customary Mechanisms

In Uganda, traditional practices were officially prohibited in 1962 in favor of a harmonized court system modeled on the British system.[51] Yet their use has continued in Uganda fulfilling a variety of different functions for communities particularly affected by war and violence.

Moreover they are widely used by many of Uganda's ethnic groups.[52] Among the Karamojong, the *akiriket* councils of elders adjudicate disputes according to traditional custom[53] which includes cultural teaching and ritual cleansing ceremonies.[54] These ceremonies are similar to those used by the Langi (called *kayo cuk*), the Iteso (called *ailuc*), and the Madi (*tonu ci koka*).[55] The Lugbara maintain a system of elder mediation in family, clan, and inter-clan conflicts.[56] In 1985, an inter-tribal reconciliation ceremony, *gomo tong* (bending the spear) was held to signify that "from that time there would be no war or fighting between Acholi and Madi, Kakwa, Lugbara or Alur of West Nile."[57] A similar ceremony, *amelokwit*, took place between the Iteso and the Karamojong in 2004.[58]

In some areas, however, these practices are used less frequently. The Baganda occasionally use the *kitewuliza*, a juridical process with a strong element of reconciliation, to bring about justice.[59] The "Annexure to the Agreement on Accountability and Reconciliation," part of the agreements signed in 2005, also lists mechanisms used by the Ankole, called *okurakaba*.[60]

People from nearly every one of Uganda's ethnic groups have reported to me that "everyone respects these traditions,"[61] and that reconciliation continues to be an "essential and final part of peaceful settlement of conflict."[62] But many, particularly young, educated Ugandans who live in the city, report that they have never participated in such ceremonies.[63]

The Acholi use a complex system of ceremonies in adjudicating everything from petty theft to murder.[64] In the current context, two ceremonies have been adapted to welcome ex-combatant child soldiers home after they have been decommissioned: *mato oput* (drinking the bitter herb), and another called *nyouo tong gweno* (a welcoming ceremony in which an egg is stepped on over an *opobo* twig). *Nyouo tong gweno* is used to welcome back anyone who has been away from his home for an extended period of time.[65] These ceremonies allow Acholi to acknowledge that this person has been accepted back into the community.

Presently, both ceremonies are being used to welcome child soldiers home.[66] In 1985, *gomo tong* was held to signify that "from that time there would be no war or fighting between [the following ethnic groups:] Acholi and Madi, Kakwa, Lugbara or Alur of West Nile."[67]

Certainly, and not surprisingly, the role played by traditional mechanisms of justice has changed.[68] External influences have altered ways in which justice is administered. Additionally, there was frequent reference to the fact that "youth" do not recognize or understand such mechanisms. The introduction of other religions, in particular Christianity, appears to have led many to reject traditional mechanisms, although many referred to the level of compatibility between their religious beliefs and Acholi traditionalism.

There is, however, some evidence of their decline.[69] "The traditional values, cultural knowledge and social institutions of everyday life are threatened."[70] The social meanings of some ceremonies that are still practiced appear to be shifting,[71] as people move farther away from their *gemeinschaft* communities. This is especially true in regions where large numbers of people have been forced from their homes and into IDP camps.[72] Among the Karamojong[73] and the Acholi,[74] cultural education through practice and social education, is beginning to decline.

It seems clear, however, that these traditional mechanisms have a great deal to offer. It was variously reported to me that "everyone respects these traditions,"[75] and that reconciliation continues to be an "essential and final part of peaceful settlement of conflict."[76] A common understanding of these symbols, ceremonies, and institutions, and their meanings remains throughout Uganda.

Others argue:

> It would be wrong to imagine that everything traditional has been changed or forgotten so much that no traces of it are to be found. If anything, the changes are generally on the surface, affecting the material side of life, and only beginning to reach the deeper levels of the thinking pattern, language content, mental images, emotions, beliefs and response in situations of need. Traditional concepts still form the essential background of many African peoples, though obviously this differs from individual to individual and from place to place. I believe . . . that the majority of our people with little or no formal education still hold on to their traditional corpus of beliefs.[77]

Finnström and others also take this into account: "These practices, far from being dislocated in a past that no longer exists, have always continued to be situated socially. They are called upon to address present concerns. Of course, like any culturally informed practice, with time they shift in meaning and appearance."[78] "Ideas about old models are often used to help shape new ones."[79]

There is some evidence of customary practices having been formalized to an extent. They are now legally provided for under legislation including Article 129 of the 1995 Constitution, which provides for Local Council Courts[80] to operate at sub-county, parish and village levels;[81] and the Children Statute 1996, which grants these courts the authority to mandate any number of things including compensation and apology.[82] The Government of Uganda recognized the potential of these practices in the recent Agreement on Accountability and Reconciliation and its subsequent Annexure, which emerged out of the Juba Peace Talks.[83]

There are no data to show how these traditional practices have assisted people in the transitional process. Most is known about how they operate and some criticism has arisen which alleges that their use in the present circumstance is in many ways non-traditional.[84]

Conclusions

There have been calls for more rigorous solutions to end the conflict in northern Uganda; among these a solution outlined by the Chief Negotiator in the conflict, Betty Bigombe, that includes increased diplomatic and financial support and possible UN Security Council involvement among others.[85] It is important to note that the UN has been conspicuously absent from the debate, except for its indirect participation in the ICC. Instead the process has been spearheaded by a group of donor countries.[86]

This solution is of particular interest because it clearly recognizes the various attempts that have been made in northern Uganda, and the problems that arise as a result, and nonetheless calls for further action. Bigombe's statement mirrors a number of concerns that arise from the discussion above. The first of these is the interaction between the mechanisms themselves. The expected outcomes of each differ considerably and the implications of each are worrying. Amnesties and ICC prosecutions convey very different messages. This proliferation of approaches in Uganda represents a pattern of policy that may undermine the confidence of those who are involved in the conflict. They may be induced to surrender because they cannot be assured of what will happen to them should their involvement in the conflict continue.

This gives rise to a pressing question of transitional justice, and a second concern: sequencing.[87] Scholars and practitioners are still trying to determine the order in which the various elements of social rebuilding ought to occur. There is an inherent tension in having both the Amnesty and ICC processes run concurrently. More than that, however, many have questioned whether any of the above mechanisms ought to be operating at all *before* the conflict is ended. As one report said, "Peace first. Justice later."[88]

Lastly, although Museveni is shrewd and clever, it is not clear whether he fully appreciated the contradictions that would arise.[89] Or, conversely, whether he did understand, and the resulting quandary is just what he had hoped for. The words of one opposition politician summarizes the problem well:

> Museveni knows that the north/Gulu/Acholi is full of opposition. If they were pacified, they would mount serious opposition [to him, politically], so it is much better to keep them disconnected and devastated politically/socially/economically. He will be looked at as a saviour when he makes a show of trying to fix the situation. Meanwhile, the opposition is made impotent.

He is promoting a scorched earth policy. Ideologically, people believe that an impoverished society is easier to manage, so it is better to keep the situation in the north in turmoil—that way, Museveni can come with a master serving spoon and everyone has to come to him. To look for anything at all, they must come to him.[90]

Notes

1. Edward Khiddu-Makubuya, "Paramilitarism and Human Rights," in *Conflict Resolution in Uganda*, ed. Kumar Rupesinghe (Oslo: International Peace Research Institute, 1989); Yoweri Kaguta Museveni, *Sowing the Mustard Seed* (London: Macmillan, 1997); Thomas P. Ofcansky, *Uganda: Tarnished Pearl of Africa* (Boulder: Westview, 1996); Abdul Nadduli (LCV District Chairman, Luweero Triangle), interviewed by author in Luweero, Uganda, November 17, 2004.

2. Dirk Berg-Schlosser and Rainer Siegler, *Political Stability and Development: A Comparative Analysis of Kenya, Tanzania and Uganda* (Boulder: Lynne Rienner Publishers, 1990), 196.

3. These include rebellions by the Action Restore Peace and Holy Spirit Movement. These are from a larger list compiled from Lucy Hovil and Zachary Lomo, "Behind the Violence: Causes, Consequences and the Search for Solutions to the War in Northern Uganda." Refugee Law Project Working Paper 11, Refugee Law Project, Kampala (February 2004), 4; Lucy Hovil and Zachary Lomo, "Whose Justice? Perceptions of Uganda's Amnesty Act 2000: The Potential for Conflict Resolution and Long-Term Reconciliation." Refugee Law Project Working Paper 15, Refugee Law Project, Kampala (February 2005), 6.

4. Tim Allen, *War and Justice in Northern Uganda: An Assessment of the International Criminal Court's Intervention* (London: Crisis States Research Centre, Development Studies Institute, London School of Economics, February 2005), 14.

5. Allen states "the scale of abduction is a matter of speculation" due to insufficient monitoring. *War and Justice*, iii.

6. Joanna R. Quinn, "Gender and Customary Mechanisms in Uganda," in *Confronting Gender Justice: Women's Lives, Human Rights*, ed. Debra Bergoffen, Connie McNeely, Paula Ruth Gilbert, Tamara Harvey (New York: Routledge, 2010), 482-519.

7. Geresome Latim (Secretary to the Paramount Chief of Acholi), interviewed by author in Gulu, Uganda, November 22, 2004.

8. Joanna R. Quinn, "The Supposed Accountability/Peacebuilding Dilemma: The Case of Uganda" (paper presented at the Annual Convention of the International Studies Association, New Orleans, LA, February 18, 2010).

9. A good illustration is the prosecution of Rwanda nationals in Belgium for their perpetration of war crimes and crimes against humanity. *Hirondelle News Agency*, "Belgium Trials 'Good Thing for Rwanda' Says Top Prosecutor," April 27, 2005, www.globalpolicy.org/intljustice/tribunals/rwanda/2005/0427belgtrials.htm (accessed February 21, 2006).

10. Carola Eyber and Alastair Ager, "Conselho: Psychological Healing in Displaced Communities in Angola," *The Lancet* 360 (September 14, 2002): 871.

11. Alcinda Honwana, "Children of War: Understanding War and War Cleansing in Mozambique and Angola," in *Civilians in War*, ed. Simon Chesterman (Boulder: Lynne Rienner, 2001), 1137-1140.

12. Ruto Pkalya, Mohamud Adan, Isabella Masinde, in *Indigenous Democracy: Traditional Conflict Resolution Mechanisms*, ed. Betty Rabar and Martin Karimi (Kenya: Intermediate Technology Development Group–Eastern Africa, January 2004).

13. Rosalind Shaw, "Rethinking Truth and Reconciliation Commissions: Lessons from Sierra Leone." *United States Institute of Peace Special Report 130* (Washington, DC: United States Institute of Peace, February 2005), 9.

14. See for example, Peter E. Harrell, *Rwanda's Gamble: Gacaca and a New Model of Transitional Justice* (New York: Writers Club Press, 2003).

15. Sabiny man studying at Makerere University, confidential interview by author in Kampala, November 7, 2004.

16. Peter Otim (Inter-Governmental Authority on Development), interviewed by author in Kampala, November 23, 2004.

17. Priscilla Hayner, "Fifteen Truth Commissions—1974-1994: A Comparative Study," *Human Rights Quarterly* 16 (1994): 597-655.

18. Middle-aged professional Karimojong man working in Kampala, interviewed by author in Kampala, November 13, 2004.

19. Geresome Latim (Executive Secretary, *Ker Kwaro Acholi*), interviewed by author in Gulu, Uganda, November 22, 2004.

20. Sverker Finnström, *Living With Bad Surroundings: War and Existential Uncertainty in Acholiland in Northern Uganda* (Uppsala: Acta Universitatis Upsaliensis, Uppsala Studies in Cultural Anthropology, 2003), 291.

21. *BBC News*, "State funeral for Uganda's Obote," October 12, 2005, www.news.bbc.co.uk/2/hi/africa/4333618.stm (accessed February 22, 2006).

22 Official (Office of the Prime Minister) confidentially interviewed by author in Kampala, October 30, 2004.

23. *BBC News*, "Uganda Votes," February 22, 2006, article available at www.news.bbc.co.uk/2/hi/africa/4721242.stm (accessed February 22, 2006).

24. John Njoroge and Flavia Lanyero, "Otunnu and FDC Officials Blocked from Visiting Besigye and Mao," see article at *Daily Monitor*, April 25, 2011, www.monitor.co.ug/News/National/-/688334/1150358/-/c27fdqz/-/index.html.

25. Joanna Quinn and Mark Freeman, "Lessons Learned: Practical Lessons Gleaned from Inside the Truth Commissions of Guatemala and South Africa," *Human Rights Quarterly* 25, no. 4 (November 2003).

26. The Republic of Uganda, *The Report of the Commission of Inquiry into Violations of Human Rights*, Appendix 10 (Kampala: UPPC, 1994), xxx.

27. Uganda, *Commission of Inquiry*, Table Three, V-VI.

28. Uganda, *Commission of Inquiry*.

29. Joanna R. Quinn, "Constraints: The Un-Doing of the Ugandan Truth Commission," *Human Rights Quarterly* 26, no. 2 (May 2004): 401-427 and Joanna R. Quinn, *The Politics of Acknowledgement: Truth Commissions in Uganda and Haiti,* (Vancouver: UBC Press, 2010).

30. The Republic of Uganda, Amnesty Act 2000, Part II, 3(1).

31. Moses Draku (Principal Public Relations Officer, Amnesty Commission), interviewed by author in Kampala, July 7, 2008.

32. Allen, *War and Justice*, 31.

33. Hovil and Lomo, "Behind the Violence," 4 and "Whose Justice?," 6.

34. Hovil and Lomo, "Whose Justice?," 6.

35. Uganda, Amnesty Act 2000, "Preamble."

36. P.K.K. Onega (Chairman of The Amnesty Commission), interviewed by author in Kampala, October 28, 2004, Kampala.

37. Hovil and Lomo, "Whose Justice?," 10.

38. Allen, *War and Justice,* 33.

39. MEGA FM producer, confidential interview with author in Gulu, Uganda, November 20, 2004.

40. Christian NGO worker, confidential interview by author in Kampala, October 28, 2004.

41. Christian NGO worker, confidential interview by author in Kampala, November 10, 2004.

42. Hovil and Lomo, "Whose Justice?," 25.

43. Hovil and Lomo, "Whose Justice?," 24.

44. Allen, *War and Justice*, 34.

45. Information has surfaced that the Chief Prosecutor approached Museveni to ask him to refer the situation. Nicholas Waddell and Phil Clark, eds., *Courting Conflict? Justice, Peace and the ICC in Africa* (London: Royal African Society, March 2008), 43. There is a great deal of debate about what this discrepancy means.

46. Allen, *War and Justice*, 39.

47. Chief Prosecutor Louis Moreno-Ocampo, "The Investigation in Northern Uganda," October 14, 2005, http://www.icc-cpi.int/library (accessed February 22, 2006).

48. Allen, *War and Justice*, 43.

49. Father Carols Rodriguez, "Public Statement," quoted in Adam Branch, "International Justice, Local Injustice: The International Criminal Court in Northern Uganda," *Dissent Magazine* (Summer 2004).

50. Jenny Cuffe, "Uganda Torn over Price of Peace," *BBC News*, March 31, 2005, http://news.bbc.co.uk/2/hi/africa/4394923.stm (accessed February 24, 2006).

51. The British Colonial Office, *Report of the Uganda Relationship Committee*, (London: British Colonial Office, 1961).

52. Joanna R. Quinn, "What of Reconciliation? Traditional Mechanisms of Acknowledgement in Uganda" (paper prepared for *Reconciliation*, a conference held by the Nationalism and Ethnic Conflict Research Centre at The University of Western Ontario, May 14-15, 2005).

53. Bruno Novelli, *Karimojong Traditional Religion* (Kampala: Comboni Missionaries, 1999), 169-172, 333-340.

54. Peter Lokeris (Minister of State for Karamoja), interviewed by author in Kampala, 18 November 2004.

55. Government of Uganda and Lord's Resistance Army/Movement, Annexure to the Agreement on Accountability and Reconciliation (February 19, 2008), Art. 21.1.

56. Joseph Ndrua, "A Christian Study of the African Concept of Authority and the Administration of Justice among the Lugbari of North Western Uganda," 42-56 (1988) (Ph.D. diss., Catholic Higher Institute of Eastern Africa).

57. Finnström, *Living*, 299.

58. Iteso focus group, conducted by author, in Kampala, August 31, 2006.

59. John Mary Waliggo, "The Human Right to Peace for Every Person and Every Society," (paper presented at Public Dialogue organized by Faculty of Arts, Makerere University in conjunction with Uganda Human Rights Commission and NORAD, Kam-

pala, Uganda, December 4, 2003) author's collection, 7; also John Mary Waliggo, "On Kitewuliza in Buganda, May 3, 2005," email correspondence, author's collection, 1.

60. Government of Uganda and Lord's Resistance Army/Movement, "Annexure to the Agreement on Accountability and Reconciliation" (Juba, February 19, 2008), Art. 21.1.

61. Interview with Sabiny man.

62. Waliggo, "The Human Right," 9.

63. Northern Uganda focus group, conducted by author in Kampala, August 23, 2006.

64. Thomas Harlacher, Francis Xavier Okot, Caroline Aloyo Obonyo, Mychelle Balthazard, and Ronald Atkinson, *Traditional Ways of Coping in Acholi: Cultural Provisions for Reconciliation and Healing from War* (Kampala: Thomas Harlacher and Caritas Gulu Archdiocese, 2006).

65. For an excellent description of *mato oput* see Finnström, *Living,* 297-299.

66. Finnström, *Living,* 297-299.

67. Finnström, *Living*, 299.

68. Joanna R. Quinn, "Here, Not There? Theorizing About Why Traditional Mechanisms Work In Some Communities, Not Others" (paper presented at the Annual Convention of the International Studies Association, New York: February 15, 2009).

69. A study funded by the Belgian government revealed that young people no longer automatically respect the elders. Allen, *War and Justice*, 76.

70. Finnström, *Living,* 201.

71. Finnström, *Living*, 298.

72. Finnström, *Living*, 201.

73. Novelli, *Karimojong Traditional Religion*, 201-225.

74. Finnström, *Living*, 76, 219; also E.E. Evans Pritchard, *Witchcraft, Oracles and Magic Among the Azande* (Oxford: Clarendon Press, 1937), 154.

75. Interview with Sabiny man.

76. Waliggo, "The Human Right," 9.

77. John S. Mbiti, *African Religions and Philosophy* (Kampala: East African Educational Publishers, 1969, 2002), xi.

78. Finnström, *Living,* 299.

79. Allen, *War and Justice*, 84.

80. The LC Courts "were first introduced in Luweero in 1983 during the struggle for liberation. In 1987 they were legally recognized throughout the country." Waliggo, "The Human Right," 7.

81. "Uganda: Constitution, Government & Legislation," [article on-line], http://jurist.law.pitt.edu/world/uganda.htm (accessed April 30, 2005).

82. Government of Uganda, *The Children Statute 1996.*

83. Joanna R. Quinn, "Accountability and Reconciliation: Traditional Mechanisms of Acknowledgement and the Implications of the Juba Peace Process" (paper presented at the conference, "Reconstructing Northern Uganda," held by the Nationalism and Ethnic Conflict Research Group, The University of Western Ontario, London, ON, April 9, 2008).

84. Adam Branch, "Ethnojustice: the Theory and Practice of 'Traditional Justice' in Northern Uganda" (paper presented at the conference, "Reconstructing Northern Uganda," held by the Nationalism and Ethnic Conflict Research Group, The University of Western Ontario, London, ON, April 9, 2008).

85. Betty Bigombe and John Prendergast, "Stop the Crisis in Northern Uganda," *The Philadelphia Inquirer*, February 21, 2006.

86. The core group comprised Belgium, Germany, Ireland, the Netherlands, Norway, Sweden, the United Kingdom, and Canada.

87. See Joanna R. Quinn, "Chicken and Egg? Sequencing in Transitional Justice: The Case of Uganda" *International Journal of Peace Studies* 14, no. 2 (Autumn/Winter 2009): 35-53.

88. Lucy Hovil and Joanna R. Quinn, "Peace First. Justice Later: Traditional Justice in Northern Uganda." Refugee Law Project Working Paper 17, Refugee Law Project, Kampala, Uganda, July 8, 2005.

89. Allen, *War and Justice*, 42.

90. Opposition politician, confidential interview by author in Kampala, November 3, 2004.

Chapter 17

Restorative Justice, RPF Rule, and the Success of *Gacaca*

Stacey M. Mitchell

The perpetrators of the genocide in Rwanda have been tried in three venues: the International Criminal Tribunal for Rwanda (ICTR), conventional courts, and in *gacaca*.[1] *Gacaca* courts were established by the government in an attempt to alleviate the backlog of genocide-related cases clogging domestic courts. In this respect, they have been successful. They have prosecuted several hundred thousand persons.[2] Compared to the pace of prosecution in Rwanda's national courts this is quite an accomplishment.[3]

Gacaca courts are depicted by the state as having a number of purposes. They are "a cornerstone for reconciliation." They are also intended to fulfill a retributive function, as well as eradicate the "culture of impunity" in Rwanda. *Gacaca* courts are meant to enable the population "to live in peace and harmony once again"; to "strengthen ties between Rwandans"; and "[demonstrate] the ability of local communities to solve their own problems." Similar to truth and reconciliation commissions, they are presented as providing a forum in which the "truth" may be fully disclosed.[4]

The *gacaca* process for genocide cases has now concluded.[5] The purpose of this essay is to assess the role politics played in the courts' ability to attain restorative justice for the victimized communities and the country.

"Ethnic" Group Politics in Rwanda

Political competition between the country's two largest demographic groups—the majority Hutu and minority Tutsi—has historically been a zero-sum contest, with violence usually accompanying the process of political reform and/or regime change.

During the years of Belgian rule the Hutu were the out-group. Ruled by a despotic Tutsi monarchy, the Hutu were denied economic and social advancement, as well as any substantial degree of political representation. In the years before independence, it was their belief in their inherent right to rule that led many Tutsi elites to challenge and resist the prospect of sharing power with the Hutu.[6]

When regime change occurred—a period known as the "Hutu Revolution"—it was accompanied by episodes of extreme inter-group violence. Thousands of Tutsi lost their lives and hundreds of thousands fled the country. With the assistance of Belgium the Hutu established a regime in which access to the political arena was essentially forbidden to the Tutsi.[7] The Hutu became dominant and the Tutsi became the out-group, a status-quo that persisted until 1994.

Violence sharply increased in the early 1990s as the country was making the transition to multiparty democracy. Because the Hutu government was also engaged in a civil war with the RPF, institutional reform became inextricably linked with the ongoing peace negotiations held in Arusha, Tanzania.[8]

The 1993 Arusha Accords mandated the creation of a transitional government wherein power was to be divided between the RPF and the major political parties in Rwanda. Because the agreement substantially reduced the power of the former ruling party—the Mouvement Rèpublicain National pour la Démocratie et le Dèveloppment—relative to the opposition, and guaranteed a substantial share of positions in the transitional government and military to the RPF, many Hutu politicians rejected the agreement outright.[9] Following the assassination of President Juvénal Habyarimana on April 6, 1994, Hutu extremists conducted a highly organized campaign of destruction aimed at the complete elimination of the Tutsi population, and moderate Hutu opposition. Over eight hundred thousand men and women in Rwanda were brutally massacred.

The genocide was ended when the RPF captured control of Kigali in July 1994. What happened next followed a familiar pattern: the Hutu government that oppressed the Tutsi was replaced by a government that set about to oppress the Hutu (and any who opposed RPF rule). Sarkin describes post-genocide Rwanda as an example of an "overthrow" model of democratization, wherein one set of ruling elites is completely replaced by another.[10] This particular mode of regime change poses severe difficulties for the process of achieving transitional justice more generally, and restorative justice specifically because it grants the new elites "the widest discretion to decide how [to] . . . deal with the past, including unfettered power to bring the perpetrators of human rights abuses to justice."[11]

The "unfettered power" enjoyed by the RPF has only increased over time. An internal struggle for power during the transitional period (1994-2003) culminated in the exodus of several Hutu and Tutsi politicians from the country. Those who resigned, fled, were disappeared or assassinated, were targeted because they resisted or were in some way critical of RPF policies.[12]

Moreover, the RPF has consolidated its power through the electoral process. An RPF coalition currently controls nearly 80 percent of the seats open to direct election in the Chamber of Deputies (an increase of roughly 5 percent over the number of seats obtained in the 2003 elections).[13] In the country's 2003 presidential election former RPF commander Paul Kagame was elected president with 95 percent of the popular vote; a performance he repeated in the 2010 election.[14] Although this latest election proceeded peacefully according to international observers, the government was heavily criticized for clamping-down on the local press and political opposition groups.[15] One independent journalist and one leading member of the opposition were murdered; others were forced to flee.[16]

Moreover the ability of political parties and civil society associations to operate freely in the country remains heavily restricted.[17] Some parties have been banned, others harshly sanctioned for engaging in "sectarian" activities. The government's authority for these actions stems from a number of laws which specifically prohibit certain types of speech, including that which promotes "divisionism" and speech which negates, minimalizes or justifies the genocide.[18] The practical effect of these laws has been to sharply curtail public discussion about events which took place during the genocide as well as the RPF's current policymaking behavior.[19]

Contrary to the principles of an open democracy, agents of the government have made it a practice to target any who challenge or question RPF rule, including members of the independent media and the opposition. Although the number of disappearances and political killings has decreased in recent years, cases of torture, arbitrary arrest and harassment continue as the recent presidential election demonstrates.[20]

More egregious by far are the human rights abuses perpetrated against the Hutu civilian population. Members of the Rwanda Patriotic Army (RPA) are believed to be responsible for the deaths of tens of thousands of Hutu killed during the genocide and in counter-insurgency operations conducted in the northwestern part of Rwanda, as well as in the Democratic Republic of the Congo.[21]

The Concept of Restorative Justice

Restorative justice is unlike retributive justice which requires "that perpetrators must be punished, to bring them to account and to give them what they supposedly 'deserve'." [22] A reliance on retributive justice for post-conflict societies is frequently faulted for its lack of attention to the "big picture," including the conditions of structural violence that preceded the conflict and the needs of the victims.[23] Restorative justice, by contrast, moves beyond castigation and individual culpability towards a larger goal of reconciliation.

Johnstone and Van Ness contend that the definition of restorative justice is open-ended, a function of the purpose(s) it is meant to accomplish and/or the types of processes necessary to achieve same. The authors distinguish between encounter, reparative and transformative conceptions of restorative justice.

Advocates of the "encounter" conception place emphasis on victim-offender interaction (to address the harm done, determine appropriate remedies etc.). Victim empowerment is considered essential to the process of healing. Here restorative justice promotes understanding, reduces uncertainty and allows victims to achieve a sense of closure.[24]

Proponents of a "reparative" conception contend that justice is not merely a matter of victim-offender interaction and individual empowerment. While these are certainly important to the reconciliation process both are not always present, nor can they be. Instead, greater emphasis must be placed on the ability of offenders to make restitution and repair the damage they have wrought on society. Unlike the encounter conception, the state is permitted to play a larger role in ensuring that justice is forthcoming.[25]

Lastly, proponents of a "transformative" conception look beyond the immediate relationship between victim and offender to address larger issues of social injustice. From this perspective, the end-game is altering the manner in which individuals conduct themselves vis-à-vis their fellow citizens. Restorative justice in this instance is conceived of as a way of life, not merely a matter of individual restitution or closure.[26]

Rather than explicitly taking sides in this definitional debate I share with Johnstone and Van Ness the assumption that all three conceptions overlap considerably. I focus instead on the ingredients they identify as crucial for the achievement of restorative justice. Paraphrasing and quoting from their work, these include:

1. An informal process that brings together all relevant stakeholders to discuss the crime(s) in question, what should be done to repair the damage, as well as resolve the conflict;

2. An emphasis placed on "strengthening or repairing relationships between people";

3. An emphasis placed on empowering victims, as well as addressing and acknowledging their injuries and needs;

4. An emphasis directed toward facilitating the perpetrators' acknowledgement of their crimes and their responsibility to make amends to achieve reintegration and reconciliation;

5. A process guided by widely-held values and principles that are considered necessary for peaceful interaction in a society (the authors include: respect, inclusion and a de-emphasis on the use of force as a means of conflict resolution).[27]

Others, including Clark, suggest that imposing one standard set of criteria on *gacaca* produces misleading conclusions. He strongly contends *gacaca* has been a constantly evolving social process that differs between communities.[28] I concur with his assertion that restorative justice criteria—such as that utilized by this study—are normative. Nevertheless Johnstone and Van Ness' criteria remain relevant as a general framework with which to examine *gacaca*, keeping in mind of course that perceptions "on the ground" regarding the ability of *gacaca* to meet its objectives must also be taken into account.

Restorative Justice and *Gacaca*

Established by Organic Law No. 40/2000, *gacaca* tribunals were made responsible for adjudicating cases that fell within the categories of genocide-related offenses outlined in Organic Law No 08/96.[29] These crimes include intentional and unintentional homicides, fatal and non-fatal assaults, and property crimes.[30]

Gacaca courts are unique in that members of local communities play a vital role as arbiters of justice (each acts as "a lawyer, a prosecutor and a witness at the same time").[31] *Gacaca* courts at the cell and sector levels included a set of judges (*inyangamugayo*), a president, a General Assembly, and a Coordinating Committee.

Defendants brought before *gacaca* included those recently accused, as well as detainees who confessed to genocide-related offenses. Depending on the crime in question and whether or not the offender confessed, punishments meted out by *gacaca* included compensation, community service, and varying amounts of prison time. Reductions in prison sentences were possible in most cases if the defendant confessed before he/she was charged, and his/her confession was judged by the court to be truthful and sincere.[32]

Important for the achievement of restorative justice is an informal process that emphasizes victim-offender interaction. Clark suggests that the participatory aspect of *gacaca* is its most significant feature. His research indicates that public ownership of the justice process and the forum for discussion *gacaca* provide are why *gacaca* are valued by many Rwandans: "Many everyday Rwandans believe that greater 'unity' is likely to result from this dialogue at gacaca. . . . Many Rwandans argue that parties at gacaca will carry this dialogue and the peaceful methods of conflict resolution embodied in the hearings into their everyday lives leading to a greater sense of cohesion in previously fragmented societies."[33]

That being said the evidence indicates that an informal environment alone is insufficient for the achievement of restorative justice. The political environment in which genocide-*gacaca* operated must be factored into any assessment of their success (or failure) as a tool for conflict resolution.

Much the general criticism voiced by scholars and human rights organizations focuses on those aspects of *gacaca* which they contend seriously infringe on internationally accepted standards of due process. These include: (1) denial of legal counsel to defendants; (2) an absence of a presumption of innocence; (3) the lack of legal training afforded the *inyangamugayo*; (4) the acceptance of hearsay testimony; (5) the exclusion of physical evidence as a means to corroborate witness testimony; and (6) the fact that defendants were often denied sufficient time to prepare their cases and adequately confront their accusers.[34]

Others question the fairness of these due process challenges. Meyerstein suggests they are a form of "symbolic violence."[35] Arguing from a more general standpoint, Snyder and Vinjamiari contend that the international community's expectation that the process of justice in transitional societies adhere to internationally accepted norms is unrealistic and ignores political realities on the ground.[36] Instead of furthering justice and a respect for human rights, a strict adherence to these standards actually hampers prospects for stability.

Drumbl questions the appropriateness of applying universal standards of criminal justice to cases involving the commission of "extraordinary crimes," which are horrific systematic crimes committed by whole societies.[37] Given their depth and severity, ordinary methods of adjudication and punishment which focus on individual rights and accountability frequently fail to achieve justice for traumatized societies. Drumbl recommends the utilization of more culture-specific methods of adjudication as a supplement. In this respect he contends *gacaca* have potential to achieve restorative justice for genocide survivors.[38]

Lastly Clark takes issue with the due process criticisms (the "dominant discourse") suggesting that NGOs like Amnesty International routinely disregarded the inherent protections *gacaca* provided participants. Certain safeguards—the mediator function performed by *inyangamugayo* and *gacaca* presidents, the fact that *inyangamugayo* deliberate *in camera* before reaching judgments, the right to appeal—protect the individual and the legitimacy of the entire process. He attributes critics' neglect of these safeguards to their preference for formal models of justice and their assumption that deterrence and retribution were (or should have been) the chief goals of *gacaca*.[39]

Many of the concerns voiced by critics also concern government interference in the *gacaca* process. To demonstrate this point, a few examples are worth mentioning.

The first of these concerns the role of the *nyumbacumi* ("persons in charge of ten households"). In an effort to streamline the *gacaca* process in late 2004, responsibility for gathering and assessing evidence was officially transferred from the General Assembly to the *nyumbacumi*. As Penal Reform International (PRI) and others contend, this "outsourcing" policy had the unfortunate effect of increasing the discretion of local officials in determining who would be tried for genocide crimes, and by extension, how easily they would be convicted.[40] Moreover: "The absence of any verificatory barriers and [no] due process created a climate favourable to exaggeration and the potential for false-accusations and . . . personal score-settling."[41] The revised information-gathering process diminished the truth-gathering function of *gacaca*, not to mention its potential for any meaningful victim-offender interaction. At many *gacaca* hearings *inyangamugayo* were left with the duty of recording the information presented with little or no debate.[42]

PRI and others attribute the role of the *nyumbacumi* to the RPF government's desire to control the *gacaca* process, albeit indirectly. A similar observation can be made of the *inyangamugayo* who are required by law to be "free from the spirit of sectarianism" as well as "genocide ideology."[43] In more practical terms this means *inyangamugayo* were expected to refrain from challenging government behavior in *gacaca* hearings.[44]

Direct government interference in *gacaca* included various forms of coercion and intimidation. However Clark contends this interference was limited by geography. In his observations of *gacaca* hearings he found that rural areas exercised greater agency with respect to the manner in which hearings were conducted, the requirements for attendance, and the topics open for discussion. In some cases RPF/RPA offenses were addressed by participants, although no RPF member was officially tried for these abuses.[45]

This latter issue points to an especially formidable obstacle that hampered the ability of *gacaca* courts to meet *all* of Johnstone and Van Ness' requirements for restorative justice: the "prejudicially narrow" scope of crimes included within their mandate.[46] Crimes perpetrated by the RPF/RPA during the course of the genocide and after were excluded from consideration in *gacaca* and have been largely ignored by Rwanda's formal courts. This failure to include these offenses has damaged any real hope of achieving reconciliation at the local and national levels.[47]

To date no member of the RPF/RPA has been brought to justice in the ICTR or *gacaca* for crimes committed during the genocide. The government claimed at one point that as many as fifteen hundred RPA members had been tried and convicted in conventional courts for human rights offenses perpetrated during the genocide.[48] Evidence obtained by human rights observers suggests, however, that very few soldiers have been prosecuted by the state.[49] The government's unwillingness to "face the music" remains despite public opinion in Rwanda that RPF agents should be held accountable for their crimes.[50]

Their exclusion from the judicial process is one of a number of factors that infringe upon another crucial ingredient for restorative justice: victim empowerment. In post-conflict societies allowing victims of atrocities to participate in the justice process is crucial as a means of achieving long-term reconciliation, and the remaining "profound objectives" Clark discusses. Sarkin contends that by permitting victims the ability to tell their stories, by granting official recognition of their suffering, "the inherent worth and dignity of the [victim] is acknowledged."[51]

In many ways genocide-*gacaca* enabled victim empowerment. Unlike conventional courts they placed greater emphasis on wrongdoings perpetrated against individual victims and by implication whole communities. *Gacaca* provided a forum in which victims were able to come forward and publicly air their grievances against the accused. *Gacaca* facilitated what Clark terms "truth-telling" and "truth-hearing" processes; both of which many survivors and suspects contend contribute to healing, justice, and reconciliation for individuals and communities.[52]

Critics, however, suggest that a number of factors substantially reduced the likelihood that victims would obtain any cathartic effect from *gacaca* proceedings. These include: personal safety issues, the mandatory nature of *gacaca*, and the limitations placed on speech which prevented victims from openly and honestly testifying for or against defendants.[53] Those who offered testimony for the defense, for example, risked being subjected to harassment, physical harm, and/or being charged by the state with "negating the genocide" or promoting divisionism.[54] Based on his extensive observations and discussions with *gacaca* participants Clark suggests that many of these concerns are valid, but their impact varied between communities and did not necessarily detract from their overall significance as a peace-building tool.

Yet for victim empowerment to have any lasting impact on creating conditions of positive peace in a country like Rwanda *all* victims must have their day in court. This has not occurred. Excluding RPF/RPA offenders from the docks impaired efforts to achieve a comprehensive truth about the genocide and/or group relations in Rwanda at the national level. At the local level, exclusion of RPF/RPA offenses detracted from the positive restorative effects the truth-telling and hearing processes provided participants.[55]

The official version of the truth—promoted in *gacaca* hearings, by the National Unity and Reconciliation Commission (NURC), in "civic education" programs in *ingando* camps[56]—attributes the Hutu-Tutsi conflict to colonial practices and "bad governments" in the post-colonial era.[57] Moreover the official truth of the genocide focuses on the wrongdoings perpetrated by Hutu and erases from popular memory the work of the *Intwali* ("the righteous"); Hutu who actively assisted in the rescue of Tutsi.[58]

On the issue of "truth shaping" it has been suggested that political elites must realize that a "multiplicity" of truths about the genocide, stemming from thousands of personal narratives, have emerged from *gacaca*. Rather than impose one version of the truth on communities, elites must respect local ownership of the truth process: "effective truth-shaping must be consultative and must reflect a wide range of people's beliefs and memories."[59] Presently local truths are divorced from the national truth about the genocide. This disconnect poses serious challenges for the ability of *gacaca* to achieve positive peace at the national level.

Johnstone and Van Ness' fourth criterion concerns offenders: their acknowledgment of their crimes, attempts to make amends and so forth. Genocide suspects in Rwanda are required by *gacaca* to participate in community service and many were obligated to pay restitution; both of these necessary to enable the accused to repair the damage done and achieve reintegration.[60] This is crucial for post-conflict societies: "reparations [which include restitution and compensation] provide a basis for rebuilding trust that may have been undermined by the offense, thereby creating the conditions for reassuming a normal place in society."[61]

When it comes to financial reparations *gacaca* fell short for obvious reasons. Rwanda is a poor country. It is not surprising that most defendants lack the resources to financially compensate their victims.[62] Owing also to government financial shortfalls the Compensation Fund for Victims of the Genocide and Crimes Against Humanity has lain dormant.[63] PRI notes: "reparations have been under consideration since 2000, issues surrounding what form compensation should take, how a beneficiary should be defined and how victims should be paid were never resolved."[64] Consequently many survivors have become disenchanted with the justice process.[65]

An additional factor worth addressing is the confession process. Whether or not defendants were able to have their sentences reduced or commuted to community service was partially due to their willingness to confess their crimes and implicate others. The result: many defendants falsely confessed to lesser crimes or falsely accused others of complicity in genocide-related offenses.[66] NGOs write of a process of "confession dealing" which occurred in prisons wherein money was exchanged between prisoners in return for accusations/confessions and agreements were made to "divide up culpability" among willing participants.[67]

More troubling is the fact that few suspects have expressed any real regret for the harm they caused their victims. In his interviews of suspects Clark found that many valued the confession process largely as a means to obtain release from prison and/or reduce their punishments. A lack of empathy, and the fact that many offenders perceived confession and acknowledgment of their crimes as a duty to the state, indicates that full perpetrator accountability in *gacaca* has not been entirely forthcoming.[68] This of course detracts from the rehabilitative quality of *gacaca*, the ability of *gacaca* to facilitate perpetrator reintegration, not to mention survivor-offender forgiveness.

The last requirement for restorative justice is a process guided by values and principles that are considered necessary for peaceful interaction in a society. These include a de-emphasis on force as an acceptable means of conflict resolution, tolerance, "morality and reverence for life."[69] *Gacaca* experienced mixed success in this regard. The therapeutic value of truth-telling and hearing for participants, and the ethos of cooperation fostered by the relatively open forum for debate, for example, will likely continue into the future. This is the hope expressed by many Rwandans. At the same time, however, the absence of RPF/RPA perpetrators in the docks and the limitations placed on speech, demonstrate a process grounded in norms of exclusion; justice for some, injustice for others.

Many of the limitations placed on *gacaca* are a function of the balance of power in Rwanda. It is therefore ironic that political elites consider *gacaca* to be a foundation for democratic peace; that *gacaca* "will have long-lasting effects on people's interactions in daily life and in the broader social and political realms."[70] *Gacaca* may have contributed somewhat to the formation of social capital at the local level. The likelihood this will translate into greater participation in the public severe, however, is sharply curtailed by the RPF ruling elite; its restrictions on civil liberties and political rights, and its penchant for coercion.

Conclusion

The purpose of this chapter has been to assess whether or not *gacaca* enable the population of Rwanda to achieve restorative justice. Many of the problems *gacaca* encountered are attributable to the current status quo of power relations in Rwanda. Single-party authoritarian rule still hangs over the heads of Rwandans in ways that curtailed the positive influences *gacaca* had on the prospects for positive peace.

An important aspect of *gacaca* concerned the historical narrative of the conflict that emerged. An accurate narrative must include information regarding the crimes perpetrated during and prior to a conflict, the identities of perpetrators and their victims, and the systemic inequalities that contributed to the conflict. Such a narrative enables government and society to come to terms with deep-seated issues of injustice in order to prevent a possible repetition of the abuses in question. As has been stated: "the past, far from disappearing or lying down and being quiet, has an embarrassing and persistent way of returning and haunting us unless it has in fact been dealt with adequately. Unless we look the beast in the eye we find it has an uncanny habit of returning to hold us hostage."[71]

However, the "expressivist" function of trials is frequently limited by rules of evidence and procedure which, in turn, are a function of a state's truth-seeking agenda.[72] Rules place limitations on the types of witnesses who can testify, the manner in which they are questioned, and the type of testimony they can give, all of which determine the kind of narrative that unfolds.[73]

Many scholars who have written about *gacaca* would likely agree with my contention that achieving a comprehensive truth about Hutu-Tutsi relations is a matter of the existing political environment. National truth differs from truth achieved at the local level; the latter reflecting the various debates and discussions that took place among participants. Whatever transformative effect these truths have, however, is limited to local communities.

In a country like Rwanda, history is everything. It determines who has the legitimate right to rule. The current discourse, reinforced by the justice system and government, stresses the collective victimization of the Tutsi at the hands of the Hutu, while at the same time overlooking the human rights abuses endured by the Hutu during the genocide, as well as under the years of RPF rule.

This current whitewashed version of history is mutually constitutive in that it permits and reinforces the appropriateness of RPF rule. They are, after all, victors in the civil war. They therefore have a legitimate right to punish the *génocidaires*. Unfortunately, this right currently extends to any who pose a threat to political stability or security in the country. At present, the RPF has little incentive to alter this view; their power depends on it.[74]

Notes

1. The ICTR tries persons formally accused of genocide and other serious crimes committed in Rwanda between January 1, 1994 and December 31, 1994. UNCTR, "About the Tribunal," http://69.94.11.53/default.htm (accessed May 15, 2011).

2. Phil Clark, *The Gacaca Courts, Post-Genocide Justice and Reconciliation in Rwanda: Justice without Lawyers* (Cambridge, UK; New York: Cambridge University Press, 2010), 51.

3. Between 1997 and 2008 just over 7,400 genocide-related cases were tried in Rwanda's conventional courts. Human Rights Watch (HRW), *Law and Reality: Progress in Judicial Reform in Rwanda* (New York: Human Rights Watch, July 24, 2008), 17. To date, only forty-eight cases have been completed in the ICTR (plus an additional sixteen pending appeal and ten acquittals). See "Status of Cases," http://69.94.11.53/default.htm (accessed August 31, 2012).

4. Official Website of the Republic of Rwanda, "*Gacaca* Courts," www.gov.rw/ (accessed April 1, 2008).

5. *BBC*, "'Gacaca' Courts Finish Work," June 18, 2012, at http://www.bbc.co.uk (accessed June 19, 2012).

6. For a comprehensive history of early political development in Rwanda, see René Lemarchand, *Rwanda and Burundi* (New York; London: Praeger Publishers, Inc., 1970).

7. Regarding the Rwanda-Belgium relationship see Lemarchand, *Rwanda and Burundi,* 109-111, 197; Hutu rule in post-independence Rwanda, see Gerard Prunier, *The Rwandan Crisis: The History of a Genocide* (London: Hurst & Co, 1995).

8. Alison Des Forges, *Leave None to Tell the Story: Genocide in Rwanda* (New York: Human Rights Watch, 1999); Timothy Longman, "State, Civil Society, and Genocide in Rwanda," in *State, Conflict, and Democracy in Africa,* ed. Richard Joseph (Boulder, CO: Lynne Reinner Publishers, 1999), 339-358.

9. Bruce Jones, "The Arusha Peace Process" in *The Path of a Genocide: The Rwanda Crisis from Uganda to Zaire,* ed. Howard Adelman and Astri Suhrke (New Brunswick, NJ: Transaction Publishers, 1999), 136-143.

10. Jeremy Sarkin, "The Tension between Justice and Reconciliation in Rwanda," 45 *J. Afr. L.* 143, 145-146 (2001).

11. Sarkin, "Tension," 146.

12. Felip Reytjens, "Governance and Security in Rwanda," in *Security Dynamics in Africa's Great Lakes Region*, ed. Gilbert M. Khadiagala (Boulder, CO; London: Lynne Reinner Publishers, 2006), 18-20.

13. Amnesty International (AI), *The Enduring Legacy of the Genocide and War,* AFR 47/008/2004 (New York; London, Amnesty International, 2004), 2.

14. HRW, "Rwanda: Attacks on Freedom of Expression, Freedom of Association, and Freedom of Assembly in the Run-up to Presidential Election," August 2, 2010, www.hrw.org (accessed September 1, 2010).

15. HRW, "Attacks."

16. US Department of State, *Country Reports on Human Rights Practices: Rwanda, FY 2009* (Washington, D.C., 2010), http://www.state.gov (accessed March 19, 2010).

17. Reytjens, "Governance," 26-29.

18. Organic Law No. 47/2001 on Prevention, Suppression and Punishment of the Crime of Discrimination and Sectarianism, www.amategeko.net/index.php (accessed March 16, 2009) and Organic Law No.33 BIS/2003 Repressing the Crime of Genocide, Crimes Against Humanity and War Crimes, www.amategeko.net/index.php (accessed March 16, 2009).

19. HRW, *Law and Reality.*

20. US Department of State, *Country Reports on Human Rights Practices: Rwanda, FY 2008* (Washington, DC, 2009) www.state.gov (accessed March 19, 2010) and *Country Reports 2009.* In 2010 opposition candidates were arrested and detained for a variety of offenses including divisionism and propagating genocide ideology. This paved the way for an easy Kagame victory at the polls. Max Delany, "Rwanda Election: Kagame Supporters Celebrate Landslide Win," *Christian Science Monitor*, August 8, 2010.

21. René Lemarchand, "Genocide in the Great Lakes: Which Genocide? Whose Genocide?" *African Studies Review* 41, no. 1 (April 1998); Des Forges, *Leave None,* 702-722.

22. Phil Clark, "Establishing a Conceptual Framework," in *After Genocide: Transitional Justice, Post-Conflict Reconstruction and Reconciliation in Rwanda and Beyond,* ed. Phil Clark and Zachary D. Kaufman (New York: Columbia University Press, 2009), 197.

23. On these and other issues associated with post-conflict retribution for Rwanda and other countries, see Rama Mani *Beyond Retribution: Seeking Justice in the Shadows of War* (New York: Polity Press, 2002); Mark Drumbl, *Atrocity, Punishment and International Law* (Cambridge; New York: Cambridge University Press, 2007).

24. Gerry Johnstone and Daniel W. Van Ness, "The Meaning of Restorative Justice," in *Handbook of Restorative Justice*, ed. Gerry Johnstone and Daniel W. Van Ness (Portland, OR: Willan Publishing, 2007), 9-12.

25. Johnstone and Van Ness, "Restorative Justice," 12-15.

26. Johnstone and Van Ness, "Restorative Justice," 15-16.

27. Johnstone and Van Ness, "Restorative Justice," 7.

28. This is contrary to the conception of *gacaca* described by the government and observers such as AI and HRW. *Gacaca Courts*, 47-80.

29. Organic law 8/96 of 30 August 1996 on the Organization of the Prosecution of Offences Constituting the Crime of Genocide or Crimes Against Humanity Committed since October 1, 1990 (August 1996).

30. Changes to the original *gacaca* law were made by Organic Law No. 16/2004 of 19/6/2004 Establishing the Organisation, Competence and Functioning of the Gacaca Courts Charged with Prosecuting and Trying the Perpetrators of the Crime of Genocide

and Other Crimes against Humanity, Committed between October 1, 1990, and December 31, 1994, Art. 51 (2004); also Organic Law No. 13/2008 of 19/05/2008 Modifying and Complementing Organic Law No. 16/2004 of 19/6/2004 Establishing the Organisation, Competence and Functioning of the Gacaca Courts Charged with Prosecuting and Trying the Perpetrators of the Crime of Genocide and Other Crimes against Humanity, Committed between October 1, 1990, and December 31, 1994, as Modified and Complemented to Date, Art. 1, 6, 7, 9 (2008).

31. National Service of *Gacaca* Jurisdictions, "The Gacaca Process: Achievements, Problems and Future Prospects," www.inkiko-gacaca.gov.rw/PPT/Realisation%20and%20future%20persective.ppt#265, 12 (accessed January 14, 2009).

32. For *gacaca's* punishment schedule see Clark, *Gacaca Courts*, 78; see also Jonathan Blagrough, ed., *Eight Years On: A Record of Gacaca Monitoring in Rwanda* (London: Penal Reform International, 2010).

33. Clark, *Gacaca Courts*, 139. This perception is supported by empirical data. According to a national opinion survey, 92 percent of the population believes that genocide-*gacaca* lays the foundations for positive peace (long-term peace) in Rwanda. National Unity and Reconciliation Commission, "Opinion Survey on Participation in Gacaca," Annex 4, 1 cited in Clark, *Gacaca Courts*, 227.

34. See HRW, *Law and Reality*; AI, *The Enduring Legacy* and *Gacaca: A Question of Justice* AFR 47/007/2002 (New York; London: Amnesty International, 2002); Sarkin, "Tension," 161-166; Avocats sans Frontierès (ASF), *Monitoring of the Gacaca Courts: Judgment Phase, Analytical Report, March-September 2005* (2005).

35. Ariel Meyerstein, "Between Law and Culture: Rwanda's *Gacaca* and Postcolonial Legality," 32 *Law & Soc. Inquiry* 467, 497-500 (Spring 2007).

36. Jack Snyder and Leslie Vinjamuri, "Trials and Errors: Principle and Pragmatism in Strategies of International Justice," *International Security* 28 (2003/2004): 5-44.

37. Drumbl, *Atrocity*, 3-6.

38. Drumbl. *Atrocity*, 94-99.

39. *Gacaca* Courts, 91-97, 154-161; also Timothy Longman, "Justice at the Grassroots? Gacaca Trials in Rwanda," in *Transitional Justice in the Twenty-First Century,"* ed. Naomi Roht-Arriaza and Javier Mariezcurrena (Cambridge: Cambridge University Press, 2006), 216-219.

40. Blagrough, *Eight Years*, 27-29; also HRW, *Law and Reality*, 12-13.

41. Blagrough, *Eight Years*, 29.

42. Clark voices a similar criticism about the increasingly legalistic character *gacaca* assumed once they began trying Category 1 offenses. *Gacaca Courts*, 214-216.

43. Both of which are vaguely defined. See Organic Law No. 10/2007 of 01/03/2007 Modifying and Complementing Organic Law No. 16/2004 of 19/6/2004 Establishing the Organisation, Competence and Functioning of Gacaca Courts Charged with Prosecuting and Trying the Perpetrators of the Crime of Genocide and other Crimes against Humanity, Committed between October 1, 1990, and December 31, 1994, as Modified and Complemented to Date, Art. 3-4 (2007); also HRW, *Law and Reality*, 20.

44. Sarkin, "Tension," 164; Blagrough, *Eight Years*, 29-31.

45. Clark, *Gacaca Courts*, 139-140, 144-145, 157-160, 211.

46. Sarkin, "Tension," 161.

47. Sarkin, "Tension," HRW, *Law and Reality*, 50-54; Clark, *Gacaca Courts*, 210-211.

48. AI, *Enduring Legacy*, 8.

49. HRW, *Law and Reality*, 51-52; also AI, *Enduring Legacy*, 8.

50. In a 2002 survey of Rwandans, Longman found that over 61 percent of respondents believed RPF members should be tried in the ICTR. Fifty-two percent of Hutu respondents and 19 percent of Tutsi respondents agreed that RPF members should stand trial in *gacaca.* Timothy Longman, "Memory, Justice, and Power in Post-Genocide Rwanda." Paper presented at the annual meeting of the *American Political Science Association*, Philadelphia, September 6, 2006, 32.

51. Jeremy Sarkin, "Promoting Justice, Truth and Reconciliation in Transitional Societies," 2 *Int'l. L. F. D. Int'l.* 112, 117 (2000).

52. Clark, *Gacaca Courts*, 186-189, 192-201.

53. HRW, *Law and Reality*, 83, 41-45; also Drumbl, *Atrocity*, 96-97 and Longman, "Trying Times for Rwanda: Reevaluating Gacaca Courts in Post-Genocide Reconciliation," *Harvard International Review* (Summer 2010): 51.

54. HRW, *Law and Reality*, 44-45.

55. Clark, *Gacaca* Courts, 123, 210-211.

56. Regarding *ingando* camps see Clark, *Gacaca Courts*, 99-107.

57. See for example National Unity and Reconciliation Commission (NURC), *The Causes of the Violence* (Kigali: NURC, 2008).

58. Blagrough, *Eight Years*, 37-40.

59. Clark, *Gacaca Courts*, 219.

60. Mark Drumbl, "Pluralizing International Criminal Justice," 103 *Mich. L. Rev.* 1295, 1316 (2005).

61. Mani, *Beyond Retribution*, 175.

62. Regarding compensation for property offenses see Blagrough, *Eight Years*, 58-60; Clark, *Gacaca Courts*, 179.

63. Clark, *Gacaca Courts*, 178-179.

64. PRI, *Eight Years*, 46.

65. *Gacaca's* ability to contribute to economic development has been overstated by the government. Clark, *Gacaca Courts*, 177. For problems with community service see Blagrough, *Eight Years*, 46-47; 60-61. Clark, *Gacaca Courts*, 183-184, 252-253.

66. ASF, *Monitoring*, 12.

67. ASF, *Monitoring*, 12; Blagrough, *Eight Years*, 35-36.

68. Clark, *Gacaca Courts*, 141, 147-148, 225. For an excellent assessment of the weaknesses of the confession process see Blagrough, *Eight Years*, 34-37.

69. Sarkin, "Tension," 159.

70. Clark, *Gacaca Courts*, 143.

71. Desmond Mpilo Tutu, *No Future Without Foregiveness* (New York: Doubleday, 1999), 28.

72. Drumbl, *Atrocity*, 173.

73. Drumbl, *Atrocity*, 176-180.

74. Longman, "Memory," 13.

Chapter 18

Gacaca and the Treatment of Sexual Offenses

Prisca Uwigabye

Gacaca courts were established by the Government of Rwanda to overcome the challenge of unification in post-genocide Rwanda. It is in line with this that the Vice-Chairman of the National Unity and Reconciliation Commission (NURC) stated: "for Rwandans: Reconciliation is not just one of the many other options for us Rwandese; it is rather a non-negotiable obligation. An obligation to give to ourselves hope for our old age, an obligation to leave to our children a better Rwanda to grow and live in."[1]

This chapter addresses *Gacaca's* record with respect to women. It asks how *Gacaca*, which highlights the impressive ingenuity and innovation of the Rwandan people,[2] has worked in practice for women, as well as what *Gacaca* means for gender-related justice. It examines the manner in which female survivors and perpetrators in Rwanda were treated throughout the process, and whether or not the hearings contributed to reconciliation and were fair given their specific gender concerns.

Assessing *Gacaca*

Gacaca courts were a response to the enormous challenges that confronted Rwanda after the genocide. Approximately 11,000 community-based *Gacaca* courts were set up and managed by almost 100,000 locally elected judges, both men and women. It is estimated that 400,000 suspected perpetrators of the genocide were convicted through the *Gacaca* process.[3]

The goals of *gacaca* include reconciliation, peace, justice, healing, forgiveness and truth.[4] However none of these goals automatically imply gender justice. This chapter focuses on the gender dimension of *Gacaca*, a topic that has been neglected in most research with few exceptions.[5]

The core objective of this study is to explain how female survivors and perpetrators viewed *Gacaca* courts and how they were affected by *Gacaca*. Other views (politicians, scholars) are also considered. The main research question is as follows: To what extent do women from diverse backgrounds in the Kicukiro district in the capital city of Kigali consider the *Gacaca* process able to promote justice and reconciliation?

This study utilized a case study approach for primary data collection. The sample size was fifty-seven persons which included female survivors and perpetrators, *Gacaca* officials, Elders, pastors, judges, and politicians. The Kicukiro district in the capital city of Kigali was selected for the following reasons: (1) the researcher's familiarity with the location; (2) the fact that *Gacaca* records in Kicukiro are considered exemplary; and (3) the district is assumed to have the highest number of recorded genocide-related killings and hosts relatively high numbers of female survivors, and suspected and convicted perpetrators of the 1994 genocide.

Gacaca in Context: History and Key Concepts

The effect of the 1994 genocide in Rwanda was atrocious: the creation of thousands of orphans and widows; large numbers of HIV/AIDS infected people; huge numbers of refugees; vandalism of property; and the destruction of Rwandan cultural values. In approximately 100 days it is estimated one million Tutsis and moderate Hutu were killed; 250,000 to 500,000 girls and women–mostly Tutsis—raped by Hutu extremists.[6]

Gacaca courts were re-established as a means to end impunity in Rwanda. They are a form of transitional justice designed to promote wider inter-personal justice, as well as reconciliation. There are three broad approaches to transitional justice—retributive, restorative, reparative—all of which were to some extent part of the justification given for *Gacaca* when it was first introduced.[7]

Gacaca as a Hybrid Institution

Traditional *Gacaca* courts were used for handling smaller crimes like theft, and simple disputes between neighbors, friends, and family members.[8] Prior to 1994 *Gacaca* had no powers to sentence wrongdoers to prison. The Government of Rwanda, however, found it useful to give this practice priority in post-genocide Rwanda in order to deal with genocide-related crimes and to achieve the various goals of transitional justice. Tiemussen agrees that present-day *Gacaca* is formally institutionalized and much more clearly linked to state structures compared to its traditional counterpart.[9]

Gacaca is, in effect, a hybrid system. It is a "neo-traditional construct" which synthesizes an institution based on customary law, with concepts drawn from criminal law and procedure derived from written law.[10] In the same vein Karbo and Mutisi agree that *Gacaca* has now been infused with Western ideas about justice.[11]

Gacaca courts were resurrected in Rwanda as a form of transitional justice that would more closely align with local values; this in comparison to the other two venues hearing genocide-related cases: Rwanda's conventional courts and the International Criminal Tribunal for Rwanda. Genocide-*Gacaca* courts were held on grass; literally under trees in the case of villages, and at playing grounds in the urban centers. Tiemussen notes that most *Gacaca* hearings maintained this conventional outdoor setting. However in practice the system functioned more like a conventional court system.[12]

There were some reservations about the ability of *Gacaca* to handle genocide-related cases. It was said its informal nature would trivialize these crimes. Moreover since the majority of Rwandans are Hutu, it was feared that *Gacaca* courts would fail to uncover the truth of the genocide. It was also believed that judges would easily be corrupted and that prisoners would make confessions just to get out of the over-crowded prisons.[13]

Women, Gender, and *Gacaca*

A Brief History of Gender Crimes and *Gacaca*

Pre-genocide *Gacaca* was a useful way to resolve offences and injuries, many of which were related to rape, theft, and vandalism. The most important thing about traditional *Gacaca* was its ability to bring people together to strengthen unity in a society. During the colonial and pre-colonial eras women had no active involvement in *Gacaca* courts. Their roles were defined by a dominant patriarchal culture wherein they could not claim their right to compensation or redress, even when they were the direct victims of a crime. An old man described traditional *Gacaca* in the following way:

> when a woman is raped, she does not go to accuse her rapist but she would have first to tell her mother or elder brother who would in turn communicate it to the father, and the father to the elders. They would call the rapist to appear before the elders, for him to be punished. That time women were marginalized at a high level.[14]

Women's Perceptions of Gender and *Gacaca*

In post-genocide Rwanda, the roles of women have tended to undermine any prior claims that Rwandese women should be treated as a weak sex, or solely as care-takers and nurturers. On the contrary, the evidence that has emerged indicates,

> [m]any women of every social category took part in the killings but the burden of the responsibility lies with educated women who took part. Such as: Rose Karushara, who beat up refugees herself; Odette Nyirabagenzi, who selected men who were to die; Athanasie Muka-rutabana, who went into the hospital with a machete; and Jullienne Kizito who worked directly with killers . . . to burn people alive.[15]

Ahead of them was Pauline Nyiramasuhuko whose participation made her the first woman ever to be charged with genocide and rape as a crime against humanity in an international jurisdiction.[16]

Considering the roles of women as defined by cultural, social, economic, and political conditions, it is observed that gender expectations and obligations have changed since the genocide and have become more meaningful and visible. According to the National Coordinator of *Gacaca*, changing perceptions of gender were due to: "The effects of the genocide for having on one hand, a large number of widows and on the other hand large numbers of women whose husbands committed genocide crimes. Around 120,000 detainees were arrested for genocide crimes, and among them women were few compared to men."[17] This is in line with academic research that suggests that there are often changes and a shift in attitudes towards gender roles after conflicts.[18]

The fact that there were female *Gacaca* judges was one of the most obvious differences. This was seen as opening up gender roles. On this point a female *Gacaca* judge stated: "After the genocide, women were elected with men to be judges, without considering class, education or status. As a poor widow without education, I was elected among other persons of integrity to contribute to this Gacaca Jurisdictions. Reconstruction of this country is not only for the educated ones or men."[19] Another female judge added: "Before the genocide, only the few women who were educated could be involved in Government activities. Even in this, the selection was based on their ethnic groups which is really the opposite to what is happening nowadays."[20]

Judging from these views, *Gacaca* has enhanced the roles that women play within their local communities. It has granted them agency, making it possible for relatively poor and uneducated women to become judges. These changes go beyond shifting gender roles, and imply some reduction of class and status barriers. This is a stark contrast to the past, which was dominated by a culture that considered men to be head of the family and the primary decision makers; a culture in which women were not confident about their public role in society.

Also significant is the fact that genocide-*Gacaca* punished gender-based crimes. In traditional *Gacaca* gender-based crimes were considered crimes against property: "Raping a woman was a serious crime in the past. If the raped woman was married, Elders in *Gacaca* would order the criminal to pay a cow to her husband, or if the victim did not have a husband, judges would give an order to the rapist to immediately marry that lady."[21] Traditionally women were regarded as the property of their men. Perpetrators of gender crimes were softly punished, sometimes to their advantage.

In the post-genocide era perpetrators actually faced the possibility of life imprisonment; this possibly standing as a deterrent to the commission of future crimes. Overall the primary difference between the perception of rape offenses in the pre-genocide and post-genocide eras is that in the former rape was considered an assault against an individual in the larger context of sexual discrimination; in the latter a systematic campaign to subdue and destroy women and girls during wartime.[22]

Gender Justice Through the Eyes of *Gacaca*

Since the 1970s, gender justice has become a central concern in international development policies and programs. A broad agenda for women has been constructed in many parts of the world with different global initiatives including those that address cultural traditions that harm women, women's economic rights, and peace and security. The prevailing view is that one set of the rights cannot be claimed without realizing the others.[23] However, it is relevant to recall for this study that gender justice needs to be a priority, especially in the context of armed conflicts and their aftermath. Typically, however, the opposite has been the case: "Gender justice is neglected in preference for achieving reconciliation driven by patriarchal interest and favoring the powerful and disenfranchising the oppressed."[24]

In the context of armed conflict, gender justice refers to: "Legal processes that are equitable . . . and which acknowledge [the] ways in which women uniquely experience harm."[25] From this point of view, the legal process of *Gacaca* did not give an opportunity only to men. Women constituted 40 percent of *Gacaca* judges.[26] The role of the female judges is viewed as being especially valuable by female survivors and perpetrators. On this point one female perpetrator stated: "Truly, I was feeling comfortable to respond to my fellow women judges who have the same level like me."[27] A survivor stated: "Approaching a woman judge in court has helped me to look forward and has given me strength to appear before the court."[28]

It is interesting that this sense of being encouraged by the presence of female judges was shared by both perpetrators *and* victims. The high proportion of female judges seems to have made it easier for these women to respond to questions, and may have helped some of them overcome their fears of being involved in the *Gacaca* process.

Gender Justice and Sexual Violence in *Gacaca*

According to some female interviewees, even though they were involved in the *Gacaca* process as judges, survivors, or perpetrators, this did not mean that their wounds and suffering, or for that matter their stigmatization, were fully acknowledged. A sixty-year old female survivor stated: "It is good that they have set up *Gacaca* to punish crimes committed during the genocide than pretending to handle gender-based crimes in private, so that we would not be shy or ashamed! Personally, I didn't feel good when I saw someone who raped me before court and other people."[29]

Some politicians highlighted the loophole in *Gacaca* regarding the manner in which rape cases were handled. One had this to say:

> They said rape trials must be in private; personally I don't know what they called private. Because in such trials, beside the victim and the rapist, there are at least seven *Inyangamugayo,* plus coordinator from *Gacaca* National court, as well as one counselor and at least one security man. Therefore you cannot convince me that something heard by nine people will remain a secret.[30]

In *Gacaca,* rape cases were handled in private to hide the identities of victims because these women were already experiencing psychological trauma that "could lead sometimes to chronic mental illness."[31] One could argue from the above testimonies that the trust of the victims and the privacy of rape hearings were defeated by the number of attendees. Because of the psychological torture endured by these women, many seemed not to have the courage to face their rapist(s) and/or suffer further stigmatization and shame from the society.

More generally *Gacaca* failed to fully acknowledge how women uniquely suffered rape during the genocide; a consequence of the manner in which sexuality is perceived in Rwanda society. Thus the privilege of appearing before *Gacaca* was far easier for men, than for female rape victims. Although laws were passed to punish those who betrayed the credibility of the closed *Gacaca* rape trials,[32] some women still doubted the confidentiality of the process. They claimed that leaks were very common and went unpunished. This deterred many from coming forward to tell their stories. Among the twelve female survivors interviewed, seven were raped during the genocide, but only one had willingly testified in front of a closed *Gacaca* hearing. Consequently justice for many rape perpetrators was not forthcoming.

Moreover the absence of victim cooperation has serious implications for the psychological well being of the victims of sexual violence. Impunity touches on psychological phenomena such as denial and silence versus acknowledgement and disclosure; shame and guilt versus rehabilitation; being stuck in the past versus the ability and the freedom to move ahead and integrate.[33] Young women in focus group discussions traced the root of their apathy to culture. Their common view was: "It's a taboo to talk about sexuality in our culture. The stigma for it is huge." These women feared their story would be leaked out and people would likely use it to mock them. Others who wanted to marry and have children in the future feared this would damage their chances. It is seen here that rape victims suffered greatly and because of cultural taboos many never came forward to tell their stories; this to the detriment of society as a whole which needs victim testimonies to eradicate the extant culture of impunity.

Women's Voices: *Gacaca*, Reconciliation, Gender, and Transitional Justice

Women's Perceptions about the Wider *Gacaca* Process

Women's involvement in the *Gacaca* process came in two forms: as judges and as witness and bystanders. Many survivors complained about experiencing foul treatment from the public. It came out that some young people attended the trials purposely to ridicule female survivors. This experience made the women feel bad, as three of six female survivors confirmed in a July 2010 focus group discussion in Gikondo. Consequently they stopped attending *Gacaca* meetings and lost their ability to influence what happened in their cases. When the President of the *Gacaca* was asked about this he stated: "Sometimes those young ones may be sent by their families to disturb people, it wasn't all the time but we asked people to respect each other."[34]

Other female participants verified a similar experience. As a consequence of the disrespectful behavior exhibited towards female participants many found it hard to express themselves at hearings. Innocent women could be found guilty because of their failure to adequately defend their innocence. Many survivors confirmed they lacked confidence and an ability to fully articulate what they witnessed. This led some perpetrators to be set free.

Female perpetrators who finished their jail terms and have been integrated back into the society complained of suffering mistrust in their communities. One stated: "We are being stigmatized even more than men who committed the same crimes despite the assurance given to us at the solidarity camp. It is a heavy burden because we receive foul look everywhere."[35]

These women suffer social sanctions because they had been pronounced guilty of playing roles incompatible not only with law, but with tradition.[36] Rwandese culture has strong expectations of peaceful behavior from women as portrayed by a local saying "*umugore ni umutima w'urugo*" ("a woman is the heart of the family"). The notion of a female war criminal or a genocide participant is incompatible with traditional gender norms. Consequently: "Violent women defined within the monster narrative are not real women because they are described as both actually evil and psychologically broken, two facets which the ideal types of womanhood in gender norms exclude."[37]

Perceptions of Women about Punishment

By law *Gacaca* punished perpetrators according to the gravity of the crime committed.[38] Female survivors however held a different view: "*Gacaca* didn't punish killers according to crimes they committed in the genocide. *Gacaca* sensitized perpetrators to own up and show remorse for reduction of their punishments. Many perpetrators took advantage of this and came out to confess and apologized. *Gacaca* also freed old people and those considered sick." [39]

The act of categorizing punishments, in particular the reductions in sentences available to perpetrators, demonstrates that the government was making national reconciliation central to its political program.[40] It also streamlined the process. This was seen as necessary given the large numbers of perpetrators still being held in Rwanda's prisons at the time.[41] However as a consequence many female survivors developed a cynical distrust of politicians and resentfully said:

> They are using the lives of the people we lost for politics. I found it hard to understand why punishments of perpetrators were reduced because they own up to confess. It increases my headache everyday.[42]
>
> Why should *Gacaca* release old people and those who were seriously sick while in France (Lyons Jurisdictions) when they were after people who committed Holocaust, they didn't consider any age exemption from sentence, some were even old at that time.[43]

They saw the categorization of punishment for killers and the release of the sick, elderly, and minors from prisons as an injustice. Many believe the punishment of the perpetrators should be commensurate to their offenses. Old age, illness or confession should *not* be used to commit crime with impunity or for that matter to enjoy a reduction in punishment. Notwithstanding, female survivors appreciated the fact that rape was defined as a Category One offense: "Laws of *Gacaca* classified rape crime in first category the same as a crime planned to exterminate Tutsi, this really helps and I think women will not encounter the same issues in the future."[44]

Although most female survivors were not content with the punishment of perpetrators and the way in which they asked for forgiveness, they supported the process overall. It was the first time Rwandans saw justice done in that way and many believed it would deter future crimes.

With regard to female perpetrators, two claimed they were innocent of the crimes of which they were accused and punished. One said: "Because of jealousy people accused me for nothing, and I was put in jail whereas I was innocent! So *Gacaca* is not for justice because people should just come up to accuse you and you get punished."[45] Other perpetrators were content with their punishment and said they were lucky not to have been killed. As one said: "We should have been killed since we killed innocent people in the 1994 Genocide. But through *Gacaca*, the Government has forgiven us and reduced our sentences."[46]

Many survivors were worried that most perpetrators simply faked their remorse and apologies in order to reduce their punishment. This is demonstrated in the testimony of the above perpetrator that, "the government has forgiven us and reduced our sentences" implying that the apology she rendered was aimed not at the family she harmed but the panel hearing her case. As discussed in a female survivors focus group, this lack of genuine remorse was demonstrated by some perpetrators who continued killing survivors after serving their reduced sentences.

With regards to restitution, *Gacaca* operated very differently. Some perpetrators were able to pay survivors. However many others were unable to do so because of poverty or because they had sold their property before appearing before *Gacaca*. Thus many who believed that property crimes would be compensated for were frequently disappointed:

> *Gacaca* is not enough to get back our property! Even if perpetrators are made to pay, the amount can't get me quarter of my property. The money given to me can't raise two rooms while a complete house of my husband was vandalized with our personal and valuable items. [47]

> Where is the compensation? The judges were corrupt and if you are poor, you are not considered. They used our situation to get money from the international community to support us but ended supporting selected few and diverting the chunk for their parochial interest. Don't you see the few lavish life around? Perhaps that is what they called compensation![48]

Restitution was not given the priority needed to promote reconciliation. The reason why *Gacaca* covered issues of restitution may be related to the way it traditionally dealt with smaller crimes like theft.[49] Restitution in the pre-genocide period was relatively simple and usually involved a single crime unlike post-genocide *Gacaca* which looked into more complex crimes that were difficult to resolve through restitution. Though restitution could not bring back the lost lives and property destroyed, if it had been given the priority it deserved, it could have softened the path of reconciliation especially for survivors.

Women's Perceptions of Their Security and Status in Relation to *Gacaca*

Among female perpetrators interviewed, five of the eight women had few concerns about their security before the genocide. After the genocide, however, they feared revenge from survivors and the Rwanda Patriotic Front (RPF).[50] By way of contrast eleven out or twelve female survivors in a focus group discussion indicated that they felt little security before or after the genocide. The pre-genocide period was crowded with devilish propaganda inciting Hutus against Tutsis. The post-genocide period was marked by the continued killing of Tutsi survivors.

Two of the eight convicted perpetrators maintained that they had been wrongly convicted and felt unhappy about the whole *Gacaca* process and claimed not to have found justice. It is clear that female perpetrators do not all share the same assumptions about what promotes their sense of security now and in the past, including in relation to *Gacaca.* However they all agreed that in the future the situation will improve, since the politics in place do not promote discrimination. From the appearance of the perpetrators, one could see they were speaking with caution in order not to trespass the threshold of *Gacaca* which had protected them.

Women's Social and Economic Position

Post-genocide Rwandan society remains heavily divided with little improvement at the grass-root level. According to female survivors and perpetrators, *Gacaca* exacerbated tensions among some families and neighbors who appeared before the court as witnesses to accused killers. Many women testified against their husbands, former husbands, brothers, and brothers in-law and are considered enemies by almost everyone in the family.

The Rwandan government created a fund—the Fonds d'Assistance aux Rescapés du Génocide (FARG)—to support genocide survivors. Some of the female survivors interviewed said they had been left without any help and that disbursement of the funds was discriminatory. Having assumed a new gender role as household head, most of these women lack skills or employment prospects, this worsening their economic status and making life unbearable.

The problems of female perpetrators were related to their involvement in the genocide and *Gacaca.* Soon after being released from prisons, some found their husbands had married other women. Consequently this led to many divorces and separations and weakening the economic status of these women because they could no longer depend on husbands to share the burden of providing for family members. The economic situation of most women was not in any good standing.

Psychological Aspects of Women's Positions

As recent research demonstrates, female victims of gender-related violence suffer serious mental health problems, including a drop in self-esteem and self confidence, as well as amnesia, headaches, and other forms of physical pain.[51] Additionally, most women survivors in Rwanda understandably didn't trust perpetrators and sometimes believed they would be attacked again as aptly stated by one survivor: "How do you trust these people who without provocation killed?"[52]

For female perpetrators, the situation is surprisingly similar. They are heavily traumatized by their crimes and the possibility of suffering vengeance and so feel uncomfortable with survivors. One perpetrator said: "I have killed my in-law, and one lady who was my neighbor, and I have asked for forgiveness but still I am not relaxed, I do not know why I am still living on this earth. My daughter will never forgive me."[53] What this woman said demonstrates how her traumatization led her to fear other people, who in turn fear her. Both survivors and perpetrators were traumatized and need to have sense of peace before they can be healed. As Staub opined, "it is not only victims but also perpetrators who need healing for reconciliation to be possible and to take place." [54] One school of thought suggests that Western psychiatry could take one hundred years to heal those traumatized by the genocide (in others words it would not be possible).[55] This school seems to have won the battle, leaving the government to leave perpetrators (and victims) to their fate to fight their trauma and suffer it alone.

Women through the Eyes of Others: Politicians, Judges, and Officials

From the perspective of the NURC reconciliation is a civic obligation of each Rwandan.[56] However female survivors and perpetrators may pay a higher price when testifying largely due to the shame and the stigma that burdens victims of sexual abuse in Rwandan society,[57] and for the fact that some lost their children and husbands and/or were raped and infected with HIV/AIDS. Asking them to reconcile is like forcing a bitter pill down their throats. However bitter pills may need to be swallowed: "There is a need for strong reactions in difficult times. Reconciliation is a bitter pill especially for raped women. But we must guarantee our future, and that of our children by sacrificing ourselves today and that is what our women have done."[58] On this point one pastor said: "Our messages on forgiveness and love for one another as Christ loves us had contributed to reconciliation."[59] A female survivor politician stated: "Reconciliation here in Rwanda is just politics! How could anyone tell me to just forgive considering what they did to us? Of course we are reconciled because we have no choice."[60]

When analyzing these statements one can generally say, from the perspective of those outside the domain of female survivors, that reconciliation has been reached in Rwanda. Yet one could argue we still have a long way to go considering the expressions from the female survivors in general.

It is of course difficult to forgive when victims still need to be healed. Reconciliation means coming to accept one another and to develop mutual relations based on trust.[61] In many cases the trust element is still missing, but as reconciliation is a process it can be viewed as positive that people manage to live peacefully side-by-side.

Conclusion

Reconciling post-genocide justice and gender justice has been the central theme of this chapter. A range of evidence was examined including original interviews with female survivors, perpetrators, and others about their perceptions of *Gacaca* courts and whether or not they considered *Gacaca* hearings to be fair and well-suited to their specific gender based concerns.

One of the key findings of this study is that women's active involvement in *Gacaca* as judges made a difference. Besides granting women a greater role in their communities, it enabled some female participants to feel more comfortable with the *Gacaca* process. Moreover many female participants got what they expected from *Gacaca* which was the truth. Though painful, many survivors appreciated the process because it enabled them to bury their family members. For some survivors, this helps because they feel they know what happened at last.

Overall, the findings of this study demonstrate that the *Gacaca* process benefited both female survivors and perpetrators. However *Gacaca* did not always acknowledge the ways in which women uniquely experienced harm during the genocide; this despite the provision of special closed hearings for sexual violence cases and a higher number of female judges. A key finding of this study is that, if restitution and some psychological sensitivity to the stigma of sexual violence and rape had been given more attention, *Gacaca* would have been more effective in prosecuting greater numbers of perpetrators. Thus while some objectives of *Gacaca* have been reached, it has generally fallen short in terms of eradicating the culture of impunity in Rwanda. Consequently, this could be a possible obstacle for victim-offender reconciliation in the future.

Notes

1. National Unity and Reconciliation Commission at http://www.nurc.gov.rw (accessed April 20, 2010).

2. Phil Clark, "Truth and Reconciliation at a Price," (August 24, 2010) http://www.rnw.nl/international-justice/article/truth-and-reconciliation-a-price.

3. Clark, "Truth"; Martin Ngoga, "The Institutionalization of Impunity: a Judicial Perspective of the Rwandan Genocide" in *After Genocide: Transitional Justice, Post-Conflict Reconstruction and Reconciliation in Rwanda and Beyond*, ed. Phil Clark and Zachary D. Kaufman (London: Hurst & Co, 2008), 321-322.

4. Phil Clark and Zachary D. Kaufman, ed. *After Genocide: Transitional Justice, Post-Conflict Reconstruction and Reconciliation in Rwanda and Beyond* (London: Hurst & Co, 2008), 193.

5. John Mutamba and Jeanne Izabiliza, *The Role of Women in Reconciliation and Peace Building in Rwanda: Ten Years After the Genocide (1994-2004) Contributions, Challenges and Way Forward* (Kigali: National Unity and Reconciliation Commission, 2005), 1-5.

6. IntLawGrrls, "Gacaca Courts in Rwanda: 18 Years after the Genocide, is there Justice and Reconciliation for Survivors of Sexual Violence?" (April 7, 2012), www:intlawgrrls.com/2012/Gacaca-court-in-rwanda-18years-after.html.

7. IntLawGrrls, "Gacaca Courts in Rwanda," 356.

8. William Schabas, "Genocide Trials and *Gacaca* Courts," 3 *J. Int'l. Crim. Jus.* 879, 891 (2005).

9. Alana Erin Tiemussen, "After Arusha: Gacaca Justice in Post-Genocide Rwanda," *African Studies Quarterly* 8, no. 1 (2004): 58.

10. Avocats sans Frontieres "Monitoring of the Gacaca Courts Judgment Phase, Analytical Report" (2005), 7.

11. Tonny Karbo and Martha Mutisi, "Psychological Aspects of Post-Conflict Reconstruction: Transforming Mindsets: The Case of the Gacaca in Rwanda," (paper Prepared for the Ad Hoc Expert Group Meeting on Lessons Learned in Post–Conflict State Capacity: Reconstructing Governance and Public Administration Capacities in Post-Conflict Accra, Ghana, 2008), 7.

12. Tiemussen, "After Arusha," 58.

13. Antoine Rutayisire, "Truth and Reconciliation Process," Woodrow Wilson International Center for Scholars (May 30, 2004), www.wilsoncenter.org/event/truth-and-reconciliation-processes-8211-global-assessment,

14. Ninety-four year old man interviewed by author in Gikondo, July 20, 2010.

15. Adam Jones, "Gender and Genocide" in *Mothers, Monsters, Whores: Women's Violence in Global Politics*, ed. Laura Sjoberg and Caron E. Gentry (London: Zed Books Ltd, 2007), 160.

16. Laura Sjoberg and Caron E. Gentry, eds., *Mothers, Monsters, Whores: Women's Violence in Global Politics*, (London: Zed Books Ltd., 2007), 162.

17. National Coordinator of *Gacaca* interviewed by author in Remera, August 16, 2010.

18. Judy El-Bushra, "Fused in Combat: Gender Relations and Armed Conflict, Development in Practice," in *Development, Women and War: Feminist Perspectives*, ed. H. Afshar and Deborah Eade, (Oxford, UK: Oxfam, 2004), 161-163.

19. Thirty-nine year old female *Gacaca* judge, interviewed by author in Kigarama, July 29, 2010.

20. Forty-four year old female judge, interviewed by author in Gahanga, July 29, 2010.

21. Eighty-nine year old woman, interviewed by author in Kigarama, July 20, 2010.

22. Sjoberg and Gentry, *Mothers, Monsters*, 143.

23. Carol Barton, "Integrating Feminist Agenda: Gender Justice and Economic Justice," *Dialogue* 48, no. 4 (2005): 76.

24. Susan McKay, "Gender Justice and Reconciliation," *Women's Studies International Forum* 23, no. 5 (2000): 561

25. McKay, "Gender Justice," 561.

26. National Coordinator of *Gacaca*, interviewed by author in Remera August 16, 2010.

27. Forty-eight year old female perpetrator, interviewed by author in Nyarugunga, July 21, 2010.

28. Forty-five year old female survivor, interviewed by author in Gikondo, July 18, 2010.

29. Sixty-year old female survivor, interviewed by author Gikondo, July 18, 2010.

30. Politician, interviewed by author in Kacyiru, July 30, 2010.

31. Helen Leslie, "Healing The Psychological Wounds Of Gender Related Violence In Latin America: A Model For Gender-Sensitive Work In Post-Conflict Contexts," *Gender and Development* 9, no. 3 (2001): 52.

32. Inkiko Gacaca, *Icyegeranyo cy'itegeko ngenga No 16/2004 ryo ku wa 19/6.2004 rigena imiterere, ububasha n'imikorere by inkiko Gacaca, Kiga-li-Rwanda*, (2007), 22

33. Nora Sveaass, "The Psychological Effects of Impunity," in *Pain and Survival*, ed. Nora Sveaass, Nils Johan Lavik, Eva Chr Fannemel and Mette Nygård (Universitetsforlaget kapittel, 1994), 213.

34. Fifty-five year old president of *Gacaca* court, interviewed by author Gikondo, July 26, 2010.

35. Fifty-three year old female perpetrator, interviewed by author in Gikondo, August 05, 2010.

36. Sjoberg and Gentry, *Mothers, Monsters*, 9.

37. Sjoberg and Gentry, *Mothers, Monsters*, 41.

38. See at http://www.inkikoGacaca.gov.rw/pdf/Organic%20Law%2027062006.pdf

39. Female survivors, interviewed by author in Kicukiro, July 25, 2010.

40. Lidwien Kapteijns and Annamiek Richters ed., *Mediation of Violence* (Leiden, The Netherlands: BRILL, 2012), 179.

41. Eugenia Zorbas, "Reconciliation in Post-Genocide Rwanda, Politics, Human Rights Right, Due Process and the Role of Gacaca Courts in Dealing with the Genocide," *Journal of African Law* 45, no. 2 (2004): 36.

42. Forty-year old female survivor, interviewed by author in Kicukiro, July 25, 2010.

43. Thirty-eight year old graduate female survivor, interviewed by author in Kicukiro, July 24, 2010.

44. Focus group discussion with female survivors, aged 60 years and more in Gikondo, July 16, 2010.

45. Forty-nine year old female perpetrator, interviewed by author in Gikondo, July 21, 2010.

46. Forty-eight year old female perpetrator, interviewed by author in Gatenga, July 21, 2010.

47. Forty-seven year old female survivor, interviewed by author in Kicukiro, July 24, 2010.

48. Sixty-one year old female survivor, interviewed by author in Gahanga, July 23, 2010.

49. Schabas, "Genocide Trials," 891.

50. Interviews by author conducted in Gikondo, Gatenga and Nyarugunga, July 21, 2010.

51. Leslie, "Healing," 52.

52. Forty-seven year old survivor, interviewed by author in Kicukiro, July 25, 2010.

53. Sixty-two year old female perpetrator in solidarity camp, interviewed by author in mayange, August 6, 2010.

54. Ervin Staub, *Genocide and Mass Killing: Origins, Prevention Healing and Reconciliation* (Amherst: University of Massachusetts Press, 2000), 377.

55. Kapteijns and Richters, *Mediation*, 185.

56. NURC, "Reconciliation Work in Rwanda," (October 2009), 15.

57. Donna Pankhurst, *Gendered Peace Women's Struggle for Post-war Justice and Reconciliation* (New York: Taylor & Francis, 2008), 187.

58. Male politician, interviewed by author in Kacyiru, July 11, 2010.

59. Pentecostal Pastor, interviewed by author in Nyarugunga, July 23, 2010.

60. Female survivor politician, interviewed by author in Gahanga, July 19, 2010.

61. Staub, *Genocide and Mass Killing*, 376.

Chapter 19

Guilty as Charged: The Trial of Former President Alberto Fujimori for Human Rights Violations

Jo-Marie Burt

On April 7, 2009, the Special Criminal Court of the Peruvian Supreme Court found former president Alberto Fujimori guilty of grave human rights violations and sentenced him to twenty-five years in prison—the maximum penalty allowed by Peruvian law.[1] This trial is truly historic: It marks the first time a democratically elected head of state has been extradited to his own country, put on trial for human rights violations, and convicted. Equally historic is the fact that dozens of human rights trials are currently under way in Peru, as elsewhere in Latin America.[2]

The Fujimori trial is all the more remarkable given domestic prosecutions of heads of state for human rights crimes are extremely rare. Peru, in contrast, has shown that national governments can hold their former leaders accountable, and that a head of state is not above the law. Interestingly enough, Fujimori remains popular among certain segments of the Peruvian public. The Fujimori trial demonstrates that with sufficient political will, domestic tribunals can prosecute high-level public officials who commit or order the commission of human rights violations. While Peru's prosecution is unprecedented in many ways, at the same time it reflects a broader global trend favoring accountability for those who perpetrated, ordered or otherwise authorized grave violations of human rights, war crimes, and crimes against humanity. This global shift toward accountability has been widely documented and analyzed.[3]

The chapter explores these dynamics in the context of Peru's transition to democracy in 2000. Transitional justice scholars have argued that transition by collapse provides the most likely scenario for criminal prosecutions following regime change: powerful economic and military elites who might oppose such trials have been weakened, and political elites may pursue a prosecutions strategy to differentiate the new regime from its predecessor.[4] This chapter highlights the role played by Peruvian civil society, primarily human rights and victims' groups; specifically their ability to unify local efforts in favor of truth, justice, and reparations and to construct international alliances in favor of accountability as the key dynamic pushing this process forward.

The Fujimori Decade

Popular discontent with "traditional" political parties fueled support for Fujimori, who promised "honesty, technology, and work" if elected to the presidency. His appeals to economic populism endeared him to the rural and urban poor. His main rival, internationally renowned writer Mario Vargas Llosa, was soon seen to be part of the traditional Lima-based elite that had ruled Peru for centuries and had proved unable to address Peru's unfolding crises.[5]

Fujimori was elected president in 1990, a time of deep political, economic, and social crisis in Peru. The two previous democratic governments had failed to stop the advance of the Shining Path, an insurgent group that launched its struggle to conquer state power in 1980. Shining Path became known for its widespread use of terrorist tactics, including assaults on unarmed civilians. The Peruvian state, meanwhile, resorted to state terror to combat terrorism, resulting in widespread human rights violations on both sides.

Fujimori's authoritarian inclinations soon became evident. In 1992, he announced his *autogolpe*, or "self-coup," in which he closed congress, suspended the constitution, and took over the judiciary with the backing of the military and powerful elites. With the assistance of former army captain and *eminence grise* Vladimiro Montesinos, Fujimori established control over virtually all governing bodies and institutions.[6] When international pressure forced Fujimori to reinstate the legislature, he created a unicameral body he easily controlled. A new constitution allowed Fujimori to seek reelection which he did successfully in 1995, and despite restoring democratic institutions, the underlying structure of power remained deeply authoritarian.[7] The regime used state power to undermine opposition movements through illegal surveillance systems, intimidation, and outright attacks. It also established near-total control over the media. According to historian Alfonso Quiroz, the Fujimori regime was likely the most corrupt in Peruvian history, with $1.5 to $4 billion lost due to corruption.[8]

Many Peruvians remember Fujimori as the president who put Abimael Guzmán—Shining Path's top leader—behind bars. Indeed, the regime's reorientation of counterinsurgency efforts achieved many important results. However, a parallel strategy was also put in place, in which clandestine military units engaged in targeted killings and forced disappearances. The most notorious of these was the Colina Group, a unit created within the military intelligence services in mid-1991, whose chief purpose was to eliminate suspected subversives. The Colina Group was responsible for a number of killings between 1991 and 1992, including the Barrios Altos massacre in 1991, and the disappearance and killing of nine students and a professor from the Cantuta University in July 1992.[9] The regime thwarted efforts to investigate these crimes by, among other things, passing two amnesty laws in 1995. Other abuses perpetrated by the regime included arbitrary detentions, and the creation of military tribunals that violated the due process rights of defendants.

In 2000 Fujimori ran for what opposition leaders charged was an illegal third term as president. The regime's effort to guarantee victory through electoral fraud was met by massive street protests, as well as international condemnation by the Organization of American States (OAS) and the US government.[10] However Fujimori weathered the domestic and international criticism and was inaugurated to a third term in 2000.

A series of scandals in the following months triggered the collapse of the Fujimori government. The first revealed that Fujimori and Montesinos were involved in a drugs-for-arms deal with the Revolutionary Armed Forces of Colombia (FARC). The second involved the public airing of a video showing Montesinos paying off opposition legislator Alberto Kouri in exchange for him switching to Fujimori's political party. Montesinos immediately fled the country. Several weeks later Fujimori too decided to flee; from his new safe haven in Japan, he faxed his resignation. The opposition in congress, reinvigorated by this chain of events, rejected Fujimori's resignation, declared him unfit to serve as president, and named leading opposition congressman Valentín Paniagua interim president until new elections could be held the following year.

Peru's Transitional Justice Challenges

Fujimori's escape to Japan, along with mounting evidence of corruption involving high-ranking officials, prompted massive citizen indignation. Additionally, human rights and victims' groups began clamoring for a truth commission to investigate human rights violations, punish those responsible, and provide reparations for victims.

The Paniagua government sought to meet these challenges through a series of measures designed to restore citizen confidence in government and international faith in Peru's new democracy. The government reorganized the country's electoral institutions to ensure free and fair elections. Efforts were made to purge the judiciary and other institutions of corrupt officials. Judges and military officers who had been sacked during the Fujimori regime were restored to their positions or provided indemnization. Congressional inquiries were launched into the crimes of the Fujimori-Montesinos mafia, and efforts were made to recuperate stolen government funds. Paniagua also created a special prosecutorial unit, the *Procuraduría Pública Ad Hoc,* tasked with working with the Public Ministry and the judiciary to prosecute corruption (but not human rights) cases.

On the international front, Paniagua determined Peru's return to the contentious jurisdiction of the Inter-American Court of Human Rights (IACtHR) (in 1999, angered by IACtHR rulings on human rights cases, Fujimori withdrew Peru from the Court's jurisdiction.) Moreover the Paniagua government acknowledged Peru's responsibility for a series of human rights violations committed during Fujimori's regime, and accepted amicable solutions or agreed to abide by the Court's rulings in some 150 cases.[11] This decision was hailed by the human rights community as a major step forward on human rights issues and restoring international confidence in Peru's democratic institutions, and would later prove critical to efforts to criminally prosecute perpetrators of human rights abuses. In November 2001 the Paniagua government ratified the Rome Statute and Peru joined the International Criminal Court (ICC).

In the meantime, momentum began to build for the creation of a truth commission. This was a key demand of the *Coordinadora Nacional de Derechos Humanos* (National Human Rights Coordinator), an umbrella group of sixty-seven human rights organizations throughout Peru. The *Coordinadora* documented human rights violations, provided legal defense to victims, and organized domestic and international campaigns to bring awareness to key problems including forced disappearances and arbitrary detentions. In the face of the failure of the Peruvian judiciary to investigate and prosecute human rights violations, the *Coordinadora* and its member organizations began denouncing cases to the IACtHR. The *Coordinadora* became an outspoken advocate for an integral model of transitional justice. Shortly after the working group was established, Sofía Macher, executive secretary of the *Coordinadora,* stated that the truth commission should be oriented around three key objectives—truth, justice, reparations—and that it should nullify the 1995 self-amnesty laws in order to facilitate criminal investigations of key human rights cases.[12] International human rights organizations, such as Amnesty International, Human Rights Watch, and the International Center for Transitional Justice (ICTJ) also supported efforts to establish a truth commission.

As these debates unfolded, in March 2001 the IACtHR handed down a ruling that shifted the terms of the discussion. The IACtHR ruled that the Peruvian state was responsible for the 1991 Barrios Altos massacre, and ordered the state to investigate, prosecute, and punish those responsible.[13] It also ordered reparations be paid to victims. Most importantly, the Court determined the 1995 self-amnesty laws violated the American Convention on Human Rights, and therefore lacked legal effect. The IACtHR previously ruled that amnesty laws violated the American Convention, but this was the first time it specifically ruled that amnesty laws, when intended to guarantee impunity for grave violations of human rights, violate victims' rights and thus lack legal effect.[14]

The ruling marked a watershed in Peru's efforts to prosecute cases of human rights violations. It opened the door for prosecutors and judges to pursue human rights cases in court. Soon after a judge ordered the arrest of two army generals and eleven members of the Colina Group implicated in the Barrios Altos massacre; additional arrests followed.[15] In addition, the Supreme Court determined that the IACtHR ruling must be put into effect by Peruvian tribunals,[16] formally paving the way for the reopening of the Barrios Altos case and other Colina Group crimes.[17] The threat of criminal sanction prompted some Colina Group members to turn state's evidence in exchange for reduced sentences, providing compelling new evidence of the direct involvement of Fujimori, Montesinos, and Hermoza Ríos in the creation and operation of the Colina Group death squad.[18]

The Barrios Altos ruling also generated new momentum for the creation of a truth commission that would engage in truth-telling and also seek to identify, prosecute, and punish those responsible for human rights violations. As these debates were unfolding, new videotapes surfaced showing Montesinos and the military top brass collecting signatures of hundreds of military officers in support of the April 1992 *autogolpe* and the 1995 self-amnesty laws. The fact that the current heads of the armed forces were among those in the video prompted demands for a major overhaul of the military. Top military leaders offered their resignations. The military emitted a statement apologizing for its past support of the Fujimori regime and pronounced its support for Peru's new democracy and the creation of a truth commission. In a message to the nation on April 17, 2001, Paniagua accepted the resignations, and announced that he would soon create a truth commission to promote national unity and reconciliation.[19]

Peru's Truth Commission

Calls for a truth commission gathered strength in the context of growing local momentum in favor of truth and justice, coinciding with a growing global trend in favor of accountability for atrocity crimes, as evident in the creation of the international tribunals for the former Yugoslavia and Rwanda and the ICC.[20] It was also evident in Latin America in renewed efforts to press for accountability in domestic courts, in international tribunals such as the IACtHR, or sometimes in foreign courts.[21] Peru also had the advantage of being able to study the experiences of previous truth commissions in Latin America and South Africa.[22]

In 2001, Paniagua emitted a decree law establishing a truth commission with the most comprehensive mandate of any truth commission to date. It was charged with investigating the causes and consequences of political violence in Peru between 1980 and 2000. It was also to "contribute to the clarification, by the corresponding jurisdictional bodies, as necessary, of crimes and violations of human rights committed by terrorist organizations or state agents, determine the fate of the victims, and identify, insofar as possible, those responsible."[23] The truth commission was additionally charged with making recommendations for reparations and institutional reforms to prevent similar crimes in the future. After assuming the presidency in July 2001, Alejandro Toledo ratified the truth commission, renaming it the Truth and Reconciliation Commission (CVR), and expanding the number of commissioners from seven to twelve.

Findings

In 2003, the CVR presented its Final Report to President Toledo. Over the course of two years, the CVR collected 17,000 testimonies, and held public hearings on a variety of topics in which victims on all sides of the conflict were able to tell their stories.[24] Major findings of the CVR included :

1. The internal conflict between 1980 and 2000 was the bloodiest in Peruvian history fueled by deep social and ethnic cleavages.

2. An estimated 69,000 Peruvians died in the political violence. Shining Path was responsible for 54 percent of violent deaths; state security forces for 37 percent; and the Tupac Amaru Revolutionary Movement (MRTA), 2 percent. The remaining 7 percent are unaccounted for.

3. Some 6,000 Peruvians were forcibly disappeared, primarily by state agents. In most cases, their fate and whereabouts remain unknown. (This figure is now considered to be 15,000.)

4. Three-quarters of the victims were rural-dwellers whose primary tongue was Quechua or another indigenous language. This is an astonishing figure given that only 16 percent of Peruvians are not primary Spanish speakers.

5. Women were victims of sexual abuse and rape by the armed forces and Shining Path, and as new widows, forced to fend for themselves and their families.

6. Fujimori was criminally responsible for the creation and operations of the Colina Group death squad and the Colina Group, including the Barrios Altos and Cantuta massacres.[25]

In light of these dramatic findings, the CVR made a series of recommendations to the state to further the justice and reconciliation process. It recommended that the state provide individual and collective reparations for victims. It also recommended the prosecution of forty-seven cases of grave violations of human rights by competent judicial authorities. The CVR cautioned the state not to use amnesties, pardons or other measures that would create obstacles for the search for truth and justice, making specific reference to the IACtHR's rulings on the subject.

Truth *and* Justice

There were intense debates within the CVR regarding the desirability and feasibility of a focus on retributive justice. Some commissioners favored a focus on truth-telling and historical memory; others the need to build criminal cases. After much debate, an integral model of transitional justice prevailed, in which retributive justice was one crucial element in a broader process of national reconciliation.[26] As noted by CVR president Salomón Lerner:

> We said: it is necessary to link truth and reconciliation, but truth cannot be achieved automatically, and truth cannot carry us automatically to reconciliation. There has to be a mediation to achieve reconciliation, that would be not the sufficient but certainly the necessary condition for reconciliation, and the necessary condition for reconciliation is justice.[27]

In its effort to fulfill its accountability mandate, the CVR established a legal unit tasked with identifying key cases that it would recommend for criminal prosecution by the Peruvian judiciary. In 2003, the CVR handed over forty-seven cases, involving more than 150 police and military officers, to the Public Ministry for prosecution. The CVR's Final Report gave renewed emphasis to criminal prosecutions and confirmed the state's commitment (at least theoretically) to an accountability agenda. The *Defensoría del Pueblo*, which was charged with overseeing the implementation of the CVR's recommendations, lodged complaints in an additional twelve cases, bringing the total number of criminal trials being prosecuted by the state to fifty-nine. While the Toledo government was criticized for moving too slowly on implementation of the CVR's recommendations, by early 2005 the Public Ministry and the Judiciary had established a special system to investigate and prosecute human rights cases.

Fujimori's Extradition

It was in this context of an expanding accountability environment that, in November 2005, Fujimori left his safe haven in Japan for Chile, where he was promptly arrested. The Peruvian government immediately announced it would seek Fujimori's extradition so he could face charges of human rights violations, usurpation of authority, and corruption in Peru. The *Procuraduría*, which had been investigating Fujimori for numerous cases of corruption, abuse of authority, and human rights abuses, quickly prepared the extradition request and worked in concert with other state agencies, ministries, and civil society groups, to ensure Fujimori's extradition.[28]

The Peruvian government's decision to denounce Japan before the International Court of Justice likely complicated Fujimori's standing with Japanese authorities. With presidential elections scheduled for April 2006, Fujimori clearly believed he could launch his political comeback from Chile. His advisors must have believed that his good relationship with important Chilean business elites would protect him; the historical conservatism of the Chilean Supreme Court, and its prior refusal to admit extradition requests, likely also played a role in their calculations.

Peru's human rights community immediately mobilized to support the extradition request. Relatives of victims and members of the *Coordinadora* made numerous trips to Chile over the course of the next two years, organizing public events, and meeting with Chilean government and judicial officials to plead their case.[29] In Chile, human rights and victims' groups actively supported their Peruvian counterparts. International human rights organizations also played an important role by providing legal arguments supporting extradition and lobbying Chilean government and legal officials.[30] The IACtHR also weighed in and urged the Peruvian state to continue pursuing legal and diplomatic measures to ensure Fujimori's extradition.[31]

In 2007 the Chilean Supreme Court ruled in favor of extradition on the basis of a handful of cases of corruption, usurpation of authority, and human rights violations.[32] Within hours of the ruling, Fujimori was returned to Peru. Local and international human rights groups hailed the decision as a major precedent for global justice efforts.[33] The Peruvian Supreme Court determined that it would first hear the cases of human rights violations, including the Barrios Altos massacre, the disappearances at the La Cantuta University, and two kidnappings. After sixteen months of deliberations, on April 7, 2009, the Court found Fujimori guilty of all counts of aggravated homicide, assault, and kidnapping and sentenced him to twenty-five years in prison. A tribunal comprised of five Supreme Court justices reviewed Fujimori's appeal, and on December 30, 2009, emitted its final ruling upholding the original sentence.

Fujimori was prosecuted in three additional public trials on a series of other charges related to corruption and misuse of public authority. He was convicted on all charges. Today, Fujimori serves out his prison sentence in a prison built especially for him on a special forces police base and of which he is the sole resident.

Guilty As Charged: The Human Rights Trial

The remainder of this chapter examines the Fujimori verdict, then explores the process itself to determine whether it avoided the shortcomings scholars have pointed out often plague criminal trials for grave human rights violations. It closes with an analysis of the impact of Fujimori's conviction on efforts to achieve accountability in Peru, and its implications for the theory and practice of transitional justice.

The verdict in the Fujimori trial was widely hailed as exceptionally thorough and analytically sound.[34] The judges noted that they applied the maximum sentence allowable by Peruvian law at the time the crimes were committed due to the "gravity and extent of the crimes," and the "nature and condition of the accused as former head of state."[35] The Court determined that the victims in both cases were not members of any terrorist organization, a request by the civil parties meant as a reparative measure to survivors and relatives of victims, who have suffered stigmatization, threats, and intimidation due to unsubstantiated accusations that their family members were "terrorists."[36]

The judges used the concept of *autoría mediata* (perpetration by means) to determine Fujimori's culpability in these crimes.[37] In Peruvian law, *autoría mediata* is attributed to those who have dominion over an "organized power apparatus" and thus have the power to order and direct its agents to commit crimes, or in this case, human rights violations.[38] In the Fujimori case, the Court considered that the prosecution had fully proven that the Fujimori, as commander in chief of the armed forces, had direct control over the Colina Group.[39]

The judges drew upon the IACtHR's 2006 ruling on the Cantuta case, as well as a 2005 ruling by Peru's Constitutional Tribunal and the Final Report of the CVR, to argue that these crimes formed part of a broader pattern of "state crimes" that could not have been committed without prior knowledge of high-ranking government and military authorities, including Fujimori.[40] The judges determined the Colina Group was active during a fifteen-month period between 1991 and 1992, and that it committed at least fifty assassinations, including Barrios Altos and La Cantuta.[41] The Court found evidence of a pattern of systematic violations of human rights, defining them as "crimes against humanity."

Dilemmas in Criminal Prosecutions

There is a rich and ultimately unresolved debate about the viability and desirability of criminal trials after mass atrocity.[42] Since Peru is a case not only in which criminal prosecutions have moved forward but a former head of state has been successfully convicted for grave human rights violations, it seems apt to explore some of the specific dilemmas of criminal prosecutions for human rights violations that have been raised in the transitional justice literature and how they have played out in the Fujimori trial.

One of these dilemmas is the question of politicization: how to ensure that the tribunal prosecuting human rights violations is impartial and removed from political pressures. Jurists concur that to avoid politicization, the prosecuting tribunal must be independently constituted for its operations, resources, and decisions so rule of law norms and due process can be fully upheld, and to avoid undue political influence or intervention.[43] Despite charges by Fujimori supporters that the trial was politically motivated, neither Fujimori nor his lawyer questioned the tribunal's impartiality. In the days following the verdict, new charges of politicization circulated in the pro-Fujimori media, including charges that the president of the tribunal, César San Martín, ruled against Fujimori motivated by revenge, since he had been fired after the 1992 *autogolpe*.[44] The public disagreed: 75 percent said Fujimori's due process rights had been respected, while 67 percent said the judges acted fairly and impartially.[45]

Indeed, domestic and international observers widely noted that this was a fair and impartial trial that scrupulously guaranteed the due process rights of the accused.[46] Fujimori was given ample opportunity to defend himself in a court of law: his lawyer was permitted to present witnesses, documents, and other evidence he deemed pertinent to the case, and he had ample time to present arguments in defense of his client and to cross-examine prosecution witnesses. Fujimori himself was allowed to address the tribunal. Moreover, the judges responded even-handedly to key challenges that emerged throughout the trial. For example, when Fujimori appeared to be ill, the Court allowed his private physician to examine him, but ordered medical exams by a Court-appointed physician to prevent undue delays.

To guarantee fairness and limit political interference, the judicial process was made as transparent as possible. The judges allowed the media direct access to the proceedings, and the trial was widely covered by the Peruvian press. The Court also permitted survivors and relatives of the victims, as well as Fujimori's relatives, friends, and political associates to sit as permanent observers. Human rights activists, academics, and international observers were also permitted to observe the process. The Court made transcripts and videotapes of each day's proceedings available to the defense and prosecution. Additionally, the Court posted brief summaries of each session on its website. This high public visibility reduced the opportunities for political interference in the trial, which was a real concern given that the sitting president at the time, Alan García, could face possible charges for human rights crimes committed during his first government (1985-1990).

This leads us to another major issue raised in the literature about retributive justice after atrocity: selectivity. This is a complex issue, raising questions not only about who should be prosecuted and with what criteria, but also whether it is desirable and even possible to prosecute all those believed to be responsible for grave human rights violations. This is an issue with which Peru continues to grapple. The success of the Fujimori trial aside, massive human rights violations occurred under the two previous presidencies of Fernando Belaúnde (1980-85) and Alan García (1985-90). Belaúnde died in 2002. García, however, not only has not faced prosecution for crimes committed during his government; he was actually re-elected president of Peru in 2006. That he has yet to face charges for any number of cases committed during his first government begs the question: in the end, is politics the determining factor as to whether prosecutions move forward in these cases? Fujimori, after all, had fallen from grace; García, on the other hand, was and remains a powerful political figure in Peru.

Implications: Peru and Beyond

By prosecuting a former head of state, Peru proved its system of justice is capable of prosecuting powerful political elites. This goes a long way toward legitimizing the rule of law in Peru, and sets an important precedent for those who violated human rights in the past and those who may do so in the future. This lesson transcends Peru, as noted by Peruvian journalist Augusto Álvarez Rodrich the day after Fujimori's conviction: "Future rulers are now forewarned that it is their duty to respect the life of all citizens and that it is not acceptable to kill—or to order someone else to do so—no matter how powerful they think they are or how 'justified' they believe their cause to be."[47]

Peru's transitional justice process also demonstrates that an integral approach to transitional justice is viable in post-conflict societies. Of course Peru's process is far from complete. There have been numerous stumbling blocks along the way. The reparations program, for example, has moved at a glacial pace. Yet any serious student of transitional justice knows that these advances are deeply circumscribed by politics. It is precisely by studying the political process in which transitional justice processes are embedded that we are able to further understand what makes criminal prosecutions more likely and sustainable.

The question remains whether the Fujimori trial will be a catalyst for the successful prosecution of other cases of human rights violations in Peru, and contribute to a virtuous cycle of accountability and respect for the rule of law, or whether it will stand as a solitary example of success that has limited impact on the behavior of judicial authorities and political elites. There are now a series of state institutions dedicated primarily to prosecuting human rights cases. Nearly forty cases have been fully prosecuted, with convictions in several instances.

However, this is only a fraction of the cases that have been denounced by victims before the Public Ministry. Many investigations remain stalled due to insufficient resources, but also, rights activists charge, to insufficient political will. Hundreds of cases have been closed by state prosecutors because of the unwillingness of the armed forces to provide access to official documents to state prosecutors that could help resconstruct the facts and identify perpetrators. In recent years there have been increasing signs of political interference in the judicialization process. Shortly after García's inauguration in 2006, the state announced it would provide legal defense to most state agents accused of human rights violations. though many victims lack legal representation. There have been repeated efforts to implement different types of amnesty laws. In 2008, Mercedes Cabanillas, an APRA congresswoman, called for a general amnesty for military and police officials accused of human rights violations. In 2010, Garcia passed Decree Law 1097, which was widely viewed as a veiled amnesty law for state agents accused of human rights violations. After domestic and international outcry the law was revoked. Successive defense ministers, army generals, and other conservative politicians lambast state prosecutors and NGOs representing the victims of human rights violations of engaging in a vast conspiracy to "persecute" the armed forces. In their view, there were no systematic human rights violations, only some "excesses" committed by unruly or stressed out soldiers or low-ranking officers.

Osiel has argued that criminal trials help create a meaningful framework for publicly exploring the traumatic memories of political violence.[48] The Fujimori trial has done that, but only to a degree. Political violence in Peru spanned two decades, three presidents, and was carried out by a variety of actors. As Lutz and Reiger have argued, in societies marked by serious cleavages, there may be less support for criminal prosecutions in cases of human rights violations, which affect only a subgroup of society, than, say, corruption, which is seen as being harmful to the whole society.[49] In such societies, they argue, criminal trials for human rights violations may reinforce these cleavages.

This does not seem to have occurred in the aftermath of the Fujimori trial. On the contrary, the tribunal that prosecuted Fujimori was widely perceived as legitimate and a majority came to believe that Fujimori was guilty of human rights violations.[50] The fact that Fujimori was also prosecuted for corruption and abuse of authority probably contributed to this view. But Peru has yet to fully settle accounts when it comes to human rights violations committed during the 1980s, as briefly aluded to above, revealing the enormous political and institutional challenges of achieving justice in the aftermath of atrocity.

Notes

1. This article is an updated version of the article (same title) published in the *International Journal of Transitional Justice* 3, no. 3 (2009): 384-405. It is the result of a collaborative research and advocacy project of George Mason University, the *Instituto de Defensa Legal*, and the Washington Office on Latin American (WOLA) made possible by the generous support of the Latin American Program of the Open Society Foundation.

2. Kathryn Sikkink and Carrie Booth Walling, "The Impact of Human Rights Trials in Latin America," *Journal of Peace Research* 44, no. 4 (2007): 427-445; Coletta Young-

ers and Jo-Marie Burt, *Human Rights Tribunals in Latin America* (Washington DC: George Mason University/WOLA/Institute for Legal Defense, 2009).

3. Ruti Teitel, "Transitional Justice Genealogy," 16 *Harv. Hum. Rts. J.* 69 (2003).

4. Carlos Santiago Nino, *Radical Evil on Trial* (New Haven: Yale University Press, 1996).

5. Carlos Iván Degregori and Romeo Grompone, *Elecciones 1990. Demonios y Redentores en el Nuevo Perú* (Lima: Instituto de Estudios Peruanos, 1991).

6. Gustavo Gorriti, "The Betrayal of Peru's Democracy: Montesinos as Fujimori' Svengali," *CovertAction Quarterly* 49 (1994): 4-12, 54-59.

7. Carlos Iván Degregori, *La Década de la Antipolítica. Auge y Huida de Alberto Fujimori y Vladimiro Montesinos* (Lima: Instituto de Estudios Peruanos, 2001); Jo-Marie Burt, *Political Violence and the Authoritarian State in Peru: Silencing Civil Society* (New York: Palgrave Macmillan, 2007).

8. Alfonso Quiroz, *Corrupt Circles: A History of Unbound Graft in Peru* (Baltimore: Johns Hopkins University Press, 2008).

9. The partial remains of some of the students were discovered a year later bearing signs of torture. Comisión de la Verdad y Reconciliación, *Informe Final* (2003): vol. v, chap. 2.19, http://www.cverdad.org.pe [hereinafter CVR].

10. Catherine Conaghan, *Fujimori's Peru: Deception in the Public Sphere* (Pittsburgh, PA: University of Pittsburgh Press, 2005).

11. Susana Villarán, "Peru," in *Victims Unsilenced: The Inter-American Human Rights System and Transitional Justice in Latin America* (Washington, DC: Due Process of Law Foundation, 2007), 95-126.

12. APRODEH, "Resumenes de prensa sobre Comisión de la Verdad," (September 2003).

13. Inter-American Court of Human Rights, *Barrios Altos Case,* Judgment of 14 March 2001, Ser. C, No. 83, Par. 1. The Court subsequently determined this ruling is valid for the entire region; Inter-American Court, *Barrios Altos Case,* Judgment of 3 September 2001, Ser. C, No. 83, par. 18.

14. Douglas Cassel, "The Inter-American Court of Human Rights," in *Victims Unsilenced,* 151-166.

15. *Resumen Semanal* 23, no. 1115 (March 21-27, 2001).

16. *Resumen Semanal* 23, no. 1116 (March 28, 2001-April 3, 2001).

17. The trial in the Barrios Altos case started in 2005. Eighteen former military officers were convicted in the Barrios Altos case in October 2010 and sentenced to between fifteen and twenty-five years in prison. Prosecutors grouped together several other Colina Group crimes, including the Cantuta massacre and two other cases. Later the Cantuta case was separated into a different trial; several Colina Group members were convicted in April 2008.

18. Ronald Gamarra Herrera, "Derechos Humanos, Justicia y Transición Democrática: el Balance Institucional," in *El Legado de la Verdad. La Justicia Penal en la Transición Peruana,* ed. L. Magarrell and L. Filippini (Lima: International Center for Transitional Justice/IDEHPUCP, 2006), 211-248.

19. *Resumen Semanal* 23, no. 1118 (April 11-17, 2001).

20. Teitel, "Transitional Justice Genealogy."

21. Ellen Lutz and Kathryn Sikkink, "The Justice Cascade: The Evolution and Impact of Foreign Human Rights Trials in Latin America," 2 *Chi. J. Int'l. L.* 1 (2001).

22. Javier Ciurlizza, interviews with author, July 2006, and Salomón Lerner, interview with author, August 2006.

23. Supreme Decree Law N° 065-2001-PCM, *El Peruano,* 2 June 2001.

24. On the CVR, see Eduardo González, "The Peruvian Truth and Reconciliation Commission and the Challenge of Impunity," in *Beyond Truth versus Justice: Transitional Justice in the Twenty-first Century,* ed. Namoi Roht-Arriaza and Javier Mariezcurrena (New York: Cambridge University Press, 2006), 70-93 and Lisa Laplante, "The Peruvian Truth Commission's Historical Memory Project: Empowering Truth-Tellers to Confront Truth Deniers," *Journal of Human Rights* 6, no. 4 (2007): 433-452.

25. CVR, *Informe Final*, vol. 2, ch. 2.3.

26. Javier Ciurlizza and Eduardo González, "Verdad y Justicia desde la Optica de la Comisión de la Verdad y Reconciliación," in *El legado de la verdad*, 86-104.

27. Salomón Lerner, interview with author in Lima, August 2006.

28. Former Anticorruption Prosecutor Antonio Maldonado, National Endowment for Democracy, July 18, 2009.

29. Gisela Ortiz and Carmen Amaro, interview with author in Lima, April 17, 2009.

30. Human Rights Watch, *Peru/Chile. Presunción Fundada: Pruebas que Comprometen a Fujimori* (December 2005). Amnesty International, *Chile, Peru. Fujimori case–the Supreme Court of Justice must Comply with Obligations of International Law* (August 2007).

31. Inter-American Court of Human Rights, *Case of La Cantuta v. Peru* (November 29, 2006).

32. This was greatly reduced from the original sixty cases for which Fujimori's extradition was initially sought. It is significant since Fujimori can be prosecuted only for cases for which he was extradited.

33. The history of the extradition process remains unexplored.

34. Sala Penal Especial, Corte Suprema de Justicia, Exp. No. A.V. 19–2001/Acumulado, *Sentencia Alberto Fujimori Fujimori* (April 7, 2009) [herein after *Fujimori*], http://www.pj.gob.pe/CorteSuprema.

35. Supreme Court Justice César San Martin, Public sentencing in the Fujimori trial, Lima, April 7, 2009.

36. Sala Penal Especial, Corte Suprema de Justicia, *Fujimori,* 707.

37. Jurist Claus Roxin is considered to be the innovator of this legal concept, which was applied in the trial of Adolf Eichmann and others.

38. There is no equivalent to *autoría mediata* in English-speaking legal systems. It is sometimes translated as "perpetration by means" of an organized apparatus of power or other instrument. Douglass Cassel, Personal communication with author, July 20, 2009.

39. Sala Penal Especial, Corte Suprema de Justicia, *Fujimori*, 655-657.

40. Sala Penal Especial, Corte Suprema de Justicia, *Fujimori*, 655.

41. Sala Penal Especial, Corte Suprema de Justicia, *Fujimori*, 483-492.

42. See José Zalaquett, "Balancing Ethical Imperatives and Political Constraints: The Dilemma of New Democracies Confronting Past Human Rights Violations," *Hastings L. J.* 43 (1992): 6-16; Juan Méndez, "Accountability for Past Abuses," *Human Rights Quarterly* 19, no. 2 (1997): 255-282; Mark J. Osiel, "Why Prosecute? Critics of Punishment for Mass Atrocity," *Human Rights Quarterly* 22 (2000): 118-147; Laurel Fletcher and Harvey Weinstein, "Violence and Social Repair: Rethinking the Contribution of Justice to Reconciliation," *Human Rights Quarterly* 24 (2002): 573-639; and Mark A. Drumbl, *Atrocity, Punishment, and International law* (New York: Cambridge University Press, 2007).

43. Martha Minow, *Between Vengeance and Forgiveness: Facing History after Genocide and Mass Violence* (Boston: Beacon Press, 1998)

44. Fiebre Naranja, *Caretas,* April 16, 2009.

45. Instituto de Opinión Pública/Pontificia Universidad Católica del Perú, "El Caso Fujimori y la Opinión Pública," *Estado de la Opinión Pública* (April 2009).

46. Human Rights Watch, *Peru: Fujimori Verdict a Rights Victory: Former President's Trial Likely to Advance Justice, Rule of Law* (April 2009) and Amnesty International, *Peru: The Conviction of Fujimori–A Milestone in the Fight for Justice* (April 2009).

47. Augusto Álvarez Rodrich, "No Matarás," *La República,* April 8, 2009.

48. Mark Osiel, "Ever Again: Legal Remembrance of Administrative Massacre," 144 *U. Pa. L. Rev.* 463 (1995).

49. Ellen L. Lutz and Caitlin Reiger, *Prosecuting Heads of State* (New York: Cambridge University Press, 2009), 281.

50. In a May 2009 poll, 62 percent said that Fujimori was guilty of human rights violations; 70 percent said that he was guilty of corruption. 58 percent opposed a pardon for Fujimori. *La República,* 11 Mayo 2009.

Afterword

Henry F. Carey

The contributors to *Trials and Tribulations* have analyzed the uneven track-record of international criminal courts with jurisdiction to try heads of states and official and military officers. The essays examine the political and legal challenges of criminal prosecutions by international tribunals since their reestablishment a half century after the international military tribunals at Nuremberg and Tokyo. The contributions, dilemmas, and moral hazards from the record of the past two decades has episodes of deterrence and punishment, but also harmful effects from selective enforcement and post-conflict polarization, instead of building the rule of law and deterrence. States both inside and out of these courts' jurisdiction have strengthened and undermined these courts, while facilitating arrests of leaders of whom they disapprove while preventing arrests of their own and their allies' current leaders. Various lessons have been learned from legal and political efforts to account for and punish those who perpetrated the gravest crimes in armed conflicts, but some would argue that the lesson is to admit that realist exceptionalism has undermined the essence of the subliminal message intended of equal protection of international law. Conversely, others emphasize that in expanding the scope of international criminal law and by punishing a significant number of high-profile cases, the tribunals confirm aspirations and nascent norms of international society, albeit in particular circumstances where the correlation of politics coincides with justice.

Of course, there have also been hard cases, such as the recent reversal on appeal of Croatian General Ante Gotovina and his colleagues for genocide during Operation Storm, which produced the largest ethnic cleansing of the post-Yugoslav wars. There have been clear instances of unprosecuted crimes against humanity, particularly the leaders from countries who have not ratified the statute of the International Criminal Court (ICC), namely India, Pakistan, Sri Lanka, Palestine (whose ability to ratify it is uncertain), Israel, the United States, Russia and China—the latter three also Permanent members of the United Nations Security Council (UNSC). At the time of writing, all indictees have come exclusively from Africa, though at least two of them came from African states parties whose leaders wanted their military rebels prosecuted.

The effects of criminal tribunals on deterrence and international peace and stability has been more problematic than how these courts are redefining and influencing what norms states must respect to preserve their reputations. By mobilizing information networks from journalists, NGOs, IGOs, and states to document and publicize violations of international criminal law, tribunals have not only documented crimes that might have gone unnoticed, they also adduce evidence to apply nascent customary international criminal law in ever more precise and systematic fashion. Yet, the patchwork of selective prosecution, compliance, and norm development is fraught with double standards, hypocrisy, selective enforcement, and neo-imperial delegitimation of the subaltern. Moreover, even if we assume the worst crimes are universally abhorred, it does not follow that formal prosecution, either politically, culturally or even legally is universally applied without question and accepted as legitimate. Not only are these courts' procedures contested politically, culturally and legally, domestic alternatives, including customary legal remedies, are often seen as more legitimate, at least by key elites and even victims. As Clausewitz might have spun them, tribunals are, or are seen, as politics (or war) by other means. Still, tribunals have raised the profile of humanitarianism by punishing some of the most notorious atrocities. The question remains whether ongoing impunity of both the powerful and the powerless will undermine or limit this potential.

International criminal tribunals are supranational institutions with significant-but-autonomy limited by geopolitics, in spite of the norm of judicial independence. They are embedded in a two-dimensional, exogenous system of global governance, ranging from formal supranational and intergovernmental institutions regulating these courts and sets of international, regional and domestic regimes offering obstacles and incentives for tribunal action and inaction. In the first dimension, intergovernmental institutions (like the UNSC), have selectively required ICC prosecution of some actors, like Libya's Qaddafi and Sudan's al-Bashir leadership, while ignoring violations by leaders of its permanent Member States and their political allies, as well as war criminals fighting ethnic uprisings. Supranational institutions (viz., European Court of Human Rights), have clarified customary international law. Supranational agents (viz., UN Secretariat, human rights treaty bodies, and the Parliamentary Assembly of the

Council of Europe) have categorized evidence of violations. The international legal system is a consequential regime affecting the law applied by tribunals. Sovereign states especially the most powerful ones, finance and constrain tribunals and the laws they apply. Domestic legal systems and their own political influences, create the need for international tribunals when they fail to prosecute their own leaders and citizens whenever they act unsanctioned combat, torture, disappearances, and other crimes with dual international jurisdiction. While there is no institutionalized, world police force to arrest war criminals before their indictments, the establishment of various criminal tribunals represents a major step toward judicial enforcement at the international system level, which is no weaker than any domestic constitutional court in enforcing its decisions by having to rely on other branches for resources and enforcement. The hybrid tribunals in particular directly rely on domestic judges and in some tribunals, domestic law The complimentary jurisdiction of the ICC makes it subordinate to domestic judicial enforcement. The UNSC-created, *ad hoc* tribunals for Yugoslavia and Rwanda have commissioned domestic trials by the former and customary justice by the latter to prosecute some originally indicted under their superior jurisdiction. International criminal tribunals operate within these two dimensions, both taking cases suggested by external states parties and/or international organizations, as well as making legal and strategic decisions on which cases to initiate undertake on their own initiative. As with domestic courts, tribunals are legal and strategic actors in their growing jurisprudence, beyond the analytic legal analysis they presumably make in good faith. The performance of the international criminal tribunals can be evaluated in terms of these endogenous, intra-tribunal politics and exogenous political-legal factors, which encompass sociological, economic, political, and cultural causes.

To acknowledge these political factors is not to demean hard labor that resulted in part from the optimism of those who have built these tribunals. The hopes expressed by UN Under-Secretary General Nicolas Michel, about the long-negotiated hybrid tribunal for Cambodia epitomizes these hopes: "Let us work together to make the Extraordinary Chambers a success. Such success will stand as a beacon in the region signaling that the sinister culture of impunity is, indeed, being replaced by a culture of accountability. It would also leave Cambodia with a positive legacy in the strengthening of the rule of law."[1] Unfortunately, the difficulty of the Extraordinary Chambers to achieve such intended goals is a cautionary tale juxtaposed by the aspirations for criminal tribunals in general to counter impunity. Criminal courts are the primary new, international law institution of the past two decades. They represent a necessary, but not sufficient condition for greater criminal regulation of international and domestic politics, beginning in the realm of armed conflict, but with potential for all types of crimes across, and where needed, inside borders. All domestic courts of importance are affected by internal and external politics, but that does not mean that the scope of legal science can make significant inroads into depoliticizing, that is, legalizing issues for which there is a consensus to proceed on a relatively apolitical basis. One of the problems of the bounded autonomy in which these courts operate is that the consensus is still missing that the courts can operate legally, without the political ramifications that ensue any time a political leader is in the defendant's dock. If sufficient success were to be engendered in legalization, politics would not disappear any more than they do from constitutional courts. However, the extent of de-politicization through rule enforcement would be expected to increase so long as the tribunals' decisions are viewed as legitimate. A major question for the past and coming decades is whether these criminal tribunals have increased or decreased the extent of *perceived* politicization. To the extent that convicted mass murders are perceived as victims of partial justice, such courts would increase politicization, even if their practice of due process was above reproach. Changing historical memory is one of the great hopes of criminal tribunals, but much depends on who, if anyone, has control over knowledge and the narrative for particular intended audiences. Contested narratives lead to one side continuing to blame the other. Sometimes, even clear condemnations of evil can morally exonerate civil societies that actively supported the guilty leaders, who are presumed to have acted alone.

Given manifold efforts at politicizing what are also inherently political institutions, many political dilemmas have emerged for tribunals from international efforts to legalize, judicialize, and criminalize the most horrific of crimes through the international criminal tribunals. At the outset, they are very expensive; yet have not always been able to implement due process in a timely manner after the past two decades of experience[2] at an annual cost of approximately $400 million. One hundred and forty million alone has been for the ICC, totaling $1 billion in the latter's first decade of existence.[3] The future establishment of regional criminal courts might replace those *ad* hoc and hybrid tribunals going out of existence. Thus, the dilemma of perceived selective prosecution could be mitigated if Africa could establish its own regional tribunal. Already, its relatively new regional human rights court held Libya responsible in 2011 for violent human rights violations, just as the African Union asked the UNSC to intervene in Libya, while rejecting the ICC's indictments in Sudan. Until Africa is no longer singled out as the only region prosecuted by the ICC, the latter will suffer a legitimacy crisis, no matter that many Africans support its work to stop the senseless wars that murder innocents. Paradoxically, the less the domestic political will of states to prosecute their own leaders, the greater their opposition, perhaps, to either regional or multilateral prosecution.

The political origins of prosecution afflicted the exemplar of success, the International Military Tribunal (IMT) at Nuremberg, was both consciously, as well as subconsciously posited as an ideal type for international criminal tribunals, consistent with the narrative that emerged by the end of the Cold War. The victorious Allies then, as with the West now, are seen as asserting victor's justice though an arrogant proclamation of moral superiority, despite their own unpunished violations. This view was not lost on Germans in 1946 any more than Serbs in 2012, particularly after Gotovina was absolved under what critics of Justice Meron's judgment call his unrealistic standard of proof of genocidal intent. The domestic criminal prosecution of Adolph Eichmann in Israel had a much more powerful impact on the German population, according to the chapter by Smith and other accounts.[4] While German public opinion was arguably swayed by guilt for responsibility some fifteen years later, following the revelations at the Eichmann trial in Jerusalem, Croatia's views of Gotovina as anything but a national hero do not appear likely to change, even if genocidal intent was somehow proven with documentation in years hence.

Still, the myth of Nuremberg as the cause of German sense of accountability has also been hard to shake, despite detailed scholarship. Years of NGO lobbying and socialization have socially constructed another important myth, that the tribunals express universally or at least general support for international prosecution by international civil society. Notwithstanding its enormously damaging decline in respect for civil liberties since 9/11, as well as its bipartisan opposition to the ICC, the United States still supports international criminal prosecution, at least of its enemies. It also has dramatically lost prestige in the past decade over its patent double standard regarding the ICC's use for Sudan and Libya, but not for countless other cases, not least of which by the United States for torture, extraordinary rendition, and indiscriminate civilian deaths for drone attacks. If the myth of the IMT at Nuremberg was socially constructed by international civil society, the prevailing conditions, which made that myth possible, will rarely be replicated: a) total military defeat and surrender, and consequent shame for and dislike of the previous regime following a war perceived as between good and evil; b) clear, documented evidence of genocide and crimes against humanity, which had been kept largely secret from the general public during their commission; c) reasonably high standards of criminal due process, d) victor's justice, which was controlled by media-controlled, military occupations, e) and purging of top leaders from the previous regime and execution or long prison sentences of convicts who could not speak to the press. Yet, as Adam Smith argues in this volume, the German public was not persuaded that the IMT prosecutions had de-legitimated the Nazi regime, let alone lead to soul-searching about their past support for this regime. In even less ideal conditions, with a peace born of military stalemate, with violations by all sides, ambiguous evidence, and outsiders unable to censor local media, even court processes above reproach are unlikely to undo political and denial processes exogenous to tribunal proceedings.

After an "illegal but legitimate" abduction, arrest, and transfer by the *Mossad* from Argentina to Israel, Eichmann's trial prompted many questions from German youth of their parents, such as, "What did you do during the War?" Indeed the "illegal, but legitimate" formulation, postulated by Anne-Marie Slaughter and others after the "humanitarian interventions" in Haiti, Bosnia, and Kosovo in the 1990s, has also been adopted in the moral vagaries of criminal tribunals. Victor's justice at Nuremberg, Tokyo, and more recently at the Rwanda tribunal, not to mention the latter's inefficiency, compared with the Yugoslav court. If one posits counter-factual speculations, the Nuremberg narrative that has emerged two decades after those trials might not have emerged had Eichmann not been "illegally, but legitimately" arrested, which might also have meant that the *ad hoc* tribunals would not have been created in the first place as a response to the two genocides of the early 1990s. What some call the "African Criminal Court," the Hague-based ICC formulated by the 1998 Rome Statute amounts to one-sided justice that is not considered legitimate at the African Union despite the obvious guilt of the accused. If the ICC indicted George W. Bush for authorizing torture, as he admitted in his autobiography, there might no longer be an ICC either, if the United States decided to retaliate. While the price of one-sided justice at Nuremberg appears not to have harmed, and may have ultimately helped the cause of international justice, postcolonial perceptions of the ICC appear too well-founded and feared may de-legitimate it unless defendants from other continents are not soon indicted.

The legitimacy of tribunal verdicts is rarely accepted by defendants or their fellow citizens. In Peru, as Jo-Marie Burt's chapter explains, a domestic criminal case against Alberto Fujimori produced only a 65 percent public perception of guilt. This might be attributable to the fact the defendant was the former president who defeated an all-too real threat from Maoist guerrillas, who made no effort to hide its terrifying crimes against humanity. Fujimori had fled Peru in the wake of various scandals and was clearly incriminated, among other evidence, by the videotape of his then Interior Minister Montesinos bribing a legislator. The longer-term impact in Peru of his trial appears muddled, as new efforts to prosecute other human rights violations have been stalled by the current ruling party and by other politicians, who want to protect not only military officers responsible, but also their own corrupt or violent acts.

Such difficulties in gaining broad acceptance of tribunal credibility and legitimacy are not unknown in situations of institutionalizing new forms of politics. Such challenges of establishing the rule of law, to replace authoritarianism, can present legitimacy crises. Yet, even that effort usually does not lack for the possibility of creating a legitimate, hierarchical state. International law and criminal tribunals as a subfield constitute what Hans Kelsen called a "primitive legal system," which lacks guaranteed enforcement, relying more on self-help by states. Many have hoped the emergence of the tribunals would increase systemic enforcement of international criminal law. Others add states that do not consent to tribunals face costs to their reputations from non-compliance, including losing specific "reciprocity-entitlements," as well as greater cooperation accruing from mutual respect for the rule of international law. Progress in any area of politics everywhere is slow. Criminal tribunals are a step upward in the long durée toward international rule of law, along with the dozen UN treaty-based, soft law institutions, which have contributed to the increasing legalization of international human rights, even before their legitimacy as law has been accepted.[5]

This slow road to progress is shown by the long effort to establish accountability of Chad's former leader Hissene Habre. In July 2012, the International Court of Justice (ICJ) held that Senegal must try him on charges of crimes against humanity committed in Chad against his alleged political opponents from 1982-1990, or be extradited to Belgium, which had issued for extradition requests. The next month, Senegal and the African Union signed an agreement to set up an *ad hoc*, criminal tribunal to prosecute Habre, who had been under house arrest since 2005 in Senegal, where he had sought refuge after he was overthrown. This suggests the African Union's opposition to international prosecution is focused on the ICC's postcolonial domination, not an assertion sovereign or head of state immunity in principle.

In April 2012, another key moment in the long evolution of the fight against impunity emerged as Charles Taylor was convicted on all eleven guilty verdicts, based on nearly five years of trials at the Special Court for Sierra Leone (SCSL). Fifty thousand pages of witness testimony proved that he aided and abetted rape, sexual slavery, pillage, and abduction and conscription of child soldiers between December 1998 and February 1999 that occurred in Sierra Leone only. He was prosecuted only for indirect effects in that country: funding criminal activities in return for conflict diamonds, and failing to stop funding the atrocities, even if he never directly ordered them. That he has not been prosecuted for more direct and greater crimes in Liberia, as well as directly ordering crimes in Sierra Leone, have left many feeling justice remains incomplete. Moreover, that the trial occurred in the Hague, instead of in Freetown, Sierra Leone, along with the other SCSL trials, for safety reasons also led many to conclude that hybrid courts cannot always have much effect inside the countries with territorial jurisdiction. Still, this news is not perceived in an unambiguous fashion. Taylor's supporters, and incredibly, there are still many in Liberia, assert that the trial was always politically motivated. They point out the postcolonial nature of the SCSL, citing the Contras, who committed war crimes in Nicaragua, while being based in Honduras and Costa Rica, but were never prosecuted because the United States supported them and because they were given amnesty for laying down their arms as part of the 1987 Esquipulas II peace process. Taylor, they assert, similarly accepted the peace agreement in Liberia and was forced into exile because of the United States' threat to have him prosecuted. Any atrocities for which Taylor may have been responsible were far less, they believe, than what the prosecutors sought to prove. This anti-colonial narrative does not only resonate in that former colony of the United States. A Wikileaks cable stated that if Taylor were not convicted, the United States considered trying him in the United

States to keep Taylor out of West Africa. The United States, in 2008, had prosecuted his son Chuckie Taylor, who was the first and probably the only US citizen to be convicted of torture perpetrated outside of the United States. In Taylor's case in Liberia, the United States paid for 70 percent of the court's expenses, which shows its motives and control over the process according to the view of the SCSL's critics.

Given these ongoing signs of progress, how can tribunals help the evolution of international law above a primitive legal system? How can they help constitute stronger norms of international criminal law? Can they help deter crime? Will they help reduce the number and severity of conflicts resulting from gross and systematic human rights violations? Certainly, there is no shortage of new headlines, which at first glance, suggests more and deeper institutionalization of international criminal justice, and with it, the possibility of more judicial protection of human rights outside of armed conflict as well.

Interpreting the Role and Effects of Tribunals

Disciplinary and paradigmatic differences account for some of the other disparate narratives about the received success or failure of international criminal tribunals. Just as public law scholars in political science and law disagree on the extent to which analytic jurisprudence is politicized or motivationally reasoned,[6] international law professors tend to perceive the development of conventional and customary international law accruing from tribunals as extraordinary and likely to end impunity. As the President of the International Criminal Tribunal for the former Yugoslavia (ICTY), Theodor Meron, noted, "All living persons indicted by the Tribunal have been or will be tried in a court of law, either at the Tribunal or in the courts of national jurisdictions. One of the greatest achievements of the Tribunal and its sister court on Rwanda was their contribution to the development of substantive, procedural and evidentiary international criminal law. That corpus of jurisprudence far outweighed that of Nuremberg," he said, "pointing out that national judiciaries in the former Yugoslavia were successfully prosecuting war crimes cases, partly owing to the Tribunal's example."[7]

By Meron's account, the fact that no one is, in theory, above the law, means crime should be deterred because no one can ever claim to have been singled out for prosecution on political criteria. Most law professor advocates often acknowledge tribunal difficulties and failures, some of them exogenous (inadequate funding, state obstruction, and low salaries leading to poor retention). To be sure, "new thinking" critics underscore perverse incentives. David Kennedy notes NATO leaders were not prosecuted for crimes in 1999 in Yugoslavia, Iraq, and Afghanistan precisely because war law is enforced: there is now a cold, calculated strategy of weighing collateral damage against proclaimed military objectives that has an exonerating quality, without those weighing the balance being present on the scene. A clean bill of health is issued by judge advocates general, who approve targeting decisions according to legal doctrine not subject to subsequent review — the ICTY determined the US-led 1999 NATO war against Serbia involved no war crimes worth any indictments, despite deliberate targeting of civilian infrastructure like reservoirs, bridges, and journalists killed in raids on the Serb broadcasting station. The latter crime was repeated over two days by Israel's November, 2012 attacks on Gaza, when the Israeli Defense Forces attacked journalists unlawfully deemed to be military targets. As David Kennedy has written of war, law, "Law can also be a weapon—a strategic partner, a force multiplier, and an excuse for terrifying violence . . . The legalization of warfare has made it difficult to locate a moment of responsible political discretion in the broad process by which humanitarians and military planners together manage modern war."[8]

The attempt to assess international criminal adjudication involves all the temptations, critiques, and promises that apply to international law generally. Hard realists will always assert that the tribunals are no more effective than what great powers permit. They regard tribunals as epiphenomena of dominant states' power and interests. Realists would attribute the unexpected UNSC referrals of cases with Sudanese defendants after just two years of the ICC's existence, and the Council's referral of Qaddafi regime defendants in 2011 to the fact that the powerful five permanent members, after some horse-trading by China and Russia with the three Western powers, authorized it in their collective and separate interests. Furthermore, the absence of any of the great powers on any ICC or ICTY charge sheet and the exclusive focus of the seven ICC trials on African defendants both illustrate power politics. The *ad hoc* tribunals were created out of the desire of great powers to be morally relevant, given their lack of interest in sending troops on the ground to curtail genocides in Bosnia and Rwanda, as well as to signal to future criminals that the less powerful will face prosecution from which the powerful will exempt themselves. Liberals and constructivists would counter moral indignation aroused by non-intervention, in the face of both the requirements of the Genocide Convention and increasing potency of the Nuremberg narrative, forced powerful states to respond—that letting the proverbial tribunal rabbit out of its cage will eventually lead to moral indignation about universal crimes perpetrated by the powerful.

Softer realists, who feel tribunals reflect the triumph of hope over experience, may admit tribunals have gained some autonomy, but still need more enforcement powers to be really effective, especially against leaders of powerful states. Tribunals are constrained not to challenge great powers by complimentary rules, used to justify non-prosecutions of the preeminently guilty in developed states. One can merely point to the August 2012 decision of US Attorney General, Eric Holder that no further investigation of torture cases, including for two deaths in Afghanistan and Iraq, was merited. The next month, Human Rights Watch documented that the United States had used water-boarding and other torture techniques on members of the Libyan Islamic Fighting Group who were captured in Afghanistan. The United States assumed and asserted they were members of *al-Qaeda* and then extraordinarily rendered them criminally to torture by Qaddafi. Not only were they not part of *al-Qaeda*, but less than a decade later, the United States later armed them to overthrow the Libyan leader, and some of these torture victims assumed leadership roles in the rebellion and the subsequent government. Soft realists like Jack Goldsmith and Eric Posner, and even Henry Kissinger, all of whom generally minimize human rights crimes, find such behavior unacceptable because torture is a *jus cogens* crime, from which there is not derogation. Unlike the Bush administration leadership, soft realists acknowledge tribunals are a reality, as with international human rights, which contends with the national interest.

Both soft and hard realists argue that international law generally, and prosecution in particular, is unreliable normatively because autonomous courts contradict national interests and power structures, which are authoritarian and unwilling to defer to independent judiciaries, except when convenient to the powerful and their interests.[9] However, classical realists such as Morgenthau and Kissinger would argue that international law, and the courts that have emerged, can be useful when applied against enemies in what is unabashedly "victor's justice," a necessary hypocrisy for realism, since the purpose of courts for realists is to punish the enemy.

Subsequent leaders in Croatia and Serbia have been willing to extradite indicted predecessors like Generals Ante Gotovina and Ratko Mladić, Presidents Slobodan Milošević and Radovan Karadzić (though NATO ally Franjo Tudjman was never indicted before he died). Nor have any Tutsis been prosecuted for war crimes by the ICTR, which the UNSC did not give jurisdiction for all the Tutsi and Hutu crimes in the Eastern Congo over the past decade, much of it orchestrated from the capital, Kigali by former Tutsi rebel leader and current autocratic President, Paul Kagame. The trials that have already occurred for these individuals have been marked by significant departures from due process, even though a due process norm, self-representation, has been invoked to justify dilatory and irrelevant cross-examination of witnesses, witness boycotts over attempts to appoint *amicus* attorneys, clear patterns of witness intimidation by security agencies leading to no-shows or illnesses after initial testimonies, insistence on defense claims to waive rules permitting witnesses to make written statements, allowing dilatory and intimidating cross-examinations with irrelevant, repetitious or threatening questions and speeches, as well as providing information that effectively reveals the names of unnamed witnesses. The result is that "In any leadership case, testimony about the crimes is more attenuated than in cases involving direct persecutors."[10] For such reasons, realists are likely to assert criminal tribunals have important biases—which liberals cannot exactly reject, but not so much because they allow the guilty to go unpunished or because a different story is presented, but because the victims' story goes under-noticed.

Liberals argue this new criminal institution induces undeniable behavioral changes, from reduced criminal behavior to discursive assertions of new prerogatives, both of which increase costs of non-compliance. Liberals, sometimes called legalists, argue tribunal goals beyond punishment, like deterrence and reconciliation, accrue from establishing rule of law and ending impunity in post-conflict societies. Institutions create regimes and organizations that provide information and offer incentives and side payments inducing increased authority of international institutions.[11] For about five years, NATO refused to arrest the majority of ICTY-indicted war criminals. Gradually, all 161 were apprehended. Many key indictments were kept sealed in order to facilitate arrests, though few of those who were publicly indicted voluntarily turned themselves in. In time, the practice of secret indictments was ended, illustrating the trend toward improvements in due process, but only after significant political and economic pressure was placed on the relevant states through withholding foreign aid and EU accession candidacies until indicted war criminals were extradited.

Constructivists emphasize potential for isolating non-state parties as for their exceptionalist normative claims. They argue identity, reputation, ideas, and social interaction induce groups to perceive power structures in terms of norms that are generated, diffused, and incorporated over time, particularly in contexts of uncertainty. Epistemic communities diffuse political norms to international organization which induce states to reformulate the meaning of their power and interests. They believe that institutions like international criminal tribunals can construct new identities. As a result of collecting evidence and connecting with communities through outreach programs and by providing solace to victims, these tribunals can go beyond just collecting facts to providing insights and identities. In particular, epistemic communities of international lawyers, human rights NGOs, and journalists interact with citizens, humanitarian NGOs, and victims who appreciate their new ideas, ideals and human rights activism.

Given all the different competing claims, none of which are consistent, there are situations where realism is dominant, but others where liberal and constructivist paradigms fit complex, contextual alternatives. To cite one example from debates about transitional justice, the indictments and arrest warrants of some leaders have prevented peace (Kony), while others (Karadzić, Milošević) may have encouraged peace. Prosecution appears to be possible in some contexts and not in others, including within the same countries over time. One constructivist, Jeffrey Checkel, conceded different paradigms have validity under different conditions. The scholarly challenge consists of identifying, hypothesizing, and testing those conditions. He suggests interaction between agents and realist and liberal structures present opportunities and moments when the power of ideas finds receptive audiences that alter predictions of either national security or interests on the one hand and legal compliance on the other.[12]

The lead British Prosecutor at Nuremberg, Hartley Shawcross, advocated many roles for tribunals, from prosecution and punishment to deterrence, rehabilitation, and teaching morality to civil society. Hannah Arendt, by contrast, maintained the only goal should be retributive, eschewing didactic, restorative, or reformation goals. Others debate the compatibility or conflicting logics of prosecution and restoring peace and security. Any assessment of international criminal tribunals depends on how narrow or ambitious are the goals they are expected to achieve. Realists assert ambitious goals amount to judicial romanticism. Liberals argue incremental evolution can gradually enhance a robust regime of rule internalization and criminal deterrence. Constructivists add that the ideas of criminal justice impel voluntary obedience. Now that ongoing litigation at most of the *ad hoc* and hybrid tribunals is almost all over, international criminal tribunals have not yet achieved deterrence, but they have punished many of the chief perpetrators of unfathomable crimes. Retribution provides some solace to victims and perhaps deters a few would-be *genocidaires*. The criminal tribunals did not inhibit the cycle of ethnic violence in the Great Lakes region; arguably, the worst war since World War II was aggravated and prolonged in small-but-significant part by international prosecution. The reaction of Sudan's President Omar al-Bashir after his ICC indictment was to expel the humanitarian NGOs and deepen ethnic cleansing. Threatening the targets of unenforceable arrest warrants can strengthen the will of indicted warriors to resist.

That states are still left to police and prosecute themselves does not mean that tribunals should never attempt to act pragmatically. Early in the history of the *ad hoc* tribunals for Yugoslavia and Rwanda, the main concern was whether or not indicted war criminals could even be arrested. US-led, NATO troops were hesitant to take risks, given the "CNN effect" for US casualties. It took almost two decades in some cases for NATO or the countries themselves to arrest all the indictees. It will take even greater institutionalization for them to deter heads of state and militaries from committing crimes. In this longer term perspective, however, such changes in international institutions underscore important landmarks on the road to progress in situations that were once considered hopeless. That could only be true without perverse incentives and unforeseen consequences at play with costs that outweigh the benefits.

Positive Signs

We know tribunals have made important gains in clarifying or contributing to customary international law. Convictions of heads of state and government must be taken seriously. The variegated array of formal and precise rules has expanded the extent to which the law is predictable, a procedurally intense and non-arbitrary process of treating criminals outside the arbitrary vagaries of politics. Established first in the 1990s to promote peace in Rwanda and former Yugoslavia, what potential do they have to contribute to peacebuilding through justice? First, no leader can be sure he will enjoy impunity. More states are starting to pay attention to these legal rules, whether or not they are actually enforced in courts, to avoid reputational costs. It may not stop an authoritarian regime because these are force-utilizing (not law-obeying) states. The incentive for autocrats committing atrocities is perverse, at least initially, because these tribunals threaten to punish them if they leave power; so, they may rationally be more apt to encourage greater violent repression. Over time, their effect on encouraging a reduction in repression and peacemaking may be curvilinear, as leaders understand that amnesties now may give them a safe exit, if they end war and atrocities, whereas holding on to power will leave them no mercy when and if they do lose power, as most, though not all, authoritarian regimes do. Taylor and Milošević became targets for prosecution only when exogenous factors were favorable, since eventually, the United States reversed its initial opposition and eventually wanted both extradited, just as even China reversed its prior opposition at the UNSC to refer al-Bashir's case to the ICC. Such exogenous factors make the efficacy of the courts more dependent on realist calculations than on liberal institutionalization or constructivist appeals to doing the right thing and tend to undermine claims to greater legalization of world politics.

For those who feel the proverbial glass is at least half full, the SCSL proved that thugs and dictators cannot feel they can act above the law. Prosecution witnesses from Sierra Leone convinced the judges that Taylor was the sponsor for the crimes in that country after receiving a fair trial in a complex case that required a large team effort to pull the case to its conclusion. It is indisputable, despite these contrasting effects, that dictators and despots, such as Slobodan Milošević and Jean Kambanda, can no longer be sure that they will enjoy legal impunity for the rest of their lives. This is to be applauded even if it is also a limited gesture. It is limited both because such leaders often feel that repression may be their only option to stay in power and *avoid* prosecution and because only a small minority of repressors will, for the foreseeable future, be likely ever to be arrested.

In the seventeen years it took the ICTY to arrest all of its 161 indicted war criminals, Serbia finally sent Radovan Karadzić in July 2008, along with former Bosnian Serb Police Commander Stojan Zupljanin in June 2008, and former top General Ratko Mladić in May 2011 after a sixteen-year manhunt. For its part, Croatia had arrested all the indicted war criminals, including the highest ranking General, Ante Gotovina. Bosnia's cooperation was completed, other than for ICTY requests for further investigations and prosecutions of fugitive support networks. For the ICTR, chief prosecutor Hassan Jallow had appealed to the UN

Mission in the Congo and UN member states to seek out and arrest some seven fugitives still at large at the time of writing.

The emerging international tribunals were part of what Richard Falk hoped would turn into a Grotian moment, which restructures international law.[13] Or was the real Grotian moment 9/11, when national security concerns have diminished respect in practice for human rights? Disappointment abounds from post-prosecution genocidal denial after tribunal prosecutions among many or most in civil society in the former Yugoslavia, as Michael Thurston's chapter shows, as well as for the greater power impunity. Furthermore, close examination of some of the great difficulties of the slow pace of prosecutions of the *ad hoc* tribunal for Rwanda, the East Timor Panels, and the Special Court for Lebanon, are apparently the rule, despite the ability of the SCSL to complete its work with prosecutions of all sides, both government and rebel paramilitary forces. The hybrid court for Kosovo did not use case precedents from the ICTY, which helped its international judges remain credible with the ethnic Serb minority, but it also undermined the claim that customary international law had been clarified by the latter, *ad hoc* tribunal. Given the hesitancy of the East Timor Panels to antagonize Indonesia with aggressive prosecutions, reviewing the hybrid courts in Cambodia demonstrates on how many levels prosecution remains problematic.

Cautionary Tale of Cambodia's Extraordinary Chambers

The Extraordinary Chambers in the Courts of Cambodia (ECCC) was created by UNSC and negotiated between the UN and Cambodia. While the primary purpose of the ECCC was to bring justice to those accused of the "the worst of worst crimes," it was acclaimed as a tool for transforming Cambodia's judicial system, as well as contributing to the healing process for victims.[14] The ECCC is the first hybrid tribunal in which international prosecutors and judges do not constitute a majority. This was an opportunity for Cambodian judicial officers to learn from the "internationalized" process, while also harboring reservations about the ability of the national counterparts to behave in an independent manner.[15] A further innovation of the ECCC is allowing victims to participate in proceedings and seek moral and collective reparations. This opens the possibility for the ECCC to also function as a truth and reconciliation process. Victims, if admitted as civil parties, may seek moral and collective reparations for the injuries they suffered as a direct consequence of the crimes alleged against the accused. Some commentators have called for a more holistic approach than that provided by the ECCC to transform Cambodian society.[16] The model adopted for allowing victim participation has been criticized for being based on an assumption that victim participation in tribunals is always therapeutic.[17] It has also raised concerns that judges may be drawn into the role of historians when deciding matters of law.[18]

To be sure, since the signing of the Paris Peace Accords in 1991, Cambodia's legal system has moved a good distance from its socialist era's "show trials." Many necessary institutions have been created, laws have been adopted, and professionals have been trained to improve the country's ability to reach just outcomes in cases of judicial accusation. However, many challenges continue to frustrate the system's ability to deliver fair trials. At the time of writing, the ECCC had finalized its first case and had begun trial proceedings for its second, which will see more senior members of the Khmer Rouge that are still alive brought to justice. However, an investigating judge resigned because of the government's opposition to further prosecutions. The German judge who resigned was controversial because he actually had been criticized for not investigating additional defendants. Curiously he had been the least involved among the judges, but his resignation may improve the chances of prosecutions. The co-investigating judge became involved when the government already stated only the five original defendants should be tried. The government made the usual argument, invoked by Carlos Menem in Argentina and Barack Obama in the United States, among others, that Cambodia should "look forward."

The proceedings to date suggest that any improvements are likely to be negligible in comparison to the problems that currently hamper the justice system in Cambodia. It is unlikely that the ECCC will leave a lasting legacy of strengthening the rule of law in Cambodia. James Goldston, Executive Director of the Open Society Justice Initiative, feared for the potentially negative quality and impartiality of judicial decision-making in Cambodia.[19] As Johanna Herman explains in her chapter, endemic corruption in the judiciary is a major obstacle to the development of a professional, independent, and impartial judiciary in Cambodia. It remains an open secret that judges and other court officers regularly accept significant bribes; by some estimates, it is the method by which the vast majority of cases are decided. The ability and willingness of the government to exercise control over the courts and its actors continues to undermine the independence of Cambodia's judiciary. According to Subedi, the absence of laws providing judges with the security and independence frustrates their ability to carry out their duties effectively.[20] The case of Mu Sochua, a sitting Member of Parliament for the Sam Rainsy Party, being successfully sued for defamation after filing a defamation complaint against the Prime Minister which was subsequently thrown out, is a recent example where the independence of the courts has been brought into question. In response to this verdict, the Director of LICADHO, a Cambodian human rights NGO that monitors trial proceedings, commented that the decision of the court was "predictably unjust" and called it a further example of the government-controlled courts being used "as a weapon against its political opponents."[21]

Examples of Endogenous Factors Affecting Tribunals

Particular criticism is directed at endogenous factors inside these tribunals, especially the alleged politics motivating some key prosecutorial decisions. Sir Geoffrey Nice, a deputy prosecutor at the Milošević ICTY trial, stated that one defendant at the ICTY presumptively guilty of genocide, as well as war crimes and crimes against humanity, was not prosecuted because the judges had made clear they did not want this particular case to become the first genocide conviction. The prosecutors tried to complain, but the judges ignored them. Sir Geoffrey reports his colleague was told by one of the judges that while they thought the defendant was indeed guilty of genocide, they did not want the first genocide prosecution to be for this low-level defendant and preferred to wait for a genocide case with a high-ranking defendant. On appeal, the court ruled that the trial court should have prosecuted the defendant for genocide. Sir Geoffrey said the judges' interest in publicity interfered with their duty to keep politics out of the courtroom.[22] Genocide convictions were also prevented in the International Court of Justice in *Bosnia v. Serbia*, according to Sir Geoffrey, because the national security archive of Serbia files were used in cases by the ICTY on the condition that they not be used by any other court and were to remain secret. This allowed the ICJ to find Serbia not guilty of genocide, as well as the loss to the public of the files.[23]

These examples of political interference are not necessarily unusual. Political scientists have long argued that decisions by domestic constitutional courts reflect non-legal factors.[24] This is due to the fact both tribunals and constitutional courts occur in political contexts, with mandates, resources, evidence, implicit and even explicit threats from states and global civil society. Former ICTY/ICTR chief prosecutor Carla del Ponte had two-full time political advisers. In 2000, she decided not to open a criminal investigation into NATO's bombing campaign in Serbia during the eleven week war the year before. The prosecutor does not comment on decision to investigate or prosecute, itself as much a political as a legal decision. One may infer del Ponte was not about to bite the proverbial feeding hand of NATO and NATO member states that had been providing documentation of war crimes by Serbs and others. Former ICC Chief Prosecutor Luis Moreno regularly met with local communities of victims to learn their reactions to ICC indictments. Similarly, judges, prosecutors and registrars, and their staff, also exercise discretion to interact with states and civil society, collecting information about perceptions of courts and utilizing prosecutorial discretion to evaluate the "interests of justice," that is political considerations in addition to the legal merits and effects of justice claims. The ICC statute, under Article 53 states it is the prosecutor's responsibility to consider "whether to initiate an investigation," and, upon investigation, to decide "that there is not a sufficient basis for a prosecution." In making these decisions, the Rome Statute states that a factor to be considered by the prosecutor is "the interests of justice." Apparently, one of the cases where the ICC prosecutor refrained "in the interests of justice" from investigating was for US torture and extraordinary rendition committed on the territories of ICC states parties, such as Afghanistan, Bosnia, Macedonia, Poland, and Romania.[25]

In the nearly two decades of the *ad hoc* tribunals, the varying terms of the hybrid courts, and the decade of the ICC, the highest marks are given to the ICTY, having arrested all the 161 indicted and clarified new precedents, which states have largely accepted as customary international law, as Larry Taulbee's chapter argues. All the tribunals have established that head-of-state immunity and other "reasons of state" are not legally acceptable. The explosion of politicized "lawfare" from opposing political forces have resulted in part from the tribunals' success in clarifying legal rules prohibiting international crimes. Most tribunals have been criticized for their cost and delays, but credited for providing due process to almost all defendants, except for those cases with *pro se* defendants. The hybrid tribunals, designed to utilize local resources and legitimacy and provide training, proved to be more expensive than anticipated since domestic systems often remained inadequately prepared and resourced. Questions were also raised with the East Timor Panels under the supervision of the UN peacekeeping mission, following the withdrawal of all the experienced Indonesian judges and lawyers and the use of prosecution witnesses who would also be defendants. Problems arose over the truth commission in Sierra Leone, which offered no amnesty for confessions, but also raised controversy over the admissibility of evidence. Delays in Cambodia over budget resources and local autonomy were resolved, but the Cambodian judicial majority has raised procedural questions about political and judicial will to prosecute, on top of the pervasive fear of potential Khmer Rouge retaliatory violence. As Kathleen Barrett discusses in her chapter, the Special Court for Lebanon (up until recently) faced interference from Syria, which was under suspicion and which was justly perceived as biased and an unnecessary cause for delay in the prosecution for the murder of the Prime Minister. Four Hezbollah members and no Syrians were ultimately indicted in 2011. They will controversially be prosecuted *in absentia* by its hybrid court. Many in legal epistemic communities have criticized the first chief prosecutor during the ICC's first decade, Luís Moreno, for failing to investigate *prima facie* war crimes and crimes against humanity occurring on the territory of states parties by heads of state or rebel leaders, like, Bosnia, Burundi, France, Jordan, Macedonia, Mexico, Moldova, the Philippines, Poland, Romania, South Africa, the United Kingdom and Venezuela. The pace of the first ICC conviction in 2012 of Thomas Lubanga was very slow and almost was dropped, while cases involving even more serious offenses hardly began at the ICC. The conditions for making tribunals more effective depends on improving such endogenous conditions, as well as exogenous factors analyzed above, such as norm double standards and unequal distribution of state power and influence.

Trials of Milošević, Saddam Hussein, and Charles Taylor exemplify the extent to which due process procedural norms and substantive law can deviate from liberal precepts and thereby introduce legitimacy gaps in their performance. The best example is the four-year trial of Slobodan Milošević, which ended with his death. There are strong suspicions that he and his agents in security agencies were intimidating witnesses and wasting trial time without much or any discipline or punishment. He bullied witnesses under cross-examination, particularly those with less education. Victims, thus, had to suffer twice, the original crimes and then the indignity of his antics dodging the evidence before the court. The ICTY appeals court did cite an ICTR decision that the right to self-representation was not absolute, "where it is in the interests of justice to appoint counsel (against the accused's will)."[26] Those circumstances were said not to have arisen in the Milošević trial while keeping the option under "review." The Court ultimately did not restrict Milošević much, such as insisting that this defendant's questions be submitted to the court for the latter to ask or insisting that a court-appointed lawyer represent, rather than just advise the defendant. Between his real and faked illnesses, improper use of smuggled medications, false documents, scripted testimony of his witnesses, leading questions, failure, intended or not, of his witnesses to appear, and dilatory cross-examination of prosecution witnesses, the Court's various deadlines for presenting its case were never met; The Court waited a year before insisting it would appoint its own *amici* lawyers to advise judges how Milošević should be represented. The Court never appointed him attorneys, though it was clear the defendant not only did not recognize the ICTY's legitimacy, but that he would make good on his stated purpose to preach a political lesson to Serbs rather than focus on the evidence brought against him. The Court finally tired of his behavior such as his harassment of rape victims, claiming they were liars, along with his revealing the identity of witnesses. However, when it tried to appoint a lawyer years later into his three-and-a-half year trial, the Appeals Chamber overruled the Trial Chamber, and the defendant continued his nauseating behavior under his right to self-representation and failed to limit the excesses of this *pro se* defense. In Armatta's conclusion:

> Milošević considered the ICTY proceedings a game. While his adversaries attempted to win by presenting facts and playing by the rules, Milošević cheated. . . . Future war crimes tribunals and the ICC must take account of the character of the people they will mostly be dealing with—ruthless men and women who have no ethical qualms about lying, perpetrating fraud, or threatening or even killing witnesses. These are people whose careers were built on deceit and manipulation. . . . It would be foolish to believe that such tyrants will accede to a

law that seeks to hold them accountable for acts they considered not subject to any law.[27]

A realist arguably would not have tolerated such misconduct. The bending over backwards to allow *pro se* defendants the right to make political speeches instead of examining evidence, along with so many other abuses, showed that the ICTY was more concerned with granting defendant rights than protecting the court's legitimacy, as well as the due process rights of that Court and the victims of such horrible crimes. It is difficult to describe such decisions on the basis of either liberal or constructivist precepts. One can see a new institution, the ICTY, undergoing political learning: that what occurred in the *Milošević* case was intolerable and should not be repeated. Yet, in the trials of Šešlej at the ICTY and Taylor at the SCSL, similar patterns were repeated, with the former arguing *pro se*, with that right upheld on appeal, while the latter was accused of bribing and intimidating witnesses, as well as revealing their identities, even if his demeanor in court was much more respectful than Milošević's.

Courts have also been faced with the prosecutors' and defendants' allegations of prosecutorial misconduct toward witnesses. While the former's complaints are more plausible, defendants like Milošević and Šešlej made formal allegations of prosecutorial misconduct. Expensive studies by independent experts had to be conducted to review allegations that more correctly applied to the complaining defendants' own conduct. Regime leaders routinely allege that prosecutors are suborning perjury, as well as threatening and bribing witnesses. Courts have to investigate these allegations and develop rules on how to respond to allegations from the mass murderers like Milošević and Šešlej. The courts have again not acted with realist principles in hiring independent experts to review and then reject the defendant allegations based on almost no evidence.

The ICTY, based on jurisprudence from the ICTY, ICTR, and the SCSL, where the issue of witness intimidation by either prosecution or defense has established models of judicial response, concluded in dismissing further action in the ICTY in the Vojislav Šešlej allegation of prosecutor misconduct. Tribunals make it necessary to hire independent, *amicus* investigators to evaluate if: a) there is credible evidence corroborating the allegations and b) a "reasonable trier of fact has reason to believe that there is sufficient evidence to sustain a conviction beyond a reasonable doubt" and if yes, then to investigate and prosecute the prosecution. According to the public document, the evidence has to be "manifestly unreliable or incredible."[28] The *amicus* cannot stop the process if the *amicus* does not believe the evidence. So, a high test exists before a case can be dismissed. Thus, the test is whether a reasonable trier of fact *could* credit evidence, which would include evidence pro and con, that is not manifestly unreliable, and that proved beyond a reasonable doubt evidence of witness misconduct. Often, prosecutors have no evidence to contradict allegations about witnesses far removed from international tribunals.

Nevertheless, the standard for recommending prosecution is a very low one. If an independent investigator finds "sufficient grounds" to prosecute, he cannot consider the difficulty of prosecution and the probability of success. An independent friend of the court must recommend prosecution, even if he believes the chances of obtaining a conviction are very low and the cost of the effort would be very high. The courts for the ICTY, ICTR, and the SCSL have concluded that a contempt prosecution, at the instigation of even a rogue defendant, against the prosecution, must proceed if in the independent investigator's judgment, a reasonable trier of fact could credit the evidence in support of the allegations and find that it could sustain a conviction beyond a reasonable doubt. Put differently, a prosecution should go forward only if the evidence is "manifestly unreliable or incredible."

As with the issue of *pro se* representation, the Appeals Chamber took a liberal or constructivist position, erring on the side of the defendant. No realist would have insisted on legal niceties to investigate implausible allegations by defendants. Nor would they have tolerated such obvious abuses as witness intimidation and bribery that were used by Milošević, Šešlej, and Taylor. Perhaps, these liberal positions are akin to political interference, a form of liberal activism. In any event, the politics of procedural and substantive issues have not followed realism.

Examples of Exogenous Factors Affecting Tribunals

Many exogenous political, economic, social and cultural factors limit these courts' effectiveness. The content of the founding statutes represented to a high degree the preferences and interests of the powerful states that created and funded the tribunals. None of them pursue crimes against humanity outside of the statutorily limited context of widespread or systematic attacks on civilian populations. Other violent human rights violations must be committed in armed conflict for these courts to proceed. All these courts are limited by what other states provide in terms of intelligence and cannot subpoena them to provide evidence they hold. Enemies of the United States generate ample evidence of crimes; allies nothing. P-5 members of the Security Council select whom to refer or not refer to the ICC, just as heads of states parties only refer cases involving their enemies. Clearly, attempts to pursue defendants from powerful states or their allies and clients would come at a cost to the court. David Forsythe has argued that it makes sense for the ICC and other tribunals to proceed slowly as they improve its institutional capacity and the rest of the world becomes acclimated to its culture and legitimacy rather than attempting the utopian and unrealistic goal of asking powerful democratic states to surrender their own citizens when these states oppose the rule of international law against their own citizen defendants.[29]

Despite increasing legalization emphasized by liberals, criminal tribunals' influence will still depend on exogenous factors, such as greater equality in state power; greater compliance by weak states with tribunals; greater cooperation by leading world powers, instead of exempting themselves from tribunal jurisdiction; broader expectation that the international law is becoming stronger; and even greater activity by non-state actors' (both NGOs and IGOs) in monitoring of international law rules.

The position on criminal tribunals of the United States, like those of the BRIC countries, is difficult to characterize as always realist, liberal or constructivist. Russia and China are just as opposed to the ICC as India and the United States, while Brazil is a state party to its statute. Still, the United States has funded most of the *ad hoc* and hybrid tribunals, and supported the Security Council's referrals of cases to the ICC from Sudan and Libya, controversially claiming humanitarian intervention as a basis for the ICC undertaking cases advocated by the United States. On December 7, 2011, US Ambassador Jeffrey DeLaurentis told the UN Security Council that,

> The ICTY has shown that it can provide fair trials, that war crimes fugitives cannot escape justice, and that victims can now expect that those who commit crimes against civilians will be held to account. . . . Mr. President, the United States continues to call on states in the former Yugoslavia to cooperate fully with the ICTY. We encourage the Government of Serbia to continue its efforts to determine how Ratko Mladić and Goran Hadzić were able to avoid justice for so many years, and to take appropriate measures against their support networks. We also look forward to cooperation from the relevant countries in the region on the apprehension of Radovan Stanković, who escaped in 2007 from prison in Bosnia and Herzegovina. . . . Turning to the International Criminal Tribunal for Rwanda, the United States welcomes the June 24, 2011 judgment in the case against the former Minister of Women's Development and five others . . . because it demonstrates that rape is a crime of violence that has been used as a tool of war by both men and women. The United States also welcomes the November 17, 2011 judgment in the case against the former Mayor of Kivumu, who had authority over the local police, yet failed to prevent the massacre of more than 1,500 people . . . 198 days after the arrest of (fugitive Bernard Munyagishari), the United States is discouraged that the nine remaining fugitives remain at large. . . . Every member state has an obligation to apprehend the remaining fugitives. The United States, along with many others, is making a concerted effort to assist other nations in bringing these fugitives to justice.[30]

Despite the positive view of the United States for criminal tribunals, anti-imperialists perceive tribunals like realists, as "complicity with power." Only two situations—Kenya and the Ivory Coast—were opened at the instance of the prosecutor. The Kenya investigation started after former UN Secretary General Kofi Annan, Chairman of the AU Panel of Eminent African Personalities, provided a secret list of suspects to the ICC and after the Kenyan parliament refused to establish a national tribunal. In Ivory Coast, it was former President Laurent Gbagbo who accepted the jurisdiction of the ICC in April 2003 under the provisions of Article 12(3) of the Rome Statute. After he was arrested, he too depicted the ICC as the "White Man's Court" and complaining about its "neo-colonialist" and "imperialist" agenda. Therefore, reverse anti-imperialism can also apply to suspected mass-murders.

International Criminal Law criminalizes some, but not all human rights and humanitarian law. Crimes against humanity must be part of a widespread or systematic attack on a civilian population. In theory, grave breaches of the Geneva Conventions enjoy universal jurisdiction in any domestic court, which is largely theoretical. Such legal and practical limitations protect great powers and their client states from tribunal prosecution for crimes against humanity, for example, any acts of torture not part of a widespread or systematic attack, or as a war crime if not occurring in armed conflict.

Finally, the oft-debated issue of amnesties for peace will not be resolved in this chapter. This does not mean that every case must bring an indictment, no matter what actions are taken regarding amnesties or prosecutions. It is no more automatic that amnesties will bring peace than it is true that indicting those at large will harm peace. The pragmatic liberal pattern suggest that the ICC suffers not so much from rogue prosecution as the United States has claimed, but intimidation by outside states signaling which cases they want pursued or not. The dilemma will also be affected by the tribunals' institutional practice. Adversaries and their mediators may claim that they can deliver peace, but the examples of Milošević and Karadzić show that former heads of state not only can be arrested without harm to domestic peace, but their indictments may also have hastened their loss of power. Both Milošević and Karadzić were de-legitimated as leaders by their indictments, leading to the electoral defeat of the former and the latter's claim to negotiate on behalf of the Bosnian Serbs. Out of office, it became easy to arrest them later. The delay may be justice delayed, but it is not justice denied.

The suddenly (spring 2012) iconic case of Joseph Kony, may illustrate the opposite effect, where peace is impeded by prosecution. The ICC's refusal to suspend his arrest warrant, despite objections from the same Ugandan government which had originally requested the ICC investigation and indictment, illustrates liberal ICC commitments to the rule of law, instead of either peacemaking or *realpolitik*. Kony refused to sign a peace agreement with the government so long as he remained an international outlaw. The internal and external credibility of the ICC would have been sorely tested had it dropped the indictment. The Prosecutor could have made a plea "in the interests of justice" under the ICC

Statute's authority. Moreover, the ICC prosecutor did not want to investigate Ugandan President Yoweri Museveni for his own alleged war crimes. However, it is not always clear that a country like Uganda or a President Museveni will more likely deliver peace any more than the ICC can deliver prosecution. For his part, Kony might not have had any sincere interests in peace than the government; nor would the President necessarily have had the ability to control subordinate troops, had the ICC opted for pursuing the peace pact. Even former ICC Chief Prosecutor Moreno stated he was not opposed to the proposed amnesty because it only applied when and if Kony's LRA guerrillas were to come out of the bush, which Kony had still not agreed to do.

Conclusions

Paradigmatic differences often account for the different interpretations of the tribunals. Realists, perceiving a negative-sum game, do not trust losses of sovereignty to an institution that by definition is supposed to be independent—though even realists can perceive just how these exogenous factors limit the autonomy of the tribunals, such as the ICTY's prosecutor's decision not to indict any NATO leader for war crimes in the 1999 bombing of Yugoslavia even when civilian targets like the employees in the national television station and infrastructure such as bridges and reservoirs were deliberately attacked. While some scholars reluctantly acknowledge the influence of realist logic in tribunal practice, [31] skeptics follow the logic of Morgenthau, Carr, and Kissinger in warning against international criminal tribunals and universal jurisdiction. Realists argue tribunals represent either the logic of legalism in an illiberal world, or the logic of emotions rather than actual consequences.[32] For example, should not one see the ICC for what it is: a court that takes cases from autocratic strategic allies of the United States, such as President Museveni of Uganda against his enemy, Joseph Kony, through whom the Obama administration has proclaimed its renewed ICC support by sending military advisers to Uganda for that effort? Or, should we interpret the ICC court's valiant pursuit of the rule of law by refusing to drop Kony's indictment, even though an incipient peace agreement was supposedly abandoned because of the ICC's refusal to drop Kony's indictment? Is the ICC continuing the armed conflicts in the Great Lakes region of East Africa, providing the basis for a just resolution of ethnic conflicts and control over lootable resources, or is it a minor player in a much larger game? Did the Security Council lengthen the war in 2011 by referring the Libyan leadership for investigation by the chief ICC prosecutor? Or did the UNSC's referral not only encourage the rebels that the great powers were behind them, as well as signal to future autocrats that human-caused, humanitarian emergencies can result in not only forcible interventions, but also prosecution for those responsible. Is Africa going to be further alienated by the ICC as it takes more cases like Kenya and Sudan, which are not referred by African state parties? Realists would answer all these questions with a skeptical view of judicial romanticism.

On the other hand, liberals and constructivists see the potential for generalized, positive-sum gains from the reciprocity practiced when and if tribunals succeed in treating all states alike. If tribunals have not yet generated an improvement in the international rule of law, it is only because sovereign states have not been willing to be subjected to the equal protection and application of the law. Regardless of the answers to such questions, the politics of international criminal tribunals, at the level of discourse, calculations, and consequences are clearly affecting international and domestic politics in both positive and negative ways, even if characterizing those roles and effects is difficult to discern. Whether that is because of democratic identity politics, transnational legal processes, or merely because criminal are the subject of debate remains an open question. Liberals and constructivists also have their own disagreements with each other over how pragmatic tribunals are to be, given all the exogenous constraints they face.

Clearly, international criminal tribunals fit the liberal and constructivist paradigms in the realm of norm creation, but realism provides a better understanding of their incomplete effectiveness and interference by states with the international rule of law. They do not substantially deter international crimes, and some states can manipulate them for their own interests because reputational costs are still too low and monitoring by IGOs and NGOs is incomplete. However this is a long process whose endpoint is not predetermined, and much will depend on how successful tribunals are in prosecuting leaders from powerful countries who are war criminals, and constant efforts at monitoring compliance are maintained by international civil society. The trajectory remains slightly upward in spite of the realist pressures from counter-terrorism that have marginalized global civil society since 9/11. Additionally, the incorporation of customary international law generated by international tribunals is proceeding in Latin American countries like Argentina and Peru. Clearly, domestic enforcement of international criminal law offers the potential of overcoming realist constraints to the international rule of law. However, so far the US and most other regions have not held their leaders criminally accountable in domestic courts, but that situation too could gradually change. Again, the danger posed by terrorism makes it more difficult to apply international criminal law to leaders instead of just to terrorists. One of the major tests will begin with domestic enforcement of human rights laws in the domestic enforcement of tribunal-generated customary law. Otherwise realism will also have its day in domestic enforcement as well.

From the viewpoint of compliance using social science methodology, the record for international criminal law is arguably even worse than respect for the Law of the Sea, human rights, and environmental law, which in turn is much worse than economic and trade law. To some extent, no set of criminal tribunals could overturn the realist logic of national security trumping law through conflict resolution by force by those unmoved by liberal or constructivist incentives and processes. Yet despite lower incentives for compliance, most statistical studies find some improvement in compliance with the prohibition of torture in state parties to the Convention against Torture.[33] However, tribunals may not generate as much voluntary cooperation against their own citizens to be criminally tried. Yet, as currently constituted, international criminal tribunals will not even have jurisdiction for most torture, which occurs in peacetime and not during the contexts required, either armed conflict or a widespread or systematic attacks on a civilian population. The extent of future socialization toward compliance, nevertheless, remains an open possibility, and certain behavior changes in actual behavior, as well as rhetoric, can be perceived, even if the average behavior would appear to be not much different.

In succeeding in punishing a number of high-profile cases, the tribunals arguably constitute what Habermas called communicative action[34] that expresses the aspirations and nascent norms of international society.[35] Beyond the confines of a specific of international cooperation, these courts are increasingly becoming norm entrepreneurs, defining the norms of coexistence among states, such that internal atrocities are seen not only as international crimes, but threats to the stability and order of international society. These courts are also redefining the attributes of what states must practice to preserve their reputations, a breach of which will prove increasingly costly. The tribunals are increasingly incentivizing and mobilizing informational networks from NGOs, IGOs, and states to document and publicize violations of international criminal law, thereby increasing exposure risks of perpetration. To be sure, the patchwork of compliance and norm communication is fraught with double standards. The contributions, dilemmas, and moral hazards from this record of nearly two decades has episodes of deterrence and punishment, but also harmful effects from selective enforcement and post-conflict polarization, instead of building the rule of law and deterrence. Still, what has begun as institutions created in the absence of humanitarian action by the powerful may come to constitute normal state attributes similar to sovereignty, whose violation will be seen as not only illegitimate, but also meriting humanitarian action to correct and punish such behavior.

Like all international laws, the powerful are often exempted, even as they enforce those laws on others, at least for a while. Over time, it can be hoped that cognitive dissonance from non-compliance by states espousing the rule of law will also increase the costs of hypocrisy among the non-compliant states, both powerful and weak ones. Otherwise, how could a realist claim that international law hardly exists and then inveigh against the emerging norm of universal jurisdiction rooted in gross violations of a universal treaty like the 1949 Geneva

Conventions?[36]? Senior members of the Bush administration do not travel to Europe, which shows that realists do not always get their way given the increasing legalization of international politics. Powerful states however may find that respecting criminal norms themselves will strengthen these norms abroad, which could accrue greater benefits over time in reducing the incidence and intensity of failing states from which trafficking and terrorism proliferate. Already, the United States has transferred cases from Sudan and Libya to the ICC via the Security Council and participated in the preparatory commission to define aggression as a future core crime to be prosecuted there. On the other hand, the future face of criminal tribunals, the ICC, has faced a host of problems after only one conviction in its first decade of billion dollar expenditures. Still at-large indictees like Kony and Sudan's President al-Bashir, who has regularly visited UN member states, some of them ICC states parties, who ignore their UN Charter obligations to implement international arrest warrants on cases referred by the UN Security Council to the ICC, as well as their obligations to the ICC statute. Some of them were on the Council at the time of the visits. Such disobedient Council states might take their example from the double standard perceived by the ICC's only prosecuting Africans while exempting African war criminals who are US allies.[37]

Still, international tribunals can be further developed internationally, just as the Courts of the Council of Europe and the European Union have strengthened far beyond the roles originally envisioned for them. Similar developments include the domestic prosecutions mandated by the ICTY in Bosnia, Croatia, and Serbia, along with Fujimori in Peru, hundreds of torturers in Argentina, and possibly, at the time of writing, Polish intelligence officials for collaborating in CIA torture and rendition. At least some armies and governments are planning their military operations with the strengthening of criminal prohibitions in mind, including the threat of prosecution domestically or internationally. That international crimes will continue does not weaken norms any more than the prevalence of murder in domestic legal systems renders their police and courts unnecessary—quite the contrary. Rather than seen as a panacea, tribunals should be considered institutions and norms embedded in a larger context. Admittedly, compliance, or the lack thereof, cannot be solely attributed to legal explanations because legal effects reflect many normative, cultural, and institutional factors, both endogenous and exogenous to these courts. Even if politics affect legal processes, legal processes also affect politics. Yet, any explanation of politics is equally incomplete if legal norms and institutionalization are not also understood. Even if some actors can evade compliance in some arenas does not mean that they will not face costs from non-compliance in that arena or in others. Ultimately, norms have ability to haunt those who wield those norms in some contexts but make exceptions for themselves in others.

Notes

1. Remarks at the Reception following the Swearing in of National and International Judicial Officers for the Extraordinary Chambers of the Cambodian Courts, July 3, 2006.

2. Kenneth W. Abbott, "International Relations Theory, International Law, and the Regime Governing Atrocities in Internal Conflicts," 93 *Am. J. Int'l. L.* 361 (1999); Judith Goldstein, Miles Kahler, Robert O. Keohane, and Anne-Marie Slaughter eds., *Legalization and World Politics*, Special Issue, *International Organization* 54, no. 3 (2000).

3. My estimate based on reviewing websites.

4. Deborah E. Lipstadt, *The Eichmann Trial (Jewish Encounters)* (New York: Schocken, 2011).

5. Goldstein et al. *Legalization and World Politics*, Special Issue, *International Organization.*

6. On the political science approach, see Martin Shapiro and Alex Stone Sweet, *On Law, Politics and Judicialization* (Oxford; New York: Oxford University Press, 2002); Jeffrey A. Segal and Harold J. Spaeth, *The Supreme Court and the Attitudinal Model Revisited* (Cambridge; New York: Cambridge University Press, 2002); For a robust defense of analytic jurisprudence and critique of attitudinal models, see Stephen Breyer, *Making Our Democracy Work: A Judge's View* (New York: Alfred A. Knopf, 2011).

7. "Members Hear Briefings by Presidents, Prosecutors of Courts Trying War Crimes in Former Yugoslavia, Rwanda," UN Security Council 10476, www.un.org/News/Press/docs/2011/sc10476.doc.htm.

8. David Kennedy, *Of War and Law* (Princeton, NJ: Princeton University Press, 2006), .1,12; see also his: *The Dark Side of Virtue: Reassessing International Humanitarianism* (Princeton, NJ: Princeton University Press, 2005).

9. For example, see Jack Snyder and Leslie Vinjamuri, "Principle and Pragmatism in Strategies of International Justice," *International Security* 28, no. 3 (2003-2004): 5-44; and Jack Goldsmith and Stephen Krasner, "The Limits of Idealism" *Daedalus* 132, no. 1 (2003): 47-63.

10. Judith Armatta, *Twilight of Impunity: the War Crimes Trial of Slobodan Milošević* (Durham, NC: Duke University Press, 2010), 44.

11. L. Raub, "Positioning Hybrid Tribunals in International Criminal Justice," 41 *N.Y.U. J. Int'l. L. & Pol.* 1013 (2009).

12. Jeffrey Checkel, "Theoretical Synthesis in IR: Possibilities and Limits," in ed. Walter Carlsnaes, Thomas Risse and Beth Simmons, *Handbook of International Relations*, 2d. ed. (London: Sage Publications, 2011).

13. Richard A. Falk, "The Grotian Moment," in *International Law: A Contemporary Perspective*, ed. Richard Falk, Friedrich V. Kratochwil, and Saul Mendlovitz (Boulder, CO: Westview Press, 1985), 7-42.

14. I am indebted to Paul Rickard, who initially drafted this discussion of Cambodia. The ECCC "will provide a good model for strengthening Cambodia's judicial": Statement by Press Secretary, Director-General for Press and Public Relations, on the Adoption of the Internal Rules for the Khmer Rouge Trials in Cambodia, The Ministry of Foreign Affairs of Japan, June 13, 2007.

15. "No Perfect Justice: Interviews with Thun Saray, Son Chhay and Ouk Vandeth," *Justice Initiatives: A Publication of the Open Society Justice Initiative* (Spring 2006), http://www.ivr.uzh.ch/institutsmitglieder/kaufmann/cont/jinitiatives_200604.pdf.

16. Wendy Lambourne, "The Khmer Rouge Tribunal: Justice for Genocide in Cambodia?" (Law and Society Association Australia and New Zealand Conference—Whither Human Rights, December 10-12, 2008, Univ. of Sydney), 9; also see Wendy Lambourne, "Traditional Justice and Peacebuilding after Mass Violence," *International Journal of Transitional Justice* 3 (2009): 28-48, in which Lambourne asserts that, in addition to holding those most responsible to account for the crimes they committed, attention also needs to be paid to the elements of truth, socioeconomic justice, and political justice in peace-building in processes.

17. See http://www.eccc.gov.kh/en/victims-support; Madhev Mohan is critical of what he considers to be "vague speculation that victim participation in international trials is always therapeutic." See Madhev Mohan, "The Paradox of Victim-Centrism: Victim Participation at the Khmer Rouge Tribunal," *ICLR* (2009): 733-775.

18. Rupert Skilbeck, "Defending the Khmer Rouge," 8 *Int'l. Crim. L. Rev.* 423 (2008).

19. James A Goldston, "An Extraordinary Experiment in Transitional Justice," *Justice Initiatives* (Spring 2006), available at http//: www.ivr.uzh.ch.

20. Surya P. Subedi, "The UN Human Rights Mandate in Cambodia; the Challenge of a Country in Transition and the Experience of the Special Rapporteur for that Country," *International Journal of Human Rights* (2011): 254.

21. Media Statement, Licadho, "Mu Sochua Verdict: Another Blow to Cambodian Democracy," (August 4, 2009), www.licadho-cambodia.org.

22. In an interview, Nice stated, "The ICTY Prosecutor did not indict all others at the top of Serb leadership in office when the Bosnian war was pursued, and thus when Srebrenica and the genocide there occurred," (February 21, 2012) http://talkbosnia.net.

23. "It should also be remembered that there are other protected document collections and individual documents which were, and still are, protected by direct agreements between Belgrade and the former OTP Prosecutor, i.e., they were not protected by the Trial Chamber. These documents are difficult now to identify but if and when Bosnia-Herzegovina decides to reopen the ICJ case it will be essential to require Serbia and/or the ICTY to produce all those documents for the ICJ." KBSA Interview of Sir Geoffrey Nice, "The Victims of Srebrenica: Living and Dead" (April 6, 2012), http://www.kbsa2000kbs.org/index.php?option=com_content&view=article&id=256:sir-geoffrey-nice-rtve-srebrenice-ivi-i-mrtvi-zasluuju-istinu&catid=45:intervju&Itemid=107.

24. See, for example, Jeffrey Segal and Harold J. Spaeth, *The Supreme Court and the Attitudinal Model* (Cambridge; New York: Cambridge University Press, 1993).

25. Henry F. Carey, *Reaping What You Sow; A Comparative Examination of Torture Reform in the United States and Israel* (Santa Barbara, CA: Praeger, 2012). Human Rights Watch concluded that the states of Afghanistan, Chad, China and Hong Kong, Malaysia, Mali, Mauritania, Morocco, the Netherlands, Pakistan, Sudan, Thailand and the United Kingdom were all implicated in detainee abuse and rendition to torture of Libyans to the Gaddafi regime. Human Rights Watch, "Delivered into Enemy Hands," Available at: http://www.hrw.org/node/109831/section/3 (Accessed September 6, 2012). So far, there has been no ICC investigation of state parties involved such as the Netherlands and the UK.

26. Armatta, *Twilight of Impunity*, 209, quoting ICTR, *Prosecutor v. Jean Bosco Barayagwiza*, Case No. ICTR-1997-19.

27. Armatta, *Twilight of Impunity*, 441-442. For video of some of these disgraceful performances, see: http://hague.bard.edu.

28. ICTY, *Prosecutor v. Vojislav Šešelj*, Case IT-03-67-T, April 10, 2000.

29. David P. Forsythe, *Human Rights in International Relations*, 3rd ed. (Cambridge; New York: Cambridge University Press, 2012).

30. Statement by Ambassador Jeffrey DeLaurentis, US Ambassador and Alternate Representative for Special Political Affairs, at Security Council Debate on International Criminal Tribunals, usun.state.gov/briefing/statements/2011/178480.htm.

31. Gary J. Bass, *Stay the Hand of Vengeance: the Politics of War Crimes Tribunals* (Princeton, NJ: Princeton University Press, 2000); Chandra Lekha Sriram, "Justice as Peace: Liberal Peacebuilding and Strategies of Transitional Justice," *Global Society* 21, no. 4 (2007): 579-591.

32. Leslie Vinjamuri and Jack Snyder, "Advocacy and Scholarship in the Study of International War Crimes Tribunals and Transitional Justice," *Annual Review of Political Science* 7 (June 2004): 345-362.

33. Unfortunately, the statistically significant coefficient is quite small. See, for example, Beth Simmons, *Mobilizing for Human Rights: International Law in Domestic Politics* (Cambridge; New York: Cambridge University Press, 2009). The original line of compliance analysis began with Stephen Poe and C. Neal Tate, "Repression to Human Rights of Personal Integrity in the 1980s: A Global Analysis," *American Political Science Review* 88, no. 4 (1994): 853-872.

34. Jürgen Habermas, *Communication and the Evolution of Society* (Cambridge: Polity, 1991).

35. Hedley Bull, *The Anarchical Society: A Study of Order in World Politics* (London: Macmillan, 1977).

36. Henry A. Kissinger, "The Pitfalls of Universal Jurisdiction," *Foreign Affairs* (July/August 2001).

37. David Kaye, "Who's Afraid of the International Criminal Court?" *Foreign Affairs* (May/June 2011).

Index

About the Contributors

Kathleen Barrett has an LLM in international human rights law and practice and is a PhD candidate in political science at Georgia State University. Her research interest is comparative justice including transitional justice, constitutions, constitutional courts, and perceived judicial corruption. Her dissertation addresses the influence of international law as reflected in the relationship between the Constitutional Courts and Legislatures in Central Eastern European countries. She has presented conference papers on topics including judicial reform in El Salvador, cross-national perceptions of judicial corruption, use of international law by constitutional courts, indigenous rights in the United States, and victim's rights at hybrid tribunals.

Susan Benesch is a leading scholar on speech in international criminal law. Susan Benesch wrote the seminar 2008 article "Vile Crime or Inalienable Right? Defining Incitement to Genocide." She teaches at American University in Washington, DC, and holds a JD from Yale and an LLM from Georgetown. She is also a senior fellow at the World Policy Institute, where she founded and directs the project "Dangerous Speech on the Road to Mass Violence," working to identify speech that helps to catalyze violence, and to find the best policy options to contain its effects without curbing freedom of expression.

Candace H. Blake-Amarante is completing her PhD in political science at Columbia University. Her areas of specialization are international relations and international criminal law. Her research focuses on how to design international legal regimes to alter the incentives of warring combatants from fighting to committing atrocities to bargaining for peace during civil wars. She is the recipient of the National Science Foundation Graduate Research Fellowship, Columbia University Graduate School of Arts and Sciences Pre-doctoral Minority Merit Fellowship, Buttenweiser Fellowship, Kluge Fellowship, and Cordier Fellowship.

Jo-Marie Burt is an associate professor of political science at George Mason University, where she is director of Latin American Studies and codirector of the Center for Global Studies. She is also a senior fellow at the Washington Office on Latin America (WOLA). She was a researcher for the Peruvian Truth and Reconciliation Commission, and has been a visiting professor at the Pontifical Catholic University of Peru. Dr. Burt is currently directing a research project on human rights and accountability efforts in Peru and is completing a book on the Fujimori trial. She has published on political violence, transitional justice, and state-society relations in Latin America, and is the author of *Political Violence and the Authoritarian State in Peru: Silencing Civil Society* (2007).

Dr. Henry (Chip) F. Carey is associate professor of political science at Georgia State University. He is the author most recently of *Reaping What You Sow: A Comparative Examination of Torture Reform in the United States, France, Argentina and Israel* (2012) and *Privatizing the Democratic Peace: Dilemmas of NGO Peacebuilding* (2012). He is also editor of *Human Rights, Civil Society and European Institutions: Thematic Debates* (2013), *Human Rights Promotion of the European Union and the Council of Europe: Case Studies* (2013) and co-editor with Stacey M. Mitchell of *International Legal Disputes: A Moot Court Approach* (2013). He was coeditor of the International Studies Compendium's Essays on International Law (2010). He regularly contributes foreign policy blogs to the World Policy and other web sites and is also editor of United Nations Law Reports.

Dr. Beth Dougherty is manger professor of international relations and professor of political science at Beloit College. Dr. Dougherty specializes in Middle Eastern politics, transitional justice mechanisms, and African conflicts. She is a Fulbright scholar and has published on the topics of transitional justice in Iraq and Sierra Leone as well as ethnic conflict.

Johanna Herman is a research fellow at the Centre on Human Rights on Conflict at the University of East London. She received her MA in international affairs from Columbia University's School of International and Public Affairs, with a concentration in human rights. She holds a BA in social and political sciences from Fitzwilliam College, Cambridge University. Her research interests include transitional justice, peacebuilding, and human rights. She is a coauthor of *War, Conflict and Human Rights* (2009) and coeditor of *Transitional Justice and Peacebuilding on the Ground: Victims and Ex-Combatants* (2012), *Peacebuilding and Rule of Law in Africa: Just Peace?* (2010) and *Surviving Field Research: Working in Violent and Difficult Situations* (2009).

Dr. Kimberly Lanegran is an associate professor of political science at Coe College in Cedar Rapids Iowa. Dr. Lanegran specializes in international organizations and transitional justice and has published on the topics of international criminal tribunals and politics in South Africa.

Dr. Olga Martin-Ortega is senior research fellow at the Centre on Human Rights in Conflict, University of East London. She conducts research in the areas of business and human rights, post-conflict reconstruction, and transitional justice. She is the author of *Empresas Multinacionales y Derechos Humanos en Derecho Internacional* (2008), coauthor of *International Law,* 6th edition (2009) and *War and Human Rights. Theory and Practice* (2009), and co-editor of *Peacebuilding and Transitional Justice on the Ground: Victims and Excombatants* (2012), *Peacebuilding and Rule of Law in Africa. Just Peace?* (2010), and *Surviving Field Research. Working in Violent and Difficult Situations* (2009). She is a founding member and sits on the Executive Committee of the London Transitional Justice Network and cochair of the European Society of International Law Interest Group on Business and Human Rights.

Dr. Stacey M. Mitchell is a lecturer at the University of Georgia, Department of International Affairs. She specializes in human rights and international criminal law and has written on the topics of genocide, genocide in Rwanda, US foreign policy towards Rwanda and the *Gacaca* courts in Rwanda. She is also coeditor with Henry (Chip) F. Carey of *International Legal Disputes: A Moot Court Approach* (2013).

Dr. Mahmood Monshipouri is an associate professor at the Department of International Relations, College of Creative Arts and Humanities, San Francisco State University. Dr. Monshipouri specializes in the Middle Eastern politics, human rights in the developing world, and globalization and identity construction in the Muslim world. He is currently working on a book on *Youth, Technology, and Democratic Uprisings in the Middle East and North Africa* (forthcoming). He is author of *Muslims in Global Politics: Identities, Interests, and Human Rights* (2009). His most recent book is *Terrorism, Security, and Human Rights: Harnessing the Rule of Law* (2012).

Dr. Kelly-Kate Pease is a professor of international relations in the Department of History, Politics and International Relations, and director of the Institute for Human Rights and Humanitarian Studies at Webster University. She has published extensively in areas related to human rights and humanitarian Intervention. Her book *International Organizations: Perspectives on Global Governance* is currently in its fifth edition, and the coauthored book *The United Nations and Changing World Politics* is in its seventh. Pease also publishes articles and chapters on human rights, humanitarian intervention, humanitarian assistance, and most recently, international criminal law. Her current research project focuses on the impact of Joint Criminal Enterprise as a mode of legal liability for holding leaders accountable for gross violations of international human rights and humanitarian law.

Joanna R. Quinn is associate professor of political science, director of the Centre for Transitional Justice and Post-Conflict Reconstruction, and director of The Africa Institute, at The University of Western Ontario. Since 1998, Dr. Quinn has been engaged in research that considers the role of acknowledgement in overcoming the causes of conflict, which has the potential to affect real and lasting change. She has written widely on the truth commissions in Uganda, Haiti, and elsewhere. Her current research considers the role of customary practices of acknowledgement and justice in Uganda and in Fiji.

Benjamin N. Schiff received his PhD from the University of California, Berkeley and is a Williams-Smith Professor of Politics at Oberlin College. He teaches international politics and related topics and has published three books on international organizations: *International Nuclear Technology Transfer: Dilemmas of Dissemination and Control* (1982) about the International Atomic Energy Agency; *Refugees unto the Third Generation: UN Aid to Palestinians* (1995) about the UN Relief and Works Agency; and *Building the International Criminal Court* (2008). With his wife, June Goodwin, he also published *Heart of Whiteness: Afrikaners Face Black Rule in the New South Africa* (Scribner, 1995) and two mass-market paperback thrillers.

Adam M. Smith is a Washington, DC-based international lawyer. He has written extensively on international law in both the academic and popular press and has worked on post-conflict justice in the Balkans, Asia, and Africa. Smith is a frequent lecturer on international justice, speaking before groups including the CIA, the Royal Institute for International Affairs, and the US Holocaust Museum and has been interviewed on the subject by the *Economist*, NPR, the *New York Times*, the BBC, *Congressional Quarterly*, *Time* and other outlets. Educated at Harvard, Oxford, and Brown, Smith has held posts at the World Bank, the OECD, and the UN and is the author of numerous articles, book chapters, and two books: *International Judicial Institutions: The Architecture of Interna-*

tional Justice at Home and Abroad (2009) (with Justice Richard Goldstone) and *After Genocide: Bringing the Devil to Justice* (2009).

Dr. Peter J. Stoett is professor in the Department of Political Science at Concordia University in Montréal. His main areas of expertise include international relations and law, global environmental politics, and human rights. His recent books include *Global Ecopolitics: Crisis, Governance, and Justice* (2012); *Global Politics: Origins, Currents, Directions* (2010); and *Human and Global Security: An Exploration of Terms* (2000). He has conducted research in Europe (including the Balkans), eastern, southern and western Africa, central America, and Asia. Dr. Stoett has taught at the UN University for Peace in Costa Rica; and the IMT Institute for Advanced Studies in Italy; and was a Fulbright Research Chair at the Woodrow Wilson International Center for Scholars in Washington, DC in 2012.

Yuki Takatori is associate professor of Japanese and the Japanese advisor for Asian studies in the modern and classical languages department at Georgia State University. Her current research focuses on the history of Japanese war crimes trials. She is the author of "Canada and War Crimes Trials: From the International Military Tribunal for the Far East to the International Criminal Court" (forthcoming), "The Forgotten Judge at the Tokyo War Crimes Trial" (2008), "America's' War Crimes Trial? Commonwealth Leadership at the International Military Tribunal for the Far East, 1946–1948" (2007), and other articles and book chapters on the Tokyo War Crimes Trial. She is also the translator, from English to Japanese, of several articles on this topic.

James Larry Taulbee is professor emeritus at Emory University, Department of Political Science. Dr. Taulbee received his PhD in political science from The Johns Hopkins University. He specializes in international law and international security policy, and has published extensively on the topics of international law and international security issues. Some of his works include *International Crime and Punishment* (Praeger, 2009), *Law Among Nations*, 10th edition (2012), and *Blood and Conscience: Genocide and Mass Atrocity in Contemporary History* (forthcoming).

Michael D. Thurston graduated from the University of Illinois in 2002, with a bachelor's degree, majoring in political science. He graduated from Loyola University of Chicago School of Law in 2005, with a juris doctorate degree. He graduated from Georgia State University in December 2010 with a master's degree in political science. He is currently a senior assistant district attorney in Clayton County Georgia, assigned to the crimes against women unit.

Prisca Uwigabye received her bachelor's degree from the Universite Libre de Kigali in administrative sciences and her master's degree in conflicts, reconstruction, and human security from Erasmus University/Rotterdam, The Netherlands. She has a strong conviction that proper accountability for sexual offenses perpetrated against women during conflict is a powerful tool to achieve reconciliation in post-conflict societies.